QlikView for Developers

Design and build scalable and maintainable BI solutions

Miguel Ángel García

Barry Harmsen

BIRMINGHAM - MUMBAI

QlikView for Developers

First published: June 2017

Production reference: 1280617

Published by Packt Publishing Ltd.
Livery Place
35 Livery Street
Birmingham B3 2PB, UK.

ISBN 978-1-78646-984-7

www.packtpub.com

Credits

Authors
Miguel Ángel García
Barry Harmsen

Reviewer
Steve Dark

Commissioning Editor
Veena Pagare

Acquisition Editor
Meeta Rajani

Content Development Editor
Aishwarya Pandere

Technical Editor
Dinesh Pawar

Copy Editor
Safis Editing

Project Coordinator
Nidhi Joshi

Proofreader
Safis Editing

Indexer
Pratik Shirodkar

Graphics
Tania Dutta

Production Coordinator
Deeplika Naik

Cover Work
Deepika Naik

About the Authors

Miguel Ángel García is a business intelligence consultant and Qlik Solutions Architect from Monterrey, Mexico. Having worked throughout many successful Qlik implementations, from inception to implementation, and performed a wide variety of roles on each project, his experience and skills range from pre-sales to applications development and design, technical architecture, system administration, as well as functional analysis and overall project execution. He currently holds the QlikView Designer, QlikView Developer, and QlikView System Administrator certifications.

His early-found passion for QlikView led him to create and host the iQlik blog, which you can find at `https://aftersync.com/blog` and has been proved to help many developers, both newcomers and experienced, in their everyday development challenges. You can follow his blog updates via Twitter on `@GarciaMMiguel` and `@iQlik`.

He also delivers advanced online Qlik training at `https://q-on.bi` and `https://masterclass.bi`, so be sure to check out the courses there to continue learning QlikView and Qlik Sense development.

> I also want to thank my family for their understanding and support throughout all the projects and endeavors I undertake. This book is dedicated to them.

Barry Harmsen is a business intelligence consultant based in the Netherlands. Here, he runs Bitmetric (`http://www.bitmetric.nl`), a boutique consulting firm specialized in the Qlik product suite. Originally from a background of traditional business intelligence, data warehousing, and performance management, in 2008 Barry made the shift to Qlik and a more user-centric form of business intelligence. Since then, he and his team have helped many clients get the most out of their investments in the Qlik platform.

Barry is one of the four Qlik experts teaching at the Masters Summit for Qlik (`http://www.masterssummit.com`), advanced training for experienced Qlik professionals. He also runs the Amsterdam chapter of the Qlik Dev Group (`http://qlikdevgroup.com/`), an open and informal gathering where Qlik professionals can share knowledge and experiences.

For his contributions to the Qlik ecosystem, Barry has been accredited by Qlik as a Qlik Luminary since 2014.

Barry and his colleagues regularly post Qlik tips, tricks, and tutorials at the QlikFix blog (`http://www.qlikfix.com`). He can also be found on Twitter as `@meneerharmsen`.

I want to thank my daughter Lucie, my sons Lex and Bob, and especially my wife Miranda for the support and patience during the writing and updating of this book.

I also want to thank the team at Bitmetric: Wesley Smit, Rik Cramer, Johan van den Bosch, and Vincent Hayward.

Acknowledgements

Writing a book is not a solo or duo exercise. This result could not have been achieved without the contributions of a great team.

Steve Dark performed the technical review of this book. His insightful comments and suggestions have added an extra dimension of quality to the book. For that we thank him. We also wish to thank Ralf Becher and Stephen Redmond, who did the technical review on the previous edition of this book.

We also want to thank Packt's team: Aishwarya Pandere, content development editor, and Dinesh Pawar, technical editor. Their guidance kept us focused and on track.

About the Reviewer

Steve Dark heads up Quick Intelligence, a business intelligence consultancy with 100 percent focus on the Qlik platform. With clients in sectors as diverse as manufacturing, pharmaceuticals, and finance, we cover and support the entire Qlik project lifecycle and ecosystem for our customers. Through the numerous successful implementations and challenges met for these clients, Steve has in depth expertise and a wealth of experience in QlikView and more recently Qlik Sense.

It is this experience that Steve shares through his blog at `http://www. quickintelligence.co.uk/qlikview-blog/` and via other channels, such as Qlik Community. This sharing of knowledge and enthusiasm for the Qlik platform has been recognized by Qlik, as they made Steve a Luminary and a Community MVP.

Steve has also been on the technical review team for *QlikView 11 For Developers*, *QlikView 11 For Developers Cookbook*, *QlikView Scripting*, and *QlikView Server and Publisher*. All of these titles are published by Packt Publishing.

I would like to thank all those colleagues and clients who have allowed me to keep doing the work that I enjoy for so long.

www.PacktPub.com

eBooks, discount offers, and more

Did you know that Packt offers eBook versions of every book published, with PDF and ePub files available? You can upgrade to the eBook version at www.PacktPub. com and as a print book customer, you are entitled to a discount on the eBook copy. Get in touch with us at customercare@packtpub.com for more details.

At www.PacktPub.com, you can also read a collection of free technical articles, sign up for a range of free newsletters and receive exclusive discounts and offers on Packt books and eBooks.

https://www.packtpub.com/mapt

Get the most in-demand software skills with Mapt. Mapt gives you full access to all Packt books and video courses, as well as industry-leading tools to help you plan your personal development and advance your career.

Why subscribe?

- Fully searchable across every book published by Packt
- Copy and paste, print, and bookmark content
- On demand and accessible via a web browser

Customer Feedback

Thanks for purchasing this Packt book. At Packt, quality is at the heart of our editorial process. To help us improve, please leave us an honest review on this book's Amazon page at https://www.amazon.com/dp/1786469847.

If you'd like to join our team of regular reviewers, you can e-mail us at customerreviews@packtpub.com. We award our regular reviewers with free eBooks and videos in exchange for their valuable feedback. Help us be relentless in improving our products!

Dedicated to our families.
Miguel Ángel García
Barry Harmsen

Table of Contents

Preface

The need for business intelligence (BI) solutions and data analysis has always existed, and so have different approaches to fulfill this need. Traditional BI software has heavily relied on techniques that have been around and persisted through the decades, but newer technologies have emerged in recent times that have been proven to be more flexible and, therefore, more adequate for the evolving environment in which they are used. QlikView is an example of these disruptive technologies, a kind of software that changes the rules of the game.

QlikView is different; that's a fact. It's different in an advantageous way. If you have worked with traditional BI software before, it might be necessary to let go of some of the preconceptions you may have regarding how BI solutions are built. If, on the other hand, you are a newcomer to the BI landscape, we will help you get the basics in order so that you get up-to-speed. In any case, rest assured that you are on the right track by having picked QlikView as your tool and this book as your guide.

The good news is, the material between these covers has been written in such a way that newcomers, BI professionals experienced in other tools, and even seasoned QlikView practitioners will find useful. This book will provide you with the knowledge required to understand how QlikView works, and the skills needed to build QlikView documents from start to finish—from loading data to building charts. Even if you have worked with QlikView before, you will find that the exercises presented in each chapter, and the recommended practices we discuss, will help you extend your knowledge and become more proficient with QlikView.

Among other features you will find on this book, some of the most important are as follows:

- The book is practical and hands-on. It is filled with examples that will let you take the theory into practice right away. We support this hands-on experience by providing a full dataset used across the entire book, and around which we build a fully-functional QlikView document that contains a dashboard, various analyses (both basic and complex to build), and reports using the Dashboard-Analysis-Reports (DAR) approach.

- In every chapter, a piece of a final QlikView document is built, which allows you to follow its evolution from start to finish. It also enables us to cover different development challenges that you may encounter in a real-world QlikView project.

- We made sure to cover both backend and frontend development, so you will find that all 15 chapters cover different topics, from scripting and data extraction to data modeling, design, charts and expressions, as well as security, and everything in between. We also talk about various best practices related to each of these topics.

All of the examples discussed in the book are complemented with solution files for the reader to follow the exercises and compare your work. The QlikView files we provide are Personal Edition enabled, which means that a purchased QlikView license is not required to open them.

Although the case and story used in the book are built around a fictional company, the data we use in our examples and final application is real. Thanks to the Open Government initiative and the Bureau of Transportation Statistics of the United States, which compiles and maintains a complete dataset about airline operations in the US, you will be able to work with real data and build a QlikView application to analyze flights, enplaned passengers, cargo, and many others across multiple dimensions, such as carriers, airports, cities, and aircraft types.

Congratulations on taking a step towards learning to develop BI applications with QlikView. Are you ready for take off? Qlik on!

What this book covers

Chapter 1, Meet QlikView, introduces QlikView and shows how it can be used to explore data. We will also learn about the technology and components behind QlikView and will be introduced to the case that is used throughout the book: HighCloud Airlines.

Chapter 2, What's New in QlikView 12, presents a summary of the changes in the QlikView software, as well as in the Qlik ecosystem in general, that happened since the previous version of this book was published in 2012. In this chapter, we will bring you up to speed with the changes over the past few years.

Chapter 3, Seeing Is Believing, help us get hands-on with QlikView by building a simple QlikView document. We will learn what dimensions and expressions are, in the context of a QlikView document. We will also learn how to build simple charts to visualize and aggregate data, and how to design a basic user interface for navigating through the QlikView document.

Chapter 4, Data Sources, will help us learn how to load data from different sources and how to extract data using the built-in wizards. We will also take a closer look at QlikView's proprietary data files.

Chapter 5, Data Modeling, explains which type of data model is best suited for QlikView. We will see which rules need to be followed when designing a QlikView data model, and will also learn how best to take advantage of the associative data model to make our documents highly dynamic.

Chapter 6, Styling Up, will help us learn how to style our QlikView documents. We will learn about the various document and sheet properties and will use them to manage the visual style of our document. We will also take a closer look at some of the most fundamental objects and learn how we can change their appearance.

Chapter 7, Building Dashboards, introduces us to the three basic types of QlikView users, and how we can best cater to their needs. We will learn about the various charting options that are available in QlikView, and will see how we can add interactivity to our QlikView documents. We will also be introduced to basic calculations.

Chapter 8, Scripting, introduces us to the QlikView scripting language and editor. We will learn about the most important script statements, and how we can use them to manipulate data and control the flow of the script. We will also be introduced to some of the most important operators and functions for dealing with various data types. Finally, we will look at the options for debugging scripts, how to organize and standardize script, and how we can reuse our scripts.

Chapter 9, Data Modeling Best Practices, expands on the knowledge about data modeling and scripting we gained in earlier chapters. We will learn how to make sure that data models are consistent and how to work with complex data models and multiple fact tables. We will also learn how to reduce storage requirements for a dataset and how best to deal with date and time information.

Chapter 10, Basic Data Transformation, focuses on how to deal with unstructured data and how to transform it for use in our QlikView data model. We will learn about basic data transformation subjects, such as cleansing data and how to restructure pivoted and hierarchical tables for inclusion in the QlikView data model.

Chapter 11, Advanced Expressions, discusses the use of variables. We will also learn how to use conditional functions and how to handle advanced aggregations.

Chapter 12, Set Analysis and Point In Time Reporting, takes a closer look at Set Analysis and will explain how it can be used for Point In Time Reporting. We will also learn about comparative analysis using alternate states.

Chapter 13, Advanced Data Transformation, returns to the topic of data transformation. We will learn about the most commonly used data architectures that can ease QlikView development and administration. Next, we will take a close look at aggregating and sorting data in the data model. In the final part of the chapter, we will learn how to take advantage of some of QlikView's most powerful data transformation capabilities.

Chapter 14, More on Visual Design and User Experience, takes another look at the visual design of our QlikView documents, and will learn how to create a consistent user interface. The second part of the chapter introduces us to some additional manners of adding interactivity to our documents.

Chapter 15, Security, shows how to secure our QlikView documents. We will see how we can allow only authorized users to open our documents and will learn how we can limit what a user can do and see within our document.

What you need for this book

To use this book, you primarily need the QlikView Desktop software. With regards to computer requirements, you will need a PC with at least Windows XP (or better), 2 GB of hard disk space, and 2 GB of RAM. A 64-bit machine is required if you want to use QlikView 12 or a higher version, and is the recommended environment for this book and QlikView development in general. If you prefer to use a 32-bit machine, you can install QlikView 11 instead.

For best understanding, a general knowledge of BI and its terminology is required. Basic understanding of databases and SQL is preferred, but not compulsory for this book.

Who this book is for

This book is aimed at developers and power users who want to learn how to develop BI applications with QlikView. Developers who have already been using QlikView for some time may find that this book contains useful tips and best practices to make more effective use of QlikView.

This book only covers QlikView Desktop; deployments to QlikView Server and Publisher are beyond the scope of this book. The book is not aimed at QlikView Server administrators.

Conventions

In this book, you will find a number of text styles that distinguish between different kinds of information. Here are some examples of these styles and an explanation of their meaning.

Code words in text, database table names, folder names, filenames, file extensions, pathnames, dummy URLs, user input, and Twitter handles are shown as follows: "Before continuing, make sure a database file named `Dimension Tables.mdb` is in the `Data Files\MDBs` folder."

A block of code is set as follows:

```
LOAD `%Origin Airport ID`,
  `Origin Airport`;
SQL SELECT `%Origin Airport ID`,
  `Origin Airport`
FROM `Origin Airports`;
```

New terms and **important words** are shown in bold. Words that you see on the screen, for example, in menus or dialog boxes, appear in the text like this: "The example we will be using is the **Movies Database**, which is an example document that is supplied with QlikView."

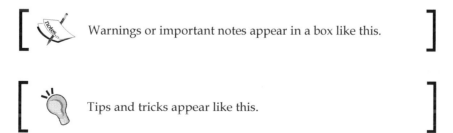

Warnings or important notes appear in a box like this.

Tips and tricks appear like this.

Reader feedback

Feedback from our readers is always welcome. Let us know what you think about this book—what you liked or disliked. Reader feedback is important for us as it helps us develop titles that you will really get the most out of.

To send us general feedback, simply e-mail `feedback@packtpub.com`, and mention the book's title in the subject of your message.

If there is a topic that you have expertise in and you are interested in either writing or contributing to a book, see our author guide at `www.packtpub.com/authors`.

Customer support

Now that you are the proud owner of a Packt book, we have a number of things to help you to get the most from your purchase.

Downloading the example code

You can download the example code files for this book from your account at `http://www.packtpub.com`. If you purchased this book elsewhere, you can visit `http://www.packtpub.com/support` and register to have the files e-mailed directly to you.

You can download the code files by following these steps:

1. Log in or register to our website using your e-mail address and password.
2. Hover the mouse pointer on the **SUPPORT** tab at the top.
3. Click on **Code Downloads & Errata**.
4. Enter the name of the book in the **Search** box.
5. Select the book for which you're looking to download the code files.
6. Choose from the drop-down menu where you purchased this book from.
7. Click on **Code Download**.

You can also download the code files by clicking on the **Code Files** button on the book's webpage at the Packt Publishing website. This page can be accessed by entering the book's name in the **Search** box. Please note that you need to be logged in to your Packt account.

Once the file is downloaded, please make sure that you unzip or extract the folder using the latest version of:

- WinRAR / 7-Zip for Windows
- Zipeg / iZip / UnRarX for Mac
- 7-Zip / PeaZip for Linux

You can access http://www.qlikviewfordevelopers.com/codebundle/ to register and download the zip package with the data and example files used throughout this book. The code bundle for the book is also hosted on GitHub at https://github.com/PacktPublishing/QlikView-for-Developers. We also have other code bundles from our rich catalog of books and videos available at https://github.com/PacktPublishing/. Check them out!

Downloading the color images of this book

We also provide you with a PDF file that has color images of the screenshots/diagrams used in this book. The color images will help you better understand the changes in the output. You can download this file from https://www.packtpub.com/sites/default/files/downloads/QlikViewforDevelopers_ColorImages.pdf.

Errata

Although we have taken every care to ensure the accuracy of our content, mistakes do happen. If you find a mistake in one of our books—maybe a mistake in the text or the code—we would be grateful if you could report this to us. By doing so, you can save other readers from frustration and help us improve subsequent versions of this book. If you find any errata, please report them by visiting http://www.packtpub.com/submit-errata, selecting your book, clicking on the **Errata Submission Form** link, and entering the details of your errata. Once your errata are verified, your submission will be accepted and the errata will be uploaded to our website or added to any list of existing errata under the Errata section of that title.

To view the previously submitted errata, go to https://www.packtpub.com/books/content/support and enter the name of the book in the search field. The required information will appear under the **Errata** section.

Piracy

Piracy of copyrighted material on the Internet is an ongoing problem across all media. At Packt, we take the protection of our copyright and licenses very seriously. If you come across any illegal copies of our works in any form on the Internet, please provide us with the location address or website name immediately so that we can pursue a remedy.

Please contact us at copyright@packtpub.com with a link to the suspected pirated material.

We appreciate your help in protecting our authors and our ability to bring you valuable content.

Questions

If you have a problem with any aspect of this book, you can contact us at questions@packtpub.com, and we will do our best to address the problem.

1
Meet QlikView

Congratulations on your decision to start learning QlikView development! You are now well on your way to building and delivering analytical applications that will help you and your organization quickly gain new insights and make fact-based decisions.

Before we dive in and start building all sorts of wonderful things, we first need to review some of the basics. This first chapter introduces us to the business end of QlikView. We will discover what QlikView is, how it's different from other tools, and how we can explore and interact with our data within a QlikView document. Of course, this being a technical book, we will also be looking at the various technical components that QlikView consists of. This chapter concludes with an introduction to HighCloud Airlines, the practical case we will be working on throughout the book in the form of hands-on exercises.

In this chapter, specifically, we will look at:

- What is QlikView?
- Exploring data with QlikView
- The technology and components behind QlikView
- HighCloud Airlines and why QlikView might be just the tool they need

First, let's look at what QlikView is, what we can do with it, and how it differs from other solutions that are available on the market.

What is QlikView?

QlikView is part of the product portfolio developed by Qlik, a company formerly known as QlikTech that was founded in Sweden in 1993 and is currently headquartered in the US. QlikView is a tool used for **Business Intelligence (BI)**. BI is defined by Gartner, a leading industry analyst firm, as:

> *An umbrella term that includes the application, infrastructure and tools, and best practices that enable access to and analysis of information to improve and optimize decisions and performance.*

Following this definition, QlikView is a tool that provides access to information and enables its exploration and analysis via a user-friendly interface, which in turn improves and optimizes business decisions and performance.

Historically, BI has been very much IT-driven. IT departments were responsible for the entire BI life cycle, from extracting the data to delivering the final reports, analyses, and dashboards. While this model works very well for delivering predefined static reports, most businesses find that it does not meet the needs of their business users. As IT tightly controls the data and tools, users often experience long lead-times whenever new questions arise that cannot be answered with the standard reports.

How does QlikView differ from traditional BI?

Qlik prides itself in pioneering an approach to BI that is different from the way other BI tools have been traditionally developed and implemented, essentially introducing a new paradigm to the BI industry which, in time, other vendors followed. With QlikView and the rest of Qlik's product portfolio, Qlik aims to put the tools in the hands of business users, allowing them to become self-sufficient and less dependent on IT to perform their own analyses.

Independent industry analyst firms have noticed this new paradigm as well. In 2011, Gartner created a subcategory for data discovery tools in its yearly market evaluation, the *Magic Quadrant for Business Intelligence and Analytics Platforms.* QlikView was named the poster child for this new category of BI tools. Over subsequent years, the market experimented a steady shift of focus from IT-led reporting to business-led self-service analytics. Gartner identified 2016 as the year the tipping point had been passed and redefined the vendor landscape on its Magic Quadrant based on this new perspective.

Besides the difference in who uses the tool — IT users versus business users — there are a few other key features that differentiate QlikView from other solutions.

Associative user experience

The main difference between QlikView and other BI solutions is the associative user experience. Where traditional BI solutions use predefined paths to navigate and explore data, QlikView's associative architecture allows users to take whatever route they want. This is a far more intuitive way to explore data. Qlik describes this as *working the way your mind works.*

An example is shown in the following diagram. While, in a typical BI solution, we would need to start by selecting a **Region** and then drill down step-by-step through the defined drill path, in QlikView we can choose whatever entry point we like — **Region**, **State**, **Product**, or **Sales Person**. We are then shown only the data related to that selection, and in our next selection we can go wherever we want. It is infinitely flexible.

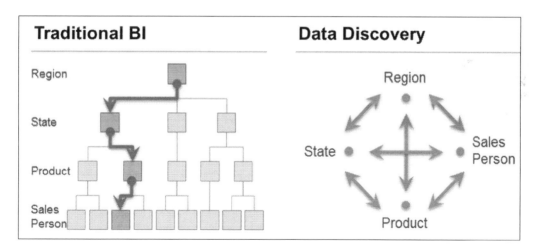

Additionally, the QlikView user interface allows us to see which data is associated with our selection.

For example, the following screenshot shows a QlikView dashboard in which two values are selected. In the **Quarter** field, **Q3** is selected and in the **Sales Reps** field, **Cart Lynch** is selected. We can see this because these values are green, which in QlikView means that they have been selected. When a selection is made, the interface automatically updates to not only show which data is associated with that selection, but also which data is not associated with the selection. Associated data has a white background, while non-associated data has a gray background. Sometimes the associations can be pretty obvious; it is no surprise that the third quarter is associated with the months July, August, and September. However, at other times, some not-so-obvious insights surface, such as the information that Cart Lynch has not sold any products in Germany or Spain. This extra information, not featured in traditional BI tools, can be of great value, as it offers a new starting point for investigation.

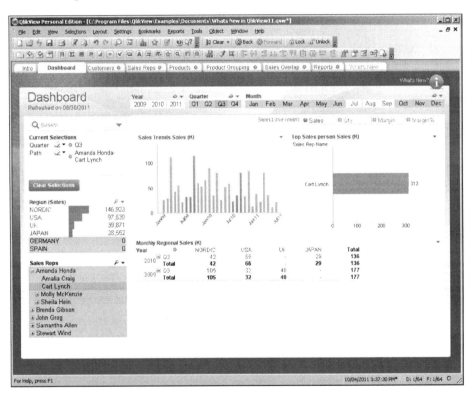

Technology

QlikView's core technological differentiators are:

- It uses an in-memory data model
- It uses an associative architecture

The fact that it uses an in-memory data model means it stores all of its data in RAM instead of using disk. As RAM is much faster than disk, this allows for very fast response times, resulting in a very smooth user experience.

The associative architecture is what makes the associative user experience, discussed in the previous section, possible. It associates every single data point in the data model with every other data point at all times throughout the entire analysis process.

Because the associative engine is built entirely in memory, every association with every data point is processed dynamically with every click.

In a later part of this chapter, we will go a bit deeper into the technology behind QlikView.

Adoption path

There is also a difference between QlikView and traditional BI solutions in the way it is typically rolled out within a company. Where traditional BI suites are often implemented top-down—by IT selecting a BI tool for the entire company—QlikView often takes a bottom-up adoption path. Business users in a single department adopt it and its use spreads out from there.

QlikView is free of charge for single-user use. This is called the **Personal Edition (PE)**. Documents created in PE can be opened by fully-licensed users or deployed on a QlikView server. The limitation is that, with the exception of some documents enabled for PE by Qlik, you cannot open documents created elsewhere, or even your own documents if they have been opened and saved by another user or server instance

Often, a business user will decide to download QlikView to see if he can solve a business problem. When other users within the department see the software, they get enthusiastic about it, so they too download a copy. To be able to share documents, they decide to purchase a few licenses for the department. Then other departments start to take notice too, and QlikView gains traction within the organization. Before long, IT and senior management also take notice, eventually leading to enterprise-wide adoption of QlikView.

QlikView facilitates every step in this process, scaling from single laptop deployments to full enterprise-wide deployments with thousands of users. The following diagram demonstrates this growth within an organization:

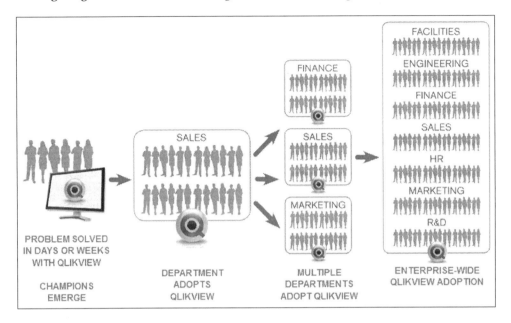

As the popularity and track record of QlikView have grown, it has gotten more and more visibility at the enterprise level. While the adoption path described before is still probably the most common adoption path, it is not uncommon nowadays for a company to do a top-down, company-wide rollout of QlikView.

Exploring data with QlikView

Now that we know what QlikView is and how it is different from traditional BI offerings, we will learn how we can explore data within QlikView.

Getting QlikView

Of course, before we can start exploring, we need to install QlikView. You can download QlikView's Personal Edition from http://www.qlik.com/us/download. You will be asked to register on the website, or log in if you have registered before.

Registering not only gives you access to the QlikView software, but you can also use it to read and post on the Qlik Community (http://community.qlik.com), which is the Qlik's user forum. This forum is very active and many questions can be answered by either a quick search or by posting a question.

Installing QlikView is very straightforward, simply double-click on the executable file and accept all default options offered. After you are done installing it, launch the QlikView application. QlikView will open with the start page set to the **Getting Started** tab, as seen in the following screenshot:

The example we will be using is the **Movies Database**, which is an example document that is supplied with QlikView. Find this document by scrolling down the **Examples** list (it is the second one on the list) and click to open it. The opening screen of the document will now be displayed:

Navigating the document

Most QlikView documents are organized into multiple sheets. These sheets often display different viewpoints on the same data, or display the same information aggregated to suit the needs of different types of users. An example of the first type of grouping might be a customer or marketing view of the data, while an example of the second type of grouping might be a KPI dashboard for executives, with a more in-depth sheet for analysts.

Navigating the different sheets in a QlikView document is typically done by using the tabs at the top of the sheet, as shown in the following screenshot. More sophisticated designs may opt to hide the tab row and use buttons to switch between the different sheets.

The tabs in the **Movie Database** document also follow a logical order. An introduction is shown on the **Intro** tab, followed by a demonstration of the key concept of QlikView on the **How QlikView works** tab. After the contrast with **Traditional OLAP** is shown, the associative **QlikView Model** is introduced. The last two tabs shown in the following screenshot show how this can be leveraged by showing a concrete **Dashboard** and **Analysis**:

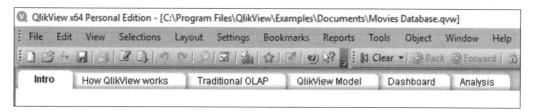

Slicing and dicing your data

As we saw when we learned about the associative user experience, any selections made in QlikView are automatically applied to the entire data model. As we will see in the next section, slicing and dicing your data really is as easy as clicking and viewing!

Listboxes

But where should we click? QlikView lets us select data in a number of ways. A common method is to select a value from a listbox. This is done by clicking in the listbox.

Let's switch to the **How QlikView works** tab to see how this works. We can do this by either clicking on the **How QlikView works** tab on the top of the sheet or by clicking on the **Get Started** button.

The selected tab shows two listboxes, one containing **Fruits** and the other containing **Colors**. When we select **Apple** in the **Fruits** listbox, the screen automatically updates to show the associated data in the **Colors** listbox: **Green** and **Red**. The color **Yellow** is shown with a gray background to indicate that it is not associated, as seen in the following screenshot, since there are no yellow apples. To select multiple values, all we need to do is hold down *Ctrl* key while we are making our selection, as shown in the following screenshot:

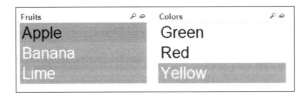

Selections in charts

Besides selections in listboxes, we can also directly select data in charts. Let's jump to the **Dashboard** tab and see how this is done. The **Dashboard** tab contains a chart labeled **Number of Movies**, which lists the number of movies by a particular actor. If we wish to select only the top three actors, we can simply drag the pointer to select them in the chart, instead of selecting them from a listbox, as shown in the following screenshot:

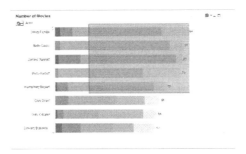

Because the selection automatically cascades to the rest of the model, this also results in the **Actor** listbox being updated to reflect the new selection, as shown in the following screenshot:

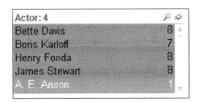

Of course, if we want to select only a single value in a chart, we don't necessarily need to lasso it. Instead, we can just click on the data point to select it. For example, clicking on **James Stewart** leads to only that actor being selected.

Search

While listboxes and lassoing are both very convenient ways of selecting data, sometimes we may not want to scroll down a big list looking for a value that may or may not be there. This is where the search option comes in handy.

For example, we may want to run a search for the actor Al Pacino. To do this, we first activate the corresponding listbox by clicking on it. Next, we simply start typing and the listbox will automatically be updated to show all values that match the search string. When we've found the actor we're looking for, **Al Pacino** in this case, we can click on that value to select it, or simply hit *Enter*, as shown in the following screenshot:

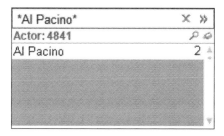

Sometimes, we may want to select data based on associated values. For example, we may want to select all of the actors that starred in the movie *The Godfather*. While we could just use the **Title** listbox, there is also another option: associated search.

To use associated search, we click on the chevron on the right-hand side of the search box. This expands the search box and any search term we enter will not only be checked against the **Actor** listbox, but also against the contents of the entire data model. When we type in `The Godfather`, the search box will show that there is a movie with that title, as seen in the following screenshot. If we select that movie and click on **Return**, all actors that star in the movie will be selected, as shown in the following screenshot:

Bookmarking selections

Inevitably, when exploring data in QlikView, there comes a point where we want to save our current selections to be able to return to them later. This is facilitated by the bookmark option. Bookmarks are used to store a selection for later retrieval.

Creating a new bookmark

To create a new bookmark, we need to open the Add Bookmark dialog. This is done by either pressing *Ctrl + B* or by selecting **Bookmarks | Add Bookmark...** from the menu.

In the **Add Bookmark** dialog, seen in the following screenshot, we can add a descriptive name for the bookmark. Other options allow us to change how the selection is applied (as either a new selection or on top of the existing selection) and if the view should switch to the sheet that was open at the time of creating the bookmark. The **Info Text** allows for a longer description to be entered that can be shown in a pop-up when the bookmark is selected.

Retrieving a bookmark

We can retrieve a bookmark by selecting it from the **Bookmarks** menu, seen here:

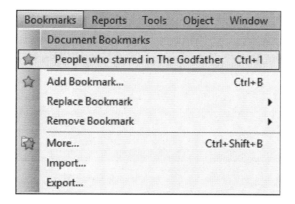

Undoing selections

Fortunately, if we end up making a wrong selection, QlikView is very forgiving. Using the **Clear**, **Back**, and **Forward** buttons in the toolbar, we can easily clear the entire selection, go back to what we had in our previous selections, or go forward again. Just like in our internet browser, the **Back** button in QlikView can take us back multiple steps, as shown in the following screenshot:

Changing the view

Besides filtering data, QlikView also lets us change the information being displayed. We'll see how this is done in the following sections.

Cyclic groups

Cyclic groups are defined by developers as a list of dimensions that can be switched between users. On the frontend, they are indicated with a circular arrow. For an example of how this works, let's look at the **Ratio to Total** chart, seen in the following screenshot. By default, this chart shows movies grouped by duration. If we click on the little downward arrow next to the circular arrow, we will see a list of alternative groupings. Click on **Decade** to switch to the view to movies grouped by decade.

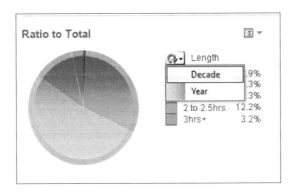

Drill down groups

Drill down groups are defined by the developer as a hierarchical list of dimensions that allows users to drill down to more detailed levels of the data. For example, a very common drill down path is year > quarter > month > day. On the frontend, drill down groups are indicated with an upward arrow.

In the **Movies Database** document, a drill down can be found on the tab labeled **Traditional OLAP**. Let's go there.

This drill down follows the path **Director** > **Title** > **Actor**. Click on the **A. Edward Sutherland** to drill down to all movies that he directed, shown in the following screenshot. Next, click on **Every Day's A Holiday** to see which actors starred in that movie. When drilling down, we can always go back to the previous level by clicking on the upward arrow, located at the top of the listbox in this example.

Director	✦ 𝒫	Table Box		昆 XI
A. Edward Sutherland		**Director** ⟋	**Title**	**Actor**
Adrian Brunel		A. Edward Sutherland	Every Day's A Holiday	Charles Butterworth
Akira Kurosawa		A. Edward Sutherland	Every Day's A Holiday	Charles Winninger
Alan Alda		A. Edward Sutherland	Every Day's A Holiday	Edmund Lowe
Alan Arkin		A. Edward Sutherland	Every Day's A Holiday	Lloyd Nolan
Alan J. Pakula		A. Edward Sutherland	Every Day's A Holiday	Louis Armstrong
Alan Myerson		A. Edward Sutherland	Every Day's A Holiday	Mae West
Albert Lewin		A. Edward Sutherland	Every Day's A Holiday	Walter Catlett
Albert Parker		A. Edward Sutherland	Follow the Boys	Andrews Sisters
Albert Ray		A. Edward Sutherland	Follow the Boys	Dinah Shore
Albert S. Rogell		A. Edward Sutherland	Follow the Boys	Gale Sondergaard
Alex Segal		A. Edward Sutherland	Follow the Boys	George Raft
Alexander Hall		A. Edward Sutherland	Follow the Boys	Jeanette MacDo...
Alexander Mackendrick		A. Edward Sutherland	Follow the Boys	Maria Montez
Alf Kjellin		A. Edward Sutherland	Follow the Boys	Marlene Dietrich
Alf Sjöberg		A. Edward Sutherland	Follow the Boys	Nigel Bruce
Alfred E. Green		A. Edward Sutherland	Follow the Boys	Orson Welles

Containers

Containers are used to alternate between the display of different objects in the same screen space. We can select the individual objects by selecting the corresponding tab within the container. Our **Movies Database** example includes a container on the **Analysis** sheet.

The container contains two objects, a chart showing **Average length of Movies over time** and a table showing the **Movie List**, shown in the following screenshot. The table is shown by default and you can switch to the **Average length of Movies over time** by clicking on the corresponding tab at the top of the object.

Average length of Movies over time		Movie List		
Movie List				昆 XI ▾
Title	**Year** ⟋	**(mins)**	**Rating**	**Director**
Tillie's Punctured Romance	1914	73	2	Mack Sennett
The Birth of a Nation	1915	159	3	D. W. Griffith
Intolerance	1916	178	3	D. W. Griffith
Rebecca of Sunnybrook Farm	1917	71	2	Marshall Neilan
Hearts of the World	1918	122	2	D. W. Griffith
Broken Blossoms	1919	95	2	D. W. Griffith
The Spiders	1919	137	2	Fritz Lang
The Last of the Mohicans	1920	75	2	Clarence Brown
Way Down East	1920	119	2	D. W. Griffith
Suds	1920	67	2	John Francis Dillon
Pollyanna	1920	60	2	Paul Powell

But wait, there's more!

After all of the slicing, dicing, drilling, and view-switching we've done, there is still one question on our minds: how can we export our selected data to Excel? Fortunately, QlikView is very flexible when it comes to this; we can simply right-click on any object and choose **Send to Excel**, or, if it has been enabled by the developer, we can click on the **XL** icon in an object's header, as shown in the following screenshot:

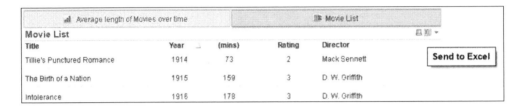

Click on the **XL** icon in the **Movie List** table to export the list of currently selected movies to Excel.

A word of warning when exporting data

When viewing tables with a large number of rows, QlikView is very good at only rendering those rows that are presently visible on the screen. When **Send values to Excel** is selected, all values must be pulled down into an Excel file. For large datasets, this can take a considerable amount of time and may cause QlikView to become unresponsive while it provides the data.

The technology and components behind QlikView

Now that we have seen how QlikView works from the point of view of a business user, it is time to get a little more technical. Let's take an in-depth look at the various components that QlikView consists of.

One of the key elements of QlikView is that it utilizes an in-memory database. Compared with a disk-based database, this offers a great advantage when it comes to performance. While disk-access time is measured in milliseconds, RAM access time is measured in nanoseconds, making it many orders of magnitude faster.

But hold on... you may say, "my hard-disk has much more space than I have RAM in my PC; won't that mean that I can only load limited amounts of data into memory?"

This is a very valid question. Fortunately, there are two factors which counter this potential problem:

- **Cheap memory and the advancement of 64-bit processors and operating systems**: While 1 MB of memory, in 1957, would have cost a staggering US $411 million, nowadays, a gigabyte can be had for less than US $5. Coupled with 64-bit operating systems, which can address much larger amounts of RAM than 32-bit systems (up to 4 TB on Windows 2012, and up to 24 TB on Windows 2016), it is feasible and (relatively) affordable to load huge amounts of data into RAM.

- **Clever compression**: QlikView utilizes some sophisticated compression algorithms (and some common sense, such as de-duplicating data) to significantly reduce the amount of memory that is required to store data. Typically, on-disk data is compressed to 10 percent of its original size when it is loaded into QlikView.

These two factors make it possible to create QlikView applications that contain hundreds of millions — even billions — of records.

The way the data flows

While the in-memory database is excellent technology, it cannot function on its own. Functionally, data flows through QlikView in the following manner:

- It starts with the source data. QlikView can load data from a large variety of sources, including ODBC, OLEDB, flat files (Excel, CSV, and so on), XML, and REST interfaces (for extracting data from web-based APIs). There are also many different connectors, ranging from big enterprise applications such as SAP to social networks such as Twitter.

- The data is loaded into QlikView using a load script. This script can be used to extract, transform, and load data into the in-memory data model or to store it to the disk in intermediary data files called QVD files.

- Data in the in-memory database is stored in an unaggregated format, meaning all aggregations are calculated on the fly. This simplifies data modeling in QlikView, as there is no need for separate aggregation tables.

- Selections made by the user automatically cascade throughout the entire data model and these changes are shown by QlikView's presentation engine.

- QlikView applications can be presented in multiple clients. The Windows application we used earlier is an example of a client; other similar examples will be covered in the next section.

When QlikView use expands

While QlikView deployments within an organization often start with a single (or few) local installations, they often do not stay that way. As the use of QlikView expands, keeping track of different versions, dealing with huge amounts of data, reloading and distributing applications, and making sure that only the right people have access to applications becomes increasingly hard when using only the Windows client.

Fortunately, Qlik offers a large range of components that ensure that QlikView can scale from a local deployment on a laptop all the way to an enterprise-wide solution. These components can be classified into three classes:

- Create content
- Reload, publish, and distribute content
- Consume content

It is also shown in the following screenshot:

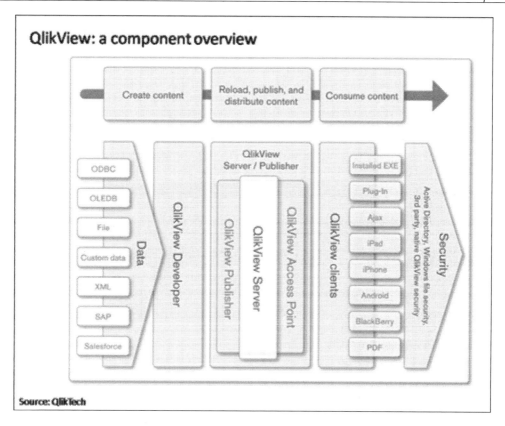

Source: QlikTech

Create content

The Windows application we used earlier to navigate and analyze the data in **Movies Database** cannot only be used to consume content, but it is also the main tool with which to create QlikView documents. As this book is focused on developers, this will be the main focus for the remaining chapters.

Reload, publish, and distribute content

When QlikView deployments expand, it becomes impractical to update and distribute files manually. Also, data is loaded into RAM when using a local Windows application to open QlikView files. When working with huge amounts of data, each PC would also need a huge amount of RAM. This might work for developer PCs, but it is hardly a cost-effective solution to outfit each user in the organization with large amounts of RAM.

Fortunately, QlikView has three components to mitigate these potential roadblocks to broader adoption:

- **QlikView Publisher**: This component can take care of reloading, reducing, and distributing the QlikView documents. Jobs can be scheduled or triggered by external events. When QlikView Publisher has not been licensed, QlikView Server can handle the task of reloading QlikView documents.

- **QlikView Server**: This is a centralized server which can load QlikView documents into memory and allows clients to interact with these documents remotely by using one of the QlikView clients. In addition to providing a central place where documents are stored, this also has the advantage of clients not needing huge amounts of RAM and CPU cores. The clients do not need to load all of the data locally and the processing power of the server is used for calculating and aggregating data.

- **QlikView Access Point**: This is a portal through which users can access their documents

Consume content

QlikView documents can be consumed in multiple ways. While this book mainly focuses on the QlikView desktop Windows application, it is interesting to take note of the other possibilities for deployment:

- **Web browser (IE plugin or AJAX client)**: When accessing a QlikView document through the web browser, the AJAX client is a safe option as it offers great flexibility as it does not require any software to be installed and works with most modern browsers. The second option is the Internet Explorer plugin. As its name implies, it is a plugin (ActiveX object) made to be used with Microsoft's Internet Explorer. While this plugin offers an experience that is closest to the native Windows application, it only works in Internet Explorer and requires the QlikView plugin software to be installed on each client PC.

- **iPad and other tablets**: Tablets can access QlikView by using the AJAX client in their browser. The AJAX client automatically detects when a tablet is being used and switches to a touch-enabled interface. This makes it possible to develop a single QlikView document which can then be rolled out to both regular computers and mobile devices.

- **iPhone, Android, and other smartphones**: Mobile devices with a smaller screen, such as most smartphones, can use a special version of the AJAX client: the small device version. Instead of displaying complete worksheets, which would be unreadable on a small screen, this client shows each of the objects (chart, table, and so on) one by one.

- **QlikView Workbench**: Using QlikView Workbench, objects from QlikView documents can be embedded within .NET-based web solutions

When going through this list of clients, you probably noticed that the AJAX client is the most versatile of all clients. While it hasn't always been that way, nowadays, the visual and functional differences between the AJAX client and the ActiveX client are small enough for the AJAX client to be considered the preferred client for the consumption of QlikView documents by users.

Meet HighCloud Airlines

It's a typical Monday morning at the office. Sara, an executive at HighCloud Airlines, arrives early to begin a busy week. Work has been hectic lately.

Ever since the start of the Euro crisis, the market for air travel and cargo in HighCloud's home market in Europe has been steadily declining. As a result, HighCloud's financial results have also been sloping downward.

A few weeks ago, in an effort to turn the company around, Steve, the CEO, launched an initiative to investigate the company's expansion into other markets. Sara and her team have been tasked with investigating the US airline market. It's a project that, if done well, might really raise the profile of Sara and the team.

Unfortunately, data from many different sources, complicated query tools, and dozens of spreadsheets have made progress slow so far. Even worse, each presentation of preliminary results has triggered a wave of new questions that cannot be answered by the existing reports and analyses. Morale within the team has been steadily dropping and Sara has noticed that Steve is increasingly annoyed by the lack of results.

Unlike the rest of the team, Sara is in an exceptionally good mood this morning. After hearing good things about QlikView, she decided to download a copy of the Personal Edition last weekend. Experimenting with it, she managed to load some data into QlikView and has even created a few charts and tables.

With her laptop under her arm and a smile on her face, she walks confidently into the CEO's office and announces, "Steve, you have to see this."

In this book, we will be following Sara and her team. We will see how they apply QlikView to their business requirements, and how their knowledge and skills, along with your own, evolve throughout the chapters. Each chapter builds on the result of the previous chapter and contains hands-on exercises, along with explanations, background theory, and examples of practical applications.

Summary

This concludes our first chapter. In this chapter, we've learned what QlikView is and how it differs from traditional BI solutions. We've also seen how QlikView works from the perspective of a business user and have had a peek at the various technical components that QlikView consists of. We concluded this chapter with an introduction to Sara and her team, and their task—to investigate if expanding to the US market might help the struggling HighCloud Airlines make a recovery.

To sum it all up, in this chapter, we have learned:

- QlikView is a BI solution that is different from traditional BI solutions because of its associative user experience, its underlying technology, and its typical bottom-up adoption path
- How to make sense of our data by selecting, filtering, searching, bookmarking, cycling, and drilling
- How the technology behind QlikView works, how it is deployed, and the various ways in which applications can be consumed
- What HighCloud's current problems are and how Sara and her team hope to help resolve them using QlikView

Now that we've been introduced to QlikView, in the next chapter we will get hands-on and will develop a small proof of concept document.

2
What's New in QlikView 12?

Since the previous version of this book was published in 2012, the Qlik ecosystem has expanded significantly. In this chapter, we will bring you up to speed with the changes over the past few years.

If QlikView 12 is your first entry into the world of Qlik then you might be tempted to skip this chapter. However, we highly recommend that, even as a new developer you, at least read the *What is new in the Qlik product portfolio?* section.

We will start with a look at some of the most important changes in QlikView 12. Although QlikView 12 Desktop is the main focus of this book, we will also discuss the changes and improvements in QlikView 12 Server and Publisher.

Next, we will take a look at the broader picture and see how the Qlik product portfolio has changed in the past few years. We will learn what these new products do and how they might fit into your Qlik deployment.

Finally, as this book is itself an update, we will finish this chapter by looking at some of the changes that were made in this revised edition of QlikView for Developers.

To summarize, in this chapter we will specifically look at:

- What is new in QlikView 12?
- What is new in the Qlik product portfolio?
- How do the products in the Qlik product portfolio fit together?
- What is new in QlikView 12 for developers?

How is QlikView 12 different from QlikView 11?

Apart from a restyled application icon, at first glance QlikView 12 looks remarkably similar to its predecessor. Under the hood, however, many improvements and fixes have been realized, and in this section we will take a high level view at some of those changes.

Common QIX Engine

The main difference compared to previous versions is that the underlying engine of QlikView has been replaced with the updated QIX Engine 2.0. This is the same engine that powers the other products in the Qlik portfolio (*Qlik Sense Enterprise and the Qlik Analytics Platform,* discussed later). Besides performance improvements over the previous version, this common engine makes it easier to share data models between QlikView and the other Qlik products, notably Qlik Sense. The shared code base of the engine also ensures that future investments that Qlik does in features, performance, security, and connectivity can be easily back ported to QlikView.

64-bit only

Where previously there were both 32-bit and 64-bit versions of the QlikView software, QlikView 12 desktop and server are only available in the 64-bit version. Since the publication of the previous version of this book was in 2012, 64-bit versions of Windows on the desktop have become commonplace (64-bit was already the norm on servers). The 32-bit QlikView desktop version, with its memory limited to 2 GB, has become outdated. If you have a hard requirement to still use a 32-bit version of the software, you will need to fall back to QlikView 11.2.

Online documentation

QlikView 11.2 and earlier included local documentation and help files. With QlikView 12 all documentation and help is found online.

For the English version of QlikView, which we will use in this book, the online help can be found at:

- QlikView 12: `http://help.qlik.com/en-US/qlikview/12.0/Content/Home.htm`

- QlikView 12.1 `http://help.qlik.com/en-US/qlikview/12.1/Content/Home.htm`

You will notice that only the version number is different in the URL.

Downloadable guides can also be found in the online documentation:

- QlikView 12: `http://help.qlik.com/en-US/qlikview/12.0/Content/Guides.htm`
- QlikView 12.1: `http://help.qlik.com/en-US/qlikview/12.1/Content/Guides.htm`

The next changes mainly impact the server side of QlikView, but they are still interesting to take note of.

Security improvements

Although not visible from the outside, Qlik has made significant investments in security around QlikView 12. Improvements include stronger encryption and better encryption handling, centralized client request handling, and XML parsing. These improvements mean that QlikView can now meet some of the more demanding security requirements within the private sector, government, and military.

Mobile touch improvements

With QlikView 12, all the functions that are available in the regular QlikView web client are also accessible on touch devices. Besides consuming applications, this means that you can now also use collaboration capabilities, create and modify objects, and export to Excel on a mobile device. You can also use swiping to scroll, or use a long-press to activate the right-click menus.

Improved clustering and scaling

QlikView 12 supports more nodes in a clustered environment, which means that in multi-node environments QlikView will be able to support more concurrent users.

Clustering improvements in QlikView 12.1

In QlikView 12.1, released in November 2016, even more improvements have been made in the area of clustering, allowing QlikView to scale to even more nodes, users, and documents.

Changes in QlikView 12.1 include improvements for dealing with high-load scenarios, such as shared file caching, offline mode for PGO files, better caching in AccessPoint, and more efficient communication between services.

QlikView 12.1 also has the option to use unbalanced nodes in a cluster (that is, using servers with differences in CPU and RAM in the same cluster). For Publisher, it is now possible to create multiple Publisher (QDS) clusters, referred to as Publisher groups, and to assigns tasks to specific nodes within a cluster.

What is new in the Qlik product portfolio?

Since the publication of the previous version of this book in 2012, the Qlik product suite has changed and expanded significantly, both through acquisitions and the introduction of new products. In this section, we will look at some of the most important changes and we will look at how these fit into the bigger picture.

Qlik Sense Enterprise and the Qlik Analytics Platform

Initially billed as `QlikView.Next` and anticipated to be an update of QlikView, Qlik Sense was launched as a new, separate product in September 2014. Regular users of QlikView will immediately notice that the frontend of Qlik Sense looks very different from QlikView:

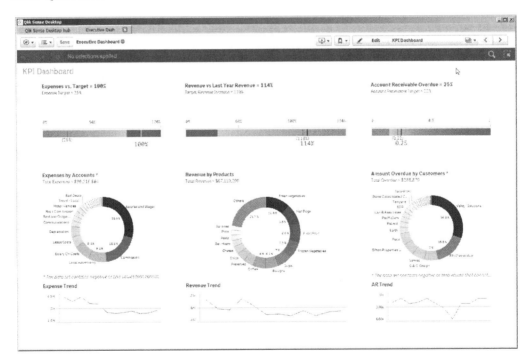

With the introduction of Qlik Sense, Qlik suddenly had two similar products out in the market, which they dubbed the two product strategy. This strategy positions Qlik Sense not as an updated version of QlikView, but rather as a separate self-service visualization solution that co-exists with QlikView. At the same time, QlikView was repositioned as the tool for 'guided analytics'.

The full Qlik marketing mantra is "*Qlik Sense is for Self-Service BI, QlikView is for Guided Analytics*".

As the two product strategy is a major aspect of the Qlik product portfolio and knowing when to apply which product is important, we will have a closer look at the similarities and differences between QlikView and Qlik Sense.

In what way are QlikView and Qlik Sense similar?

Both QlikView 12 and Qlik Sense share the same underlying QIX Engine. They both use the same scripting and expression language. Skills that you have gained (or will gain, using this book) in these areas in QlikView can be directly transferred to Qlik Sense.

In what way do QlikView and Qlik Sense differ?

The main technical differences between QlikView and Qlik Sense are in the frontend presentation and server implementation or, simply put, the things sitting on top of and around the QIX Engine.

Qlik Sense is based on the latest technologies and it employs a web-first approach. It has responsive design, which means that objects automatically adjust to your screen size and device type. This makes it work very well on mobile devices. Qlik Sense also has extensive API's that can be used to automate, extend, or embed the product. All of the development in Qlik Sense takes place on the Qlik Sense Server. As with QlikView, a desktop version, called **Qlik Sense Desktop**, is available. In contrast to QlikView, this desktop version is mainly used as a trial version instead of a development environment. Qlik Sense also has a cloud version, called **Qlik Sense Cloud**.

QlikView is based on proven, but older, technologies. It is Windows-centric and uses a desktop-first approach, with a more pixel-perfect oriented design (that is, if you define a chart to be 500 pixels wide, it will always be 500 pixels wide). Compared to Qlik Sense, a developer can quite easily build very sophisticated, custom-styled applications without any additional programming. For example, QlikView applications can perform specific actions (such as showing or hiding an object, making a selection, selecting a sheet, and so on) when certain conditions are met or events are triggered. QlikView applications are developed in the QlikView Desktop application and deployed to the QlikView Server for consumption by users.

Although Qlik Sense does not have many options for customization or advanced application design out of the box, those who possess web development skills will be able to build very sophisticated applications using the Qlik Sense APIs and the Mashup, Widget, and/or Extension functionalities. The barrier to entry is higher, but a developer who is both skilled in QlikView/Qlik Sense and web development will be able to get far more out of Qlik Sense than they will out of QlikView.

What does this mean for users?

As mentioned before, the distinction between the products, according to Qlik, is that *"Qlik Sense is for Self-Service BI, and QlikView is for Guided Analytics"*. What this means from a user-perspective is that Qlik Sense is more geared towards situations where you do not want to, or cannot, predefine everything upfront. This gives more space to the user to build their own charts, sheets and presentations, and so on, to answer their own questions. Questions that you could possibly not have anticipated. This exploration can be done on either centrally managed, governed data models, or on data that the user adds into Qlik Sense. Building charts and other objects is mainly a drag and drop affair, with very little coding or expression writing. Qlik Sense is an ideal environment for engaged users who want to explore, but have limited technical abilities.

In situations where you need predefined business applications, that is, applications with a thought-out data model, sheets, charts, and calculations that are consumed by end users then QlikView is the preferred option. Qlik refers to this as *"Guided analytics"*. Users can still explore, filter, slice, and dice the data and use it to answer their questions, but adding new visualizations is decidedly less smooth than it is in Qlik Sense.

It is important to keep in mind that the two scenarios described previously mainly relate to the casual user experience. An experienced Qlik developer will just as easily answer a new question with QlikView as with Qlik Sense. In fact, many experienced Qlik developers still say that they prefer QlikView if they want to get something done fast.

What is the Qlik Analytics Platform?

The **Qlik Analytics Platform (QAP)** can be considered a 'headless' version of Qlik Sense Enterprise. Or, more accurately, Qlik Sense Enterprise is the QAP with some additions, such as the Qlik Sense Client.

The QAP contains the QIX Engine and API's, but lacks a frontend. From a licensing perspective, it is quite attractively priced compared to Qlik Sense Enterprise. This makes the QAP ideal for (OEM) companies that want to embed the software and create their own frontend.

Qlik NPrinting

Qlik NPrinting used to be offered as a third-party add-on to QlikView, but it was acquired by Qlik in February 2015.

NPrinting is an add-on product that can be used to create and distribute static reports based on data and visualizations from QlikView and Qlik Sense. In contrast to many other report writers, which usually only output to PDF, NPrinting can output to many popular file formats, for example, Microsoft PowerPoint, Excel, and Word, but also HTML and PDF. Reports can be scheduled and automatically distributed through multiple channels. Users can also subscribe to reports using the **Newsstand** portal.

NPrinting received an extensive overhaul in version 17. QlikView 12 is only supported from version 17 and up.

Qlik Web Connectors

Over the past few years, cloud-based data sources have steadily increased in popularity. In order to easily load (some of) these data sources into QlikView or Qlik Sense, Qlik offers the Web Connectors as a separate add-on. The Qlik Web Connectors were sold as a third-party add-on under the name QVSource by Industrial CodeBox, until Qlik acquired the company in May 2016.

The Qlik Web Connectors provide preconfigured connectors to load data from sources such as Facebook, Twitter, Google Analytics, Microsoft Dynamics CRM, MailChimp, or SugarCRM.

Besides the paid Web Connectors, Qlik also offers a free, generic REST Connector. We will learn more about this connector in *Chapter 4*, *Data Sources*.

Qlik GeoAnalytics

Qlik GeoAnalytics is Qlik's most recent acquisition. It was previously known as **IdevioMaps** and was added to the portfolio in January 2017 when Qlik purchased parent company Idevio. Qlik GeoAnalytics is a separate add-on that adds geospatial visualization capabilities to QlikView and Qlik Sense.

Qlik DataMarket

Acquired by Qlik in November 2014, and relaunched as a Qlik branded product in April 2015, Qlik DataMarket offers data as a service. With Qlik DataMarket, you can easily import external reference data into QlikView (and Qlik Sense) and combine it with internal data. Available data ranges from weather and demographics to exchange rates and financial information.

DataMarket is a subscription-based service, but it also has a free tier. Data from DataMarket is loaded into QlikView using the DataMarket Connector. We will look into this connector in more detail in *Chapter 4*, *Data Sources*.

How do the products in the Qlik product portfolio fit together?

We have seen that the Qlik product portfolio has expanded significantly in the past few years. At the time of QlikView 11 for Developers, there was only QlikView. Nowadays there is a complete range of products and add-ons.

The following diagram gives a high-level overview of how all the products fit together. The base is QlikView and the QAP, both of these use the same QIX Engine. The QAP underpins Qlik Sense Enterprise, which adds a frontend client and collaboration features. NPrinting can be used for static reporting on either QlikView or Qlik Sense. The Qlik Web Connectors, Rest Connector, and DataMarket let both QlikView and Qlik Sense ingest external, web-based data. Geographical analysis in both QlikView and Qlik Sense can be done with the Qlik GeoAnalytics add-on.

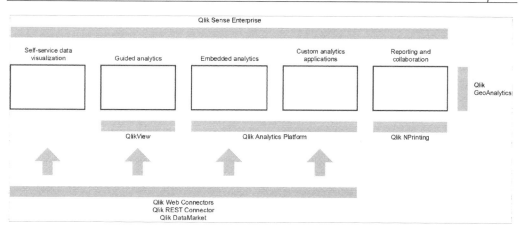

What is new in QlikView 12 for Developers?

The previous version of this book, *QlikView 11 for Developers*, has been out since 2012. The book has been very well received and we know that you should not change a winning formula. Besides this chapter and *Chapter 4, Data Sources* which introduces some new data sources, little has been changed other than correcting the various errata that have been collected through the years.

We also decided to change the book's title to be version-agnostic, since most of the concepts we aim to teach in the book apply for the software in general and are not dependent on the version (11, 11.2, 12, and so on). We also made sure the exercises are also relevant not only for QlikView 11 or QlikView 12, but for QlikView in general. However, there may be small UI changes between versions, but from what we've experienced those UI differences are not very significant at the time of writing.

Since QlikView and Qlik Sense share the same QIX Engine, this also means that the concepts we discuss related to backend and data modeling best practices, as well as expressions, apply to both products. However, the frontend exercises are QlikView-specific.

Summary

A lot has happened in the world of Qlik since the previous version of this book was published in November 2012. In this chapter, we've caught up with the most important changes in QlikView 12. We have learned how the Qlik ecosystem has expanded and how all of these products fit together in the bigger picture. We have also gotten a high level overview of the changes that were made in the revised version of this book.

In the next chapter, we will get hands-on with QlikView 12 and we will develop a small proof-of-concept document.

3
Seeing is Believing

As we've seen in the previous chapter, HighCloud Airlines has a particular need: to be able to analyze the US airline market from different perspectives, be able to create reports that help them better understand what the situation is, and evaluate if entering that market is a good strategy. Sara took the risk and showed the CEO what they could potentially do with QlikView and he was impressed by what he saw. After their meeting, Sara was asked to arrange a formal proof-of-concept session.

This chapter will not only follow a QlikView team working on the **Seeing is Believing (SiB)** phase of the pre-sale process, along with the HighCloud Airlines executives evaluating it, but it will also help us learn some basic concepts about developing QlikView documents.

So, let's get our hands on the subject and start creating. There is no better way to learn than by *doing*, and this chapter will be the initial platform on which we will base our QlikView development experience. It will help you build your first business discovery app with QlikView, completely hands-on from the start.

On a technical level, after going through the tutorial presented in this chapter, you will be able to:

- Understand the steps required in the construction process of a QlikView document
- Identify what dimensions and expressions are within the context of a QlikView document
- Build charts to visualize and aggregate data
- Design a basic user interface for navigating through the QlikView document

What is a SiB?

A SiB (an acronym for Seeing is Believing) is the proof-of-concept session in which, during the pre-sale process, the technical capabilities of the QlikView software are demonstrated to the prospective customer. The way we demo QlikView at this stage usually involves creating a targeted QlikView document that uses the customer's actual data in a limited amount of time.

That's why, in this chapter, we will build a QlikView document based on real and useful data, focused on HighCloud Airlines' line of business. The dataset we will use is publicly available and covers information about airline operations in the US. The original data files have been downloaded from The Bureau of Transportation Statistics of the United States website (http://transtats.bts.gov), and have been pre-processed so that we can focus on the main concepts this chapter is intended to outline. As the book evolves, we will introduce more advanced concepts so that, in the end, we are able to work with the original data files throughout the whole processing phase.

Because of the nature of the SiB phase, the analytical application should be developed rather quickly by the QlikView team. Since it will mainly be focused on technical features and data discovery functionalities, some design details (such as color, style, object positioning, and so on) have been left out for now. However, these details will be covered in their own good time, later in the book.

Preparing the workspace

Before we start, we need to make sure we have everything we'll need throughout the chapter.

Since the previous chapter covered the QlikView Desktop installation process, we assume that it is already installed on your machine by now. If not, please take a moment to install it before continuing.

Setting up the folder structure

We will create a Windows folder structure with which we'll work throughout the book. This set of folders will help us organize the various files we'll be using and arrange them by the specific role these files play in our project.

 The files provided along with the book are already structured with the folders we need. If you have already copied the original files, you can skip the outlined process.

A typical QlikView deployment scenario will include different types of files, but for now we'll just focus on two of them:

- The source data files
- The QlikView document

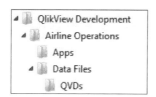

> **Downloading the example code**
>
> You can download the example code files for all Packt books you have purchased from your account at http://www.packtpub.com. If you purchased this book elsewhere, you can visit http://www.packtpub.com/support and register to have the files e-mailed directly to you.

Follow these steps to set up the environment:

1. Create a Windows folder with which you will work throughout the entire book and call it `QlikView Development`. Place it in the location of your choice.
2. Inside this folder, create another one. This folder will specifically be used to store the set of files we will work with. You may name the new folder as `Airline Operations`.
3. Inside the `Airline Operations` folder, create two additional subfolders, one called `Data Files` and the other called `Apps`.
4. Inside the `Data Files` folder, create yet another folder and name it `QVDs`. The final folder structure is depicted in the following screenshot:

```
▲ 📁 QlikView Development
   ▲ 📁 Airline Operations
        📁 Apps
      ▲ 📁 Data Files
           📁 QVDs
```

5. Copy the QVD files corresponding to this chapter into the `Data Files\QVDs` folder.

Our environment is almost set up. The only thing left is to create the QlikView document.

Creating the QlikView document

To create the QlikView file we will use to build our app, follow these steps:

1. Launch the QlikView program.
2. Click on the **File** menu and select **New**.

3. The **Getting Started** wizard dialog may instantly appear, asking you to select a data source. We will, for now, ignore it. Click on **Cancel**.

   ○ Don't worry if this dialog window doesn't appear when launching QlikView.

4. Go to the **File** menu again and click on **Save as...**. We will save the document inside the `Airline Operations\Apps` folder and name it `Airline Operations.qvw`.

Now that we have our environment ready, let's move on to create our analytical application.

 QlikView documents are often referred to as 'applications' or 'apps' as they offer a much more interactive experience than the term 'document' would imply. In this book, we will be using the terms 'document', 'application' and 'app' interchangeably.

Creating the app

We can think of a QlikView document as being composed of two major elements:

- The dataset that the user analyzes: This is the backend of our QlikView document and includes all of the source tables needed to build a data model, as well as the logic to update its source data.

- The user interface through which the user analyzes the data: This is the frontend of our analytical app and includes the objects contained in the document (like a listbox to make selections and filter data), or the charts and tables used to visualize the information.

In hand with the elements described above, we will break the construction of our QlikView document into two major phases:

- Constructing the data model
- Designing the user interface

However, before moving on to create our QlikView document, we should have a clear understanding of the business-side requirements for our app, so the construction and design phases are fully focused towards meeting those requirements.

The requirements

In our SiB scenario, HighCloud Airlines executives have determined that they would benefit from a business discovery application that helps them answer questions around the following topics:

- Number of flights across time
- Number of transported passengers
- Amount of transported cargo (mail and freight)
- Most-used routes

At the same time, the application should allow the user to choose airline and aircraft dimensions, as well as origin and destination airports, cities, and states.

Now that we have our goals clearly defined, let's move on to the construction phase.

Constructing the data model

The tutorial in this chapter is designed to focus mostly on creating the analysis interface of our QlikView document. However, a fundamental part of QlikView development is to construct an appropriate data model to support the various analyses required in the application. The dataset we will work with in this chapter will help us describe the most important concepts we need to consider when building the data model.

What is a data model?

The heart of a QlikView application is its data model. It is composed of the different source tables that contain the information and data used to measure a company's performance. The data model is constructed by using QlikView's scripting language.

A correctly-built data model will associate all of its tables in a way which allows us to manipulate the data however we like. This means that the creation of analysis objects (charts) across different dimensions depends mainly on how the data model is built and how its tables are associated (how they are linked to each other).

Loading the fact table

To start building our data model, we will load the fact table of our source data files into QlikView.

A fact table is a table that contains the measurements across which we'll make the analyses. The fact table is, at the same time, the central part of the data model.

 A data model can contain more than one fact table. We'll deal with the implications regarding schema design in *Chapter 5, Data Modeling* and *Chapter 9, Data Modeling Best Practices*.

Follow these steps to load a fact table:

1. Go to the **Edit Script** window by pressing *Ctrl + E* or by selecting **File | Edit Script...** from the menu bar.

2. In the **Edit Script** window, we will initially have 10 lines of code, all starting with the word SET. Those are the initialization variables for some common formatting options. We will leave them as they are for now.

3. At the bottom of the **script editor**, we will see a set of tabs containing specific functions regarding script generation. Make sure the **Data** tab is active and mark the **Relative Paths** checkbox, as shown in the following screenshot:

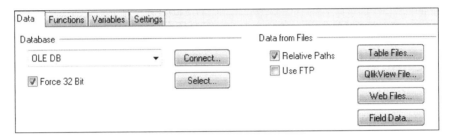

4. Position the cursor a few lines below the initialization statements and click on the **Table Files...** button to bring up the **Open Local Files** wizard. Browse to the Data Files\QVDs folder we created in the previous section and select the Flight Data.qvd file, as shown in the following screenshot. Click on **Open**.

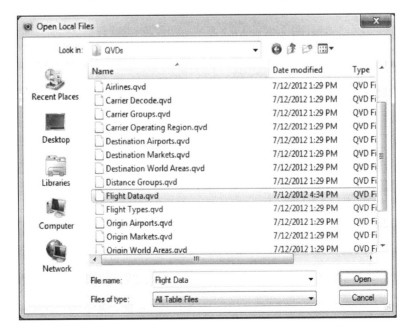

The QVD file we are using is in an optimized format for use with QlikView and, as noted previously, is the result of processing the original data files that are provided in CSV format. We will dive deeper into what these files are, and how to create them, as the book evolves.

5. The **File Wizard** dialog now appears. The **File Type** option will be set to **Qvd** (on the left pane) automatically, as shown below. Click on **Finish** to close the window.

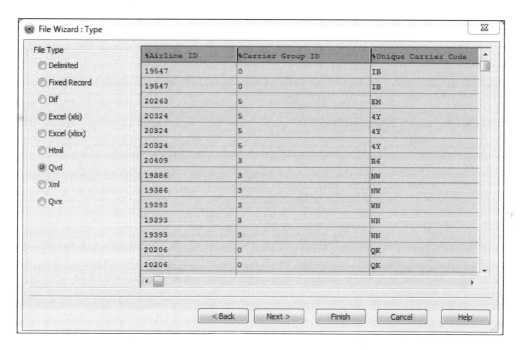

Afterwards, the Load statement is automatically created and inserted into the **Script Editor** window at the cursor's position.

Since we enabled the **Relative Paths** option, the Directory; statement is placed before the Load statement. We can delete this instruction since it is not relevant in our script.

6. The next thing we'll do is assign an internal name to the loaded table and call it Main Data. To do this, type [Main Data]: (don't forget the colon) right above the Load statement.

Brackets are required to enclose the table name because it contains special characters, in this case a blank space.

The script will look like the following:

```
[Main Data]:
LOAD
        ...Field Names...
        ...Field Names...
        ...Field Names...
FROM
[..\Data Files\QVDs\Flight Data.QVD]
(qvd);
```

The Load statement is composed of:

- The names of the fields we want to load from the source table.

- The From statement, specifying the location of the file we want to read. The location can be specified either as a full path or a relative path.

- The attributes we set about the file for QlikView to load it appropriately. In this case, this part contains only the string (qvd). In other cases it may include other important properties. We will cover this in more detail in *Chapter 4, Data Sources*.

7. We will now reload the script for the data to be loaded into the QlikView document so we can start working with it. However, before we do that, it's a good practice to hit the **Save** button so we do not lose the changes if the script execution goes wrong.

   After saving the file, locate the **Reload** button, shown in the following screenshot, in the toolbar at the top and click on it.

8. After the script execution, the **Sheet Properties** window will appear. We will use it in the next section, but for now just click on **OK** to dismiss it.

Our data model now contains the **Main Data** table.

Playing with listboxes

The first object we will look at in this tutorial is the listbox. A listbox is the most basic of all QlikView objects and contains all the occurring values for a given field in the data model. As demonstrated in *Chapter 1, Meet QlikView*, a listbox is used to make selections in the document and filter the data.

To start using this object and better understand its function, bring up the **Sheet Properties** dialog window by right-clicking in a blank space inside the sheet area, then selecting **Properties...** from the context menu. Once the **Sheet Properties** window is open, make sure the **Fields** tab is active.

From the **Available Fields** list on the left, add the **Carrier Name**, **Origin City**, **Origin Country**, **Origin State**, **Destination City**, **Destination Country**, and **Destination State** fields to the **Fields Displayed in Listboxes** list on the right by highlighting each of them and clicking on the **Add >** button.

 To highlight all of the required fields at once, click on the first one and press the *Ctrl* key before selecting the others.

The following screenshot shows the **Sheet Properties** dialog window:

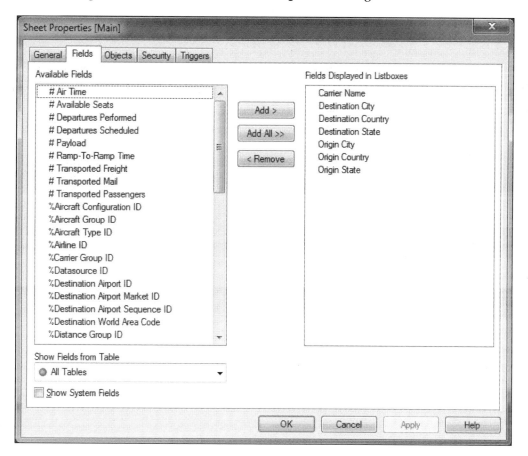

Click on **OK** to apply the changes.

The procedure we followed above will add one listbox for each of the fields we selected. Let's take a moment to position them in our workspace.

The listboxes will initially all be placed on top of each other. Go to the **Layout** menu and click on **Rearrange Sheet Objects** and they will be dispersed across the screen space.

Sometimes it's necessary to click on this command more than once because the objects don't get properly distributed at first. So, if necessary, click on **Rearrange Sheet Objects** two or three times until all of the seven listboxes we added are properly spread throughout the screen space.

You can also click and drag individual objects to position them in the place you want them on the screen. Make sure to click on the caption bar of the object to be able to drag it.

Aligning listboxes

Another way of rearranging the objects is by using the alignment commands found in the **Design** toolbar. Enable the **Design** toolbar, which is disabled by default, by selecting **View** | **Toolbars** | **Design** from the menu bar. To use the alignment buttons, select two or more objects at once by clicking on them while pressing the *Shift* key.

In the previous chapter, we talked about how listboxes work, so you should now be familiar with it and the color-coding used to mark selected, associated, and excluded values respectively. Even so, let's use some of the listboxes added above and reinforce these concepts.

Let's click on the **Adana, Turkey** value in the **Origin City** listbox. This action will filter the dataset to show only information regarding flights departing from **Adana, Turkey**. We can instantly see how the selected value will turn green. The rest of the listboxes will also be updated to show the data that is associated with the specific value we just selected. The values associated with our selection will have a white background and the data that is excluded (that is, those values that have no relation with our selection) will be shown with a gray background. The new selection state is depicted in the following screenshot:

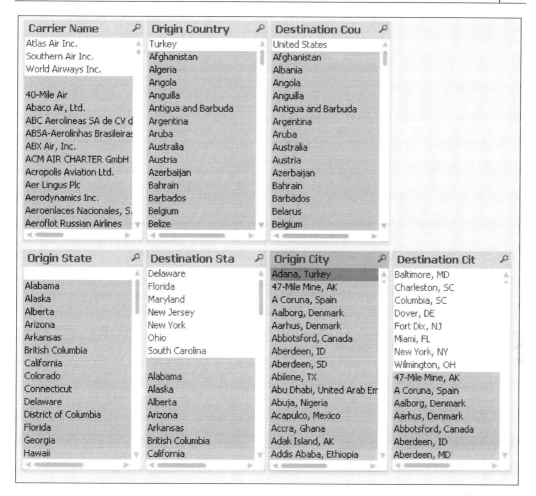

Which carriers have logged flights departing from **Adana, Turkey**? In which cities and states are those flights arriving? These questions are easily answered by QlikView's associative engine by simply selecting a value in the **Origin City** listbox. One click gives us multiple answers.

After a selection is made, QlikView updates the charts and objects in the document to match that particular request. This selection process is similar, in a way, to making filters in an Excel table. It's also similar to making a query in a database, but with the code part laid aside.

Using the associations presented in the previous screenshot, we can confidently make the following affirmations:

- Only three carriers have reported flights from **Adana, Turkey**. All other carriers have not.
- Only seven U.S. states have been destinations to flights departing from **Adana, Turkey**, in the analyzed dataset.
- We can also see, in the screenshot, the eight cities where those flights arrived.

Click on the **Clear** button, shown in the following screenshot, in the **Navigation** toolbar to reset the selection state.

Associating additional tables

At this point, the sole table we loaded provides a lot of usable information about airline traffic for us to analyze. However, while there is a lot of data, there are only a few descriptive values. Instead, the table contains references (identifiers) to values stored in other tables. We need to integrate additional tables into the data model which will provide the description to those identifiers and, by doing so, we will enrich the meaning and context of our data and allow for more insight into the analyses we make.

Structuring the script

In order to add more tables to the data model, we need to add the corresponding Load statements to the script. In order to keep things tidy, we will separate some of these Load statements and store them in different tabs in the **Edit Script** window. That way, we will keep our script well-structured. Since we already have a Load statement (the one we created in the previous section), let's place it in its own tab.

Go to the **Edit Script** window (*Ctrl + E*) and position the cursor on the line directly above the name we assigned to the first table ([Main Data]). Then, go to the **Tab** menu and select **Insert Tab at Cursor…**. The **Tab Rename Dialog** window will appear, in which we will type Main Data, to name the new tab, and click on **OK**. The code we generated previously will be moved to this new tab.

Now, let's load the remaining tables. We'll start by adding the **Carrier Groups** table, using the following steps:

1. Activate the tab on the far right, which should be the one named **Main Data**, and select **Tab | Add Tab...**. In the **Tab Rename Dialog** window, type `Airlines` and click on **OK**.

2. Click on the **Table Files...** button and browse to the `Carrier Groups.qvd` file located in the `Data Files\QVDs` folder. Highlight it and click on **Open**.

3. The **Qvd** file type should automatically show as selected in the left pane of the **File Wizard: Type** window. Click on **Finish** to close the dialog window.

4. Remove the `Directory;` instruction and assign a name to the table by typing `[Carrier Groups]:` right above the `Load` statement.

Take a moment to follow steps 2 through 4 for the remaining tables, which are listed below, but assign a different table name to each of them in step 4.

> Before adding a new `Load` statement, make sure the cursor has been placed in a new line in the **Script Editor**.

We will add the tables contained in the following files to the following tabs:

*   Airlines tab:
    *   `Airlines.qvd`
    *   `Carrier Operating Region.qvd`
    *   `Flight Types.qvd`

*   Aircrafts tab (follow step 1, above, to create it):
    *   `Aircraft Groups.qvd`
    *   `Aircraft Types.qvd`

*   Airports tab (follow step 1, above, to create it):
    *   `Distance Groups.qvd`

> **QlikView** script is followed from top to bottom and then left to right across the tabs. As a best practice, each new source table should be placed in its own tab whenever possible.

After adding these tables and reloading the script (as just described), we can press *Ctrl + T* to bring up the **Table Viewer** window, which shows the newly constructed data model as in the following image:

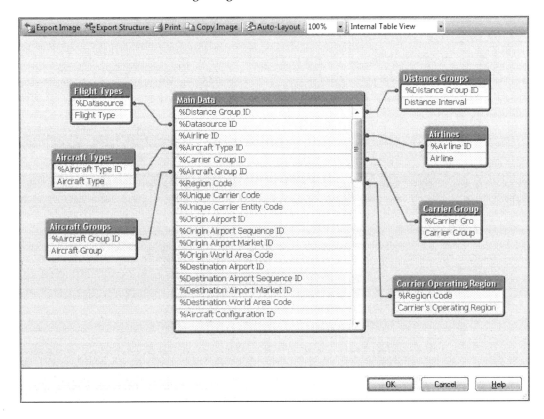

Each blue-bordered box represents a loaded table, and it lists the fields contained in that table. We can also see a blue line that shows the connection between any two tables and marks the associations generated by QlikView in the data model.

> To rearrange the layout of the data model in the **Table Viewer** window, click on the **Auto-Layout** button or click and drag the table titles.

The rule for two tables to be linked is simply that they must share a field with the same name. As a developer, you can use alias field names to link or unlink tables and ensure the created associations are correct. **Table Viewer** is very helpful when verifying table associations.

[

There is another rule for constructing data models: Two tables should be linked by only one field. If they have two or more fields in common, a **Synthetic Key** will be created which can be a potential issue that needs to be addressed. We'll cover these rules in depth in *Chapter 5, Data Modeling*.
]

Creating the dashboard tab

In this section, we will see how we can enhance the analytical capabilities of our QlikView document by adding interactive charts.

First, we will add a new sheet and name it Dashboard. From the design toolbar, locate the **Add Sheet** button, shown below, and click on it.

To rename the new sheet, right-click on its background area and select **Properties...**. Then, from the **Sheet Properties** window, activate the **General** tab, locate the **Title** field, and type Dashboard. Click on **OK**.

[

If the design toolbar is not visible, go to **View | Toolbars | Design** on the menu bar.
]

Creating and positioning the filters and user controls

We will start by adding user controls in the form of listboxes to our new sheet.

Right-click on a blank space of the sheet area and click on **Select Fields...**. Then, add the following fields to allow filtering: **Year**, **Quarter**, **Month**, **Carrier's Operating Region**, **Carrier Group**, **Aircraft Group**, and **Flight Type**.

After adding the specified fields, click on **OK**.

We will adjust some of the properties in the created listboxes, starting with the **Year** listbox. Right-click on it and select **Properties...** from the context menu.

The changes we will make to this listbox are set in the **Presentation** tab of the **Properties** dialog window. Adjust the following settings:

1. Set the **Alignment** to `Center` for both **Text** and **Numbers**.
2. Uncheck **Single Column**.
3. Mark the **Fixed Number of Columns** checkbox and set it to `3`.
4. Uncheck the **Order by Column** checkbox.
5. Click on **OK** to apply the changes.

Follow the earlier procedure for the **Quarter**, **Month** and **Carrier's Operating Region** listboxes, changing only the **Fixed Number of Columns** setting as follows:

- Set it to `2` in the **Quarter** field
- Set it to `6` in the **Month** field
- Set it to `3` in the **Carrier's Operating Region** field

Let's now reposition these listboxes appropriately on the screen space, and resize them if needed. We should have them placed in a way more or less similar to those in the following screenshot:

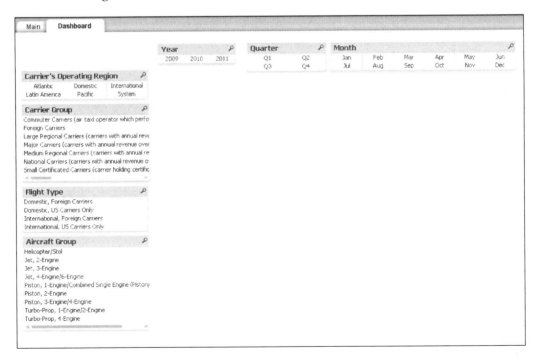

Optimizing the screen space

As you may have noticed, we still need to include a few more fields for filtering, but don't have much space available (since we must reserve the main part of the screen for charts and tables). We will make use of an additional object type to optimize the screen space used by listboxes: the search object.

The search object will allow the user to search for information related to airlines and carriers, as well as aircrafts. All of this by using only a small space on the screen.

Click on the **Create Search Object** button, shown below, located on the design toolbar.

From the **New Search Object** dialog window, we can specify which fields the object search will go through when the user types a search string. We will enable the search across **Selected Fields**, so make sure the corresponding radio button is selected, highlight the fields to be added, and clicking on the **Add>** button.

The following fields need to be added: **Aircraft Type**, **Airline**, **Carrier Code**, **Carrier Name**, **Destination City**, **Destination Country**, **Destination State**, **Origin City**, **Origin Country**, **Origin State**, and **Unique Carrier**.

The order in which the fields are added is not important.

Click on **OK** and reposition the search object, shown below, to the upper-left corner of the screen by clicking on the magnifying glass and dragging it with the mouse.

The way the **Search** object works is outlined below:

1. The user clicks inside the **Search** object and types a search string. A search string is any word(s) or set of characters the user is interested in finding within the loaded data.

2. All field values containing the specified search string will be listed below the search box. The matching search string will be highlighted in yellow and grouped by the field in which the value is found. For example, the following screenshot shows results for the search string South:

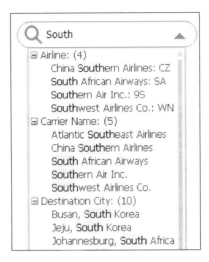

3. When the total matching values in any given field exceed a certain number (10 by default), all of the corresponding values will be collapsed. Otherwise, they will all be listed. You can change the default limit value from the **Presentation** tab of the **Properties** dialog window.

Now that our search object and listboxes are set up, let's create a few charts.

Number of flights over time

Our first analysis object will be a bar chart which will show the number of logged flights per year.

Locate the **Create Chart** button, shown in the following screenshot, in the design toolbar and click on it.

The **Create Chart** wizard will appear. In the **Window Title** field, enter Traffic per year. From the **Chart Type** section, select the **Bar Chart** option (the first one to the left) and click on **Next**.

The next dialog window is **Dimensions**. A dimension is a field across which data is aggregated on the chart.

From the list on the left, locate and highlight the **Year** field and add it to the **Used Dimensions** list by clicking on the **Add >** button. After that, click on **Next**, as shown in the following screenshot:

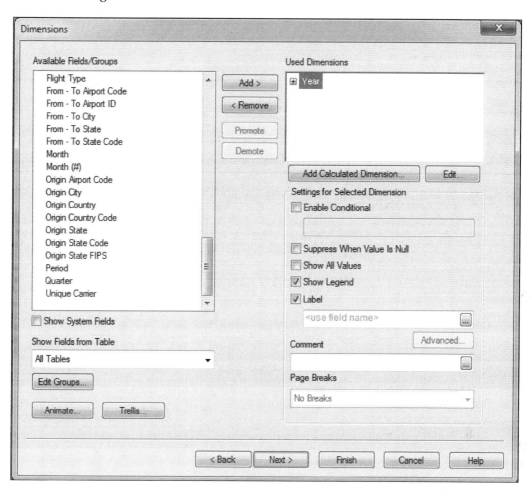

We will now deal with the expression, which is the formula QlikView will use to calculate the metric we want. In this case, we want to get the total (a sum aggregation) number of flights performed. In the **Edit Expression** dialog, which opens automatically after clicking on **Next** in the previous window, type:

```
Sum ([# Departures Performed])
```

The **Edit Expression** window is shown in the following screenshot:

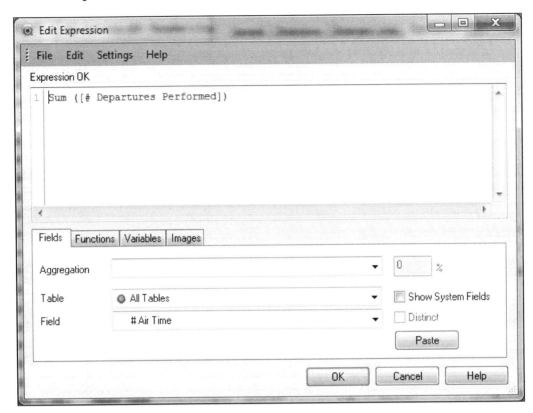

Click on **OK** to continue.

> **Building the expression**
>
> You can either type the expression directly or use the drop-down fields at the bottom of the **Edit Expression** window. When using the drop-down method, click on **Paste** after selecting the desired fields.

We will assign a label to our expression by entering # of Flights in the **Label** field of the **Expressions** dialog.

We will continue making a few additional adjustments to our chart in a moment, but for now we'll just click on **Finish** to exit the **Create Chart** wizard, which is composed of several tabs. You should see something similar to the following screenshot:

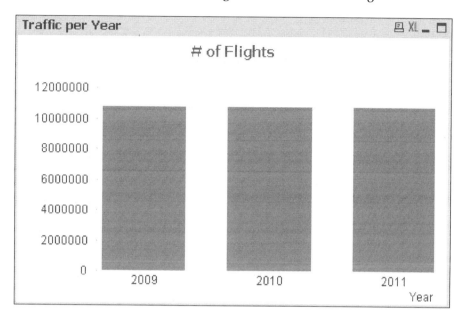

We will now go back to the **Properties** dialog (right-click on the chart and select **Properties…**), which contains the same options as the **Create Chart** wizard, and make the following adjustments to our chart:

1. From the **Caption** tab, uncheck the **Show Caption** option.
   - The **Caption** tab is the right-most tab in the **Properties** window. You might need to use the slider buttons at the top-right corner to make it visible.

2. From the **Number** tab, select **Integer** as the number format.

3. From the **Axes** tab, enable the **Show Grid** checkbox from the **Expression Axes** section (the one at the top, since there are two **Show Grid** checkboxes).

4. Also from the **Axes** tab, change the **Primary Dimension Labels** orientation to **Diagonal**.

After clicking on **OK** to apply the above changes, resize and reposition the chart on the screen to occupy an appropriate part of the upper space of the window. What we should have so far is:

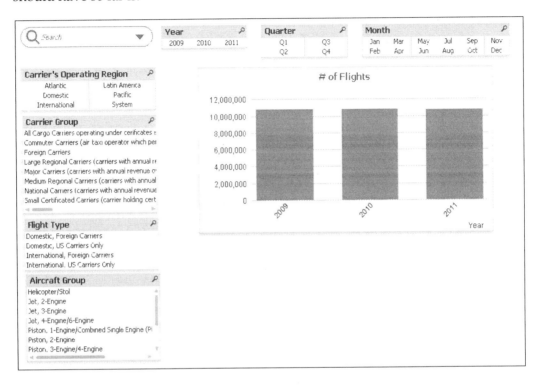

With the above user interface, a user can now start making queries, filter data, and see how the chart updates with every new selection. We can, for example, ask a question like: How many flights per year have been performed by foreign carriers? How many of those flights were domestic and how many were international?

However, let's enhance the functionality a bit more.

One chart and multiple analyses with cyclic expressions

We will now add one more level of interactivity to our chart by using a **Cyclic Expression** group. Having a cyclic expression means the user will have the ability to interactively change the measure or formula used in a chart.

The cyclic group we will create will hold expressions to calculate the number of flights, number of enplaned passengers, total freight, and total mail transported.

To create a cyclic expression, right-click on the **Traffic per year** chart and select **Properties...** from the context menu.

Since we already have the first expression created, we will continue by beginning to create the second one. Activate the **Expressions** tab and click on the **Add** button. In the **Edit Expression** dialog window, type the following expression:

```
Sum ([# Transported Passengers])
```

Click on **OK** and set the label for this expression as # of Enplaned Passengers.

Make sure this second expression is highlighted and click on the **Group** button. This will automatically create the cyclic group for our expressions.

Click on the **Add** button once more and add the following expression:

```
Sum ([# Transported Freight])
```

The label for this expression will be Transported Freight. Make sure the new expression is highlighted and click on the **Group** button again.

Click on the **Add** button again to add our last expression:

```
Sum ([# Transported Mail])
```

The label for this expression will be Transported Mail. Make sure the new expression is highlighted and click on the **Group** button again.

Finally, go to the **Number** tab and make sure that all of our expressions are formatted as **Integer**. Click on **OK** to apply the changes.

After following this procedure, our chart will have the ability to change its active expression (metric) through a cycle button (in the form of a circular arrow) that will be placed at the lower-left corner of the object.

The user can select the measure that he/she wishes to activate by either clicking on it directly to sequentially change the chart's expression, or by clicking on the little black down-arrow to display the drop-down menu from which the desired expression can be selected.

 We can also activate the drop-down menu by right-clicking anywhere inside the cycle button.

Our chart should look like the following screenshot:

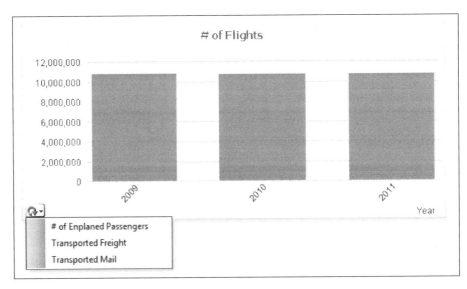

Adding a time drill-down group

Using the same chart object as in the previous section, we will now make use of a different kind of dimension: **Drill-down Group**. We will change the **Year** dimension with a hierarchical group that will contain the **Year** and **Month** fields.

First, right-click on the bar chart created above and select **Properties...**. Activate the **Dimensions** tab, then locate the **Edit Groups...** button at the lower-left corner and click on it.

The **Groups** dialog window will pop up. Click on the **New...** button and, from the **Group Settings** dialog window, enter Time as the **Group Name**, making sure the **Drill-down Group** radio button is selected.

From the **Available Fields** list on the left, locate the **Year** and **Month** fields, and add them to the **Used Fields** section on the right by highlighting them and clicking on the **Add>** button. Make sure the fields are added in the correct order.

Using an alternate label

By default, each field will use its own name as the label in the chart. However, we can specify a different label for each of them by typing it on the **Label** field at the bottom of the **Used Fields** list. For now, we will use the default label.

The **Group Settings** dialog window should now look like the following:

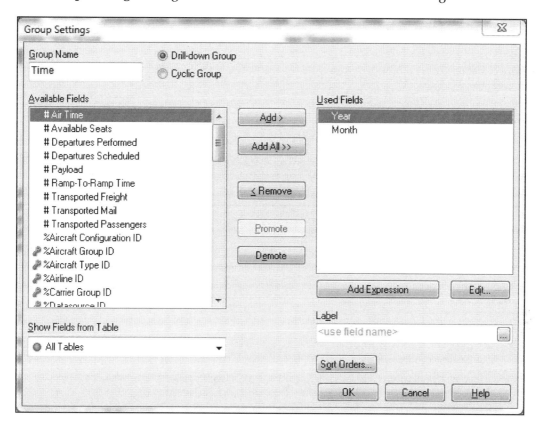

Click on **OK** to apply the changes in the **Group Settings** dialog, and click on **OK** again to close the **Group** window.

 If the fields are not added in the correct order, use the **Promote** and **Demote** buttons to rearrange them.

You will now see the newly created group in the **Available Fields/Groups** list in the **Dimensions** window. Highlight it and add it to the **Used Dimensions** list by clicking on the **Add>** button. Then, remove the one we previously had (**Year**) by highlighting it and clicking on the **<Remove** button.

Click on **OK**.

We now have a bar chart showing the number of flights per year. We can drill down to see a monthly trend by clicking on one of the bars, which initially represents a year. Another way of drilling down is by making an in-chart lasso selection covering one of the bars. Our chart should look like the following screenshot:

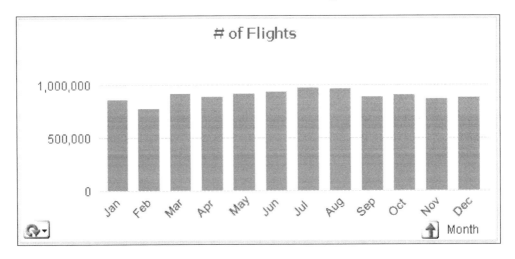

> **Navigating back up**
>
>
>
> When drilling down, you can go back to the previous level in the **Drill-down Group** by either clicking on the up-facing arrow next to the field name in the legend box (down to the right), or by clicking the **Back** button on the navigation toolbar.

With the functionality presented in this section, as well as in the previous one, the user is free to decide how he/she wants to visualize the data: selecting, slicing, drilling, and swapping as per his/her convenience. Also, the space taken up by one single chart can be used to make a lot of different analyses with just a few clicks.

> Besides drill-down groups, we can also create cyclic groups for the user to interactively change a chart's dimensions. This is similar to what we did with the cyclic expression. The procedure to create a cyclic group dimension is the same as the one described above for drill-down groups, we just select **Cyclic Group** instead of **Drill-down Group** in the **Group Settings** dialog window.

Top 10 routes

We will now add a chart in the form of table to display the top routes in terms of number of flights, enplaned passengers, transported freight, and transported mail. Let's call it Top 10 Routes.

Start by clicking on the **Create Chart** button from the design toolbar. From the first dialog in the **New Chart** wizard, select the **Straight Table** icon, shown below, as **Chart Type** and set **Window Title** to Top 10 Routes. Click on **Next**.

In the **Dimensions** window, add the **From – To City** field to the **Used Dimensions** list and click on **Next**.

We will add the following four expressions and their corresponding labels:

- Flights: Sum ([# Departures Performed])
- Passengers: Sum ([# Transported Passengers])
- Freight: Sum ([# Transported Freight])
- Mail: Sum ([# Transported Mail])

After adding the expressions, make sure to set **Total Mode** to **No Totals** for all four of them. This is done by selecting the corresponding radio button at the lower-right corner of the window.

 The **Total Mode** setting is unique to each expression, so we need to highlight each of the expressions from the list and change its **Total Mode** one at a time.

The **Total Mode** section is shown in the following screenshot:

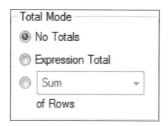

Click on **Next** two times to open to the **Presentation** dialog window. Once there, enable the **Max Number (1 – 100)** checkbox and set it to 10.

Click on **Next** three times to get to the **Number** dialog window and make sure to set all of the expressions to the **Integer** format.

Click on **Finish** and, after rearranging and resizing the objects, we should have the following:

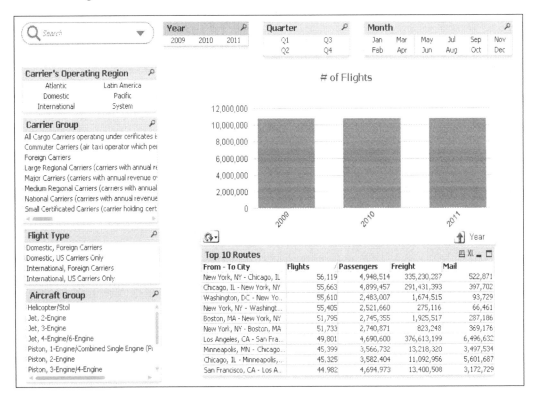

For the table to actually show the top values, we need to sort one of the four expression columns in either ascending or descending order. To do that, double-click on the header cell of the column you want to sort. The first time the column is sorted, it will use the ascending order. You can double-click it again to sort in descending order.

Now that we have prepared a QlikView document, we can explore and discover the data contained in it. We can interact with our document, make selections, and use the charts to make sense of the information.

Summary

We have just started creating and building analytical applications with QlikView. Although the data model we used was simple to build, we covered the basic concepts a developer should consider when designing it.

The main objective of this chapter was to show you the basics of QlikView development from the design perspective, to create basic objects, and to change different properties to make them more functional.

This chapter helped you learn how to load source tables from QVDs, to associate different source tables to create a data model, and to identify dimensions and expressions in the context of a QlikView document.

It also showed you how to create a user interface with user controls to filter data and make selections. Finally, we learned how to create charts and tables that have a high degree of interactivity.

In the next chapter we will learn how we can load data from different data sources.

4
Data Sources

We've completed the "seeing is believing" phase with big success. We've shown HighCloud Airlines the potential value that QlikView can bring to their business and how they will be able to give their raw data the meaning that their business requires to make everyday decisions. Now, the natural question that arises after seeing what QlikView can do on the frontend is: what type of database does QlikView require to work?

The straight answer to this question is simply that QlikView does not necessarily require a specific database or **Data Warehouse** (**DWH**) to pull data from. It can benefit from using a DWH, but that is not required. However, the data must reside somewhere in order to be able to pull it into QlikView, visualize it, discover patterns in it, and build all kinds of charts with it. That "somewhere" can be almost any standard database, flat file (for example, `.xlsx` or `.csv`), web page, web service, and so on, or even any combination of these.

When building the data model for the application created in the previous chapter, we used tables stored in a **QlikView Data Format** (**QVD**). However, as pointed out, this data can be stored and managed in a wide range of different systems. Therefore, it requires different methods for extraction. That's where data sources come in. In this chapter, you will learn:

- How to load data from different sources
- How to extract data using the built-in wizard
- What QVD and QVX files are
- How to load data from disparate sources

Although there are many different **Database Management Systems (DBMS)** out there, we can, for our purposes, group them into four different categories:

- Those that provide connectivity via ODBC/OLE DB drivers (we'll talk about what these are in a moment)
- Those that use proprietary systems with no standard connectivity
- Those that are located on the Web and connected to via APIs
- Those that are not necessarily DBMSs but, rather, have tables stored in plain files, such as Excel, CSV, TXT, XML, and the like

We'll discuss some key points in each of these categories so that we have a general understanding of the implications we must consider.

Using ODBC and OLE DB drivers

First, what do the acronyms mean?

- **Open Database Connectivity** (ODBC)
- **Object Linking and Embedding Database** (OLE DB)

You may already know what these are, and we will not go into the details of how these drivers work on the inside, but in general terms, we can think of them as query translators that enable communication between an application (such as QlikView) and the DBMS. Since they have been in use for a long time, almost all major DBMS vendors provide access via ODBC and/or OLE DB drivers.

Installing the drivers

When you use a printer, it requires you to install a driver on your computer so that the documents you send to print can be received and printed properly. The same is true with DBMS drivers. You need to install the corresponding driver on the machine you will be sending queries from in order for them to be accurately translated and properly processed by the DBMS, which will, in turn, respond to it by sending the requested set of data.

 Some common drivers will be installed along with the Windows installation. So, depending on the driver, you might not need to install any additional drivers.

A very important point you must consider when installing ODBC and OLE DB drivers is the architecture. In most cases, you will find the driver installation packages for both 32-bit and 64-bit operating systems. The 64-bit version is preferred, but, if that is not available, the 32-bit version can also be used with QlikView.

Accessing custom data sources

OLE DB and ODBC are the most common types of connectivity you will find in corporate environments. However, there are certain data sources that cannot be accessed naturally via any of these standards. For these few (but increasing) scenarios, QlikView provides the ability to integrate what are called **custom data sources**, extract data from them, and manipulate it like any other source.

We can access custom data sources just as we access any other common database: with a connector or a driver. In this case, we can either build our own custom provider or buy it from a third-party seller. The former typically requires using C or C++ code to create the communication architecture between the custom data source and QlikView. Qlik provides a **Software Development Kit** (**SDK**) to facilitate the construction of these programs, sometimes even including sample code.

An example of a custom data source would be `Salesforce.com`. The connectivity for Salesforce is provided by Qlik via a free, add-on, `.dll`-based adapter and allows rapid extraction of the data stored in this popular CRM system. This `.dll`-based adapter is what we call a connector, which serves the same purpose as an ODBC/OLE DB driver.

Another common example of a custom data source, which has been increasingly used in QlikView deployments, is the SAP platform. At an additional license fee, Qlik provides a set of `.dll`-based QlikView connectors you can use to access SAP data (R/3, mySAP, and BW). This connector is SAP-certified and comes with built-in wizards to query the database. It even includes prebuilt QlikView applications, which will certainly help you build the script you need to extract any required table. It's especially useful when you don't know how tables are related or don't actually know the technical names of the fields in a table, which is also very common.

The final example of custom data sources that we want to mention is the Qlik DataMarket Connector (shown as follows). This connector can be downloaded separately from Qlik and gives you access to an online collection of data curated and maintained by Qlik.

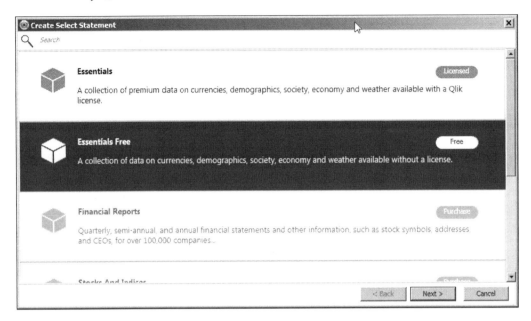

Qlik DataMarket mainly contains data on currencies, stocks, demographics, economy, weather, and company information. DataMarket is offered on a subscription basis, but also has a free tier (Essentials Free) with some high-level information.

Accessing web resources via APIs

With the increasing popularity of cloud solutions, more and more data sources are located on the Internet. Typically, these data sources are accessed via an **Application Program Interface (API)**. Examples of sources include social media sites such as Facebook, Instagram, Twitter, and also business applications such as Microsoft Dynamics CRM and SugarCRM.

Qlik offers two add-ons to QlikView that enable you to extract data from (online) resources via an API: the Qlik Web Connectors and the Qlik REST Connector.

Qlik Web Connectors

The Qlik Web Connectors were known as QVSource before it was acquired by Qlik in May 2016. The Qlik Web Connectors offer out-of-the-box connectors to specific platforms and applications, removing the need to develop these connectors in house. The connectors are offered as a subscription based add-on and are licensed on a per connector basis. Examples of connectors available in the Qlik Web Connectors collection are Google Analytics, Facebook, Twitter, YouTube, Microsoft Dynamics CRM, POP3/IMAP mailboxes, and MailChimp.

Qlik REST Connector

While the Qlik Web Connectors offer ease of use, short implementation time, and a full range of data sources, some organizations may wish to build their own connectors. The reasons for this can include avoiding additional license costs or unavailability of a required connector. This is where the Qlik REST Connector may offer a solution. The Qlik REST Connector is a free add-on to QlikView; it allows QlikView to connect to and extract data from REST APIs.

The Qlik REST Connector opens up a wealth of opportunities to extract data from web services into QlikView. For example, the following screenshot shows how QlikView can connect to the airport service of the **Federal Aviation Administration (FAA)** to retrieve the current status for major US airports, including known delays and weather data:

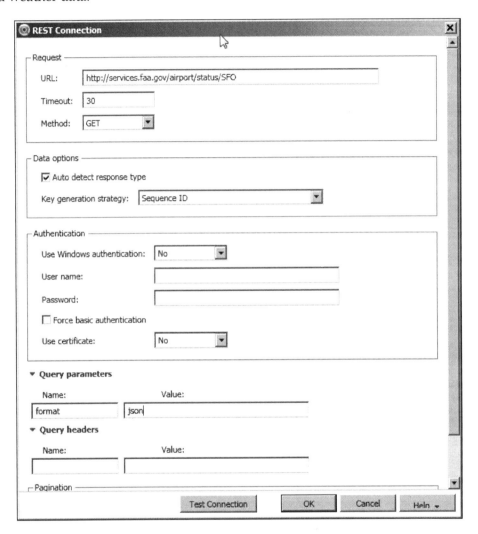

 More information on the FAA API can be found at
`http://services.faa.gov/docs/services/airport/`.

Reading table files

The fourth type of data source you will find consists of the most common table files, such as Excel, CSV, TXT, XML, or even HTML. For these types of data sources, one requirement would be that their content is in a readable, understandable structure. It will be easier to extract data from them if they are constructed in the form of a traditional table, that is, only rows and columns (like any table in a database). However, sometimes these files could contain extra information that is not actually part of the core table (such as headers or footers), and therefore, additional transformations via script are required.

 In *Chapter 10, Basic Data Transformation*, we will talk about some techniques for dealing with unstructured table files.

The ability to read table files is especially useful when we want to mix information from the DBMS and data generated by the business user that might not be stored in a database. Examples include, budget forecasts, external market indicators, and so on.

Extracting data – two hands-on examples

In this section, we will go through the steps required to extract data into a QlikView document. The extraction process through which we pull data into the QlikView document consists of:

- Connecting to the database
- Querying the database
- Reloading the QlikView script

We will provide two examples of data extraction using two different data sources:

- A Microsoft Access database
- A table file

Extracting data from MS Access

Our first example will demonstrate how to extract data from an MS Access database. It will be a good example since the connection process is very similar to that used when connecting to most major DBMSs. We will be using one of the drivers discussed in the previous section, and covering the steps required in the entire process.

Before continuing, make sure a database file named `Dimension Tables.mdb` is there in the `Data Files\MDBs` folder. If not, proceed to create the folder, if necessary, and copy the file.

Configuring the driver

Drivers for MS Access databases are often installed, by default, with the Windows OS. The default drivers are built for 32-bit architectures, but that won't be a problem for us since, as pointed out earlier, QlikView can make use of any 32-bit driver.

Connectivity to an MS Access database is provided by Microsoft either through ODBC or OLE DB drivers. At this point, we must decide which of the two types of driver we want to use. Since the connection setup via the OLE DB driver is more straightforward, we will opt for that method. However, we will take a moment to briefly describe the configuration process for ODBC drivers.

 The following process is not necessary when using OLE DB drivers, and for the purpose of our example, we can skip these steps.

How to set up an ODBC connection

In order to create the ODBC configuration, we need to go to the **ODBC Data Source Administrator** window. Access this window via **Control Panel | Administrative Tools | Data Sources (ODBC)**.

Once in the **ODBC Data Source Administrator** window, we'll go to the **System DSN** tab so that the configuration we set is visible for any user of the machine, and then we'll click on **Add...**, as shown in the following screenshot:

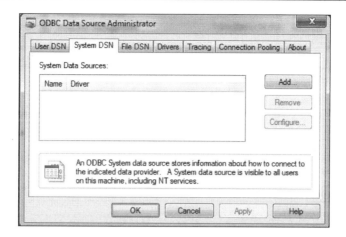

Accessing a 32-bit ODBC Data Source Administrator from a 64-bit machine

If you are using a 64-bit machine and need to configure a 32-bit ODBC driver, you will need to access ODBC data source administrator from a different location. Go to the `%systemdrive%\Windows\SysWoW64` folder and launch the `Odbcad32.exe` file. Otherwise, only 64-bit drivers will be available to configure.

The **Create New Data Source** window appears, which is where we will be able to select the driver we want to use, as shown in this screenshot:

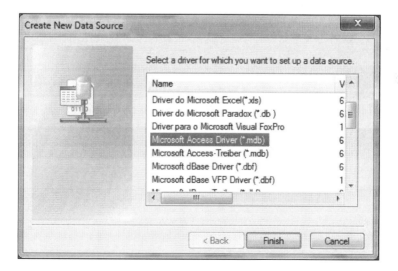

After clicking on Finish, the configuration window will appear. Depending on the driver you select, the configuration and parameters required for the connection will vary. However, the configurations for almost all drivers on this, and all of the following dialog windows, are very simple, with self-explanatory fields.

After configuration, an ODBC connection can be used from QlikView in the same manner as the OLE DB connection, just by selecting ODBC instead of OLE DB when creating the connection string, which is described in the following section.

Let's now continue with our example using the OLE DB driver. If you followed the process just described, click on **Cancel** to follow the OLE DB procedure instead.

Creating the OLE DB connection string

The connection string is basically a set of instructions and specifications with which QlikView will establish the communication with the database. It contains the database name or network location, the driver name, as well as the credentials with which we will access the database (username and password), if needed.

The connection string is created from QlikView, so the next thing we will do is open the QlikView document `Airline Operations.qvw` that we created earlier in *Chapter 3, Seeing Is Believing*. We will add new tables to the data model, this time extracting them from MS Access, to continue exploring how QlikView's built-in extraction capabilities work.

Once the QlikView document is opened, go over to the **Edit Script** window (*Ctrl + E* or **File | Edit Script...**). We've already worked briefly with this window, and this time, we will make use of the **Database** section in the **Data** tab.

Activate the **Airports** tab and position the cursor on the last line, below the existing `Load` statement. From the **Database** section, select **OLE DB** from the drop-down menu, and click on the **Connect...** button, shown in the following screenshot:

The **Force 32 Bit** checkmark is used to specify that QlikView should look for 32-bit drivers, instead of looking for 64-bit drivers, installed on the computer. It is relevant for both ODBC and OLE DB drivers.

If you need to use a 32-bit driver then please mark this option before clicking the **Connect...** button so that QlikView uses the correct connection engine. In all cases in which the 64-bit driver is available, it is advisable to use that instead, since using 32-bit drivers might significantly reduce performance over the 64-bit equivalent.

The **Data Link Properties** window, which is composed of several tabs, will appear. The first tab (**Provider**) shows a list of all the available OLE DB drivers. Here, we will select **Microsoft Jet 4.0 OLE DB Provider**. Once selected, click on **Next** to move to the **Connection** tab, in which we will specify the database file we want to connect to, as shown in the following screenshot:

Click on the browse (**...**) button, placed between number **1** and number **2**, to select the database file we have stored in the `Data Files\MDBs` folder.

Since the database file does not require logon credentials, we will leave the **User name** and **Password** fields blank. The **Blank password** checkmark should be selected as well.

We will now click on **Test Connection** to make sure the connection is established. A message will indicate if the test went well and, if so, we may now click on **OK**. If not, we need to make sure the configuration is correct and verify that the database file is accessible.

Scrambling user credentials

For databases that require logon credentials, the username and password will be stored in the connection string either as plain text or as scrambled text. To store them as scrambled text, select the **Scramble User Credentials** checkbox, in the **Settings** tab of the tool pane in the **Script Editor** window before generating the connection string.

After clicking on **OK**, you should see the newly generated connection string as part of the script.

It is possible to have several connection strings in the same QlikView document. This allows you to pull data from different sources. Each time a new connection string is found during the script execution, the previous connection is automatically disconnected. We can also use the disconnect; statement to explicitly drop the previous database connection before connecting to the next one.

Connection string portability

In some circumstances, we might need to create several QVW files for extracting several tables from a particular database. An elegant and administration-friendly approach is to store the connection string in a text file, residing in a folder that is reachable from your QVW files. Import this connection into every QVW via an include statement (from the **Edit Script** window, go to **Insert | Include Statement**). The benefit of this approach is that, if the connection string changes, you only need to modify it in one place, and all of the corresponding QVW files will automatically use the updated connect statement.

Querying the database

Now that we have established communication with the database via our connection string, we can begin retrieving data from it using the SQL. QlikView makes it easy for us to create the SELECT statements to build our queries.

The Create Select Statement wizard

The SELECT statement is used to pull data from the database into our QlikView document, and tells the DBMS the specific set of data we want. We could just type it manually, but instead we will use the **Create Select Statement** dialog in order to find the table we want to read as well as the fields we need, and automatically populate the required QlikView script.

Since we've already created the connect statement, we can go ahead and click on the Select button from the **Data** tab. The **Create Select Statement** dialog window will appear. This window is used to specify the database, table, and fields we want to load. After we click on **OK**, the corresponding SELECT statement will be generated.

Let's look at the components of this particular window so that we know what each option does. The following screenshot shows the **Create Select Statement** dialog window:

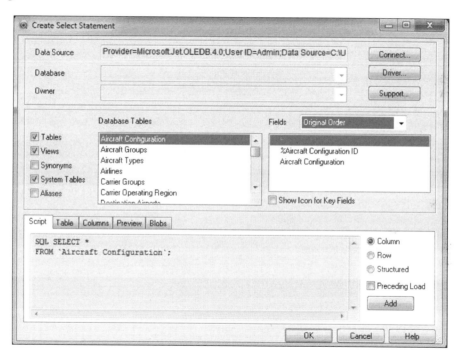

We can split the window into three horizontal panes. In the top pane, we specify where the tables we want to read are located. We have a **Database** drop-down field and an **Owner** field of this database. We also have three buttons to the right, in this top pane:

- **Connect…**: This button lets you create another connection. It is rarely used since the current window is usually opened after a connection is already created.

- **Driver…**: This button provides some information about the driver you are currently using.

- **Support…**: This button opens a pop-up window, which may or may not contain data, but it is intended to provide information about the database.

In the middle pane, we can choose what will become the core of our SELECT statement: the table and fields we will read.

On the left side of this middle pane, we have several checkmarks that will allow us to filter the list of tables we see to the right. We can select to see only **Tables**, **Views**, both, and so on. Once we apply the appropriate filter, we can move on to pick the table we need. Note that the list is alphabetically ordered, so you can type the first letter of the table you want to find, to automatically scroll to the section where the tables whose names begin with the specified letter are listed, and then scroll further down until you find it.

After highlighting the table, we can move on to the next section of this middle pane, which is the list of fields which the selected table contains. In this section, we have an additional option which is the ability to sort the listed fields by **Text Order** or by the **Original Order** on which they are stored in the database.

Note that we will always see a star symbol at the top of the list. We can highlight this "wildcard" character if we want to pull all of the fields contained in the table. In case we want to load only a few, but not all of the fields, we can do that by highlighting each of them individually and not with the star symbol.

 When selecting the particular fields you want to include, use the *Ctrl* key after each click/highlight so that you can pick more than one.

We can also click on **Show Icon for Key Fields**, if we want to identify the fields that are defined as key fields in the database.

And finally, we have the bottom pane, which at the same time is divided into several tabs. Let's go through each of them briefly:

- **Script**: This tab will give a preview of what the wizard will create based on our selections from the panes above:
    - ° To the right, we have additional options to specify how we want the script to be generated (**Column**, **Row**, or **Structured**). We can also add a **Preceding Load**, which lists the resulting fields individually and makes them available for QlikView-side operations.
    - ° We also have an **Add...** button; it basically allows the creation of several SELECT statements involving several tables at the same time without needing to click on **OK** and return to the **Create Select Statement** window for each one.

- **Table**: This tab is used to view general information about the selected database table.

- **Columns**: This tab will provide specific information about the properties of the fields that make up the table.

- **Preview**: This tab will show a preview of the table, consisting of the first few rows.

- **Blobs**: This tab provides the ability to bundle objects contained in a **Binary Large Object** (**Blob**) field into the QlikView application. This feature is only supported when using an ODBC connection (OLE DB is not supported for this).

Adding the airport tables

Even though the Access database contains all the dimension tables used in the airline operations data model and more, we will only extract the tables corresponding to the origin and destination airports and incorporate them into our application.

Using the **Create Select Statement** wizard described earlier, create the SELECT statement to extract the Origin Airports table with both the %Origin Airport ID and Origin Airport fields. Make sure to create a script in the form of, column with each field name listed in preceding load for us to manipulate it further, if needed.

The following screenshot shows the configuration we need in the **Create Select Statement** dialog for this particular example:

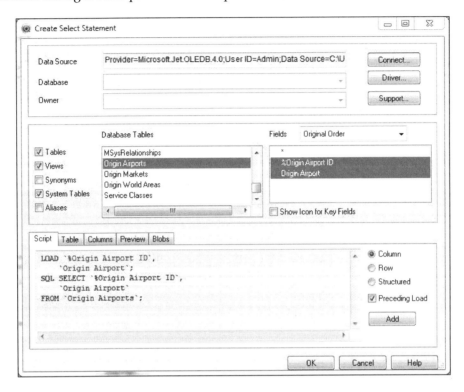

The resulting script is as follows:

```
LOAD '%Origin Airport ID',
   'Origin Airport';
SQL SELECT '%Origin Airport ID',
   'Origin Airport'
FROM 'Origin Airports';
```

Did you notice how we didn't use the star symbol when selecting the list of fields to retrieve, even when we needed to pull all fields? This is a best practice, to ensure that only the required fields are returned by the query, and no more. Suppose, for example, that a new field is added to the source table. If we used the star symbol to query the database, we would automatically retrieve this new field even when it's not necessary for our data model, wasting valuable bandwidth in the process.

Follow the same process to add the script needed to load the Destination Airports table.

Reloading the script

We now have a query to execute, and need to reload the script to actually pull the data into our QlikView document (and into RAM for as long as the QlikView document is open). We can select **File | Reload**, press *Ctrl + R*, or click on the **Reload** button from the toolbar.

After this, as we've seen previously, a **Script Execution Progress** window, shown as follows, appears and shows feedback about the loading process. It also tells us after reading a table how many rows it fetched, among other things.

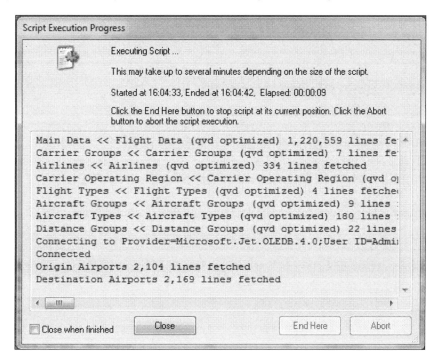

By default, the close checkmark, at the bottom-left of the window, is enabled. It tells QlikView to close the progress window immediately after finishing the script execution. It is sometimes useful to disable this property, so we can get an overview of the entire process after it is finished. You can either uncheck the option right from this window or change the parameter via **Settings | User Preferences | Keep Progress Open after Reload**. You will know that the script execution has ended when the **Close** button becomes enabled. Click on **Close** to dismiss the dialog.

Since we executed the reload operation from the **Edit Script** window, the **Sheet Properties** dialog appears immediately after script execution, with the **Fields** tab active by default. As we saw in *Chapter 3, Seeing Is Believing*, through this window we can add fields to our workspace in the form of listboxes and start reviewing what we got from the query we ran.

 This dialog does not appear when launching the reload from outside the script editor. If that is the case, you can access it by right-clicking on a blank space of the sheet area and then clicking on **Select Fields…**.

Click on **OK** to dismiss the **Sheet Properties** dialog window.

The resulting data model

If we press *Ctrl + T* at this moment, **Table Viewer** will appear and we will be able to see the resulting data model. The data model now consists of the tables we added previously, in *Chapter 3, Seeing Is Believing*, and the two tables we added from the MS Access database.

 The **Table Viewer** is also available via **File | Table Viewer…**, or by using the corresponding toolbar button available in the design toolbar.

The following screenshot shows the resulting data model:

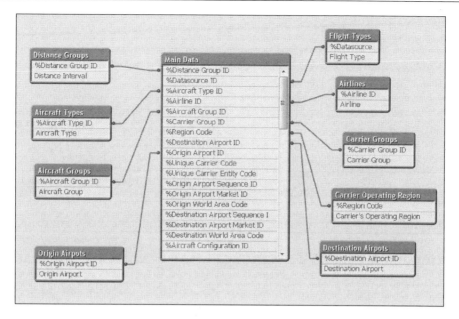

Table Viewer is a great tool to analyze the data model and check table associations. In the next chapter, we will describe in more detail how we can take advantage of it.

> It is important to note that at this point, we are using prepared source tables in our data model for introductory purposes, so everything falls into place without much effort. In the later chapters, we will cover in more detail how the data model is constructed via a script.

After reviewing **Table Viewer**, click on **OK** to dismiss it, and make sure to save the changes we made to the application before moving on to the next section.

Loading a table file

We have now covered data extraction from a typical database via ODBC and OLE DB. QlikView is also able to load data from a table file, such as an Excel, CSV, TXT, and XML file, among others.

Let's go through an example of loading a CSV file so that we can describe the steps and dialog windows involved. We will load two additional tables in the CSV format with the purpose of demonstrating that no matter what the source is, at the end (that is, once added to the QlikView document and data model) all tables are equal. The new tables are in the Origin Markets.csv and Destination Markets.csv files, so make sure you have them in Data Files\CSVs.

We will add this table to the same data model used in the previous section, so if you already closed the Airline Operations.qvw document, please open it again. Go to the **Edit Script** window, activate the **Airports** tab, and position the cursor on the very last line. Next, click on the **Table Files...** button from the **Data** tab in the tool pane below. The **Open Local Files** dialog will appear, in which we must select the file we want to load. In our case, we will first browse and select the file named Origin Markets.csv and then click on **Open**.

A new window pops up. It will be the equivalent of the **Create Select Statement** dialog we previously discussed. Here, we will define some configuration options about how the Load statement will be created.

This configuration is separated into several steps in the dialog window. We will go through the most important sections of this wizard.

Specifying the file attributes

The first step is defining the attributes of the file we are reading, as well as the fields we want to include. In the following screenshot, we can see the contents of the **File Wizard: Type** section:

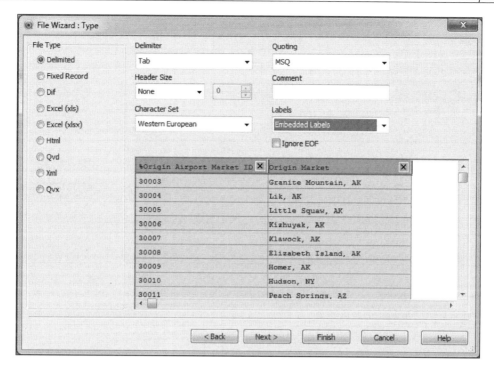

We can divide this window into three panes; the first (left pane) contains radio buttons for us to select the corresponding **File Type**. The second pane, to the upper-right of the window, contains various settings about the file attributes. These settings will vary depending on the file type. Finally, we have a preview pane at the bottom; it reflects how the table file will be interpreted by QlikView with the configuration we are setting on the two other panes. The preview pane provides immediate feedback after we modify any of the configuration options in the rest of the window.

The **File Wizard** tries to determine the **File Type** automatically, and it is pretty accurate. However, you can easily change it in case it got it wrong, by selecting the corresponding radio button. As you can see, the file types that can be loaded using this wizard include: **Delimited** (CSV, TSV, and so on), **Fixed Record** (when the file does not contain a specific character as a separator, but is consistent with its column widths), **Excel** files, **Html**, **Qvd** (QlikView datafiles, like the ones we used in *Chapter 3, Seeing is Believing*), **Xml**, and **Qvx** (QlikView eXchange format).

As part of this example, we will further discuss the settings involved when reading a CSV (delimited) file. The configuration for the rest of the file types is very similar to this, so we will not go into detail for each of them.

The CSV attributes

Since our CSV file is a delimited file, it is possible to select which character is used as a separator. This is done via the **Delimiter** drop-down field.

The **Quoting** schema to be used can also be specified, with the available options of **Standard**, **MSQ**, and **None**. By default (that is, using **MSQ**), straight double quotes (" ") and straight single quotes (' ') are permitted for field values, but with one condition: they must be in both the first and the last non-blank character of a field value.

In case the table file has more than one line as the header record, you can specify it in this same window, with the option to set it as a number of lines or number of bytes.

QlikView can also recognize comment lines in the file, when we specify the character(s) which identifies a comment line by typing it in the **Comment** field.

The other options we can set are: whether the file has the field names defined in the header row (**Embedded**) or not, and whether QlikView should ignore an end of file mark (**Ignore EOF**).

A word on quoting

If a cell contained in the table being read has only one quotation mark, or if the quotation marks are not in the first and last non-blank character position, the script reload will not be correctly executed and the file will not be properly read.

The following diagram shows three different scenarios that can be encountered when reading text files with quotes. The first two will either result in an incomplete read, or the table will contain "dirty" data. The third scenario will be read correctly. Pay special attention to the value of the third record in Field B of the input table for each scenario.

We need to emphasize this point because, for example, in the first scenario stated previously, QlikView will not alert about a possible misinterpretation of the input table. Instead, it will simply mark the dirty record as the end of the file and finish the extraction, with all of the subsequent records being left out. This potential issue is not always apparent in the preview pane of the **File Wizard**, as the offending character may be further down in the table. Look out for the listboxes containing mixed types of content, as this might be a sign that the described issue is present.

The solution to the first and second scenarios is to change the **Quoting** schema to **Standard** or **None** from the **File Wizard: Type** window.

Previewing

The **Preview** pane, as stated previously, will show how the file will be read by QlikView with the configuration we have defined. We can also use this pane to rename fields and/or exclude columns from the extraction.

To change a field name from the **Preview** pane, simply click on the cell containing the field name (dark gray, with an X mark on its right side), and type the new field name. If the file we are currently loading does not contain field labels, QlikView defaults them to something like @1, @2, and so on depending on the column number.

To continue, make sure you've defined the settings as depicted in the screenshot shown at the beginning of this section.

After we've set these configurations, we are done with this window. Let's click on **Next** to continue with the following step in **File Wizard**.

The transformation step

The second step in the **File Wizard** is the **Transform** process. Since, for now, we are not going to make any transformation to our file, we are going to skip this step. However, it is important that you know how and when this can be useful for you. *Chapter 10, Basic Data Transformation*, covers this topic more in depth.

Let's just say, for now, that the transformation step is used when loading files that are not in a format consistent with a traditional table (that is, pure and clean rows and columns). The **Transform** dialog is shown here:

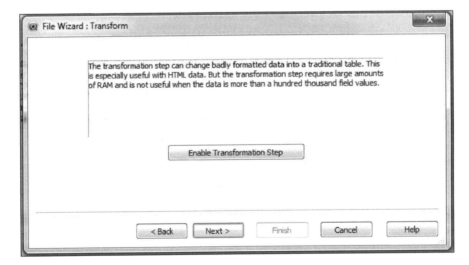

As you can see, there is a warning about using this feature: it requires a large amount of RAM. If your source file is large, you might not find this **Transform** wizard useful, and other techniques will need to be employed to process the source data.

Click on Next once more to skip the transformation step, and move to the third step in the File Wizard.

Refining the input table

There are several options that can be defined to treat a table file and transform/convert it in the loading process. This is done in the **File Wizard: Options** step, depicted in the following screenshot:

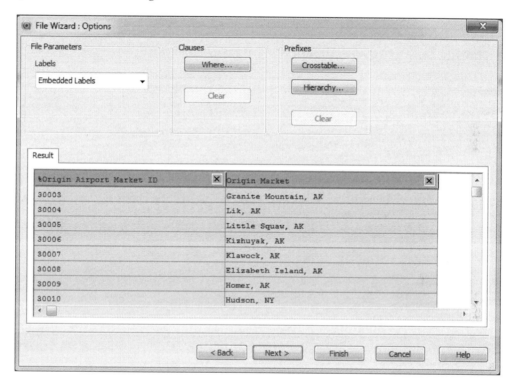

We can set options such as **Where...**, specify QlikView to treat the table as a **Crosstable...**, or interpret it as a **Hierarchy....** We will not use any of these options when loading the Origin Market table, but we will describe their components and functions for introductory purposes.

The Where clause wizard

A `Where` clause is used when we need to exclude records from the input table. We can specify on which condition these records should be left out. When clicking on the **Where...** button from the **File Wizard: Options** window, the following dialog will appear:

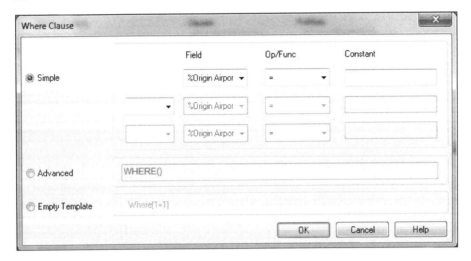

The **Simple** configuration allows us to set the commonly used conditions of Field – Operator – Value. For example, `Field A is X` will exclude all records from the input table that have the value `X` in `Field A`. The operators available in this wizard are shown in the following screenshot:

The **Advanced** option allows us to write the desired `Where` clause by hand, whereas the **Empty Template** will only add a `Where` clause similar to the following:

```
Where (1 = 1)
```

This will not exclude any records, but you can manipulate it after the script is created.

 We will talk about using the advanced `Where` clause in *Chapter 8, Scripting* and *Chapter 9, Data Modeling Best Practices*.

The crosstable

QlikView is also able to convert cross tables (a table where there is a column for each dimension in a range) to traditional tables. For the file we are loading in this example, we won't need this function, but it's important that you know about it since this table structure is very common, particularly in budget spreadsheets. An example of a cross table is shown here:

Department	Jan	Feb	Mar	Apr	May	Jun
A	160	336	545	152	437	1
B	476	276	560	57	343	476
C	251	591	555	195	341	399
D	96	423	277	564	590	130

These tables, because of their structure, are not appropriate for a QlikView data model. We will discuss this topic further in *Chapter 9, Data Modeling Best Practices*, along with other transformation options and hierarchy tables.

The resulting script

For now, let's continue to the next step in the **File Wizard**. Click on **Next** from the **File Wizard: Options** window, and the **File Type: Script** dialog will appear.

This window basically lets us take a look at the generated script with the configurations set in the previous steps. Additionally, we can set a `Max Line Length` parameter to make the script easier to read once it is pasted into the script editor, or enable the **Load All (*)** option, which will generate a script that indistinctively loads every field in the source table.

If you have previously changed field labels, or excluded some fields from the load (using the **File Wizard: Type** window), you should not use the **Load All (*)** option, since it will override those previous settings.

The **File Wizard: Script** dialog window is shown in the following screenshot:

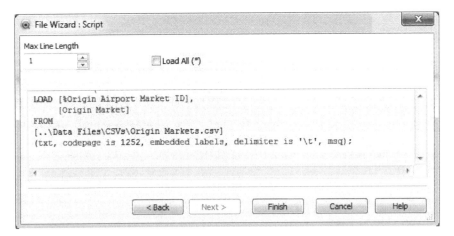

Let's leave these options as they are for now, and click on **Finish**. The script will be generated and added to the **Edit Script** window.

 Please note that when reading data from a plain table file, we do not use a SELECT statement but only a LOAD statement. That is because the SQL SELECT statement is only used to send the appropriate command to the ODBC, OLE DB, or some other data connectivity drivers, and query the database. Since we are only loading a local file, no driver is being used, and the built-in QlikView extraction functionality is used to pull data into our document.

We can now reload the script, and the table will be pulled into QlikView and treated like any other table from any other source, hereafter.

Save before reloading

The reload operation will execute every script statement, and there will be times when the script execution will fail for a number of reasons. Therefore, it's a good practice to hit **Save** before actually reloading the script. In some cases, when the reload fails, changes since the last save are lost. We have now loaded the `Origin Market` table. Take a moment to do the same with the `Destination Markets` table and include it in our data model. Afterwards, save and close the QlikView document.

QVD and QVX files

We have now gone through the process of loading data from traditional databases and simple table files. In this section, we will take a deeper look at the QVD and QVX file types, which are used by QlikView to store and read data in an optimized format. We will talk a little more about both of these types, and the benefits and uses of each of them.

QVD files

QlikView Data (QVD) files are used to extract and store data into and from QlikView. This means that whichever table you read from whichever database, you can store it in the QVD format before or after any transformations you perform on the table. The special characteristics of this file type are:

- It contains only one logical table.

- It uses a special algorithm to compress the data, achieving compression rates of up to 90 percent, depending on the fields' cardinality of the underlying data.

- When reading a QVD table file in QlikView, the loading speed is anywhere from 10 to 100 times faster than when loading from a database. When the table file is being read without applying any transformations, QlikView performs an optimized load (superfast mode).

One of the main advantages of using QVD files is that, once you have a QVD on your disk, the table can be exploited by more than one QlikView application. This reduces the load on the database server, and optimizes QlikView resources and development time. This process is called QVD staging and is discussed further in *Chapter 13, Advanced Data Transformation*.

The QVD file will also be particularly useful when dealing with incremental load scenarios which are discussed in *Chapter 13, Advanced Data Transformation*.

QVX files

QlikView Data Exchange (QVX) files are used for data input from external systems into QlikView. The main difference with respect to the QVD file is that QVX is a public format and can be created from external interfaces. It can be considered as the format in which custom data sources (described earlier in the chapter) send data to QlikView via the custom connector. Data retrieval becomes optimized when complying with QVX specifications, although not as optimized as QlikView's own QVD.

Loading an Inline table

There is yet another way of adding a table to a data model, and it's one that is especially useful for small tables that do not necessarily reside in a database, for example, those that contain a custom description of an entity. With an Inline table, the data is entered directly into the **Edit Script** window. The process to input an Inline table is outlined here.

From the **Edit Script** window, go to the **Insert** menu and select **Load Statement | Load Inline**. The **Inline Data Wizard** will appear as shown in the following screenshot:

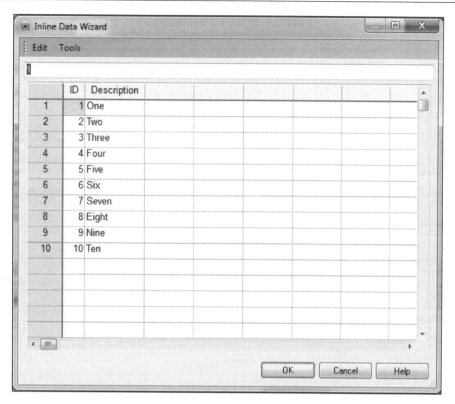

The window is similar to a spreadsheet, with rows and columns.

 To enter heading labels, double-click on the header cell.

We can start typing data into the cells, and after we are finished entering the content of the table, we can click on **OK**.

Importing document data to the inline table

It is possible to enter, within the **Inline** wizard, a list of values contained in a field that is already stored in RAM. This is done via the **Import Document Data** wizard. To bring up this wizard, go to the **Tools** menu from the **Inline Data** wizard and select **Document Data....**

The resulting script for our input table would be similar to the following:

```
LOAD * INLINE [
    ID, Description
    1, One
    2, Two
    3, Three
    4, Four
    5, Five
    6, Six
    7, Seven
    8, Eight
    9, Nine
    10, Ten
];
```

The advantage of this approach is that you will not need to maintain a separate table (whether on a database or a table file) when dealing with a small table of this sort. Keep in mind that the values will be hardcoded in the script. Whenever you need to change them, it can only be changed in the script.

Summary

We covered the most basic extraction capabilities that QlikView provides. We also described the different data sources you can access from QlikView and provided a few tips for dealing with input tables.

At the same time, the technical team at HighCloud Airlines are now able to assess that QlikView can load data from disparate sources, and see the different options they will have at their disposal with QlikView regarding data sources. They also have one of the most important differentiators of QlikView software; that is, its ability to read and process data stored in disparate sources, combine them, associate them, link them, and store them all in one location (the QlikView document) to enable a complete insight and analysis for QlikView users.

In the next chapter, we will learn how we can turn our extracted data into a proper data model.

5
Data Modeling

Up until now, we've seen the HighCloud Airlines team becoming familiar with QlikView and its powerful analytic capabilities and data association engine. The time has come to establish how their first production application will be developed, starting with its very core: the **Data Model**.

We've constructed a data model in the preceding chapters using pre-processed tables, so it was an easy task. In this chapter however, we will dig into the hows and whys of data model design in QlikView, exploring different scenarios and learning about the inner workings of QlikView's associative engine. This enables us to take the most advantage of the dataset we will be analyzing.

In this chapter, you will learn about:

- Which type of data model is best suited for QlikView
- The different "rules" that need to be followed when designing data models for a QlikView document
- How to best take advantage of the associative data model to make your documents highly dynamic
- How to work with tables and the associations between them

Dimensional data modeling

We will first take a moment to review a little bit of theory, and even some history. If you are already familiar with dimensional modeling, feel free to skip to *The associative data model* section. Otherwise, read on to see how the data models used in transaction processing systems came to be, why these data models are hard to query, and how an alternative modeling technique solves these problems.

 This section is largely based on Ralph Kimball's article, *A Dimensional Modeling Manifesto*. The full version can be found at http://www.kimballgroup.com/1997/08/02/ a-dimensional-modeling-manifesto/.

Back in the day

When computers first appeared on the scene, the methods for storing, retrieving, and modifying data were still in their infancy. For example, when storing a customer order, it was likely that all of the data from the paper order form was directly copied into a single record or file.

While it was convenient to have the data digitally available, people quickly realized that storing and manipulating the data was not. As each record was stored on its own, it was hard to keep the data consistent. Imagine customer addresses and product information being repeated on every order, and you will agree that updating and keeping the data consistent is a painful exercise.

To counter these issues, and save expensive storage space, developers started to apply their own optimizations, often splitting data out into separate tables. While this approach was a step in the right direction, it also came with a downside. The algorithms for linking and working with these tables needed to be embedded within the applications, adding significant complexity.

Relational databases and ER modeling

Fortunately, **Relational Database Management System (RDBMS)** came to the rescue by the early 1980's and solved part of the problem. These were systems dedicated entirely to storing, retrieving, and modifying data.

At the same time, the **Entity-Relationship Modeling (ER modeling)** technique became fashionable. ER modeling aims to remove all redundancy from the data model. This technique greatly improved and simplified transaction processing. For example, instead of needing to update the same customer address information in each separate record, only a single update to a customer address master table is made. This customer address is then referenced in other tables using a customer address key, a field which uniquely identifies each customer address.

While all of these advancements greatly improved the efficiency of inserting and updating information in a transactional database, it also made it increasingly harder to get information out of it. For example, consider the following table containing attributes related to **Aircraft Types**:

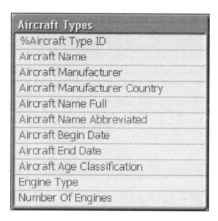

If we were to model the information in this table using ER modeling, the data could be normalized into the model, as you can see in the following screenshot:

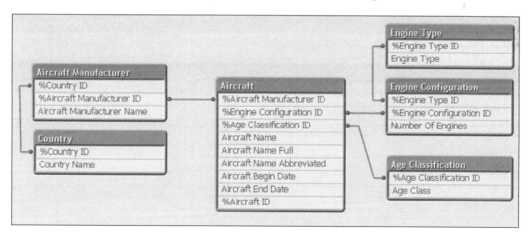

This is only some of the information relating to aircrafts. Imagine if we'd model all of the information we're interested in (airports, carriers, countries, flights, personnel, and so on), we might end up with dozens, or even hundreds, of tables!

When dealing with database sources other than a data warehouse or data mart, this is the most likely scenario we will encounter, and it might get even more complex. For example, the SAP ERP system has thousands of tables for all of the different entities it handles.

Dimensional modeling

When ER models get too complicated to query, dimensional modeling can offer a practical solution. A dimensional data model is composed of a single fact table. This fact table contains a compound primary key, with separate keys linking the fact table to the dimension tables.

These dimension tables contain descriptions and attributes that provide context to the metrics stored in the fact table. Dimensions often contain data on multiple hierarchical levels that are "flattened" (or denormalized) into a single table. For example, in our **Aircraft Types** dimension table, we have both **Aircraft** and **Aircraft Manufacturer** in the same table.

In addition to keys to the dimension tables, fact tables also contain measures. For example, metrics such as transported passengers or available seats are often additive, allowing them to be summed over various dimensions. An example would be: transported freight per aircraft type per month, in which transported freight is a fact, while aircraft type and month are dimensions that add context to the measure.

 A fact table does not always need to contain metrics. When storing an event, such as when a salesperson has visited a company, we only store the keys to the relevant dimensions (salesperson, company, and date) in our fact table.

The star schema

The fact and dimension tables are usually combined into a star schema. This name is used because, with some imagination, the data model resembles a star. An example of a star schema is shown in the following screenshot:

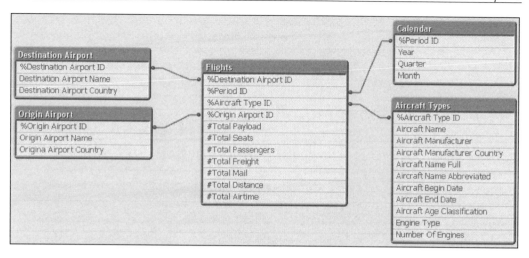

The **Flights** table is the fact table, containing all of the measures as well as links to the surrounding dimension tables. A big advantage of the star schema is that it can be easily understood, and business users can easily recognize the names of the tables and how they relate to each other.

The snowflake schema

In the earlier example, each dimension table is completely denormalized. There is a second type of dimensional model in which dimensions are not necessarily fully flattened. This is called a snowflake schema as (again with some imagination) the diagram resembles a snowflake. An example is depicted in the following screenshot. It is basically the same schema as the previous example, but the **Aircraft** dimension is not completely denormalized.

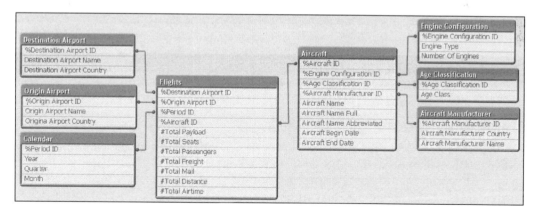

In an RDBMS, the snowflake schema is sometimes chosen when trying to save disk space, as it removes duplicate values from the dimension tables. Since QlikView automatically removes duplicates from the data model, using a snowflake schema is generally not a preferred approach.

Creating the dimensional model

So, how do we go from an ER diagram to a dimensional model? The first thing to understand is that an ER diagram does not directly translate into a single star schema. A transactional system often contains data used across many different business processes. For example, think of how many different business processes and functions a typical ERP system supports: accounting, human resources, manufacturing, supply chain management, and customer relationship management, just to name a few. The data for all of these processes is usually stored in a single ER schema.

The first step in converting from an ER schema to a dimensional schema is dividing the ER schema into separate business processes. Each of these business processes will be modeled into a separate star schema.

The next step is to declare the granularity of the business process (for example, a single flight or one salary payment). We then group the measures that are used in the business process into a single fact table.

After that, the remaining tables are flattened into dimension tables and directly linked to the fact table using a single key. It is possible for the same dimension table to be used in multiple star schemas. This is called **conformed dimension**. For example, the employee dimension can be used in the context of Airline Operations as well as in the payroll context.

In QlikView, we can use QVD files to store conformed dimensions. For example, we can store the **Aircraft Type** dimension into a QVD file and use that file in any application that requires information about the **Aircraft**. This way, data consistency is ensured across applications.

Dealing with multiple fact tables

As described previously, each business process is modeled into a separate star schema. When dealing with multiple fact tables in a single QlikView application, loops and synthetic keys can occur. To solve this problem, fact tables can be concatenated, or a link table can be added. The techniques for how to achieve this are described in *Chapter 9, Data Modeling Best Practices*.

Dimensional models in QlikView

In QlikView, the main benefit of using a dimensional model is increased response time. QlikView just works faster when there are fewer links between tables. A second benefit is that a dimensional model is very easy to understand, and can be extended gracefully. It is very easy to add new facts (as long as they share the same granularity), new dimensions, or extend existing dimensions.

As QlikView works better with fewer links between tables, you may wonder if it might work even better when we just use a single flat table. If fewer links is better, no links must be best, right? As with many things, the answer to this question is "It depends." The next diagram shows a generalized list of the pros and cons of various modeling approaches in QlikView:

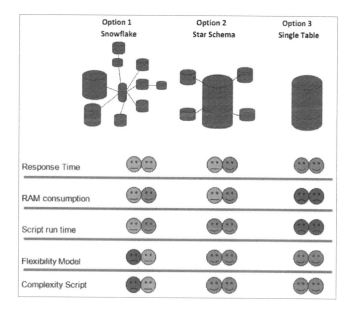

Overall, in our experience, the star schema is the preferred model as it offers a good balance between the various trade-offs.

 If you want to learn more about dimensional modeling, an excellent book to consider is *The Data Warehouse Toolkit: The Complete Guide to Dimensional Modeling* (Second Edition), Ralph Kimball and Margy Ross, Wiley publication, ISBN: 0471200247.

The associative data model

After reviewing the theory of dimensional data modeling, it is now time to apply those concepts to how QlikView works. By now, we know that a QlikView document is, in general terms, used to visualize data. This data can come from disparate sources: a database, Excel files, a legacy system, or even the Web. But how do we put all this data together? The answer is: through the associative data model.

The associative data model can be said to be equal in structure to a dimensional model. However, a data model of any type in QlikView becomes an associative data model because it not only contains the different source tables from which the charts get the data, but also keeps them associated in a way which allows the QlikView document and its users to consume information and aggregate data cross dimensionally in any possible way. In a QlikView data model, all of the field values from all of the tables in the model are automatically associated among themselves based purely on the field names.

Let's look at the Airline Operations data model built in an earlier example, from *Chapter 4, Data Sources*:

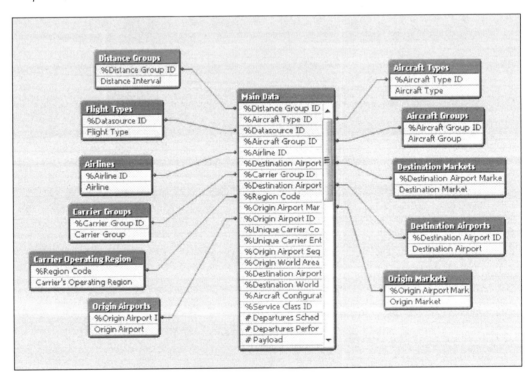

In the previous screenshot, we can see how the fact table (that is, the **Main Data** table) is directly associated with all of the other dimension tables. The purpose of these dimension tables is to provide context to the values stored in the fact table. Furthermore, the dimension tables are not only associated with the fact table, but at the same time they are indirectly associated with each other through the fact table.

With the data model shown we can, for instance, cross-reference the **Origin Airport** with the **Destination Airport** (via the **Main Data** table) and get the **Distance Interval** value between any two of them. These three fields are stored in three different dimension tables in the data model, and the fact that they are associated allows QlikView to naturally perform this cross-dimensional reference and support the associative analysis we just described. This is shown in the following screenshot:

Origin Airport	Destination Airport	Distance Interval
Belaga, Malaysia: Belaga Airport	San Juan, PR: Luis Munoz Marin International	10500-10999 Miles
Joinville, Brazil: Joinville Airport	Guam, TT: Andersen AFB	10500-10999 Miles
Miami, FL: Miami International	Shaw River, Australia: Shaw River Airport	10500-10999 Miles
Saipan, TT: Francisco C. Ada Saipan International	Joinville, Brazil: Joinville Airport	10500-10999 Miles
Bengkulu, Indonesia: Fatmawati Soekarno	San Antonio, TX: San Antonio International	10000-10499 Miles
Diego Garcia, British Indian Ocean Territory: Di...	Mena, AR: Mena Intermountain Municipal	10000-10499 Miles
Mahe Islands, Seychelles: Seychelles Internatio...	Phoenix, AZ: Phoenix Sky Harbor International	10000-10499 Miles
Miami, FL: Opa-locka Executive	Sungei Tekai, Malaysia: Sungei Tekai Airport	10000-10499 Miles
New York, NY: John F. Kennedy International	Arrabury, Australia: Arrabury Station	10000-10499 Miles
Phoenix, AZ: Phoenix Sky Harbor International	Mahe Islands, Seychelles: Seychelles Internatio...	10000-10499 Miles
Sungei Tekai, Malaysia: Sungei Tekai Airport	Miami, FL: Opa-locka Executive	10000-10499 Miles
Teterboro, NJ: Teterboro Airport	Latrobe, Australia: Latrobe Valley	10000-10499 Miles
Atlanta, GA: Hartsfield-Jackson Atlanta Internati...	Hat Yai, Thailand: Hat Yai International	9500-9999 Miles
Augustus Downs, Australia: Augustus Downs Air...	New York, NY: John F. Kennedy International	9500-9999 Miles
Carroll, IA: Arthur N Neu	Adelaide, Australia: Adelaide International	9500-9999 Miles
Colombo, Sri Lanka: Bandaranaike International...	Houston, TX: George Bush Intercontinental/Hou...	9500-9999 Miles
Columbus, IN: Columbus Municipal	Singapore, Singapore: Singapore Changi Intern...	9500-9999 Miles

Title bar: *Distance Intervals between airports*

In an associative data model, any field can act as a dimension in a chart. They can all be used within expressions to aggregate their data too.

Guidelines for table associations

In order to design and build a data model in QlikView, we need to understand how the associations between tables are created. We also need to consider some basic rules to avoid performance and data consistency issues. In this section, we will describe and review these guidelines.

How associations are created

QlikView creates associations between tables in a simple and straightforward manner: through the field names. This means that, for any given set of tables, an association is automatically created between two of them if they both contain a field with exactly the same name. Simple enough.

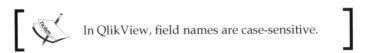 In QlikView, field names are case-sensitive.

Based on this concept, we can say that QlikView will automatically build up the data model with its respective associations even if the developer does not explicitly define how the tables are linked to each other. However, this functionality requires that the source tables contain the correct field names. Since this scenario seldom occurs, especially if we are loading tables from several different source systems, the most basic and fundamental tool for the data model design in QlikView is **Renaming fields**.

Renaming fields

There are two main reasons for a developer to rename a field:

- To ensure that two tables are associated through the correct fields when originally these two tables did not share a field with the same name, but a link does in fact exist between them.

- To prevent unwanted associations between tables when they share a field with the same name but that field does not actually represent the link between them.

To rename a field, we can simply use the as keyword in the Load script to assign an alias to the original field name. For example, take the following Load script, in which we hypothetically load the Airport descriptions:

```
[Origin Airports]:
LOAD
    Code              as [Origin Airport ID],
    Description    as [Origin Airport]
FROM
[..\Data Files\QVDs\Airport Descriptions.qvd]
(qvd);
```

What this code does is load the table contained in the Airport Descriptions.qvd file. This table has two fields: Code and Description. In this case, we are changing the original names from Code to Origin Airport ID and from Description to Origin Airport.

This way, we are ensuring an association between the Origin Airports table and any other table containing either a field named Origin Airport ID or one named Origin Airport. At the same time, we are ensuring that the table doesn't associate with other tables which contain fields named Code or Description.

Renaming fields with the Qualify statement

The Qualify keyword can be used to qualify field names with their corresponding table name, which basically renames the specified fields in the form of tablename. fieldname, thus ensuring no unwanted associations are created.

Let's look at our previous example in which we needed to rename the Code and Description fields. We can rename these fields by using the Qualify keyword as follows:

```
Qualify Code, Description;

[Origin Airports]:
LOAD
   Code,
   Description
FROM
[..\Data Files\QVDs\Airport Descriptions.qvd]
(qvd);
```

The above Load statement will result in a table with two fields: Origin Airports. Code and Origin Airports.Description.

As you can see, we have specifically entered, as the Qualify statement parameter, the two fields which we want to rename. In some cases, we might need to rename a long list of fields, making it impractical to list them all in a Qualify statement. Luckily, the Qualify statement allows the use of wildcard characters in the fieldlist parameter. For example, we can use a star symbol to specify that all subsequently loaded fields should be qualified. We can also combine the star symbol with a string or with a question mark symbol (another wildcard character) to specify that a set of fields that match a given criteria are to be qualified. For instance:

- Qualify Code, Description;: This command will only qualify fields named Code or Description

- Qualify "*ID";: This command will qualify all fields whose name ends with ID

- Qualify *;: This command will qualify all fields that are loaded from that point forward

Sometimes, the Qualify feature is required to be activated for only part of the script but then should be turned off after loading certain tables. To do that, we can simply use the Unqualify statement, specifying the field names in the same way as described previously.

In some cases, we are required to turn on qualification for all fields except one or two (for example, the key fields). To accomplish that, the Qualify and Unqualify instructions can be used in conjunction, like in the following example:

```
Qualify *;
Unqualify Key_Field1, Key_Field2;
```

The above combination of instructions will cause all fields loaded from that point forward to be qualified with their corresponding table name, except the fields named Key_Field1 and Key_Field2. This is useful when we want to ensure key fields are not affected by the Qualify instruction.

 Remember that a Qualify instruction can be turned off at any point in the script with a corresponding Unqualify statement.

Avoiding data model conflicts

With the simplicity QlikView provides in building the associative data model, it's very likely we will sometimes find one of the following two issues:

- The creation of what is called "Synthetic Keys" (described in the next section)
- The creation of circular references in the data model

Both of these issues need to be avoided since they can cause performance degradation in the QlikView application, along with data inconsistency.

Dealing with synthetic keys

When any two tables share more than one common field, QlikView creates a complex key, or synthetic key, to try and associate both tables through the combination of all of the common fields between them. This takes the form of an additional table containing the shared fields and an additional key field added to all involved tables.

An example of a data model with synthetic keys is presented in the following screenshot:

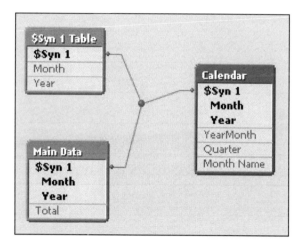

As you can see from the earlier screenshot, the data model is primarily composed of two tables: **Main Data** and **Calendar**. These two tables have two fields in common: **Year** and **Month**.

Because of QlikView's associative engine, the two tables are automatically linked through both fields, creating a complex key out of the combination of their values.

There is also a third table in our data model, called **$Syn 1 Table**. This is the synthetic table which stores the combination of values for the two fields which, as pointed out, form the synthetic key.

The presence of synthetic keys in a data model can cause the application to have slow response time and sometimes even consume all available resources. Therefore, they need to be avoided when possible.

There are several methods we can use to remove synthetic keys:

- We can rename those fields that are a part of the synthetic key but should not be a part of the association between the two tables.

- We can remove conflicting fields from one of the two tables. To remove a field, we just erase the corresponding line of code from the Load script.

- We can create an explicit complex key with the concatenation of all common fields that actually represent the link between the two tables.

  - After creating the new complex key, we can remove the conflicting fields from either table.

The following flowchart shows the decision process a developer should follow to decide which of the methods mentioned earlier should be used:

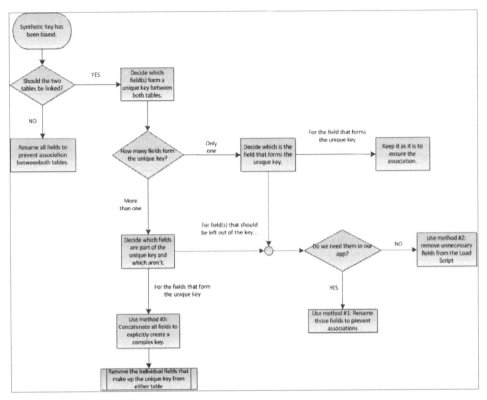

Dealing with Synthetic Keys – Flow Chart.

Getting back to our synthetic keys example shown earlier, let's see which of these workarounds would best solve our problem. If we follow the flow chart, we can arrive at the following conclusions:

- Yes, the tables should be associated with each other
- The unique key is formed by two fields
- The fields that constitute the unique key are **Year** and **Month**

Therefore, we should use the third method and create a complex key using the **Month** and the **Year** fields. At the same time, we will need to remove the individual fields from one of the tables.

We decided the unique field was composed of both fields because if we had used only one of them, the key would not be unique. That is:

- If we had used the field **Year** as our key, one record in the fact table would be associated to 12 records in the **Calendar** table, since there are 12 months corresponding to one year.

- Likewise, if we had used the field **Month** as our key, one record in the fact table would be associated to as many records as the number of years exist in the **Calendar** table.

A relation between a fact table and a dimension table should always be at the same granularity.

Creating a composite key

While we are at it, let's see how we are going to create the composite key needed in our simulated scenario to solve the synthetic key issue.

First, you should be familiar with the values that exist in each of the fields at play. Let's assume the following:

- The **Month** field has the following values:

  1, 2, 3, 4, 5, 6, 7, 8, 9, 10, 11, 12

- The **Year** field has the following values:

  2010, 2011, 2012

Complex keys can be created from the Load script. The following script will create the corrected data model by loading both tables, creating the complex key in both tables, and removing the conflicting fields from the **Main Data** table while keeping them on the **Calendar** table:

```
[Main Data]:
Load
    Year & '|' & Month as YearMonth,
    Total
From FactTable.qvd (qvd);


Calendar:
Load
    Year & '|' & Month as YearMonth,
    Month,
    Year,
    Quarter,
    [Month Name]
From Calendar.qvd (qvd);
```

We are using the ampersand operator to merge the values from the two fields into one. We then assign an alias to the new calculated field by using the as keyword.

Adding a delimiter to concatenated fields

It's always a good idea to add a separator between fields when concatenating them to ensure data consistency. For example:

```
Year & ' | ' & Month    as YearMonth
```

The resulting data model, created using compound keys, is shown in the following screenshot:

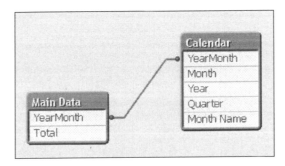

The synthetic key has been successfully eliminated from the data model and the associations between both tables have been explicitly defined.

Dealing with circular references

Similar to how synthetic keys are created, a circular reference can also be the result of unwanted associations in our data model and, as such, they can be fixed using the same principles described earlier. But before getting into how to solve them, let's first see what they are.

We can think of the data model as a map that shows the paths through which we can walk to get from one point to another. For instance, considering the data model seen in the previous section, the only path to get from the fact table to the **Calendar** table is the **YearMonth** route. This means in order to get there you must know what **Month** and **Year** you are looking for in the **Calendar** table.

However, when the data model becomes more and more complex, with a larger number of tables, and more and more destination points, we might also get to a point where we have more than one route connecting point A to point B. All roads lead to Rome, they say. Well, in our case, we must always have one road between any two points. Otherwise, we would be having a circular reference.

To better understand what a circular reference is, let's look at the following data model:

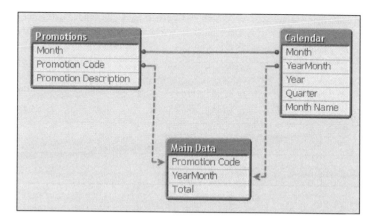

As you can see, a circular reference exists when the connections among the tables simulate a circle and we have two routes to get from any given point to another. For example, we can get from the **Main Data** table to the **Calendar** table either directly, through the **YearMonth** route, or by going first to the **Promotions** table and then moving to the **Calendar** table.

This is an issue that needs to be addressed, and one that can create severe data inconsistency problems, performance degradation, and even crashes.

To solve the presented scenario, and based on how we deal with synthetic keys in the flow chart, we should start by asking which of the created associations are correct and which aren't. In this case, the association between the **Promotions** table and the **Calendar** table is incorrect since the **Month** field stored in the former table does not necessarily represent the month in which the promotion was used, but rather the month in which the promotion was created. They just happen to have the same name.

Most of the time, as in the earlier example, we will find that the problem arises from unwanted associations and the issue is easy to solve (through the first method from the section on synthetic keys). Other times, there are design challenges that need to be analyzed thoroughly.

In *Chapter 9, Data modeling best practices*, there is a full section dedicated to address the main design challenges a developer could come across when designing a data model.

Now, let's quickly describe how the Table Viewer window works and how it can become our best ally when data modeling.

The Table Viewer window

We already had a small peek at the **Table Viewer** window in previous chapters. As this feature is very useful when analyzing our data models, let's take a more in-depth look. To illustrate, consider the data model seen in the following **Table Viewer** window:

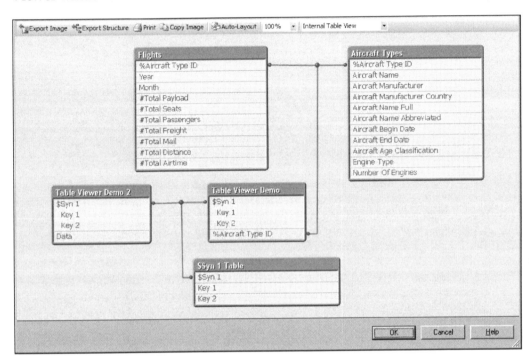

The **Table Viewer** window can be opened by selecting **File | Table Viewer** from the menu bar, or by pressing *Ctrl + T*.

The table viewer shows the tables (boxes) and their associations (connectors). When more than two tables are associated via the same key, it will be indicated with a small blue dot in the connector line.

The layout of the tables and connection points can be changed by clicking and dragging the header and connection point, respectively. Tables can also be resized when hovering over and dragging their edges. Of course, it is not mandatory to create a clean layout for your data model, but it is recommended as it makes a diagram easier to understand.

A lot of information about our data model can be learned from the **Table Viewer** window.

Table information

When hovering the mouse cursor over a table header, a tool tip is shown to display the name of the table and the number of rows, fields, and key fields. This can be used to do a quick sanity check on the loaded data. Optionally, when a comment is set for the table (using the COMMENT TABLE script statement), the corresponding comment is also shown in the tool tip. For example, the following screenshot shows the tool tip for the **Aircraft Types** table:

```
Aircraft Types
Rows: 378
Fields: 11
Keys: 1

Dimension containing information on aircrafts, including engine
types and configuration and manufacturer
```

Field information

When the mouse cursor hovers over a field name within a table, it gets even more interesting.

```
%Aircraft Type ID [Key]
Information density: 100%
Subset ratio: 42%
Tags: $key, $numeric, $integer

Primary key of the Aircraft Type dimension
```

The following information is shown in the previous screenshot:

- The name of the field. Optionally, if the field is a key field, a qualifier is shown enclosed in square brackets. This qualifier indicates the following levels of key quality:

    ○ [Perfect Key] indicates that every row contains a key value, and that all of these key values are unique. At the same time, the field's subset ratio is 100 percent. This qualifier should be seen in dimension tables, where every key should uniquely identify a single record.

    ○ [Primary Key] indicates that all key values are unique, but not every row contains a key value or the field's subset ratio is less than 100 percent.

    ○ [Key] indicates that the key is not unique. This qualifier is usually seen in fact tables, where the same dimension value may be associated with many different facts.

- **Information density** of the field, which indicates the percentage of rows that contain a non-null value.

- **Subset ratio**, which shows the percentage of all distinct values for a field in the table compared to all the distinct values for that field in the entire data model. It is only relevant for key fields since they are present in multiple tables and do not all share the same value. Subset ratios can be used to easily spot problems in key field associations. For example, when the combined total of subset ratios for multiple tables is 100 percent, this may indicate that there are no matching keys between these tables.

- **Tags**, which show the tags applied to the field. Some of these, such as tags that indicate if the field is a key field or tags indicating the data type of the field, are automatically generated. Other tags can be manually applied.

- Optionally, any comment set on the field is also shown.

Table preview

While looking at ratios and such will give us some good insights into the data in our model, it is sometimes easier to just look at the raw data. By right-clicking on a table and selecting **Preview**, a preview of the first 1,000 table rows will be shown:

Table viewer menu

The menu of the **Table Viewer** dialog contains some other useful functions:

- The **Export Image** command lets us save a picture of the data model in PNG or BMP format.

- The structure of the QlikView document can be exported using the **Export Structure** button. This creates three text files: one for the tables, one for the fields, and one for the mappings between fields. Of course, these text files can be loaded back into QlikView for further analysis.

- We can also **Print** a picture of the data model or copy a picture of the data model to the clipboard using the **Copy Image** button.

- The **Auto-Layout** feature automatically arranges the tables. While it attempts to generate a coherent layout, in our experience it usually fails. Manually positioning the tables is still our preferred method.

 The layout of tables in the Table Viewer generally persists even when the document is closed and re-opened. However, changing the data model slightly can make the tables in the Table Viewer appear in different locations than the ones previously defined.

- The zoom level on which the diagram is displayed can be set using the corresponding drop-down box. By default it is set to **100%**.

Of special interest is the drop-down box that switches the view between **Internal Table View** and **Source Table View**.

Internal Table View is the default option and shows how the data is stored in QlikView. If synthetic keys are created, they are shown in this view. However, **Source Table View** shows how QlikView reads the data, and when synthetic keys are present in the model they are not shown in this view. Instead, multiple connectors between tables are displayed.

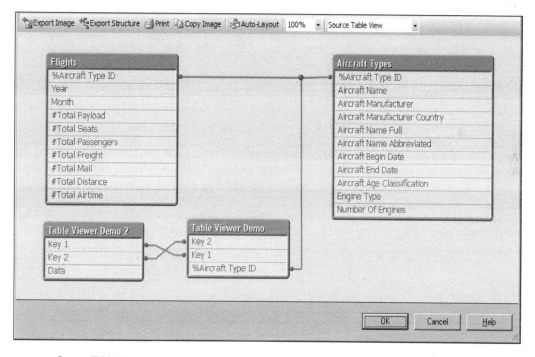

Source Table View, compare this to the Internal Table View shown at the start of this section

Summary

We've come to the end of the chapter and we hope you found the provided guidelines useful and applicable to your particular scenarios.

We learned what dimensional modeling is, how it differs from ER modeling, and why it is a good idea to use this modeling technique in QlikView. We also saw how to take advantage of the information provided by the Table Viewer dialog, how the associative data model really works, and how it does what it does.

We even got an overview of the basic rules for creating associations in QlikView and how to deal with the conflicts in data modeling

By now, we have a clear understanding of how the data model for the HighCloud Airlines document should be designed. We will continue providing tips for efficient data modeling and design in later chapters. But first, in the next chapter, we will take a more in-depth look at styling our QlikView documents.

6
Styling Up

Up until now, our focus has been more on loading data into QlikView and building the data model than on actually visualizing the information. It's about time we started working on the frontend of our document and present the data in the form of a dashboard.

Besides presenting useful insights, a very important aspect of a business dashboard is that it should be visually appealing. Our users will be accessing the document every day, so we had better give them something nice to look at while they are drinking their morning coffee.

Our course of action for now will be to take advantage of QlikView's customization flexibility to style up our document, brand it with HighCloud's corporate identity, and set up the general layout on which we will ultimately place our charts.

In this chapter, we will cover the following topics:

- Setting up the workspace
- Understanding and changing the sheet's properties
- Managing our sheet object's appearance
- Using some of the most fundamental objects for selecting and filtering data
- Placing, resizing, and aligning the sheet objects

But before we start, a word of warning.

Just because you can, does not mean you should.

Design is obviously a very subjective thing. However, there are some general design principles that will ensure your QlikView document is easy on the eyes and also easily understood by the user.

The main principle is: **minimize non-data pixels**. This is a principle introduced for print by Edward R. Tufte and brought to the digital age by Stephen Few. This principle states that we should focus on showing the data, while minimizing or de-emphasizing those pixels that do not represent data. Examples of non-data pixels include borders, grid lines, drop shadows, 3D objects, and glossy reflections. For those interested in data visualization and dashboard design, we highly recommend Stephen Few's book *Information Dashboard Design*, (First Edition), *O'Reilly Media*, ISBN: 0596100162.

Of course, the main objective of this book is to teach you how to develop QlikView solutions. For that reason, we want to let you explore as many options as possible. Unfortunately, this also means that sometimes, while showing you the technical workings of a feature, we might also be showing you things that could be considered bad visual design. Ultimately, the decision to use certain visualizations or design principles lies with you; so keep a critical mind.

Design requirements

When we start building the frontend of a QlikView document, we should always begin by defining two fundamental characteristics:

- The screen resolution on which most users will access the document
- The general style and layout of the document

We need to set a standard screen resolution right from the start because it will ultimately determine the placement and size of the objects across the screen. If we build the document targeting a screen resolution higher than that which users have on their machines, they will probably need to use the scroll bars too often. On the other hand, if we target our document to a screen resolution lower than our users' screen resolution, they will see a lot of empty space. Both of these situations will be an inconvenience that our users will need to deal with every day, so we don't want that to happen.

Having a predefined resolution in the document does not keep the user from accessing a document using a lower (or higher) resolution monitor. QlikView allows users to "zoom" a screen to a different size using the **View | Fit Zoom to Window** and **View | Zoom** options. However, using these options can lead to alignment and display issues. It is better to avoid them if possible.

For the HighCloud Airlines document, we will use a screen resolution of 1280 x 1024, since it's the one our primary users (top executives) have set on their monitors.

At the same time, it's been determined that we will divide the frontend layout into four main panels:

- The top panel will be used to place time-related user controls as well as the HighCloud logo
- The left-side panel will hold a majority of the listboxes used to filter the data
- The central area will be used to place the different charts and visualizations
- The right-side panel will have other special objects (that we will discuss later on)

The four main panels are shown in the following diagram:

Time-related user controls and logo		
List boxes used to filter data	Charts and visualizations	Special objects and other controls

The general style of the document should also reflect the HighCloud corporate identity. We will achieve this by:

- Using the official HighCloud logo, seen below. This will be visible at all times and from all worksheets in the document.

- Setting the **Background Color** to white.
- Using the following corporate colors to set different layout object's appearance:

Color name	Color code (RGB)
HighCloud Blue	0, 112, 192
HighCloud Brown	73, 68, 41

The Document Properties window

The **Document Properties** window is where document-level settings are defined. Using this dialog window, we will ensure that HighCloud's logo is embedded into every worksheet of the document. We will also divide the screen space into the panels described previously and set the default **Background Color** option to white. The **Document Properties** window is shown in the following screenshot:

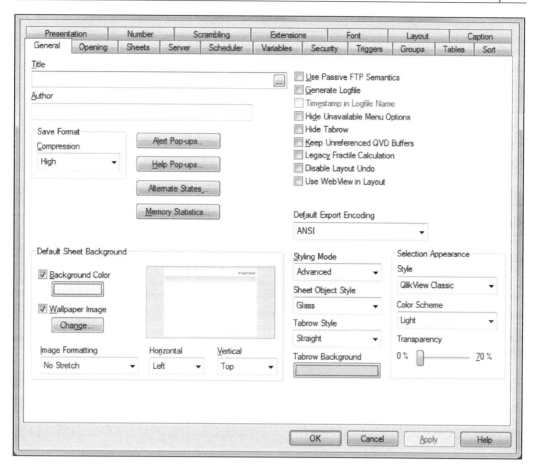

With these design requirements in mind, we will start setting up the document's appearance by following these steps:

1. Open the `Airline Operations.qvw` document we've been working with and go to the **Dashboard** tab.

2. As the document needs to fit the default corporate resolution of 1280 x 1024, select **View | Resize Window | 1280 x 1024** from the menu bar.

3. Then, open the **Document Properties** window by pressing *Ctrl + Alt + D* or by selecting **Settings | Document Properties** from the menu bar.

4. Navigate to the **General** tab and enable the **Wallpaper Image** checkbox. Then, click on the **Change...** button.

5. Browse to the `Airline Operations\Design` folder, select the `HighCloud_Background.png` image, and click on **Open**.

6. From the **Default Sheet Background** section of the **Document Properties** window, locate the **Vertical** drop-down and select the **Top** option from the list. The **Horizontal** drop-down will keep the default value, which is the **Left** option.

7. Finally, close the **Document Properties** window by clicking on **OK**.

We've now set the QlikView application window to match the required size of our document. This way, we can ensure that the sheets we design will fit entirely on the target monitors without any scrolling.

When using the **View | Resize Window** functionality, it is always advisable to also check on the target environment to see if there will be any toolbars or other objects eating into the screen real estate.

Next, we've added a background image which already includes the HighCloud logo, as well as the pre-defined panel divisions that will help us position the objects. All of the sheets we create from now on in our document will automatically have the defined background.

In *Chapter 14, More on Visual Design and User Experience*, we will look further into how we can create and use these background images.

After following the previous procedure, our **Dashboard** sheet should look like the following screenshot:

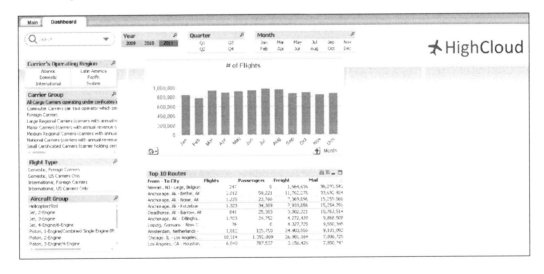

The Sheet Properties dialog

Just as there are document-level properties, we can also set properties at the sheet- and object-level. Let's have a quick look at the **Sheet Properties** dialog.

Open this window by right-clicking on an empty space in the **Dashboard** worksheet and selecting **Properties...**.

The following screenshot shows the **Sheet Properties** dialog:

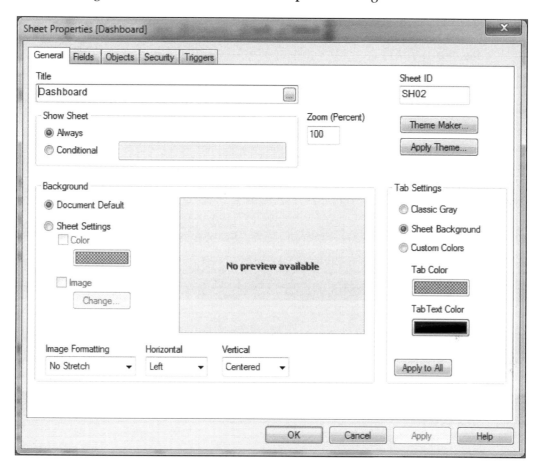

As its name implies, the **Sheet Properties** dialog can be used to set various properties of a worksheet. Let's quickly review the available options.

On the **General** tab, the following properties are of interest:

- **Title**: This property can be used to set the title that appears in the tab row. In addition to static text, this can also be a calculated value.

- **Show Sheet**: This property can be used to conditionally hide/show the sheet. For example, we can use an expression like `GetSelectedCount([Carrier Name]) = 1` to only show the sheet when a single carrier is selected.

- **Sheet ID**: This property is the internal ID of the sheet. This ID can be used to reference the sheet from other objects in the document, for example, to activate the sheet by clicking on a button object.

- **Background**: We can either use the **Document Default** option, which we set in the previous section, or override the default by setting a sheet-specific **Color** and/or **Image** selection.

- **Tab Settings**: This property can be used to set any desired **Tab Color** or style.

We've previously worked with the **Fields** tab, which is an easy way to add multiple listboxes to the sheet. Simply select the required fields from the **Available Fields** listbox and double-click (or click **Add >**) to include them in **Fields Displayed in Listboxes**.

The **Objects** tab shows all of the objects that are present on the worksheet, even those that are conditionally hidden. From this tab, we can directly open the individual object's **Properties...** dialog or even **Delete** any of them. The **Objects** tab is shown in the following screenshot:

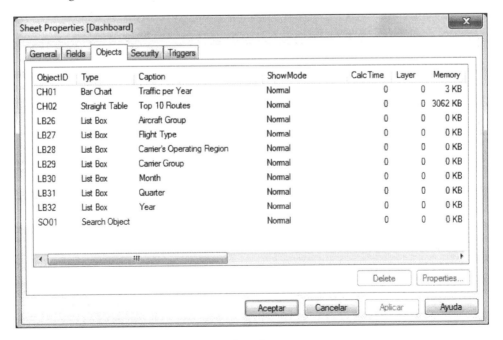

It's also worth noting the **Calc Time** and **Memory** columns in the **Objects** tab. These can be used to optimize our document by identifying which objects have the most impact on performance, or are using up a lot of memory.

The **Security** tab is used to set what users are allowed to do on the corresponding sheet. We are also able to propagate the security settings to all sheets if the **Apply to All Sheets** checkbox is marked. Additionally, when the **Read Only** checkbox is enabled, no selections can be made on the sheet.

Triggers are events to which QlikView can react with **Actions**. When used on sheets, a trigger can be set to respond to events such as activate and deactivate, meaning it will run when entering or leaving the sheet, respectively. Triggers will be discussed in more detail in *Chapter 14, More on Visual Design and User Experience*.

Setting the object properties

It's now time to peek into some of the object-level properties that affect the QlikView document's appearance. The properties we are most interested in at this point are:

- Caption colors
- Caption font

Let's see what these are.

Caption colors and style

By default, almost every object in the QlikView document has a caption bar at the top, unless we choose to explicitly hide it. Since the caption bar will be visible for most of our objects, let's apply a touch of corporate identity by setting the default caption color to **HighCloud Blue** and by selecting a custom styling mode.

Changing the caption colors

Follow these steps to apply a new formatting style to caption bars:

1. Right-click on any of the listboxes on the sheet, for example, **Carrier's Operating Region**.
2. Select **Properties...** and navigate to the **Caption** tab.

Two types of caption colors can be set: one for when the object is **Inactive** and one for when the object is **Active**. An active object is the one on which the user has last clicked, while all of the others are inactive. Since we are not interested in visually identifying the current state of an object, we will apply the same color for both options:

1. Click on the **Background Color** button on the **Inactive Caption** section to open up the **Color Area** dialog window.

2. Make sure the radio buttons corresponding to **Solid Color** and **Fixed Base Color** are selected.

3. Click on the colored square next to the **Fixed** radio button to open the **Color** dialog window.

4. Add the **HighCloud Blue** color to the **Custom colors** section by entering the RGB codes 0, 112, 192 into the respective **Red**, **Green**, and **Blue** inputs and click on the **Add to Custom Colors** button.

5. While we're here, let's also add the **HighCloud Brown** color to the **Custom colors** section. Do this by first selecting the second color placeholder from the left, under the **Custom colors** section, then enter the RGB codes 73, 68, 41 into the **Red**, **Green**, and **Blue** inputs respectively. Finally, click on the **Add to Custom Colors** button.

6. Select the **HighCloud Blue** custom color again from the **Custom colors** section and click on **OK** to close the **Color** dialog window.

7. Click on **OK** to close the **Color Area** dialog window as well.

Now that we've changed the **Background Color** option for the **Inactive Caption** section, we can repeat the same process to set the **Text Color** option of the **Inactive caption** section to white. Once this is done, we've done our fair share of clicking. Fortunately, we can take a different time-saving approach for changing the **Background Color** option of the **Active Caption** section:

1. Right-click on the **Background Color** option in the **Inactive Caption** section and select **Copy**.

2. Right-click on the **Background Color** option in the **Active Caption** section and select **Paste All**.

3. Repeat the same process for the **Text Color** option in the **Active Caption** section.

 Note that the last copied color remains on QlikView's clipboard even when other objects or text are subsequently copied.

The following screenshot shows the **Inactive Caption** and **Active Caption** sections:

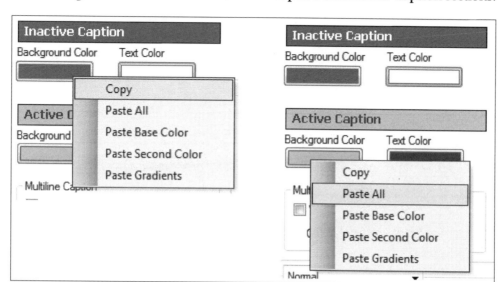

We've now set the colors used by the caption bars for this particular listbox. We will first need to tweak a few other settings before applying this style to every object caption in our document.

The Color Area and Color dialog windows

The **Color Area** and **Color** dialog windows that we've just worked with are used everywhere throughout QlikView to set the color formatting of a variety of object components.

Besides the static, solid color that we used, it is also possible to use gradients of one or two colors. Furthermore, the colors used do not always need to be fixed, they can be based on a dynamic calculation as well. A use case for this is to show a red color when a certain value is below target, and a green one when it is above the target. Calculated colors are set by using an expression with QlikView's color functions, examples of which are Red(), LightGreen(), Yellow(), and so on. In addition to these standard, pre-defined colors, any custom color can be represented using the RGB() function.

The following screenshot shows the **Color Area** dialog window:

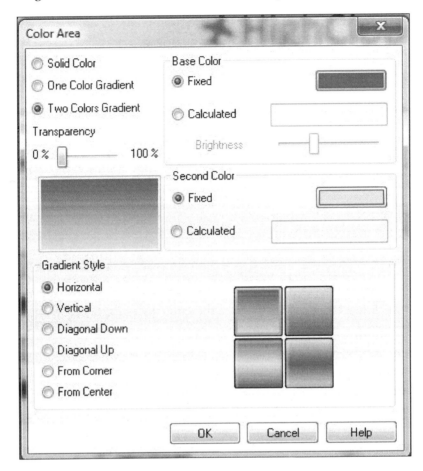

Note that the gradient used in the previous image is an example only, it is inadvisable to use these types of candy-colored gradients in your documents.

Setting the caption font

At 10 points, the default caption font in QlikView is quite big. Let's change the caption font by following these steps:

1. From the **Properties** dialog window of the **Carrier's Operating Region** listbox, click the title's **Font** button on the **Caption** tab.

2. Set the **Size** to 9 in the **Font Dialog**. The font name and font style will be kept as default (**Tahoma**, **Bold**).

3. Click on **OK** to apply the changes and close the window.

Setting the content font

Besides setting the caption font, we will also change the font used to display the listbox values. To do this, follow these steps:

1. Right-click on the **Carrier's Operating Region** listbox and select **Properties....**

2. Navigate to the **Font** tab.

3. Change the font **Size** to 9.

4. Click on **OK** to close the **Properties** window.

Setting the global font

An interesting feature in the **Font Dialog** wizard is the option to set a global **Default Font** option, found in the lower-left corner of the **Font Dialog**. By selecting either **List Boxes, Chart, etc.** or **Text Objects/Buttons** under **Default Font**, we can apply the currently selected font to all new objects of the selected class.

The **Font Dialog** window is shown in the following screenshot:

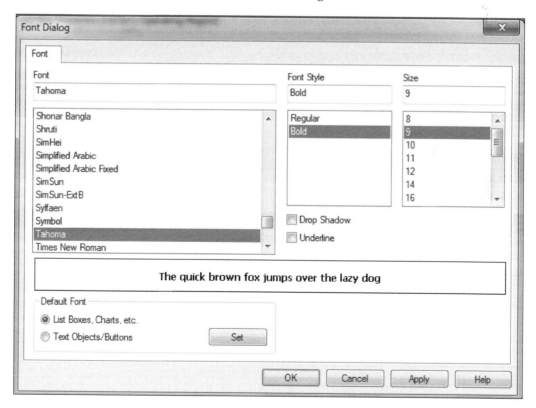

This setting is available from both the caption's font dialog and the content's font dialog.

Propagating the object appearance

By following the previously described procedures, we have set the appearance for a single listbox. To apply the same configuration to all of the remaining listboxes, right-click on the one we already configured, select **Properties...** from the context menu, and go to the **Layout** tab.

At the upper-right corner of the dialog window you will see an **Apply to...** button. Click on it and the **Caption and Border Properties** dialog window will appear. Make sure to mark the following options:

1. The **Apply properties to...** checkbox should be enabled.
2. Select the **Objects in this document** and **All object types** radio buttons.
3. Mark the **Set as default for new objects in this document** checkbox.

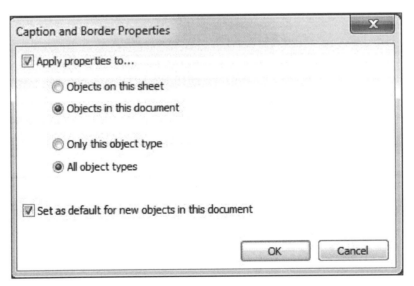

4. Click on **OK** on the two remaining dialog boxes to apply the changes.

Setting the default Sheet Object Style

The captions, as we've styled them now, still have a very basic look. As we noted at the start of this chapter, having a clean, basic style is not necessarily a bad thing, and in many cases is preferred. For now, however, we'll make our presentation a little bit flashier by setting another default **Sheet Object Style**, using the following steps:

1. Open the **Document Properties** dialog by selecting **Settings | Document Properties** or by pressing *Ctrl + Alt + D*.

2. Make sure the **General** tab is active.

3. Set the **Styling Mode** option to `Advanced`.

4. Set the **Sheet Object Style** option to `Glass`.

5. Click on **OK** to apply the settings.

The object captions now have a glass-like appearance and rounded corners. The **Advanced** styling mode allows us to make additional changes to an object's style, such as setting rounded corners.

There are several pre-defined object styles available through the **Sheet Object Style** menu. The following screenshot shows how each available combination of **Styling Mode** and **Sheet Object Style** looks:

Hiding captions

Because of the data in them, some of the listboxes, such as **Year**, **Quarter**, and **Month**, do not really need captions. We can hide these captions by right-clicking on the listbox, selecting **Properties...**, and unmarking the **Show Caption** checkbox on the **Caption** tab.

Working with listboxes

Currently, our QlikView document contains the following listboxes in the **Dashboard** sheet:

- **Carrier's Operating Region**
- **Carrier Group**
- **Flight Type**
- **Aircraft Group**
- **Year**
- **Quarter**
- **Month**

Let's see how we can add listboxes and change their properties.

Adding listboxes

Lets add another listbox representing the **Carrier Name** field by right-clicking on the worksheet and selecting **Properties...** (or by pressing *Ctrl + Alt + S*, which is the shortcut for the **Settings | Sheet Properties** menu command). Next, open the **Fields** tab, locate the **Carrier Name** field under the **Available Fields** list, and click on **Add >** to add it as a new listbox.

Many routes lead to Rome

To add an object to a worksheet, there are three basic methods: using the menu, using the toolbar, or using the pop-up menu:

Menu: By selecting **Layout | New Sheet Object**

Toolbar: By using the **design** toolbar

Pop-up: By right-clicking on a blank space within the worksheet and choosing the desired object from the **New Sheet Object** submenu

The examples throughout this book will use a different method each time, but of course you are free to choose your preferred method.

In a moment we will discuss the positioning of the objects we are adding, but for now let's add another listbox, this time using a different method:

1. Right-click anywhere on the sheet and select **New Sheet Object | List Box**.

2. Select **Aircraft Type** from the **Field** drop-down list.

3. Click on **OK** to close the dialog window.

The List Box Properties dialog

Besides the default settings, there are quite a few other options that can be set for listboxes. In this section, we will review the most common of these options. Right-click on any listbox and select **Properties…** to open the **List Box Properties** dialog window.

>
> While the customization of the listboxes' appearance is quite flexible, one of the options that cannot be changed, at least not out-of-the-box, are the colors used to identify selections. Green always means selected, while white and gray mean associated and excluded values respectively.

The General tab

As the name implies, the **General** tab contains general options for the listbox. Notable options are:

- **Title**: This option is used to set the **Title** label to be different from the default field name. The **Title** label can also be set based on a calculated value.

- **Object ID**: While the title shows the pretty-print frontend name, the **Object ID** option contains the name under which the listbox is known to QlikView. This ID can be used to reference the listbox from other QlikView objects.

- **Always One Selected Value**: This checkbox is only available when a single value is selected at the time we open the **Properties** dialog. This option locks the listbox so that it can only have one value selected at any given time.

- The **Show Frequency** and **In Percent** checkboxes: These options are used to display the absolute number of times that each value appears in the active data set. When **In Percent** is checked, the relative number of appearances versus the total is shown.

The Expressions tab

The **Expressions** tab lets us add calculations and mini charts into listboxes, for example, adding the number of departures to the **Carrier Name** listbox by using the expression Sum([# Departures Performed]). The following screenshot shows the **Carrier Name** listbox with an expression in place:

Carrier Name (# Departures)	
	367
ABSA-Aerolinhas Brasileiras	2,261
ABX Air, Inc.	1,404
ACM AIR CHARTER GmbH	116
Acropolis Aviation Ltd.	24
Aer Lingus Plc	9,821
Aeroflot Russian Airlines	2,744
Aerolineas Argentinas	1,691
Aerolineas Galapagos S A Aerogal	1
AeroLogic GmbH	927
Aeromexico	1
Aeroservices Executive	3
Aerosur	1,159
Aerosvit Ukranian Airlines	1,346
Aerovias Nac'l De Colombia	949
Air-India	2,652
Air Alsie A/S	45

The Sort tab

The **Sort** tab is commonly found across many objects. It offers the option to order the data using any of the following sort orders, outlined in descending order of priority:

- **State**: This option sorts values based on the selection state of the items. Ascending will put all selected or associated items at the top, followed by all non-selected items. Descending performs the opposite sorting. Auto Ascending puts all selected items at the top, but only if the listbox is not big enough to show all of the values at the same time. If all of the values are visible, no sorting has been performed.

- **Expression**: This option sorts the values based on the result of an expression. For example, we could sort carrier names based on the number of departures they have performed.

- **Frequency**: This option sorts the values based on how often the value appears in the dataset.

- **Numeric Value**: This option sorts the values based on the numeric values of each item.

- **Text**: This option sorts the values based on the alphanumerical representation of each item.

- **Load Order**: This option sorts the values based on the order in which the items were loaded into QlikView.

The Presentation tab

The **Presentation** tab lets us change some of the presentation aspects of the listbox. Some of the important options are as follows:

- **Selection Style Override**: This option allows for some (limited) variations on the selection style. For example, it's possible to replace the green background on selected items with a checkbox.

- **Single Column**: This option forces QlikView to use only a single column to list the corresponding field values, even if space is available for multiple columns.

- **Suppress Horizontal Scroll Bar**: When values are longer than the width of a listbox, a horizontal scroll bar is automatically created. Checking this option prevents that from happening.

- **Fixed Number of Columns**: When the **Single Column** checkbox is deselected, this option can be used to set a fixed number of columns for the listbox.

- **Order by Column**: When this option is checked, sorting is performed by column, instead of by row.

- **Alignment**: This option is used to set the alignment of **Text** and **Numbers** within the listbox.

- **Wrap Cell Text**: This option wraps text over multiple lines (as set in the **Height** input box). This can be useful for lengthy instances of text that need to be completely visible.

Suppress Horizontal Scroll Bar

Now might be a good time to suppress the horizontal scroll bar on the **Carrier Group**, **Aircraft Group**, **Aircraft Type**, and **Carrier Name** listboxes.

The Number tab

Like the **Sort** tab, the **Number** tab is used by many different objects. It allows us to control how the listbox content looks by using either predefined or custom formats. For example, if we always want numbers to be displayed with two decimals, we can follow these steps:

1. Check the **Override Document Settings** checkbox.
2. Select the **Fixed to** radio button.
3. Enter 2 in the **Decimals** input box.

By clicking on the **Change Document Format** button, a dialog is opened that lets us set the default number format for every individual field at the document level. This means we will only need to specify the format once, and it will be used everywhere within our document. This option is also available via the **Document Properties** dialog window (**Settings** | **Document Properties** | **Number**).

The Font tab

The **Font** tab is also a common one, and its purpose is very straightforward. We already worked with these properties earlier in the chapter while changing the caption font.

The Layout tab

Just as with the others, the **Layout** tab is also one that is used for nearly every object in QlikView. As the name suggests, it allows us to set various layout options.

The different properties available through this tab are directly affected by the document styling mode (**Simplified** or **Advanced**). The **Advanced** styling mode adds more options for styling borders and enables the possibility for rounded corners to be set.

 Since the **Advanced** styling mode is more comprehensive, this section assumes the **Advanced** styling mode is turned on.

Important options on this tab are as follows:

- **Use Borders**: This checkbox is used to enable/disable the object's border.
- **Shadow Intensity**: This option selects whether a shadow effect should be added to the object, and if so, specifies its intensity.
- **Border Width**: This option sets the width of the border, when enabled.

- **Rounded Corners**: This checkbox is used to set whether rounded corners should be used. By (de)selecting individual corners, we can specify which corners should have a rounded effect.

- **Layer**: This option is used to establish the ordering to be used when multiple objects are overlapping. In case of complex, overlapping objects, a **Custom** layer can be used. In this case, higher numbers overlap lower numbers.

- **Apply To...**: This option is used to apply the current format to other objects. We used this function before to apply the same caption layout to every object in the document.

- **Theme Maker** and **Apply Theme**: This option stores the current format in an external theme file. This file can then be used to apply the same format to objects in other documents. Creating and applying themes will be described in more detail in *Chapter 14, More on Visual Design and User Experience*.

- **Show**: This option allows us to either always show the object, or to apply a condition which must be fulfilled for the object to be shown. An example of this would be to use the expression GetSelectedCount([Aircraft Group]) = 1 to the **Aircraft Type** listbox so that it is only visible when a single aircraft group is selected.

- **Allow Move/Size**: Deselecting this option locks the object's size and position.

- **Allow Copy/Clone**: Deselecting this option prevents the object from being copied.

The Caption tab

The **Caption** tab is also a common tab across all QlikView objects. We used it before to set the listbox caption colors and fonts, but it contains a few other interesting options:

- **Multiline Caption**: This option wraps the caption text over the number of lines defined through the **Caption Height** field.

- **X-pos**, **Y-pos**, **Width**, and **Height**: While it is easier to just drag, align, and size objects using the mouse, these options let you define the size and location of an object with pixel-level precision. These options can be set for both the **Normal** and the **Minimized** state of the object.

- **Caption Alignment**: This option defines how the display text is aligned in the caption.

- **Special Icons**: This option adds icons to the caption which perform specific actions. An example of these icons would be the one used to send the chart's data to Excel. It is not advisable to add too many icons as this may clutter the interface. When many icons are needed, it is better to select only the **Menu** icon. This option creates an icon that shows a drop-down menu with all of the available actions.

- **Allow Minimize** and **Auto Minimize**: The **Allow Minimize** option enables an object to be minimized. This setting will add a minimize icon to the caption, much like the one on a regular Windows window. When **Auto Minimize** is also marked, different objects with this setting enabled can be interactively and alternately switched between the restored and the minimized states. This means that, when restoring a minimized object, another currently restored object will be automatically switched to the minimized state for the new object to take its place.

- **Allow Maximize**: This option enables an object to be maximized. It adds a maximize icon to the caption, in the same style as in a regular Windows window.

- **Help Text**: This option adds a question mark icon to the caption that, when clicked, will show a pop-up message with the entered help text. The **Help Text** option can contain calculated expressions as well.

This concludes the side-step into the various listbox properties. Don't worry if you didn't memorize all of them at first, we'll encounter them often enough in the rest of the book.

The Multi Box

While listboxes are a very convenient way to quickly make selections, the downside is that they can also take up a lot of space. This is where the multi box offers an alternative. The multi box displays each field on a single line, alongside a drop-down that expands to allow selections to be made.

Let's add a multi box that contains some extra information on flights, by following these steps:

1. Select **Layout | New Sheet Object | Multi Box...**.
2. In the **Title** input field enter Flight Information.
3. From the list of **Available Fields**, double-click the fields **From – To City**, **Origin City**, **Origin Country**, **Destination City**, **Destination Country**, and **Distance Interval**.
4. Go to the **Sort** tab and select **Distance Interval** from the list of **Fields**.

5. In the **Sort by** section, uncheck the **Text** option, and mark the **Load Order** checkbox.

6. Click on **OK** to apply the settings and close the **Multi Box Properties** page.

The resulting multi box should look like the one shown in the following screenshot. Notice how the list of values is expandable when clicking on each field. Also note that the sort order for the **Distance Interval** is no longer alphabetical, but uses the order in which the values were loaded into QlikView:

During this exercise, you may have noticed that, unlike the listbox, the **Sort** tab for the multi box contains multiple fields and that we can set different sort orders for each field. This is also the case for the alignment options on the **Presentation** tab and the number format options on the **Number** tab. This is not only true for multi boxes, but for any object that contains multiple dimensions and/or expressions, such as table boxes and charts.

The Current Selections Box

QlikView lets us select data in many different ways: listboxes, clicking in charts and entering search terms, just to name a few. While this is incredibly flexible, it can also become hard to see which information is actually selected at any given moment.

Fortunately, QlikView has an option to show the user exactly which selections are currently applied to the data: the **Current Selections** dialog. To open this dialog, we simply need to press *Ctrl + Q* or select **View | Current Selections** from the menu bar. This floats the **Current Selections** dialog window on top of our worksheet. Once we have had a glance at the **Current Selections** window, we can close the dialog.

It is sometimes useful to permanently display the **Current Selections** dialog. This is where the **Current Selections Box** object comes in handy. To add a **Current Selections Box** object to our **Dashboard** sheet, follow these steps:

1. Select **Layout | New Sheet Object | Current Selections Box**.

2. Click on **OK** to apply the settings and close the **New Current Selections Box** dialog window.

The resulting **Current Selections Box** will look like the following screenshot. Notice how every selection you make is added to the displayed list. Also note that we did not change any of the settings in the **Current Selections Properties** dialog, you may want to review the options yourself at a later time.

Making selections from the Current Selections Box

Besides being a great place to quickly look at the applied filters, the **Current Selections Box** option also allows us to interact with the selections in the following ways:

- Erasing filters: By clicking on the corresponding erase icon for any of the displayed fields, the selection over that field will be cleared.

- Modifying selections: By clicking on the drop-down icon, a list of that corresponding field's values will be displayed, from which we can further refine our selection and select other values, just like with a listbox.

- By right-clicking on each of the displayed filters, we can issue additional commands such as **Select Excluded**, **Select All**, **Clear**, or **Clear Other Fields**.

Adding a Bookmark Object

When using QlikView, we invariably come across some selections that we want to return to at a later time. We can create a bookmark by using the menu (**Bookmarks | Add Bookmark**), using the toolbar, or by pressing *Ctrl + B*. Another option is the **Bookmark Object**. This object lets us create and remove bookmarks from within the worksheet space.

Let's add a bookmark object to our **Dashboard** sheet by following these steps:

1. Right-click anywhere on the worksheet and select **New Sheet Objects | Bookmark Object**.
2. Enter Bookmarks into the **Title** input box.
3. Mark the **Show Remove Button** checkbox.
4. Under **Button Alignment**, select **Vertical**.
5. Click on **OK** to create the bookmark object.

Aligning and resizing sheet objects

When we look at the results so far, we will notice that it looks very unorganized (as seen in the following screenshot). The objects are all over the place and are not aligned with the background. Of course, this is not very convenient for the user, so let's see how we can solve it.

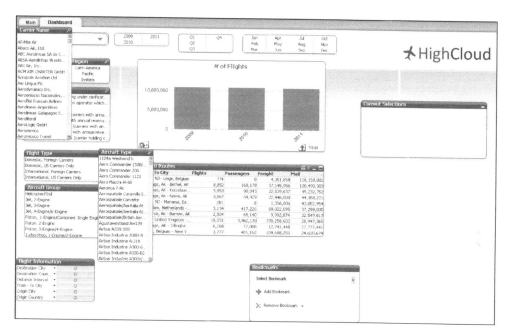

Selecting objects

To select a single object, simply click on its caption. To select multiple objects, activate all of them by either clicking and dragging around them with the mouse cursor ("lassoing"), or by clicking on their captions while keeping the *Shift* key pressed.

Moving objects

Objects (or a selected group of objects) can be moved by clicking on the caption bar and dragging them to the desired location. Objects without a caption (for example, the listboxes showing **Year**, **Quarter**, and **Month** that we created earlier) can be dragged by holding *Alt* and clicking and dragging anywhere on the object. This method also works for objects with a visible caption, and even for objects where **Allow Move/Size** is disabled.

Holding *Ctrl* while pressing the arrow keys moves the active object(s) 1 pixel at a time. Use *Ctrl + Shift* to move them in 10-pixel steps.

Resizing objects

To resize an object, click and drag one of its edges (left, right, top, or bottom) until it fits the required size. You can also use any of the object's corners.

To resize more than one object at once, activate all of them. When resizing one of the selected objects, all of the selected objects will adopt the new size, either vertically, horizontally, or both.

Resizing a Multi Box

Resizing a multi box can be somewhat tricky. Unlike the other sheet objects, if we click and drag one of the object's edges, we can get unexpected results. For example, if we click and drag the right edge and try to make the object smaller, we will, in fact, make it smaller in size but a scrollbar will appear, meaning some part of the object has actually been hidden.

If, on the other hand, we click and drag the right edge and try to make the object larger, it will result in no apparent change.

The key to resizing multi boxes lies in resizing the cells instead. A multi box can be broken into cells, one containing the field label and one containing the field values. By placing the cursor on the right edges of those cells, rather than on the edges of the object, we will be able to click and drag to resize them and, at the same time, resize the entire object.

Hover over the left side of the drop-down icon and watch for when the cursor changes its shape. Click and drag to resize the **Label** cell. Hover over the right edge of the value cell to resize it as well. Resizing cells can be a bit "fiddly," moving the mouse just a little bit may switch between resizing the cell and resizing the object. The following image shows which cursor is associated with which action:

Cursor	Action
↔	Resize cell
⇔	Resize entire object

Aligning sheet objects

To align the objects on the screen, activate the desired objects and use the aligning buttons in the design toolbar. Right-clicking on any of the selected objects also brings up the alignment options, seen in the following screenshot:

If the design toolbar is not shown in your tool dock (it is turned off by default), you can enable it by selecting **View | Toolbars | Design** from the menu.

Do a little house keeping

Let's tidy up our current dashboard using the previously described methods. See if you can get the end result to look like the following screenshot:

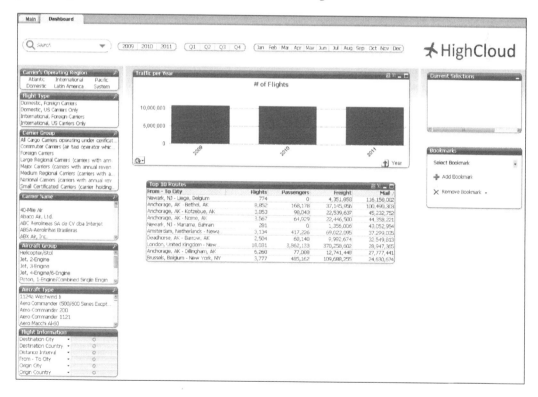

You may notice in the screenshot that I made some other changes. Besides aligning and sizing the objects, I also fixed the following things:

- Removed the border from the **Search** box.
- Changed the fixed number of columns from the **Quarter** listbox to 4.
- Changed the fixed number of columns from the **Month** listbox to 12.
- Added a caption to the **Traffic per Year** chart.
- Right-aligned the expression labels in the **Top 10 Routes** chart.

See if you can apply these changes as well.

Creating and applying a default color map

Now there is only one thing left to do to finish styling up our document: apply the standard HighCloud color scheme to our charts.

Defining chart colors

We'll start by applying the HighCloud colors to the **Traffic per Year** chart. Follow these steps:

1. Right-click on the bar chart and select **Properties...**.
2. Navigate to the **Colors** tab.
3. From the **Data Appearance** section, click on the first color button under the **Colors 1-6** list, and the already familiar **Color Area** dialog will appear.
4. Change the **Base Color** to the already defined **HighCloud Blue** and close the **Color Area** window.
5. Then, click on the second color button from the color map and change it to **HighCloud Brown**.
6. Click on **OK** to close the **Chart Properties** window.

Once we've changed the color map, our chart will adopt the new colors in the order that was defined. At this time, only one color (**HighCloud Blue**) is used by the chart. However, we will use the same color map for all of our future charts, and some of them will indeed require more of the defined colors.

Setting the default color map

Let's now see how we can use that previous definition and set it as the default scheme for all of our charts:

1. Right-click on the **Traffic per Year** chart again and select **Properties....**

2. Navigate to the **Colors** tab and click on the **Advanced...** button. You will now see the following dialog:

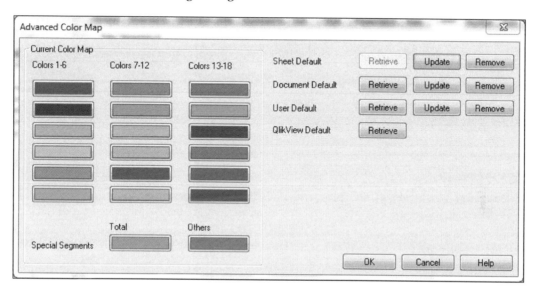

The **Advanced Color Map** dialog window lets us retrieve and update the default color map on a number of levels:

*   **Sheet Default**: The color map is only used for objects within this sheet.

*   **Document Default**: The color map is used for all of the objects within this document.

*   **User Default**: The color map is used for all of the objects that the current user creates. This is very useful when you have a corporate style that you want to apply to all of your charts across all of your documents.

*   **QlikView Default**: This is the default QlikView color map.

*   These settings can only be retrieved but not overwritten.

Setting a new default color map does not overwrite the color settings on objects that were already created. Those settings would need to be updated manually. In *Chapter 14, More on Visual Design and User Experience*, we will look at how we can use themes to override the entire look of a QlikView document, including styles that were set manually.

As we only want to apply the color scheme to this document, we will be updating the **Document Default** color map by following these steps:

1. Click on the **Update** button corresponding to **Document Default**.
2. Click on **OK** to close the **Advanced Color Map** dialog.
3. Click on **OK** to close the **Chart Properties** dialog.

The default color map used by the document has been set and it will be automatically applied to all future charts we create.

Summary

We've come to the end of the chapter, in which we learned to set document, sheet, and object properties. We've also learned how to add a background to aid the frontend layout, and also to apply a corporate identity to our document and set a default color map.

We learned how to create and use different objects, such as the listbox, the Current Selections Box, the Multi Box, and the Bookmark Object.

After preparing and setting the style used by the document, we can now continue to create and use the different data visualization objects available in QlikView. In the next chapter, we will look at building the charts and tables which will be used for dashboards, analysis, and reports.

7
Building Dashboards

By now we have a data model, a styled frontend, and a layout design. It's now time to populate our document with charts, tables, and other data visualization objects.

We will first look at the various types of QlikView users, and what they typically look for in a QlikView document. After that we will look at the different chart options available, along with a few other sheet objects, and use them to extend our dashboard. We will also take a more in-depth look at the ways in which we can create basic calculations in the various objects.

Specifically, in this chapter you will learn:

- The three basic types of QlikView users, and how best to cater to their needs
- The various charting options available in QlikView
- Other sheet objects that can be used to add interactivity to our QlikView documents
- How to create basic calculations

Let's get started!

User types

The data model within a single QlikView document can be used to serve the information needs of a wide range of users, from the executive to the operational level. As different user groups have different information needs, QlikView documents are often built using the **Dashboards**, **Analysis**, and **Reports** (**DAR**) approach. Of course, with a limited number of user types, it is inevitable that they are painted with a broad brush. Most QlikView users will fall into more than one user category. Let's take a look at each of them.

Dashboard users

Dashboards offer a quick, bird's-eye view of information. They are often used by executives and middle-management to gauge performance of a limited number of **Key Performance Indicators** (**KPIs**) against predefined targets.

Data displayed in dashboards is usually aggregated at a high level. Drill-downs to more granular data, while technically not a problem in QlikView, are purposely limited. When dashboard users spot an anomaly in the data, they may simply ask an analyst to dig deeper.

Typical data visualization on a dashboard includes speedometers and traffic lights to provide, at a quick glance, the current status of the defined KPIs. The following screenshot depicts a typical, albeit cleanly formatted, dashboard:

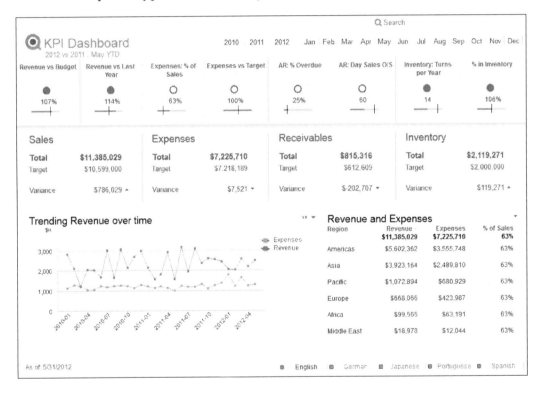

Analysts

While dashboard users commonly want to have a general view on their performance at a glance, analysts are the ones who really dig into the data. They will try to uncover not only what happened, but also why it happened. To do this, they require access to the complete dataset with no detail left out; they also need to be able to query it in many different ways.

In QlikView, this translates to having several listboxes for easy data filtering, along with many different charts offering comprehensive and insightful views of the data. Many analysts will also create their own visualizations whenever they need to answer a specific question, or will make extensive use of **What-If** scenarios to test and predict an outcome based on changes in certain variables.

Typical data visualizations used in analysis include scatter, bar and line charts, and pivot tables. The following screenshot shows an example of a typical analysis sheet:

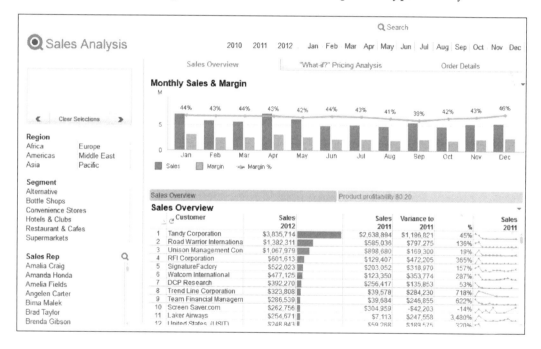

Report users

In QlikView, reports are considered to be more or less static displays of information in a tabular form. Reports can serve multiple purposes; for instance, they can be used to provide users at the operational level with the information they need in their daily activities. They can also be the end-point of an analytical exercise.

Typical data visualizations at the report level are straight tables and pivot tables. The following screenshot shows a typical report:

Number of Orders					14,369					
Order #	Order Date	Customer	Invoice #	Products	Sales Price	Sales Qty	Revenue	Margin
112683	2010-08-23	Homebound	315436	Great Cranberr	$0.00	27,500	$0.00	-$3,905.00
123888	2010-10-25	Homebound	328968	Great Cranberr	$0.00	27,500	$0.00	-$3,905.00
113727	2010-09-10	Icon	316995	Blue Label Car	$0.00	12,500	$0.00	$0.00
124664	2010-11-12	Icon	330498	Blue Label Car	$0.00	12,500	$0.00	$0.00
213740	2011-08-31	Salamander Junc	117107	Blue Label Car	$0.00	7,500	$0.00	$0.00
211183	2011-09-14	Healtheon	118326	Landslide Hot	$2.28	7,126	$16,247.28	$6,424.80
203053	2011-03-25	Healtheon	103089	Landslide Hot	$2.28	6,480	$14,774.40	$1,982.88
113711	2010-09-11	Scientific Atlanta	317070	Blue Label Car	$0.00	6,250	$0.00	$0.00
113712	2010-09-11	Scientific Atlanta	317105	Blue Label Car	$0.00	6,250	$0.00	$0.00
214783	2011-09-09	Healtheon	118060	Landslide Hot	$2.28	5,834	$13,301.52	$5,259.93
214796	2011-09-20	Healtheon	118892	Landslide Hot	$2.28	5,834	$13,301.52	$5,259.93

Applying the DAR principle to Airline Operations

Now that we've gone through the theoretical part of QlikView use cases and user types, it's time to get practical again. To continue, open the `Airline Operations.qvw` file we've been working on. We will build our exercises upon the previously created data model and frontend.

> If you've not followed each exercise in previous chapters and don't have an up-to-date document, don't worry. Take the file named `Solution_Chapter 6_Airline Operations.qvw`, which is located inside the `Airline Operations\Apps` folder; create a copy for back up, and rename it to `Airline Operations.qvw`.

When we look at the document we have built so far, we will notice that this does not yet cover the Dashboard, Analysis, and Report use cases. That's why, in this section, we will expand on the various charts that are available in QlikView, while also applying the DAR principles.

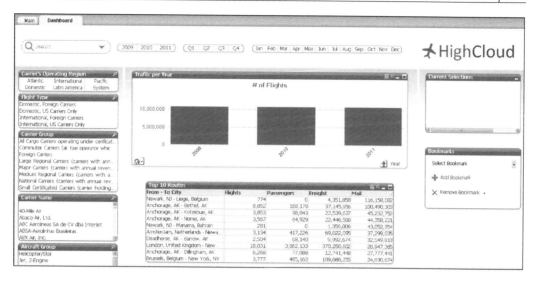

First, though, we need to take a better look at the business requirements set by HighCloud Airlines.

Document requirements

After requirement workshops and interviews with the HighCloud Airlines' executive team, Sara has distilled the following KPIs:

- **Load Factor** %: This gives the number of enplaned passengers versus the number of available seats

- **Performed versus scheduled flights**: This gives the number of flights that were performed versus those that were actually scheduled

- **Air time** %: This gives the time spent flying versus total ramp-to-ramp time

- **Enplaned passengers** (in millions): This gives the number of transported passengers, in millions

- **Departures performed** (in thousands): This gives the number of flights performed, in thousands

- **Revenue Passenger Miles** (in millions): This gives the total number of miles that all passengers were transported, in millions

- **Available Seat Miles** (in millions): This gives the total number of miles that all seats (including unoccupied seats) were transported, in millions

- **Market Share**: This is based on transported passengers

Besides these requirements, there is a need to further analyze the data. While the workshop and interviews weren't conclusive about the exact analytics requirements (they rarely are), there was consensus that at least the following areas should be investigated:

- Trend analysis of the number of flights, transported passengers, freight, and mail through time
- Top 10 routes based on the number of flights, enplaned passengers, freight, and mail
- The number of passengers versus available seats (Load Factor %) across flight types
- The relationship between transported passengers, mail, and the number of flights

In addition, the current metrics currently shown on the **Dashboard** sheet should be moved to the new analysis section.

It was also decided that the following two reports should be available:

- Aggregated flights per month
- KPIs per carrier

Creating the Analysis sheet

The first sheet we will create is the **Analysis** sheet; as the current **Dashboard** sheet already contains a few of the metrics that we want on that sheet, first, let's change the name of the sheet from **Dashboard** to **Analysis**:

1. Right-click anywhere on the sheet workspace and choose **Properties**.
2. Navigate to the **General** tab and enter Analysis in the **Title** input field.
3. Click on **OK** to close the **Sheet Properties** dialog.

While we're at it, rename the **Main** sheet to Associations. This sheet will help users to find associations on the data across many different fields. We might need to reposition the listboxes to fit our new layout.

Sheet handling

The design toolbar at the top of the screen contains some useful commands for dealing with worksheets.

The first icon on the left adds a new sheet. The second and third icons move the currently active sheet to the left or the right on the tab row. The last icon is used to open the properties dialog for the currently active sheet.

The same functionality can also be found under the **Layout** menu. This menu additionally contains the **Remove Sheet** function, which will remove the currently active sheet.

Just as a quick review to keep our focus, the following requirements were defined for the **Analysis** sheet:

- Trend analysis of the number of flights, enplaned passengers, freight, and mail through time

- Top 10 routes based on the number of flights, enplaned passengers, freight, and mail

- The number of passengers versus available seats (Load Factor %) across flight types

- The relationship between enplaned passengers, mail, and the number of flights

Adding a new chart

Now that we have a general layout to start from, it is time to add another chart to the **Analysis** sheet. As you might remember from *Chapter 3, Seeing is Believing*, a new chart can be added by selecting **Layout | New Sheet Object | Chart** from the menu, right-clicking on the worksheet and selecting **New Sheet Object | Chart**, or clicking on the **Create Chart** button on the toolbar.

This opens the first page of the **Chart Properties** dialog: the **General** tab. On this tab we can set some general settings for the chart, such as what the display text in the caption (**Window Title**) should be, and, more importantly, what **Chart Type** we wish to create.

Another interesting option in this window is the **Fast Type Change** option. This option allows the user to dynamically switch between different types of charts, for example, we may switch between a bar chart and a straight table.

> **Yes, pivot tables and straight tables are charts in QlikView**
>
> It might seem a little (or very) counter-intuitive, but pivot and regular (straight) tables are considered charts in QlikView.

Bar Chart

One of the required charts in our document should display number of passengers and number of available seats by flight type. We will use a bar chart to visualize this metric. Follow these steps to create it:

1. From the **Chart Type** section in the **New Chart** dialog window, select the **Bar Chart** option (the first one to the left) and click on **Next**.

2. The next dialog is the **Dimensions** dialog. From the list on the left, locate the **Flight Type** field and add it to the **Used Dimensions** list by clicking on the **Add >** button. After that, click on **Next**.

3. We will now enter an expression to get the total number of enplaned passengers. In the **Edit Expression** dialog that opens automatically after clicking on **Next** in the previous window, type the following expression and click on **OK**:

```
Sum ([# Transported Passengers])
```

4. We will assign a label to our expression by typing # of Passengers in the corresponding **Label** field.

5. We will add a second expression to calculate the number of available seats. Do this by clicking on the **Add** button, which will open up the **Edit Expression** window again.

6. Enter the following expression and click on **OK**:

```
Sum([# Available Seats])
```

7. Enter the label # of Available Seats into the **Label** field.

8. Let's have a look at the intermediate result; click on **Finish**.

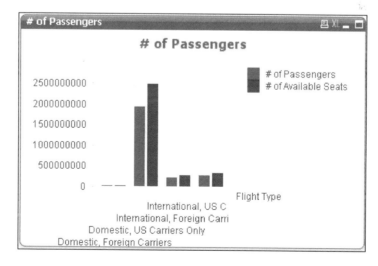

When we look at this chart, we notice that it's quite hard to read. The numbers are really large, all those zeroes occupy a lot of space. Besides that, the title text and caption both say the same thing and do not reference the second expression in the chart.

 We should also note that the corporate colors have been correctly assigned, since the default color map in place was defined in the previous chapter.

Let's correct these issues by changing the following settings in the **Properties** dialog:

1. On the **General** tab, set the **Window Title** field to `# of Passengers/ Available Seats (x 1 million) by Flight Type`. Next, uncheck the **Show Title in Chart** checkbox.

2. On the **Expressions** tab, select the **# of Passengers** expression and tick the **Values on Data Points** checkbox. Next, highlight **# of Available Seats** and also check the **Values on Data Points** checkbox. Modify both expressions' definition by dividing the result by one million. The expressions will now be:

   ```
   Sum ([# Transported Passengers]) / 1000000
   Sum ([# Available Seats]) / 1000000
   ```

3. On the **Style** tab, change the **Orientation** to horizontal (right icon).

4. On the **Presentation** tab, set the **legend's font format** to **Tahoma**, with a **Regular Font Style**, and with the **Size** set to **8** by first clicking on the **Settings** button, and then clicking on the **Font** button in the **Legend Settings** dialog window.

5. On the **Axes** tab, under **Expression Axes**, check the **Show Grid** checkbox. Change the **Font** format for both **Expression Axis** and **Dimension Axis** to **Tahoma**, with a **Regular Font Style**, and with the **Size** set to **8** using their respective **Font** buttons.

6. On the **Number** tab, hold down the *Shift* key and select **# of Passengers** and **# of Available Seats** from the list of **Expressions**. Next, select **Fixed to** under **Number Format Settings** and set the **Decimals** field to **1**.

7. On the **Layout** tab, uncheck the **Use Borders** option.

8. Click on **OK** to close the **Chart Properties** window.

The resulting chart should look similar to the following screenshot:

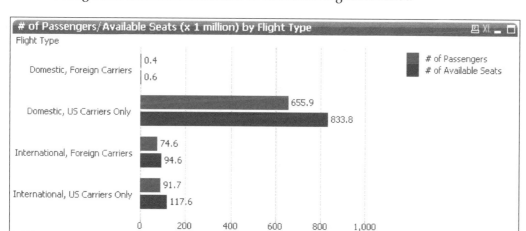

Now that we have formatted our chart, we can copy these settings to another chart using the **Format Painter Tool**. To do this, activate the object for which formatting needs to be copied and then click the **Format Painter Tool** button in the design toolbar. Next, click the target object to apply the format. Use it to copy the formatting options we set previously and apply them to our **Traffic per Year** chart.

Additional bar chart properties

In the previous example we went over the most common bar chart properties. As you may have seen in the various dialog windows, QlikView offers a lot of additional options and settings. Let's look at a few notable options available for bar charts.

Style

On the **Style** tab, you can add a 3D, shadow, or gradient **Look** to your bar chart. Additionally, you can change the **Orientation** option, as we did in the example. Choosing a horizontal orientation can make text labels much more readable. Arguably the most important option on this tab is the **Subtype** option; this lets you change the bar chart from **Grouped**, in which two bars corresponding to one dimension value will be shown side by side, to a **Stacked** arrangement, where the two bars will be stacked on top of each other.

Presentation

Notable options on the **Presentation** tab are the **Bar Distance** option, which controls the distance between bars in a group, and the **Cluster Distance** option, which controls the distance between groups of bars. For the last option to work there needs to be multiple dimensions or expressions.

Expressions and the Edit Expression window

Before we look at the other chart types and objects that QlikView has to offer, it is time to have a more in-depth look at **Expressions** and the **Edit Expression** window.

Expressions

By now you may have noticed that QlikView expressions can be used just about everywhere throughout the program, from chart expressions to expressions for setting colors or window titles. This functionality makes QlikView very flexible. Expressions in QlikView are very similar to formulas that you may know from Excel, or functions that you may know from SQL.

The Edit Expression window

The **Edit Expression** window is used to enter expressions. Whenever you see an ellipsis character (**...**) accompanying an input box, it means you can click on it to enter an expression.

Let's open the **Edit Expression** window now and have a closer look:

1. Right-click the **# of Passengers/Available Seats** chart and choose **Properties...**.
2. Select the **Expressions** tab and highlight the **# of Passengers** expression from the list on the left.
3. Click on the **...** button next to the **Definition** input box.

The **Edit Expression** window is shown in the following screenshot:

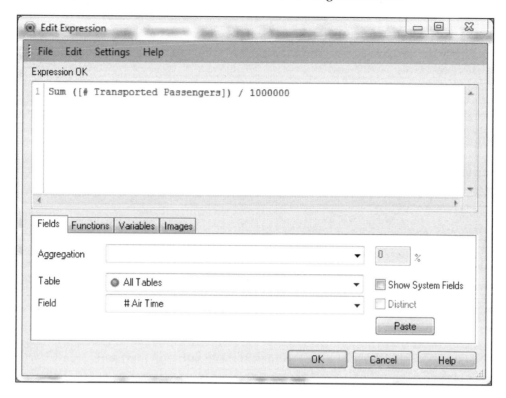

The **Edit Expression** window contains a big input field in which expressions can be entered directly. Once you have familiarized yourself with the various expression functions and their syntax (we'll cover many of them throughout the book), you will realize that this is the fastest way to enter an expression. The **Edit Expression** window automatically checks the syntax of the entered expression; if an error is found, the expression will be underlined with a red squiggly line and the text **Error in expression** will be displayed.

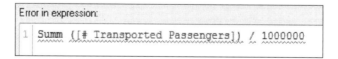

Be aware that the automatic syntax check does not always work flawlessly; with advanced expressions, the editor will sometimes indicate that an error is present when in fact there is none.

At the bottom of the expression editor, a few tabs can be found. Let's quickly see what each of these tabs does.

Fields

The **Fields** tab enables "clicking together" an expression by selecting an **Aggregation** function, such as sum, avg, min, max, and the field to which it should be applied. The **Table** dropdown can be used to filter the field list to those belonging to a particular table.

When the **Distinct** checkbox is marked, only unique values will be considered in the aggregation. This can be useful when, for example, we want to count the number of distinct customers, instead of their total number of appearances in the database.

When all selections have been made, the expression can be entered into the **Edit Expression** input field by clicking on the **Paste** button. Note that the code will be pasted where the cursor presently is, and will replace any highlighted text in the expression.

Functions

While the **Fields** tab makes it possible to create expressions using just the mouse, it is fairly limited in the type of expressions it can create. The **Functions** tab, however, contains a comprehensive list of available functions, grouped by **Function Category** and **Function Name**.

Selecting a particular function will display its syntax in a box. The selected function can be entered into the expression input field by clicking on the **Paste** button, but the corresponding parameters have to be set manually.

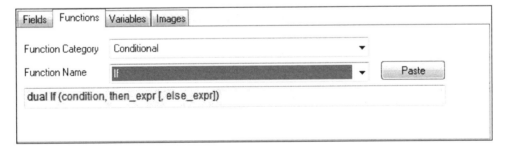

Variables

As we will see later in this chapter, variables can be used to store expressions and values. The advantage of this approach is that we can use an expression in many places, while only maintaining it in a single place.

If, for example, instead of directly typing the # of Passengers expression into the input field we had created a variable containing its definition, we would be able to select that variable from the drop-down list on the **Variables** tab and achieve the same result.

Images

A QlikView expression does not always have to be text or a calculation. There are some objects, for example, the **Text Object** or even a **Straight Table**, that are also able to display the result of an expression as an image.

The **Images** tab makes it easy to select images that are built into QlikView, or which have been bundled into the document via script. Simply select an image name from the **Image** drop-down list or, more conveniently, from a visual menu of images by clicking on the **Advanced** button.

Clicking on the **Paste** option will enter a string referencing the corresponding image into the expression input field. These string values can also be used within expressions. For example, the following expression will compare the **Target** field using the `if` function. If the value is greater than 100, a green upwards arrow will be displayed, otherwise a red downwards arrow will be shown.

```
if(Target > 100, 'qmem://<bundled>/BuiltIn/arrow_n_g.png',
'qmem://<bundled>/BuiltIn/arrow_s_r.png')
```

Click on **Cancel** in the **Edit Expression** dialog window to close it without saving any changes and close the **Chart Properties** window as well.

The Expression Overview window

With expressions in so many locations, it can be hard to keep track of them all. This is where the **Expression Overview** window comes in handy; it offers a central location to manage all expressions being used in our QlikView document.

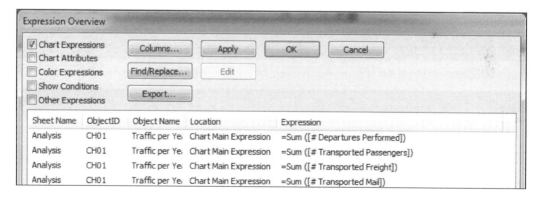

The **Expression Overview** window can be opened by pressing *Ctrl + Alt + E* or by selecting **Settings | Expression Overview** from the menu bar.

By default, only **Chart Expressions** in the QlikView document are shown. This list can be expanded or narrowed down by (de)selecting the checkboxes for each expression type.

It is possible to edit an individual expression by highlighting it from the list and clicking the **Edit** button. Bulk updates are possible, using the **Find/Replace** button. Be very cautious when using this function, as unintended changes can occur.

Line Chart

The **Line Chart** works very much like the bar chart that we looked at earlier. So, instead of creating a new line chart, we will convert one of the already built bar charts into one.

Bar charts versus line charts

While bar and line charts are considered interchangeable by many, there are actually specific use cases in which it is advisable to use one over the other. **Bar charts** are best used to compare different categories, for example, for comparing different Flight Types. **Line charts** are best used to detect trends in series that have an order, such as dates or steps within a process.

Let's follow these steps to convert the **Traffic per Year** chart from a bar chart into a line chart:

1. Right-click the **Traffic per Year** chart and select **Properties...**.
2. On the **General** tab, under **Chart Type** select **Line Chart** (second icon from the top left).
3. Click on **OK** to apply the settings.

The resulting line chart is shown in the following picture.

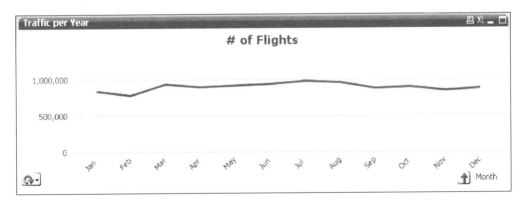

Notice we have to select a year for the months to be shown. In this case, we have selected 2011 in the **Year** listbox.

While this already looks quite nice, we will make a few extra changes:

- As we are more interested in the trend than in the exact values, the axis does not necessarily need to start at **0**
- We will add dots on the actual data points so it is clear for the user where to point their mouse cursor in case they do want to see the exact values
- The numbers on the Y-axis are quite big; we will format the numbers so that they are shown in thousands, millions, or billions depending on the selection

Follow these steps to apply the changes:

1. Right-click on the **Traffic per Year** chart and select **Properties...**.
2. Navigate to the **Axes** tab and deselect the **Forced 0** checkbox.
3. Activate the **Expressions** tab and click on the plus icon next to the circular arrow to display the list of expressions.
4. For each expression, individually mark the **Symbol** checkbox under the **Display Options** section and select **Dots** from the drop-down list.
5. Open the **Presentation** tab and set the **Symbol Size** option to **4pt** under the **Line/Symbol Settings** section; this sets the size of the dots.
6. Open the **Number** tab and select all expressions by clicking on the first expression (# of Flights) and then holding *Shift* while clicking on the last expression (Transported Mail). All expressions will be highlighted.
7. In the **Thousand Symbol** input field enter x Thousand.
8. In the **Million Symbol** box enter x Million.
9. In the **Billion Symbol** box enter, you guessed it, x Billion.
10. Click on **OK** to apply the changes and close the **Chart Properties** dialog.

The resulting line chart is shown in the following screenshot:

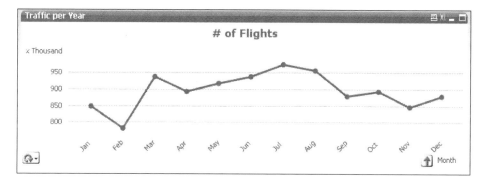

As you can see, the actual trend can be easily perceived and the individual data points are much more visible. Additionally, the scale on the y axis now contains much shorter numbers. The advantage of setting values for thousands, millions, and billions is that the y axis scale will automatically adjust to the appropriate range when updating the chart based on user selections.

Additional line chart properties

While in the previous example we looked at the most common line chart attributes, there are some additional settings in the **Chart Properties** dialog that are interesting to take note of.

Expressions

On the **Expressions** tab, the **Accumulation** option can be used to display a moving total. This means that instead of presenting individual values, each new value is added to the sum of all previous values. In the following chart, instead of the individual amount of flights for each month, we see the total cumulative amount of flights as of each period:

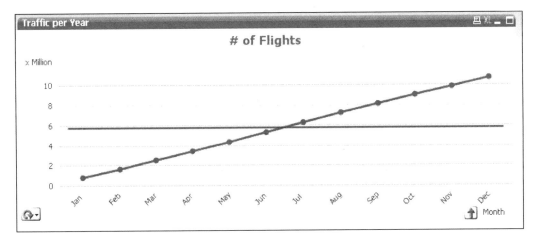

The other line you see in the chart represents the **Average**; this option and is set under the **Trendlines** section.

Style

On the **Style** tab, you can change the **Look** option of the line chart. Besides some 3D effects, an interesting visualization is the area chart (fourth icon from the top). Another useful setting, though admittedly not as useful as it is for bar charts, is the **Orientation** option. This allows you to change the orientation from vertical to horizontal.

Presentation

The **Presentation** tab offers options to change how the data is presented within the chart. Useful options are under the **Line/Symbol Settings** section; with these options we can change the **Line Width** option of the chart as well as the size of the symbols (as we saw when we added the dots in the previous chart).

For charts that have many values on the X-axis, a useful option is the **Chart Scrolling** option. By checking the **Enable X-Axis Scrollbar** checkbox and setting a value for the **When Number of Items Exceeds** parameter, a scrollbar is added to the chart whenever the number of values on the X-axis exceeds the specified amount.

Arguably the most useful option in this tab, however, is found under the **Reference Lines** section. This option can be used to integrate additional, straight lines to the line chart. A practical example would be to add a target reference to compare each data point to a predefined objective.

By clicking on the **Add** button, the **Reference Lines** dialog opens. Here we can set an expression for the reference line, set its label, and change some other settings with regard to formatting. The following screenshot shows an example of a static 900,000 flights target line, but of course a dynamic target could also be used if it is included in the data model:

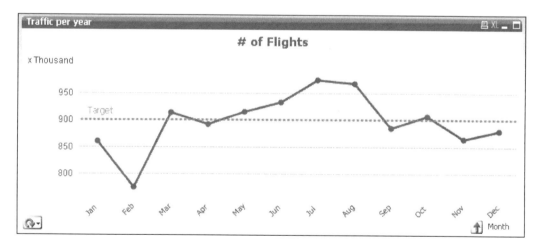

Combo Chart

Though it sounds fancy, the Combo Chart is nothing more than a combination of the bar and line charts that we used earlier. It brings together all the properties of both charts.

Let's look at how this combined chart works by converting the **# of Passengers /
Available Seat (x 1 million) by Flight Type** chart that we created earlier:

1. Right-click on the bar chart and select **Properties…**.

2. From the **General** tab, change the **Chart Type** option from **Bar Chart** (top left
   icon) to **Combo Chart** (third icon from the left).

3. On the **Expressions** tab select the **# of Passengers** expression. Next, deselect
   the **Line** checkbox under **Display Options** and select the **Bar** checkbox.
   Disable the **Values on Data Points** option as well.

4. Next, select the **# of Available Seats** expression. Then, deselect the **Line**
   checkbox and mark the **Symbol** checkbox. Select the **Diamonds** option
   from the drop-down list on the right. Disable the **Values on Data Points**
   option as well.

5. Click on **Add** to open the **Edit Expression** window and enter the following
   new expression and then click on **OK** to close the editor:

   ```
   Column(1) / Column(2)
   ```

6. Enter Load Factor as this expression's **Label**.

7. With the new expression highlighted from the expressions' list, deselect the
   Line checkbox and enable the **Values on Data Points** option.

8. Navigate to the **Presentation** tab and set the **Symbol Size** option to **4 pt**.

9. On the **Number** tab, select the **Load Factor** expression and set the **Number
   Format Settings** option to **Fixed to 1 Decimals** and mark the **Show in
   Percent (%)** option.

10. Click on **OK** to close the **Chart Properties** dialog.

The end result should look like the following chart:

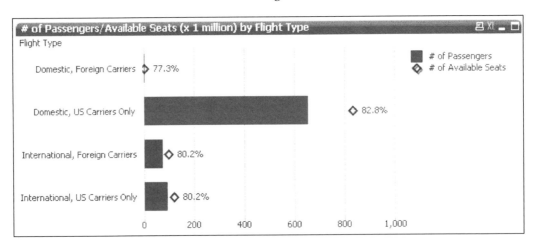

One thing you may notice is that while we entered three expressions, only two are visible in the chart. This happens because we did not select any display mode for the **Load Factor** expression. However, we did activate the **Values on Data Points** checkbox, and that is why the value for **Load Factor** is shown in the chart.

You may also wonder about the expression that we used to calculate the **Load Factor** value:

```
Column(1) / Column(2)
```

This expression tells QlikView to divide the result of the first expression by the result of the second expression. You will understand that the order of the expressions should not be changed in order for this to work reliably.

Container

By now, with three charts already created, our worksheet is becoming somewhat cluttered again. Time to do another round of reorganizing. The option of choice this time will be a container object in which we will group multiple objects together in the same screen space. The user will then be able to interactively switch between objects.

Let's put all three charts (or, two charts and a table) into the container object by following these steps:

1. Go to **Layout | New Sheet Object | Container** in the menu bar.

2. On the **General** tab, select the three items corresponding to our charts from the **Existing Objects** list (**Traffic per Year**, **Top 10 Routes**, and **# of Passengers**).

In the **Existing Objects** list, objects are prefixed with their **Object ID**, for example, **CH03 Traffic per Year**.

3. Click on **Add** to place them in the **Objects Displayed in Container** list to the right.

4. Go to the **Presentation** tab and select **Tabs at bottom** from the **Appearance** drop-down menu.

5. Go to the **Layout** tab and deactivate the **Use Borders** option.

6. Click **OK** to close the **Container Properties** dialog and create the new object.

The resulting container is shown in the following image. Notice how we can switch between charts by clicking the tabs on the bottom row.

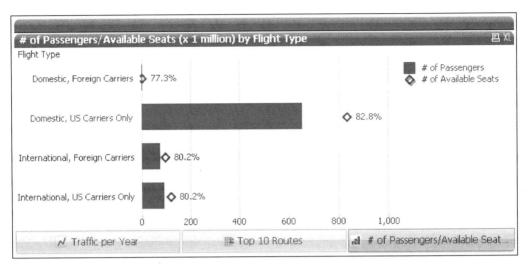

You will also notice that the original charts are still on the worksheet, making it look even messier. We will remove these old objects by right-clicking on each of them and selecting the **Remove** option. A pop-up window will appear asking to confirm deletion of either only the selected object or all linked objects. Click on the **Delete Selected** button as shown in the screenshot below:

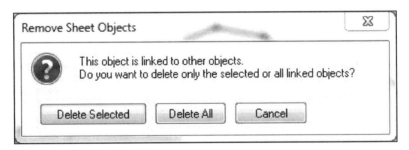

The reason this dialog message appears is that there are now two instances of the same object, and QlikView treats them as linked objects (one object sharing the same properties and IDs, but in different locations). We will look at linked objects in more detail later on in this chapter.

After we've removed all the duplicate charts and have properly aligned the container object, we will remove the container's caption by following these steps:

1. Right-click on either the container's caption or one of the buttons on the bottom row and select **Properties…**.

2. Go to the **Caption** tab and deselect the **Show Caption** option.

3. Click on **OK** to apply the settings and close the dialog window.

It is important to click on the container heading or buttons; otherwise we would not be opening the container properties but the properties of the currently active chart. Now we have space to add even more charts!

Scatter Chart

One of the analysis requirements we have to meet is to provide an insight into the relationship between the number of passengers, number of transported mail, and the number of performed departures at the carrier level. To visualize this we will add a scatter chart by following these steps:

1. Go to **Layout | New Sheet Object | Chart** in the menu.

2. From the **New Chart Object** window, set the **Window Title** to:

   ```
   Transported passengers vs mail
   ```

3. Disable the **Show Title in Chart** option and select the **Scatter Chart** (bottom left icon) option in the **Chart Type** section from the **General** tab. Then click on **Next**.

4. Select **Carrier Name** from the **Available Fields/Groups** list and click on the **Add >**button to add it to the **Used Dimensions** list. Click on **Next**.

5. On the **Expressions** tab, select **# Transported Mail** from the **X** listbox and **# Transported Passengers** from the **Y** listbox.

6. Mark the **Bubble Chart** checkbox and enter the following in the **Bubble Size Expression** input field:

   ```
   Sum([# Departures Performed])
   ```

7. Click on **Next** twice.

8. On the **Style** tab, under the **Look** section select the third icon from the top in the right column (above the "glossy" bubbles that are selected by default) and click on **Next**.

9. On the **Presentation** tab, deselect the **Show Legend** checkbox and click on **Next**.

10. On the **Axes** tab, mark the **Show Grid, Show Minor Grid**, and **Label Along Axis** checkboxes under X-axis as well as under the y axis. These options add a visible grid to the chart as well as place the labels alongside the axes, which takes less space. Click on **Next**.

11. On the **Colors** tab, enable the **Persistent Colors** checkbox. This setting ensures that dimensions (in our case carriers) keep the same color even when the selection changes. Click on **Next**.

12. On the **Number** tab, select all three expressions and set the **Number Format Settings** option to **Integer**. Enter x 1 thousand in the **Thousand Symbol** field, x 1 million in the **Million Symbol** field, and x 1 billion in the **Billion Symbol** field.

13. Click on **Finish** to apply the settings and close the dialog.

The resulting chart is shown in the following screenshot. The Y-axis shows the number of transported passengers while the X-axis shows the amount of transported mail. The bubble size indicates how many flights (departures) have been performed by each carrier.

We can immediately see there are carriers that only transport mail, such as **United Parcel Service**, and those that only carry passengers, such as **Southwest Airlines Co**. In fact, most carriers seem to either do one or the other, not both.

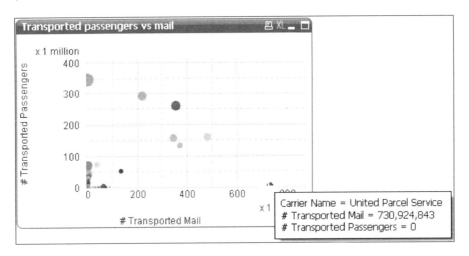

Make a few selections on the **Carrier's Operating Region** listbox and you might gain some interesting insights. Also notice how the unit of the chart's scale changes between selections because we set the **Thousand, Million**, and **Billion Symbol** fields.

In our example, we used the **Simple Mode** option to create the expressions for the scatter chart. As the name implies, this allows for only simple expressions to be formulated. We can switch to the Advanced Mode by checking the **Advanced Mode** checkbox on the **Expressions** tab. This will change the view to the regular **Expressions** tab that we saw on earlier charts.

 It is important to keep in mind that when dealing with scatter charts the expression that is defined first will be used for the X-axis, the second expression will be used for the Y-axis, and the third expression will always be used to set the bubble size.

Button

Now that we have set up the basic structure and the charts for our analysis sheet, it is time to add a few buttons for the user to interact with. QlikView allows us to execute an action, or a sequence of actions, when a button is clicked.

Let's start with a practical example. During analysis, a user will often want to clear their entire set of selections, or undo and redo single steps in their selection. Follow these steps to add a button that will clear the user's selections:

1. Go to **Layout | New Sheet Object | Button** in the menu bar.
2. On the **General** tab of the **New Button Object** window, enter `Clear Selections` in the **Text** input field.
3. Change the **Color** option to *HighCloud brown*, which was defined in the previous chapter and should be part of the custom colors available on the **Color** window.
4. Switch to the **Actions** tab.
5. Click the **Add** button, select the **Clear All** option from the **Action** list on the right, and click on **OK**.
6. Click on **OK** to close the **Button properties** dialog.

We have now created a single button that, when clicked, will clear all current selections.

As we saw while creating the button, there are a wide variety of actions that can be assigned to it. These actions can also be chained, so that one click on a button triggers a sequence of actions. The following screenshot shows a sequence of actions in which we first clear all selections, switch to a predefined sheet, and finally make a selection in a predefined field:

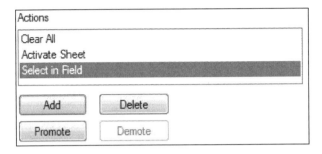

Of course, we still have to create the buttons for undoing and redoing a selection. The corresponding actions are found as **Back** and **Forward**, respectively. Take a minute to create the buttons for these actions as well and align them under the **Current Selections** box. If everything goes correctly, you should end up with something like this:

Test each button to make sure they are doing what they are supposed to do.

Statistics box

A **statistics box** is a convenient way to quickly perform a series of statistics on a single, numeric field. For example, the following shows the total, average, minimum, and maximum distances in a single statistics box.

1. Let's follow these steps to add the statistics box to our analysis sheet: Right-click anywhere on the worksheet and select **New Sheet Object | Statistics Box...**.

2. On the **General** tab, select **Distance** from the **Field** drop-down menu.

3. Double-click on the **Total count** option in the **Displayed Functions** list to remove it, since it will not be relevant.

4. Go to the **Number** tab and select all **Functions** by holding the *Shift* key while clicking on the first and last item in the list. Set their number format to **Override Default Settings** and **Integer**.

5. Click on **OK** to create the statistics box and position it below the buttons we created earlier. Move the bookmark object to a lower position if necessary.

Now whenever we make selections, the **Distance** statistics box will automatically show the various statistics calculated over all the individual records in the fact table.

With the added statistics box object, and after appropriately resizing and positioning objects, the analysis sheet should now look like this:

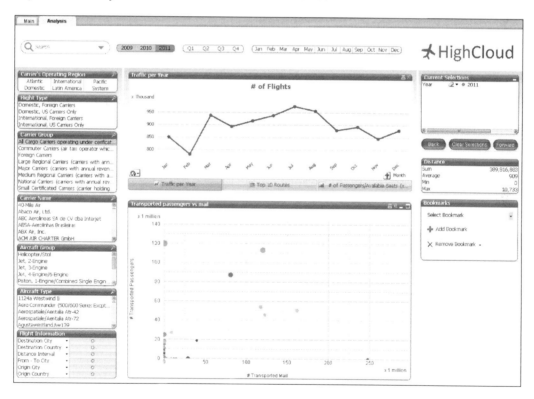

The **Analysis** sheet now meets all the current requirements. The objects we've created while building this sheet are the bar, line, and combo charts, a scatter plot, buttons, and a statistics box. We've also learned how to organize objects using a container and have had a closer look at chart properties, expressions, the expression editor, and expression overview.

Of course, QlikView has many other objects and functions that we can use in our documents. Let's move to our next sheet and discover some more of what QlikView has to offer.

Creating the new Dashboard sheet

Now that we have finished the first iteration of our analysis sheet, it is time to start creating the new Dashboard sheet. As was defined before, we will need to visualize the following KPIs and metrics:

- **Load Factor** %: This gives the number of enplaned passengers versus the number of available seats
- **Performed versus scheduled flights**: This gives the number of flights that were performed versus those that were scheduled
- **Air time** %: This gives the time spent flying versus total ramp-to-ramp time
- **Enplaned passengers** (in millions): This gives the number of transported passengers, in millions
- **Departures performed** (in thousands): This gives the number of flights performed, in thousands
- **Revenue Passenger Miles** (millions): This gives the total number of miles that all passengers were transported, in millions
- **Available Seat Miles** (millions): This gives the total number of miles that all seats (including unoccupied seats) were transported, in millions
- **Market Share**: This is based on enplaned passengers

As we want to have a consistent interface throughout our sheets, let's first set up the new sheet and common objects by following these steps:

1. Add a new sheet by selecting **Layout** | **Add Sheet...** from the menu.
2. Right-click on the new sheet workspace and select **Properties...**.
3. On the **General** tab, set the **Title** of the sheet to Dashboard and click on **OK** to close the dialog.
4. Right-click on the tab area of the new **Dashboard** sheet and select **Promote Sheet** to place the **Dashboard** sheet to the left of the **Analysis** sheet.

5. Then, navigate to the **Analysis** sheet.

6. Repeat the following process for each of the objects shown in the following screenshot. Right-click and select **Copy to Clipboard | Object**, select the **Dashboard** tab, and right-click on an empty space and select **Paste Sheet Object as Link**.

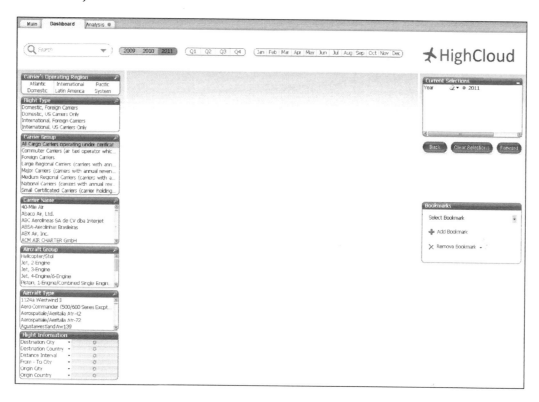

Now, when we switch between the **Dashboard** and **Analysis** tabs, we can see that the surrounding listboxes, current selection box, buttons, and bookmark object remain consistent; only the contents in the center area of the screen will differ from one tab to the other.

Linked Objects

When we created the **Dashboard** sheet in the previous exercise, we used the **Paste Sheet Object as Link** command instead of **Paste Sheet Object** to paste the copied objects to the new sheet.

The difference between these two options is that using **Paste Sheet Object** creates a copy of the object, which is independent of the source object. The **Paste Sheet Object as Link** option, on the other hand, creates an additional instance (or linked object) of the source object. Any changes made to the layout properties of a linked object will be applied to all other linked objects, with the exception of size and position.

> The size and position of linked objects can be updated manually by right-clicking on the object and selecting **Linked Objects | Adjust Position of Linked Objects**.

When the same object is used in many different places, such as listboxes that appear on every sheet, using linked objects can make maintenance a lot more convenient.

> **Drag and drop to copy or create linked objects**
>
> Objects can also be copied or linked by dragging and dropping.
>
> To copy an object, hold down the *Ctrl* key while clicking on the object's caption and drag the object. A small green plus sign on your cursor will indicate that you are copying an object. Release the mouse cursor on an empty space on the worksheet to create a copy.
>
> Creating a linked object works very similarly to copying an object. Hold down *Ctrl + Shift* while clicking on the object's caption. A small chain icon on your cursor indicates that you are linking an object. Drag and release the mouse cursor on an empty space on the worksheet to create the linked object.
>
> Of course, we can also create copies or linked objects on sheets other than the source sheet. To do this, instead of dragging the object to an empty space on the worksheet, drag it to the tab corresponding to the target sheet. The object will appear in exactly the same position as the source object, but on the other sheet.

Let's see how linked objects work by following these steps:

1. On the **Dashboard** tab, create a copy of the **Carrier Name** listbox by holding down the *Ctrl* key, clicking on the header, and dragging the listbox to an empty space on the worksheet.

2. Right-click on the new copy and select **Properties...**.

3. On the **General** tab, set the **Title** of the listbox to Copy.

4. On the **Font** tab, set the **Font Style** to **Bold** and the **Font Size** to **16**.

5. Click on **OK** to close the **Properties** dialog.

6. Now, create a linked object of the listbox **Aircraft Group** by holding down *Ctrl + Shift*, clicking on the header, and dragging the listbox to an empty space on the worksheet.

7. Right-click on the new linked object and select **Properties...**.

8. On the **General** tab, set the **Title** to `Linked Object`.

9. On the **Font** tab, set the **Font Style** to **Bold** and the **Font Size** to **16**.

10. Click on **OK** to close the **Properties** dialog.

The result shows the difference between copied and linked objects. Changes that were made to the copied **Carrier Name** listbox have not been applied to the original, while changes that were made to the linked **Aircraft Group** object were also applied to the original. In fact, they have even been applied to the **Aircraft Group** listbox on the **Analysis** sheet as well.

Let's undo the changes we've made by pressing *Ctrl + Z* until we are back to the original layout.

Beware of deleting linked objects

When deleting a linked object, a popup will ask if you want to only delete the selected object, or if you want to delete all objects. Beware of selecting **Delete All**; all instances of the object will be deleted, even those located on other sheets.

Gauges

After our little detour on linked objects, let's start building the dashboard by adding three gauge charts, one showing a global indicator of **Load Factor** %, the second showing **Performed vs Scheduled Departures ratio** value, and the third showing the **Air Time** % value.

1. Start by adding a new chart object with the **Create Chart** button located on the design toolbar.

2. From the first dialog window, make sure to select **Gauge** as **Chart Type**.

3. In the **Window Title** field, enter Load Factor % as the name of the chart and click on **Next**.

4. This chart type does not make use of dimensions, so we'll skip this window and click on **Next** once more to get to the **Expressions** dialog window.

> If a dimension is present in the gauge chart, the gauge will show the value for the first sorted value in the dimension field. Always ensure, that no dimension is selected. This is especially important to keep in mind when using **Fast Type Change** on charts.

5. Add the following expression in the **Edit Expression** dialog window and click on **OK** to continue:

   Sum ([# Transported Passengers]) / Sum ([# Available Seats])

6. The expression that we just created will calculate the percentage of occupied seats compared to those that were available on each flight.

7. The **Label** we'll assign to this expression will be the same as the **Window Title** field that we previously defined: Load Factor %.

8. Click on **Next** three times, until you are at the **Presentation** window, and set the following configuration under the **Gauge Settings** section:

   ° **Min** and **Max** values will be 0.5 and 1 respectively

   ° From the **Segment Setup** section, we will add two more segments by clicking on the **Add...** button twice

   ° Deselect the **Autowidth Segments** checkbox at the bottom of the window

When selected, the **Autowidth Segments** function automatically sizes the segments based on the Min and Max values of the gauge. We want to avoid this as we want to set the values ourselves.

We should now have four segments and will set up each of the four segments is in the following manner:

- **Segment 1**:
  - ○ **Lower Bound**: 0.5
  - ○ **Color** set to **Two Colors Gradient** with the **Base Color** option set to **Red** (R:255; G:0; B:0) and the **Second Color** option set to **Orange** (R:255; G:128; B:0)
  - ○ Color **Gradient Style** option should be set to **Vertical**

- **Segment 2**:
  - ○ **Lower Bound**: 0.625
  - ○ **Color** set to **Two Colors Gradient** with the **Base Color** option set to **Orange** (R:255; G:128; B:0) and the **Second Color** option set to **Yellow** (R:255; G:255; B:0)
  - ○ Color **Gradient Style** option will be set to **Vertical**

- **Segment 3**:
  - ○ **Lower Bound**: 0.75
  - ○ **Color** set to **Two Colors Gradient** with the **Base Color** option set to **Yellow** (R:255; G:255; B:0) and the **Second Color** option set to **Light Green** (R:128; G:255; B:128)
  - ○ Color **Gradient Style** option will be set to **Vertical**

- **Segment 4**:
  - ○ **Lower Bound**: 0.85
  - ○ **Color** set to **Two Colors Gradient** with the **Base Color** option set to **Light Green** (R:128; G:255; B:128) and the **Second Color** option set to **Green** (R:0; G:255; B:0)
  - ○ Color **Gradient Style** option should be set to **Vertical**

In these steps we configured the gauge to display values from 50 to 100 percent. Within this range we defined four separate segments, each with their own color. You may have noticed that we only set the lower boundary for each segment; this is because the upper boundary is automatically defined by the lower boundary of the following segment, or by the upper boundary of the gauge. In our example, **Segment 1** runs from 50 to 62.5 percent (although we specified the limits in decimal form, that is, 0.5 and 0.625), **Segment 2** covers the area ranging from 62.5 to 75 percent, and so on.

The boundaries that we've defined in our example may appear arbitrary. In a real-world situation, ideally we would be setting these boundaries based on targets set by the business.

Let's continue setting up our gauge.

1. Still on the **Presentation** tab, enable the checkboxes corresponding to **Show Scale**, **Show Labels on Every Major Unit**, **Hide Segment Boundaries**, and **Hide Gauge Outlines**.

2. Set the value of **Show Scale** to **6 Major Units**, set the value of **Show Labels on Every** to **1 Major Unit**.

3. Click on **Next** three times, until you get to the **Number** dialog window, set the format to **Integer,** and mark the checkbox corresponding to **Show in Percent** (%).

4. Click on **Next** to open the **Font** dialog window and set the **Size** to **8**.

5. Click on **Finish** to create the chart.

The result should be the following gauge chart:

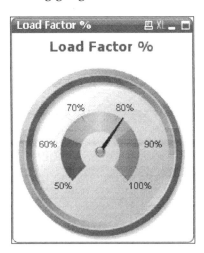

As at this point it's hard to see what exact number the chart is presenting, we'll add a **Text in Chart** attribute to show the corresponding result value using the following steps:

1. Bring up the **Properties…** dialog window again by right-clicking on the **Gauge chart** option and activating the **Presentation** tab.

2. Locate the **Text in Chart** section and click on the corresponding **Add...** button. This brings up the **Chart Text** dialog, which is shown in the following screenshot:

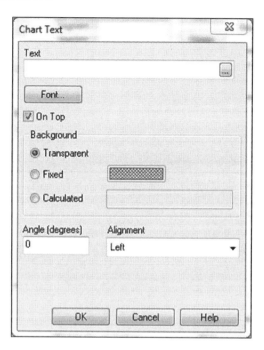

3. We'll add an expression in the **Text** field. Open the **Edit Expression** window by clicking on the **...** button.

4. Type the following expression and click on **OK**:

```
=Num (Sum ([# Transported Passengers]) / Sum ([# Available
Seats]), '##.#%')
```

 It's important to add the equal to sign at the beginning of the expression; otherwise it will not be interpreted as an expression but rather as literal text.

The expression we just created calculates the **Load Factor** % value and formats it as a percentage using the Num() function. Let's finish the text.

5. From the **Chart Text** window, make sure to set the **Alignment** option to **Centered** and change the **Font** option to **Tahoma**, **Font Style** to **Regular**, and **Size** to **14**.

6. Click on **OK** in all of the dialog windows that remain open to apply the changes.

Initially, the added text will be placed at the upper-left corner of the object and we'll need to relocate it. To do that, follow these steps.

1. Activate the gauge object by clicking on the caption. Then, press *Ctrl + Shift*.

   This will show a red border line around the text we want to move as well as around the other chart components (that is, the chart area itself, the legend, if any, and the title).

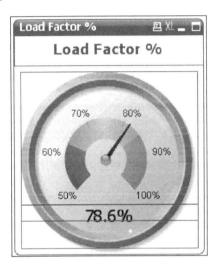

2. Use your mouse to drag the text we added to an appropriate location in the chart and size it accordingly, as shown in the previous screenshot.

Resizing chart components

You can also resize, as well as relocate, other chart components, such as titles and legends, with the *Ctrl + Shift* method described earlier. Be aware that resizing chart component can be a bit "fiddly"; you may have to try a few times before you get it right.

One final adjustment we are going to make to this chart is to remove the caption bar and border and to make the background of the chart fully transparent. To do this we use the following steps:

1. Right-click the gauge chart and select **Properties…**.
2. Navigate to the **Colors** tab and move the **Transparency** slider (under the **Frame Background** option) to **100**%.
3. Navigate to the **Layout** tab and disable the **Use Borders** option.
4. From the **Caption** tab, deselect the **Show Caption** checkbox.
5. Click on **OK** to close the **Chart Properties** window.

The end result should be a gauge chart that looks like this:

Cloning the object for re-use

Since we have already created a gauge chart with several specific configurations, let's make use of it to create a new one without having to do the whole process over again.

Right-click on the gauge chart we created previously and click on the **Clone** option. A new copy of the object will be created exactly as the previous one; the only thing we will need to do is re-position it and change its expression and title, as well as the text in the chart.

Right-click on the new cloned object and select **Properties...** to make the following changes:

1. In the **General** tab, the **Window Title** field will be Performed vs Scheduled.

2. The expression we will use is:
   ```
   Sum([# Departures Performed]) / Sum([# Departures Scheduled])
   ```

3. The label for the expression is the same as the **Window Title** field: Performed vs Scheduled.

4. On the **Presentation** tab, change the following settings:

   ° Set the **Max** value for the gauge to 1.2
   ° Set the **Show Scale** value to **8 Major Units**
   ° Set the **Show Labels on Every** value to **1 Major Unit**
   ° Highlight the **Text in Chart** expression that we added previously and click on the **Edit...** button. Change the expression to:
   ```
   =Num(Sum([# Departures Performed]) / Sum([# Departures Scheduled]), '##.#%')
   ```

Adding Air Time %

The final gauge that we will be creating is the **Air Time** %. Now that you have seen how to create a new gauge and how to clone an existing one, take a chance and see if you can create this gauge yourself:

1. The **Window** and **Expression Title** fields should be `Air Time %`.

2. The expression to calculate the **Air Time** % is as follows:

   ```
   Sum ([# Air Time]) / Sum ([# Ramp-To-Ramp Time])
   ```

3. The **Max** value for the gauge should be `1`.

4. The **Show Scale** value should be set to **6 Major Units**.

5. The **Show Labels on Every** value should be set to **1 Major Unit**.

After applying the changes and rearranging the objects, our dashboard should look like this:

More Gauge styles

While we selected the default speedometer look for our three gauges, QlikView has a few other styles as well. These styles can be selected from the **Styles** tab of the **Chart Properties** dialog.

The following screenshot shows, pictured from left to right and top to bottom, a speedometer, vertical speedometer, thermometer, traffic light, horizontal thermometer, and digital digit gauge. These objects are included in this chapter's solution file on the **Gauge Styles** tab.

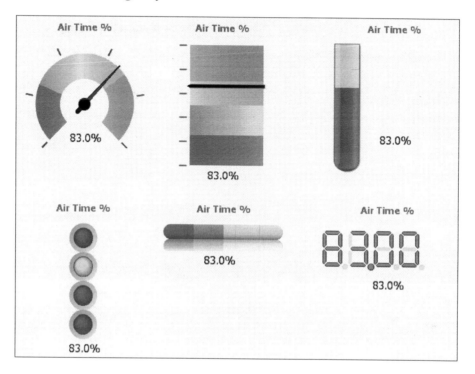

Adding a Text object

Now that we have added the gauges, it is time to add the following four metrics:

- Enplaned passengers (in millions)
- Departures performed (in thousands)
- Revenue Passenger Miles (in millions): the number of miles that paying passengers were transported
- Available Seat Miles (in millions): the total number of miles that paying passengers could have been transported, based on airplane capacity

To display these metrics, we will be using **Text Objects**. A text object can be used to display a static or calculated text and, somewhat counter-intuitively, images as well.

Let's follow these steps to create the first text object that will display Enplaned Passengers:

1. Right-click anywhere on an empty space in the worksheet and select **New Sheet Object | Text Object**.

2. In the **Text** input box enter the following expression:

   ```
   =Num(Sum ([# Transported Passengers]) / 1000000, '#,##0.00')
   ```

3. Move the **Transparency** slider, at the bottom of the window, to **100**%.

4. Go to the **Font** tab and set the **Font** option to **Tahoma**, **Font Style** to **Bold**, and **Size** to **16**.

5. On the **Layout** tab, enable the **Use Borders** checkbox.

6. On the **Caption** tab, check the **Show Caption** checkbox and define the **Title Text** field as `Transported passengers (millions)`.

7. Set the **Horizontal Caption Alignment** option to **Centered**.

8. Mark the **Wrap Text** checkbox under **Multiline Caption**.

9. Click on **OK** to close the dialog window.

After some resizing, the resulting object should look like the following screenshot.

Looking at the steps we went through to create this text object, you may have noticed a few things:

- The expression we used was prefixed with an = (equal to) sign. This is to tell QlikView to treat the entered text as an expression and evaluate it accordingly, instead of treating it as a static text.

- The **Text** object does not have the **Number properties** tab which is often seen on other objects, that is why we used the `Num()` function to properly format the expression output.

- By checking the **Wrap Text** option we can create a multiline caption, this can be very useful when we have long caption texts and limited horizontal space.

Now that we have created the first text object, take a few minutes to create the remaining three. Remember that you can press *Ctrl* and drag the mouse pointer to copy an object, so you do not have to create each text object from scratch. The caption's display and expressions are shown in the following table.

Caption	Expression
Departures performed (in thousands)	=Num(Sum ([# Departures Performed]) / 1000, '#,##0.00')
Revenue Passenger Miles (in millions)	=Num(Sum ([# Transported Passengers] * Distance) / 1000000, '#,##0.00')
Available Seat Miles (in millions)	=Num(Sum ([# Available Seats] * Distance) / 1000000, '#,##0.00')

After creating all four text objects, position them under the gauges in the following manner:

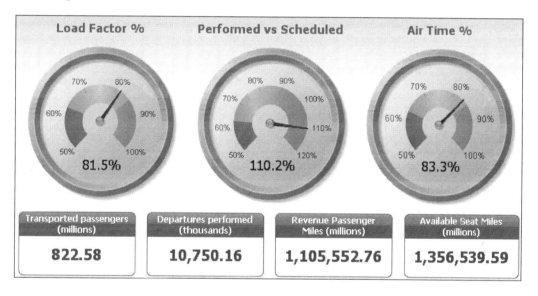

Using a Text Object to display an image

As we said at the start of this section, a text object can also be used to display an image. For example, we may want to display a small "warning" icon on our **Enplaned Passengers** text object whenever the amount of passengers is lower than 1 million. We can achieve that by following these steps:

1. Go to **Layout | New Sheet Object | Text Object** in the menu bar.

2. Do not enter any text; instead, select the **Image** radio button located in the **Background** section and click on **Change....**

3. Next, navigate to the `Airline Operations\Design` folder and select the `warning.gif` image file.

4. On the **Layout** tab, set the **Layer** to **Top**.

5. Click on **OK** to close the dialog window.

6. Position the warning icon over the **Transported passengers (millions)** text object so that it looks like the following screenshot:

One thing to make note of is the **Layer** setting. By setting it to **Top**, we ensure that the icon is always superimposed over the **Transported passengers (millions)** text object. This is important, otherwise we will not be able to select it using the mouse. Furthermore, if we hadn't set the **100%** transparency in the **Transported passengers** text object, having the icon in a lower layer would prevent it from being visible to the user.

 Remember that we can always access any object's properties via the **Objects** sheet of the **Sheet Properties** dialog (*Ctrl + Alt + S*).

The current result is almost what we want. However, you'll notice that the icon is displayed, even though there are more than 1 million transported passengers, which is the specified limit. Let's take a moment to fix it by using the following steps:

1. Right-click on the warning icon and select **Properties...**.

2. Go to the **Layout** tab and select the **Conditional** radio button under **Show**.

3. Enter the following expression:

```
Sum([# Transported Passengers]) < 1000000.
```

4. Click on **OK** to close the **Text Object Properties** dialog window.

Now the warning icon will only be shown when the specified condition is met; that is, when the number of transported passengers is lower than 1 million. To test it, you can make a few selections, for example, by selecting the year **2011** and **Piston, 1-Engine/Combined Single Engine** from the **Aircraft Group**.

Adding these type of visual cues to our dashboard will make it easier for the users to spot potential issues.

Adding actions to a Text object

Another interesting feature of the Text object is that we can assign actions to it, essentially making it function as a button.

Creating custom-style buttons

By combining a text object with a custom image (or icon) and assigning an action to it, we can create a custom-style button.

We could use this button-like functionality to allow for quick navigation across the document. For example, a text object could be used to switch to a detail sheet when a user clicks on it from a general-level dashboard. In the next example, we will assign an action that will open the **Analysis** sheet when a user clicks on one of the text objects:

1. Go to the **Analysis** sheet.

2. Bring up the **Sheet Properties** window by pressing *Ctrl + Alt + S*.

3. On the **General** tab, set the **Sheet ID** to SH_Analysis and click on **OK** to close the dialog.

4. Go back to the **Dashboard** tab.

5. Right-click on the **Transported passengers (millions)** text object and select **Properties…**.

6. Go to the **Actions** tab and click on the **Add** button.

7. Select the **Layout** option from the **Action Type** section and select the **Activate Sheet** option from the **Action** section. Then click on **OK**.

8. From the **Actions** tab, locate the **SheetID** input box and enter SH_Analysis. Click on **OK**.

9. Repeat steps 5 to 8 for each of the three remaining text objects.

Now, whenever the user clicks on one of the text objects, the **Analysis** sheet will be automatically activated. Note that instead of the sheet's name we used the **Sheet ID** to refer to the **Analysis** sheet. As explained earlier, object IDs are used internally to reference objects.

Gauges can have actions assigned to them as well, using the **Actions** tab of the **Properties** window. A typical use case for this is to let the user drill down to a detailed view for a single KPI or metric. For example, we could create a detailed sheet specifically for the **Load Factor** % metric to analyze it from many different angles (over time, by airline, and so on.) and then reference it from the corresponding gauge chart.

Adding a Pie chart

The final metric that we want to display on our dashboard is Market Share. This metric is based on the number of enplaned passengers per carrier, relative to the total. We will use a **Pie Chart** to visualize this measure. Let's follow these steps:

1. Right-click on an empty space in the sheet and select **New Sheet Object | Chart**.

2. On the **General** tab, select the **Pie Chart** option as the **Chart Type**, the third icon from the left on the bottom row, and click on **Next**.

3. On the **Dimension** tab, select **Carrier Name** from the **Available Fields/ Groups** list and click on the **Add >** button to add it to the **Used Dimensions** list. Click on **Next** to continue.

4. In the **Edit Expression** dialog, enter the following expression and click on **OK**:

   ```
   Sum([# Transported Passengers])
   ```

5. Enter **Market Share** in the **Label** input box.

6. From the **Expressions** tab, enable both the **Relative** and the **Value on Data Points** checkboxes.

7. Click on **Finish** to create the pie chart.

The result should look like the following screenshot:

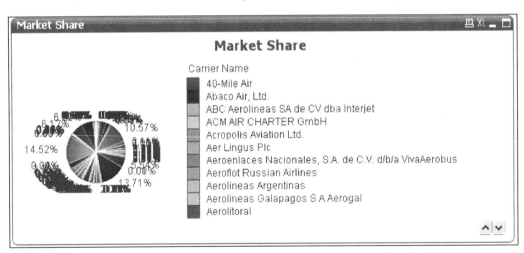

You will notice that this does not look like a pie chart at all. Maximizing the chart to full screen does show the pie, but it is unusable this way. The reason for this is that there are simply too many dimension values; with hundreds of airlines the chart looks more like a candy-cane than a pie.

Dimension Limits

As the goal of this chart is to display who the big players on the market are, we will modify the chart so that it will only show the airlines that make up 50 percent of the market. All other airlines will be grouped in an **Others** group.

Follow these steps:

1. Right-click on the pie chart and select **Properties...**.

2. Go to the **Dimension Limits** tab.

3. Mark the **Restrict which values are displayed using the first expression** checkbox.

4. Select the **Show only values that accumulate to** radio button and set the corresponding value to **50% relative to the total**. Enable the **Include Boundary Values** checkbox as well.

5. Click on **OK** to close the properties dialog.

The updated pie chart should look like the following screenshot:

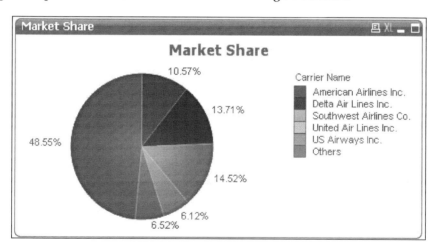

We now see that there are actually only five airlines that, put together, account for 50 percent of transported passengers. Also note that the amounts are shown as a percentage, even though the expression we used returns an absolute number (amount of passengers transported). This is because we have set the **Relative** checkbox on the **Expressions** tab, which makes QlikView automatically calculate the relative amount versus the total amount for each slice.

The **Dimension Limits** option we have used to achieve this is a very useful feature that was introduced in QlikView 11 and enables us to control the number of dimension values handled by a chart.

In the **Dimension Limits** window, all dimensions available in the chart are listed to the left. Simply highlight the desired **dimension** to which the **Dimension Limits** configuration should apply to and select any of the following settings to control the number of dimension values displayed:

- From the **Show only** option we can select **First**, **Largest**, or **Smallest** x values
- From the **Show only values that are** option we can select **Greater than**, **Less than**, **Greater than or equal to**, or **Less than or equal to** a certain value, which can be given as:
    - A percentage relative to the total
    - An exact amount
- From the **Show only values that accumulate to** option we can select a certain value, which can be given as:
    - A percentage relative to the total
    - An exact amount

The difference between the second and the third options is that the former evaluates the individual result corresponding to the dimension's value, while the latter evaluates the cumulative total of that value by either sweeping from largest to smallest or vice versa. This can be used, for instance, in a **Pareto analysis** in which we would present all carriers that make up the 80 percent of the flights, leaving all the rest out.

 Dimension limits can only be set based on the first expression. In case the chart has more than one expression, the rest are not taken into account.

Additional options can be set when working with dimension limits:

- **Show Others**: When this option is enabled, all dimension values that are found off-limits will be grouped into an **Others** category, which will be visible on the chart.
- **Collapse Inner dimensions** can also be used in conjunction with the **Show Others** setting to either hide or display subsequent dimensions' values on the **Others** row, in case the chart has further dimensions than the one highlighted. This is useful mainly on straight tables.

- **Show Total**: When this option is enabled a new total row will be displayed, which is independent from the **Total Mode** control of the **Expressions** tab. This means you can set the **Total Mode** option to perform an operation over the rows, while the **Dimension Total** will hold the actual total, considering on and off-limit dimension values.

 The **Show Total** configuration from the **Dimension Limits** window is virtually treated as a new dimension value. This opens the possibility for having subtotals in a straight table.

- **Global Grouping Mode**: This option determines if the restrictions defined should be calculated considering the inner dimensions or based on a sub total, disregarding the remaining dimensions.

You may have noticed already that this option is not only found on pie charts but on all charts, with the exception of the gauge chart and pivot tables.

Adding the dimension value to the data point values

While looking at the pie chart we created, you may notice that it is somewhat inconvenient to have to switch between the pie slices and the legend to see which slice represents which carrier. Fortunately, there is a little "hack" that we can apply to place the labels on the data points as well. Follow these steps:

1. Right-click on the pie chart and select **Properties...**.
2. Go to the **Expressions** tab, and select **Add** to add a new expression.
3. Enter the following expression:

   ```
   if(count(distinct [Carrier Name]) = 1, [Carrier Name], 'Others')
   ```

4. For the **Label** field of the expression, enter `Carrier` and enable the **Values on Data Points** option.
5. On the **Presentation** tab, uncheck the **Show Legend** checkbox.

While we're at it, let's apply some extra styling:

1. On the **Font** tab, set the **Size** to **8**.
2. On the **Layout** tab, uncheck the **Use Borders** option.
3. On the **Caption** tab, uncheck the **Show Caption** option.
4. Click on **OK** to close the **Properties** window.

Now the carrier names, along with their respective market share, are shown directly on the pie slices. Since there is no need for a legend anymore, we have disabled it. The expression that we used: `if(count(distinct [Carrier Name]) = 1,` `[Carrier Name], 'Others')` uses a conditional function to check if the current slice corresponds to a single carrier by counting the distinct number of carrier names (`count(distinct [Carrier Name]) = 1`). If the count equals one, the carrier name is used; if not, it must mean that we are looking at the "others" slice of the pie, so the "**Others**" label is applied. Our finished dashboard should now look like the following screenshot:

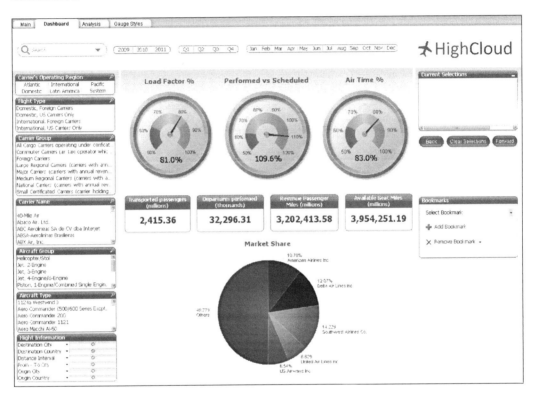

We've now finished the dashboard sheet. We re-used quite a few objects from the **Analysis** sheet, and added gauges, text objects, and a pie chart. Besides creating new objects, we were also introduced to linked objects, actions, and dimension limits.

Let's move on to the last sheet, the **Reports** sheet.

Creating the Reports sheet

Now that we've created our **Dashboard** and **Analysis** sheets, it is time to create the final sheet from our DAR setup: the **Reports** sheet.

As was defined in the requirements, we will be creating the following objects:

- Aggregated flights per month
- KPIs per carrier

But before we begin creating new objects, let's first take a quick look at how we can re-use the expressions that we have created earlier.

Variables

By now you may have noticed that we are using the same expressions in many places. While we could simply type in the same expression every time, this approach has two disadvantages:

- We risk introducing (minor) variations in the way expressions are calculated. For example, one "revenue" expression might contain sales tax while another does not.

- It makes maintenance harder; if the way an expression is calculated changes we'd have to change it in many different places in our document, though the **Expression Overview** window can help us simplify that task.

Enter **variables**. Variables make it easy to store expressions (and other statements, but more on that later) in a central location from where they can be referenced anywhere in our document.

Let's start by creating a variable to store the expression for the **Load Factor** % KPI:

1. Go to **Settings | Variable Overview** in the menu, or click *Ctrl + Alt + V*, to open the **Variable Overview** window.

2. Click on **Add**, enter `eLoadFactor` in the **Variable Name** input box, and click on **OK**.

3. While you would expect it, the new variable is not selected by default after creation. Highlight the **eLoadFactor** variable and enter the following in the **Definition** input box:

   `(Sum ([# Transported Passengers]) / Sum ([# Available Seats]))`

4. In the **Comment** box, enter the description as `The number of transported passengers versus the number of available seats.`

---

[195]

5. Click on **OK** to close the **Variable Overview** window.

6. Go to the **Dashboard** tab.

7. Open the properties for the **Load Factor** % gauge by right-clicking on the object and selecting **Properties...**.

8. On the **Expressions** tab, replace the definition for the **Load Factor** % expression with `$(eLoadFactor)`.

9. On the **Presentation** tab, replace the expression defined in the **Text in Chart** with:

   ```
   =Num($(eLoadFactor), '##.#%')
   ```

10. Click on **OK** to close the **Chart Properties** dialog.

Now, when you look at the **Load Factor** % gauge, you will notice that visually nothing has changed. Behind the scenes, the gauge is now referencing the centrally managed **eLoadFactor** variable. If we were to change this variable in the **Variable Overview** window, the change would automatically be reflected in the gauge.

There are a few points about the steps we used that you will want to take note of:

- **Enclosing the expression in parentheses**: As we want to make sure that the expression always gets calculated in the right order, we enclose it in parentheses. Imagine, for example, we had an expression `vExample` containing `10 + 5` without parentheses. If we were to use that variable in an expression containing a fraction, for example, `$(vExample) / 5`, the wrong result would be returned (`11` instead of `3`).

- **Not prefixing the variable expression with an equals sign**: When the expression in a variable definition is prefixed with an equals sign (=), the variable gets calculated globally. In our example this would mean that the **Load Factor** % value is calculated once for the entire data model. When used in a chart, all dimensions would be ignored and the expression would just return the same global value for each dimension. As we obviously do not want this to happen, in this example we do not prefix our expression with an equals sign.

- **Dollar Sign Expansion**: Enclosing a variable (or an expression) between a dollar sign and parentheses (Dollar Sign Expansion), as we did on the chart's expressions, tells QlikView to interpret the contents, instead of just displaying the contents. For example, `$(=1 + 1)` will not return the static text `1 + 1`, but will return `2`. We will look at Dollar Sign Expansion in more detail in *Chapter 11, Advanced Expressions*. For now, it's sufficient to note that, when referencing variables, we should use the Dollar Sign Expansion syntax in order for them to be interpreted.

- **The variable name begins with an e**: This is for administration purposes mainly. Having a consistent naming convention helps you, as the developer, as well as any other third-party, to easily identify the purpose of any given variable. We commonly use the following prefixes when naming variables:

  ○ `eVariableName`: When the purpose of the variable is to serve as an expression definition

  ○ `vVariableName`: When the purpose of the variable is to store a value, whether static or calculated

The Expression Overview window in action

Of course, creating variables for often-used expressions requires knowing which expressions will be used often. This is not always known beforehand. Fortunately, as we have seen earlier, we can use the **Expression Overview** window to find and replace expressions in a document. Let's see how this approach works by swapping the **Performed vs Scheduled** KPI with a variable:

1. Select **Settings | Variable Overview** from the menu, or click *Ctrl + Alt + V*, to open the **Variable Overview** window.

2. Click on **Add**, enter `ePerformedVsScheduled` in the **Variable Name** input box, and click on **OK**.

3. Highlight the **ePerformedVsScheduled** variable and enter the following in the **Definition** input box:

   `(Sum([# Departures Performed]) / Sum([# Departures Scheduled]))`

4. In the **Comment** box, enter `Ratio between scheduled and performed flights`.

5. Click on **OK** to close the **Variable Overview** window.

6. Open the **Expression Overview** window by selecting **Settings | Expression Overview** from the menu, or by pressing *Ctrl + Alt + E*.

7. Be sure to mark all different expression types from the filtering controls in the window.

8. Click on the **Find/Replace** button.

9. Enter `Sum([# Departures Performed]) / Sum([# Departures Scheduled])` in the **Find What** input box.

10. Enter the following in the **Replace With** input box:

    `$(ePerformedVsScheduled)`

11. Disable the **Case Sensitive** checkbox and click on **Replace All**.

12. Click on **Close** to close the **Find/Replace** dialog.

Of course, using this method relies on the expressions being entered identically in all places with no spaces out of place. In reality this will not always be the case, you may have to perform a more generic search and perform some manual editing instead of using the **Find/Replace** option.

If everything went well, you should be able to see the updated expressions for the **Performed vs Scheduled** gauge chart on the **Dashboard** sheet.

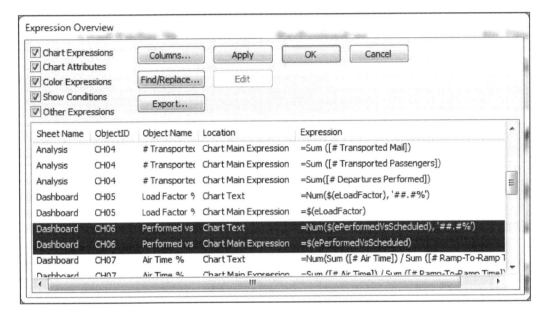

Now that we've seen how to create a new variable and how to retroactively update hard-coded expressions to variables, it is left as an optional exercise to you, the reader, to update the remaining expressions. The rest of this chapter will reference the variables names, but you can also use the expression; the result will be the same.

Should you want to update the remaining expressions, their corresponding definitions are shown in the following table.

Variable name	Expression	Description/Comment
eAirtime	(Sum ([# Air Time]) / Sum ([# Ramp-To-Ramp Time]))	Time spent flying versus total ramp-to-ramp time
eEnplanedPassengers	(Sum ([# Transported Passengers]) / 1000000)	Total enplaned passengers in millions
eAvailableSeats	(Sum ([# Available Seats]) / 1000000)	Total available seats in millions
eDeparturesPerformed	(Sum ([# Departures Performed]) / 1000)	Total departures performed in thousands
eRevenuePassengerMiles	(Sum ([# Transported Passengers] * Distance) / 1000000)	The total number of miles (in millions) that all passengers were transported
eAvailableSeatMiles	(Sum ([# Available Seats] * Distance) / 1000000)	The total number of miles (in millions) that all seats, including unoccupied seats, were transported

Now that we've seen how we can create variables and how we can use them to re-use expressions in our document, let's create the **Reports** sheet.

Copying sheets

While building the **Dashboard** sheet, we created a new sheet and copied linked versions of all the relevant objects. Another approach is to copy an existing sheet and remove all the unnecessary objects from it. We will take this approach to create our initial **Reports** sheet:

1. Go to the **Analysis** sheet.
2. Right-click on an empty space on the worksheet and select **Copy Sheet** from the context menu.
3. Open the **Sheet Properties** window for the new copy of the **Analysis** sheet by pressing *Ctrl + Alt + S*.

4. Rename the sheet by entering `Reports` in the **Title** input box from the **General** tab. Click on **OK** to close the **Properties** dialog.

5. From the new sheet, remove the objects that we do not need: the container object and the scatter chart at the center, and the distance statistics box.

Now we're ready to start adding our reporting objects.

KPIs per airline, origin, and destination country

Our first requirement is to create a table that shows **Load Factor** %, **Performed vs scheduled flights**, and **Air time** %. We also want to be able to alternate the dimension so we can see these KPIs by **Airline**, **Origin Country**, and **Destination Country**.

Cyclic and Drill-down groups

Since we want to be able to switch between dimensions in our table, we will be using a cyclic group. As we saw before, cyclic groups can be used to dynamically switch the dimension of a chart. We can cycle through the dimensions by clicking on the circular arrow, or by selecting a specific dimension by clicking on the drop-down arrow or right-clicking on the circular arrow.

In *Chapter 3, Seeing is Believing*, we described a way to create drill-down and cyclic groups. However, there is another approach, which we will follow here:

1. Select **Settings | Document Properties** from the menu bar to open the **Document Properties** window.

2. Go to the **Groups** tab and click on **New**.

3. Make sure that the **Cyclic Group** radio button is selected in the **Group Settings** dialog window.

4. Enter `Airline_Origin_Destination` in the **Group Name** input box.

5. Select the **Airline**, **Origin Country**, and **Destination Country** fields from the list of **Available Fields** and click on **Add >** move them under the **Used Fields** list.

6. Click on **OK** to close the **Group Settings** dialog window.

7. Click on **OK** to close the **Document Properties** window.

We have now created a cyclic group called **Airline_Origin_Destination** that we can use as a dimension in our charts.

 When creating a cyclic group, make sure to select the **Cyclic Group** radio button from the **Group Settings** dialog window. By default this radio button is set to the **Drill-down Group** value.

A few interesting things to take note of:

- In the **Group Settings** dialog, the **Label** input box can be used to override the display label of the field.

- Besides fields from the data model, an expression can also be used to define a field. This field can be added using the **Add Expression** button and will behave as a calculated dimension.

- In our example, we opened the **Group Settings** dialog via the **Document Properties** window. It can also be opened via the **Edit Groups...** button, which can be found on the **Dimensions** tab of chart objects. This method is probably more convenient, as it fits better into the workflow of creating a new chart object; it is the one we previously discussed in *Chapter 3, Seeing is Believing*.

A drill-down group is created in the same way as a cyclic group, the only difference is that the fields in the **Used Fields** list are not cycled through, but represent the various levels in a drill-down hierarchy. The top field is the highest aggregation, while the lowest field has the most detail. Our **Traffic per Year** chart uses a drill-down group based on time; its defined hierarchy consists only of two fields: **Year** and **Month**.

It is advisable to ensure that only fields that have a "proper" hierarchy are used for drill-down groups.

Straight table

What is known as a straight table in QlikView is in fact a regular table. It can contain dimensions and calculated expressions, which makes it the ideal candidate to display our KPIs.

> **Straight table versus Table box**
>
> New QlikView developers often confuse the straight table with the table box. While a straight table can contain both dimensions and expressions, a table box, which is created by selecting **Layout | New Sheet Object | Table Box** from the menu bar, can only contain dimensions. This makes it unsuited to display calculated aggregations. The table box can be very useful to display a quick list of possible combinations of fields in the data model, though.

Let's follow these steps to create our KPI straight table:

1. Go to **Layout | New Sheet Object | Chart** in the menu bar.

2. On the **General** tab, select the **Straight Table** option in the **Chart Type** section (bottom right icon).

3. In the **Window Title** input box, place the following expression and click on **Next**:

   ```
   ='KPIs per ' &GetCurrentField(Airline_Origin_Destination)
   ```

4. On the **Dimensions** tab, select the **Airline_Origin_Destination** cycle group from the **Available Fields/Groups** list and double-click on it to move it to the **Used Dimensions** list.

5. Click on **Next** to go to the **Expressions** tab.

6. Create three new expressions using the predefined variables (or enter their expressions directly, if you did not create the variables) and their corresponding labels:
   - **Load Factor** %: `$(eLoadFactor)`
   - **Performed vs Scheduled flights**: `$(ePerformedVsScheduled)`
   - **Air time** %: `$(eAirTime)`

7. Click on **Next** twice to go to the **Presentation** tab.

8. Change the **Alignment** settings for all three expressions so that **Label** and **Data (Text)** are set to **Right** and **Label (Vertical)** is set to **Bottom**.

9. Under the **Totals** section, select the **Totals on Last Row** radio button.

10. Under **Multiline Settings**, mark the **Wrap Header Text** checkbox.

11. Click on **Next** to go to the **Visual Cues** tab.

12. For all three expressions, set the **Upper >=** value to 0.85 and the **Lower <=** value to 0.5.

13. Click on **Next** to go the **Style** tab.

14. Set **Stripes every Rows** to 1 and click on **Next** to go to the **Number** tab.

15. Set the **Number Format Settings** option for all three expressions to **Fixed to 1 Decimals** and enable the **Show in Percent (%)** checkbox.

16. Click on **Next** three times to go to the **Caption** tab.

17. Tick the **Auto Minimize** checkbox.

18. Click on **Finish** to create the straight table.

The result should look more or less like the following screenshot:

Airline	Load Factor %	Performed vs scheduled flights	Air time %
Comair Inc.: OH	74.5%	108.6%	71.0%
Seaborne Aviation: SEB	70.6%	97.4%	71.0%
Air Wisconsin Airlines Corp: ZW	71.1%	94.6%	70.7%
Pinnacle Airlines Inc.: 9E	76.3%	96.7%	70.7%
Chautauqua Airlines Inc.: RP	72.6%	96.3%	70.4%
	78.6%	**110.2%**	**83.3%**

KPIs per Airline

Most of the settings will seem pretty straightforward by now, except for the following expression that we used for the **Window Title** input box:

```
='KPIs per ' & GetCurrentField(Airline_Origin_Destination)
```

In this expression, we used the GetCurrentField function. This function takes the name of a cycle or drill-down group, **Airline_Origin_Destination** in our example, and returns the name of the currently active field. When you cycle through the three dimensions, you will notice that the table's caption changes to reflect the active dimension.

Note that the GetCurrentField function returns the name of the field in the data model, regardless of it being overridden by the **Label** field. If this value needs to be changed, we should either change it directly in the data model or change it by using a conditional function in the expression.

Another thing you may notice in the final result is that some values have a hyphen symbol (–) instead of a value. This happens when the result of the expression is null or missing. We can illustrate this by creating a temporary table box containing the **Airline**, **# Departures Performed**, and **# Departures Scheduled** fields. We will see that, while **40-Mile Air** has actually performed flights, none of them were scheduled. This means that the **Performed vs Scheduled flights** KPI cannot be calculated (division by zero is not possible).

Airline	# Departures Performed	# Departures Scheduled
40-Mile Air: Q5	1.00	0.00
40-Mile Air: Q5	2.00	0.00
40-Mile Air: Q5	3.00	0.00
40-Mile Air: Q5	4.00	0.00
40-Mile Air: Q5	5.00	0.00
40-Mile Air: Q5	6.00	0.00
40-Mile Air: Q5	7.00	0.00
40-Mile Air: Q5	8.00	0.00
40-Mile Air: Q5	9.00	0.00
40-Mile Air: Q5	10.00	0.00
40-Mile Air: Q5	11.00	0.00
40-Mile Air: Q5	12.00	0.00
40-Mile Air: Q5	13.00	0.00
40-Mile Air: Q5	14.00	0.00

Note that, in a table box, each possible combination of values resulting from the enabled fields will occupy one row. All table records in the data model resulting in the same combination of values are grouped into a single row. In our example, **40 Mile Air** could have 10 records with **1.00 Departures Performed** and these will all be grouped into a single row in the table box.

If we want an exact count of the number of rows for each combination of dimensions, we need to use a straight table and include the count function as an expression.

Not all expressions are numbers

A nice feature of straight tables (and pivot tables as well) is that not all expressions need to be numbers. Take a look at the **Expressions** tab of the **Chart Properties** window and you'll see a drop-down menu labeled **Representation**. By default this is set to **Text**, but there are other interesting options:

- Image: This option works in the same way as the text object we used earlier. For example, we could use this setting to display an upward arrow when a certain indicator is showing positive results, or a downward arrow in case of negative performance.

- Circular Gauge: When using this option, we are able to embed a circular gauge chart, similar to the ones we added to the **Dashboard** sheet, into the table cells. The in-cell chart will keep most of the functionality that a typical gauge chart offers.

- Linear Gauge: A circular gauge takes up quite a bit of vertical space, making it less suited for use within tables. The linear gauge, which mainly occupies horizontal space, doesn't share this downside and is therefore better suited for use within table cells.

- Traffic Light Gauge: This option shows a traffic light with the corresponding value lit up. Alternatively, this can show a single light with the associated color of the expression's value.

- LED Gauge: This option shows the expression's value using an LED-style display.

- Mini chart: This option displays a trend using a line-based (sparkline, line with dots, and dots) or bar-based (bars and whiskers) mini chart. It requires an additional dimension on which the trend is based, for example, month.

- Link: This option is used to enable hyperlinking in the table cells. In this case a `<url>` tag must be used within the expression to separate the cell display text and the actual link. For example: `=Company &'<url>'& [Company URL]`.

These options are useful to add visual cues to the otherwise plain table and help the user spot trends quickly within the table.

The following screenshot shows a table with a linear gauge, a traffic light, and mini chart embedded in the cells. This object is included on the **Other representations** tab in this chapter's solution file.

Aircraft Group	Linear gauge	Load Factor %	Traffic light	Performed vs scheduled flights	Mini chart	Air time %
Turbo-Prop, 1-Engine/2-Engine		61.7%		121.0%		77.0%
Jet, 2-Engine		81.0%		103.0%		83.1%
Piston, 2-Engine		46.6%		129.3%		83.5%
Piston, 1-Engine/Combined Single En...		34.8%		701.9%		85.2%
Jet, 3-Engine		69.4%		122.7%		87.5%
Turbo-Prop, 4-Engine		-		281.7%		89.8%
Helicopter/Stol		35.7%		29.5%		91.0%
Jet, 4-Engine/6-Engine		82.0%		907.4%		93.0%
Piston, 3-Engine/4-Engine		-		-		95.6%
		81.0%		109.6%	83.0%	83.0%

Note that when tables are exported to Excel, images such as gauges or mini charts will not be included in the export.

Pivot tables

Moving on to our second requirement for the report sheet, we now have to create a table that shows enplaned passengers and departures performed across the **Carrier Group**, **Airline**, **Year** and **Month** dimensions. This table should show totals for each year, and subtotals for each carrier group.

To create this table we will use a pivot table, which offers more flexibility over a straight table when working with multiple dimensions. Let's follow these steps to create our table:

1. Right-click on an empty space in the worksheet and select **New Sheet Object | Chart**.

2. On the **General** tab, select the **Pivot Table** option in the **Chart Type** section (top-right icon) and click on **Next**.

3. On the **Dimensions** tab, select **Carrier Group**, **Airline**, **Year**, and **Month** from the **Available Fields/Groups** list and add them to the **Used Dimensions** section by clicking the **Add>** button.

4. In the **Edit Expression** dialog enter the previously defined expression for **Enplaned Passengers** $(eEnplanedPassengers), and define the **Label** field as Enplaned passengers (millions).

5. Add a second expression to calculate departures performed: $(eDeparturesPerformed), and define the corresponding **Label** as Departures Performed (thousands).

6. Click on **Next** twice to go to the **Presentation** tab.

7. Add a drop-down selection box for the **Carrier Group**, **Airline**, and **Year** dimensions by selecting them in the **Dimensions** and **Expressions** listbox and checking the **Dropdown Select** checkbox.

8. In the same way, enable the **Show Partial Sums** checkbox for the **Carrier Group** and **Airline** dimensions.

9. The **Enplaned passengers (millions)** and **Departures performed (thousands)** expressions will have the **Alignment** label set to **Right**.

10. Mark the **Wrap Header Text** checkbox and set the **Header Height** option to 3.

11. Click on **Next** three times to go to the **Number** tab.

12. For the **Enplaned passengers (millions)** expression, set the **Number Format Settings** option to **Fixed to** and set it to **3 Decimals**.

13. For the **Departures performed (thousands)** expression, set the **Number Format Settings** option to **Fixed to** and set it to **2 Decimals**.

14. Click on **Next** three times to enter the **Caption** tab.

15. Enable the **Auto Minimize** checkbox.

16. Click on **Finish** to create the pivot table.

Once the pivot chart is created it will initially have all dimension values collapsed, and only the first one will be visible. Use the plus icons to the side of each dimension cell to expand it to the underlying level of aggregation. When a dimension value is expanded, you can use the minus icon to collapse it.

Because we set the **Drop-down Select** option on **Carrier Group**, **Airline**, and **Year**, we can open a pop-up listbox by clicking on the downward arrow in the header of these fields. In big pivot tables, this makes searching for particular dimension values a lot easier.

By right-clicking on the column header and selecting **Expand all** or **Collapse all**, we are able to expand/collapse all corresponding dimension values at once.

One of the advantages of pivot tables is the ability to not only list dimension values as rows, but display them as columns as well, creating a cross-table:

1. Expand any of the **Carrier Group** values to show the **Airline** column.

2. Now, expand any of the **Airline** values to show the **Year** column.

3. Click and drag the **Year** column to place it above the **Enplaned passengers (millions)** column; this should place all the corresponding values at the top horizontally. It is worth noting that it can sometimes require a bit of patience to get the field placed in the right location.

The resulting pivot table should look like the following screenshot.

Enplaned passengers (millions)

Year	2009		2010		2011	
Carrier Group	Enplaned passengers (millions)	Departures Performed (thousands)	Enplaned passengers (millions)	Departures Performed (thousands)	Enplaned passengers (millions)	Departures Performed (thousands)
Commuter Carriers (air...	12.691	749.76	12.531	730.85	12.370	733.96
Foreign Carriers	67.966	561.50	71.336	585.75	75.025	595.57
Large Regional Carriers...	7.605	234.44	1.551	70.46	0.400	41.01
Major Carriers (carriers...	617.952	7,165.88	606.961	6,567.00	599.764	6,129.19
Medium Regional Carri...	0.284	7.84	0.623	17.19	1.201	25.15
National Carriers (carri...	74.068	1,466.55	108.726	2,210.71	130.076	2,663.80
Small Certificated Carri...	5.667	587.45	4.808	590.42	3.740	561.46
-	0.016	0.37	-	-	-	-
Total	786.250	10,773.78	806.536	10,772.38	822.576	10,750.16

In many ways, the pivot table is similar to the straight table. However, you may notice that there are a few differences:

- In a pivot table, expressions can be "rolled up" with subtotals (using the **Show Partial Sums** setting) for different levels.

- It is possible to drilldown to a deeper level by clicking on the expand icons. This can be overridden, however, by enabling the **Always fully expanded** checkbox on the **Presentation** tab, which will make the table to always show all possible dimension values.

- A cross-table can be created by dragging dimensions, like we just did with the **Year** dimension. We can prevent this from happening by unchecking the **Allow Pivoting** checkbox on the **Presentation** tab of the **Chart Properties** window.

Auto minimize

We have now created two chart objects in our **Reports** sheet, a straight table and a pivot table. These two tables do not necessarily need to be consulted at the same time. Additionally, these objects would both benefit from being sized as large as the screen space allows, so it's a good idea to display them one at a time.

Fortunately, while creating the tables we enabled the **Auto Minimize** option (located on the **Caption** tab) for both of these objects. When the **Auto Minimize** option is set for an object, it is automatically minimized whenever another object is restored. For this to work, the corresponding objects must have the **Auto Minimize** option enabled.

Let's make sure that both objects can utilize the maximum amount of space by following these steps:

1. Minimize both the straight table and pivot table.

2. Position and resize the minimized tables in the space between the buttons and the **Bookmarks** object.

3. Now, restore the straight table by double-clicking on its minimized icon.

4. Resize the table so that it occupies all the available space in the center of the screen.

5. Next, restore the pivot table by double-clicking on its minimized icon. At this point, the straight table should be automatically minimized; if it is not, then check the **Auto Minimize** checkbox on the **Caption** tab for both objects.

6. Expand the fields in the pivot table and size it so that it uses all available space in the center of the screen.

The resulting **Reports** sheet should look like the following screenshot:

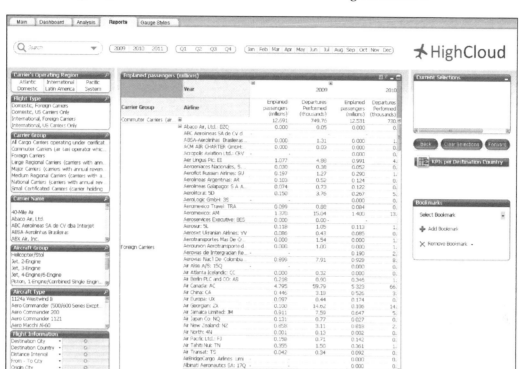

The Report Editor window

Our observant readers may have noticed that the menu bar also includes a **Reports** option. If we did not need it to create these reports, what does it do then?

While the "reports" we created in the **Reports** sheet show detailed information in tabular form, they are limited to single tables. Another disadvantage is that these reports can only be shared with others that have access to the QlikView document, or by exporting them to Excel, in which case proper formatting will be lost.

Enter the **Report Editor**. The **Report Editor** window lets us design static reports that can be used for printed distribution or saved to PDF files. While the Report Editor is far from being a pixel-perfect reporting solution, it can be quite useful to quickly create some static reports.

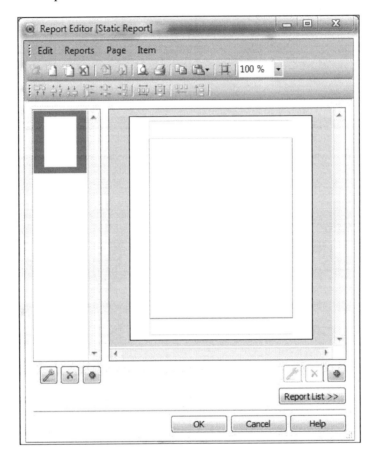

Let's see how the **Report Editor** window works by building a small report:

1. Go to **Reports | Edit Reports** in the menu.
2. From the **Report Editor** window, click the **Add...** button to create a new report.
3. Enter Static Report as the **Name** for our new report and click on **OK**.
4. Click on the **Edit>>** button to begin editing the report.

We are now shown a single, empty report page. We can add objects to this page by simply dragging them from our QlikView document. The implication of this is that, to display an object on our report, it must also exist within our document.

 In the following example, we will be using objects that we have already created on our **Dashboard**, **Analysis**, and **Report** tabs. In your own environment, you might create a separate, hidden tab where you create and store objects that are exclusively used for static reports. Such objects could be formatted differently as well. For example, where we would want sort and selection indicators on our objects used on a dashboard, we would want to suppress these on the "reporting" object. That way, they are not shown in the static report.

We will now add a few objects to our empty report:

1. Drag the **Flight Type** listbox from the app and into the **Report Editor** window.

2. Go to the **Dashboard** tab and drag the **Market Share** pie chart into the **Report Editor** window.

3. Next, go to the **Analysis** tab and drag the **Traffic per Year** line chart into the **Report Editor** window.

4. Select **Page | Page Settings** from the menu bar of the **Report Editor** window.

5. Activate the **Banding** tab and check the **Loop page over possible values in field** checkbox.

6. Select **Flight Type** from the drop-down box and click on **OK**.

7. Click on **OK** to close the **Report Editor** window.

We have now created a very simple report that loops over all values in the **Flight Type** field and creates a single page showing the corresponding **Flight Type**, **Market Share**, and **Number of Flights**. A shortcut to the report is placed under the **Reports** menu.

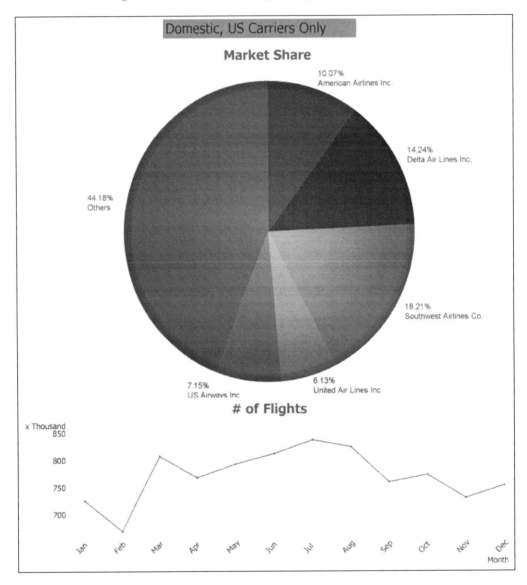

Other options in the **Report Editor** window to take note of:

- **Single versus multi page**: When creating a new page for a report, we can decide if it should be single page, or multi page. The multi page version is useful for printing tables that wrap over multiple pages.

- **Report Settings | Header/Footer**: It is used to set headers and footers for our report. It has a few default variables that can be shown, such as page number, date, time, filename, report name. An image can be included as well; this can be useful to add a logo on our reports.

- **Report Settings | Selections**: Instead of basing our report on the current selection in our document, we can also clear all selections or define a bookmark as a starting point. Besides selections, we can use the Banding function to loop the report over all possible values of a field. By setting Banding at the report level, instead of applying it to a single report page, it is applied to all pages in the entire report.

Although it is technically a "static report", it's also dynamic because the report output, either a printed page or a PDF file, will be generated the moment the user executes the report by selecting it from the **Reports** menu. This means that all selections the user has in place when creating the report will also be applied to the output, unless otherwise specified via the **Report** settings.

Now that we have created our **Reports** sheet and have created a static report, this chapter is almost at its end. The new objects we encountered in this section are the straight table, table box, and pivot table. Besides these objects, we also learned about variables, cyclic and drill-down groups, auto minimizing, and the Report Editor.

Now let's go to the final part of this chapter, in which we will take a short look at some of the objects that have not been covered in detail.

Other charts

Over the course of this chapter, we looked at the most common charts found within QlikView. There are, however, some charts that we did not use, and we will use this final section to take a quick glance at them. Do not worry though; with the knowledge you picked up earlier in this chapter you should have no problem creating these charts as well. Examples of these charts are also included on the **Other Charts** tab of this chapter's solution file.

Radar Chart

The **Radar Chart** can be used to depict information that is cyclical in nature. For example, the following screenshot illustrates the number of enplaned passengers per month. In this example you can clearly see that travel increases during the summer months:

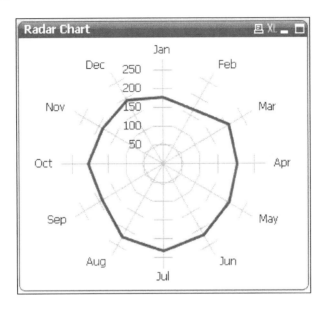

Mekko Chart

The **Mekko Chart** is basically a bar chart with the ability to handle an additional dimension. Our example, shown in the following image, displays the number of enplaned passengers by **Flight Type** and **Year**. The width of the bar is determined by the relative amount versus the total, considering the first dimension: **Flight Type**; and the segment distribution within the bar is determined by the relative amount versus the total, considering the second dimension: **Year**. Looking at this chart we can clearly see that most passengers are being transported on **Domestic, US Carrier Only** flights, and that the number of passengers transported is roughly equally distributed over the years.

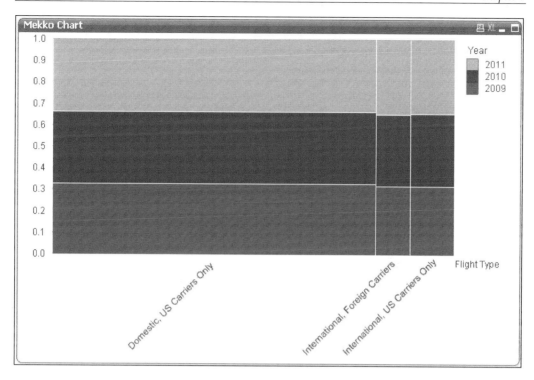

Grid Chart

A **Grid Chart** can contain three different dimensions. In the following example, we've used the **Year**, **Quarter**, and **Flight Type** dimensions. The bubble size represents the number of transported passengers. By taking a closer look, and probably with some imagination, we can spot the same discoveries we made in the first two charts. Bubble sizes are bigger in **Q2** and **Q3**, indicating increased travel during the summer. We can also easily see that most passengers are being transported on **Domestic, US Carriers Only** flights. Additionally, we can see how **Q3** has been smoothly increasing over the last three years.

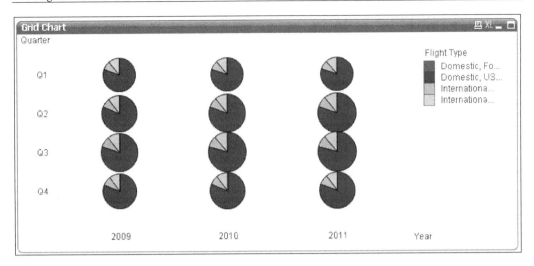

Funnel Chart

A **Funnel Chart** is often used in sales reports to visualize the "sales funnel", that is, which sales opportunities are in which phase of the sales process. The following screenshot shows an example chart that shows the various stages in the sales process and how many clients are present in that phase:

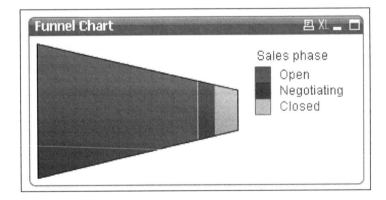

Block Chart

A **Block Chart** can be used to display hierarchical information, by displaying blocks within blocks. In our example, the size of the block corresponds to the number of passengers that were transported. Each block represents a destination city, and they are all grouped into bigger blocks according to their corresponding countries.

In this example we can clearly see that the majority of passengers have arrived somewhere in the **United States**. Within the US, we can see that **Atlanta, GA** and **Chicago, IL** are the most popular destinations.

By comparing blocks within the chart, we can see that the combined total number of people traveling from US to **Canada**, **Mexico**, and the **United Kingdom** is smaller than the number of people traveling to **Atlanta, GA**.

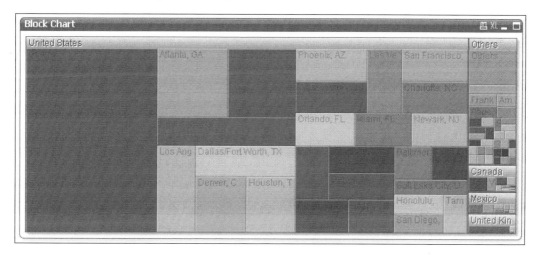

Trellis Chart

The **Trellis Chart** is not really a separate chart, but a chart option that exists on all charts; with the exception of the straight tables and pivot tables. It creates a grid in which a separate chart is created for each distinct value of the first dimension. To facilitate easy comparisons between charts, each chart's axis uses the same scale.

In the following chart, we have created a chart with two dimensions: **Flight Type** and **Month**. We have enabled the **Trellis Chart** option for the first dimension. The result is a chart that shows, within a grid, a separate chart for each **Flight Type**. Each separate chart shows the **Load Factor** % per **Month**.

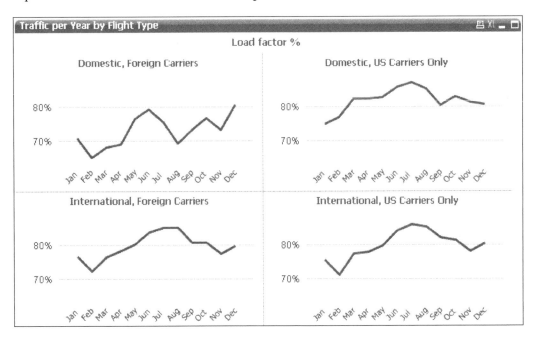

The **Trellis** option can be set by going into the **Chart Properties** of a chart. On the **Dimensions** tab you will find the **Trellis** button; clicking this brings up the **Trellis Settings**, shown in the following screenshot:

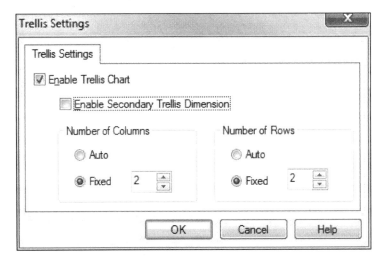

To create a trellis chart, we click on **Enable Trellis Chart**. Optionally, we can manually set the **Number of Columns** and/or **Number of Rows** options.

 With the exception of the trellis and the block chart, you will find that whenever you are thinking of using any of the charts (radar, mekko, funnel, or grid), there is usually a better solution that uses a bar, line, or scatter chart.

Summary

This has been an intense chapter, but you've hopefully achieved a deeper understanding of data visualization in QlikView and familiarized yourself with the basics of building frontend dashboard, analyses, and reports in QlikView.

We started with the **Analysis** sheet, for which we created basic data visualization objects like bar, line, combo, and scatter charts. We also learned how to create container objects, statistics boxes, and buttons, and explored more in-depth chart properties, expressions, the expression editor, and expression overview.

Next we built the **Dashboard** sheet, where we learned how to create gauges, text objects, and pie charts, while also learning about linked objects, actions, and dimension limits.

The final sheet that we built was **Reports**; here we learned how the straight table, pivot table, and table box objects are created. Additionally, we also learned about variables, cyclic and drill-down groups, auto minimizing, and the Report Editor.

We concluded this chapter by looking at some of the chart types that weren't included in our QlikView document, and what the typical use case for these chart types is.

In the next chapter we will take a better look at scripting. Before moving to the next chapter however, you may want to take a little time to explore the various charts and their options for yourself. While we have tried to show you as much as possible, there is still a lot more to discover.

8
Scripting

In the previous chapter, we looked at building the frontend objects for use in dashboards, analyses, and reports. While it may be tempting to keep working on the frontend, we still have a bit of work to do on the backend. Very often input data is not in the exact same format as is required in the target data model, so in this chapter we will look at how we can use QlikView's built-in scripting language to transform our data.

We will first look at the script editor and some of the most important script statements, and see how we can use them to manipulate tables and control the flow of the script. This is followed by a look at some of the most commonly used functions for dealing with conditions and various data types. As QlikView scripts can get quite big and complex we will look at some ways in which we can debug our scripts. Next, we look at how we can properly organize and standardize our scripts so that they are easy to understand and maintain. We conclude this chapter by looking at how we can re-use parts of our script within and between our QlikView documents.

In this chapter, specifically, we will learn about:

- The Script Editor
- The most important script statements and how to use them to manipulate tables and control the flow of the script
- Operators and functions for dealing with various data types
- The options for debugging your script
- How to organize and standardize your script
- How to re-use your script

The Script Editor

As we saw in *Chapter 3, Seeing is Believing, Chapter 4, Data Sources*, and *Chapter 5, Data Modeling*, the script editor is where a lot of the magic happens. In this chapter, we will be taking an in-depth look at the various functions that are available in this environment.

We will again be expanding the `Airline Operations.qvw` document that we worked on in the previous chapters. When you've opened the document, let's open the script editor by selecting **File** | **Edit Script** from the menu or by pressing *Ctrl + E*.

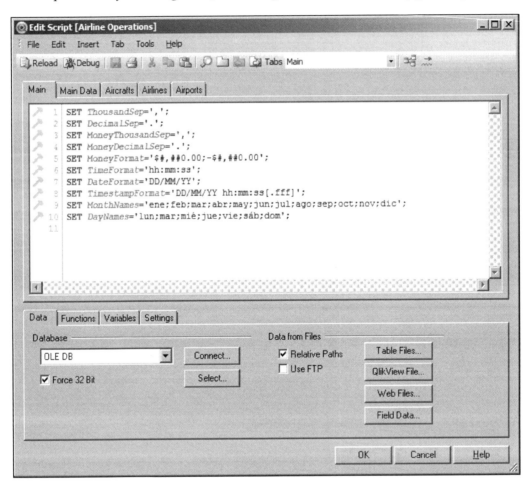

You will notice that the script editor consists of the following areas:

- A menu bar
- A toolbar
- A script pane
- A tool pane

Menu and toolbar

The menu offers a wide range of options, for some of which the toolbar offers shorthand icons. For now, the most important options to take note of are:

Function	Description
**File	Reload**	Runs the entire script to reload the data
**File	Save Entire Document**	Saves the entire document, not just the script
**Tab	Add Tab**	As we have seen, QlikView scripts can be organized using tabs; this function adds a new tab
**Tab	Rename**	Renames the currently selected tab
**Tab	Promote**	Moves the currently selected tab to the left
**Tab	Demote**	Moves the currently selected tab to the right

Script pane

The area that draws the most attention is the big, white area — the **script pane**. This is the main working area of the script editor. When a new QlikView file is created, the new script is populated with a **Main** tab and a few lines where number interpretation variables are added. These lines tell QlikView how to interpret various numbers and are generated automatically based on your operating system settings.

When looking further at the script pane we can see that the lines are numbered and that the editor has syntax highlighting. Based on their meaning, words in the script have a different color or font decoration. For example, we see that the word **SET** is shown in bold, blue text while the text immediately behind it is shown in italic, grey text. It is important to note that QlikView statements always end with a ; (semicolon).

 The exception to this rule are control statements, such as the IF .. THEN .. ELSE, DO LOOP, FOR .. NEXT, which are used to control the flow of the script. We'll learn about control statements later in this chapter.

Tool pane

In the previous chapters, we only used the **Data** tab of the **tool pane**.

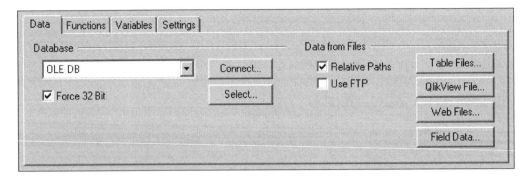

When looking at the pane we will notice that there are some additional tabs:

- The **Functions** tab gives a categorized overview of all the script functions within QlikView. Further on, in this chapter we will have an in-depth look at some of these functions.

- The **Variables** tab shows user and system variables. This tab is populated after each reload, so in a new document it will be blank.

- The **Settings** tab contains some additional settings with regards to system access and password scrambling.

Now that we have had a first look at the script editor, let's get a little more hands-on and look at how we can create scripts.

Script statements

A QlikView script is made up of a sequence of statements. These statements are typically used to either manipulate the data, or to conditionally control the way in which the script is executed. For example, we may want to combine two tables together, or skip over a part of a script if a condition is not met.

It is important to note that QlikView script is executed in a sequential order. This means that script is executed top to bottom, and left to right.

Building the aircraft dimension table

In *Chapter 3, Seeing is Believing*, we started building a small QlikView document to analyze airline operations data. We loaded a fact table and some dimension tables. All this data was loaded from QVD files, without any need for modifications. Of course, this is a scenario that you are not likely to encounter in the real world. In this example we will look at a scenario that is a little more plausible, I focusing on the Aircraft Type dimension. Instead of a single, tidy Aircraft dimension, there are multiple source files:

- `Aircraft_Base_File.csv`: This file contains information on airplanes that were in the database up to and including 2009

- `Aircraft_2010_Update.csv`: This is an update file containing airplanes that were added to the database since 2010

- `Aircraft_Group.csv`: This file contains attributes used to group airplanes; the type of engine and the number of engines

Take a minute to look through the CSV files. Notice that the column `AC_GROUP` in the `Aircraft_Base_File.csv` file references the column `Aircraft Group ID` in the `Aircraft_Group.csv` file. The format of the `Aircraft_2010_Update.csv` file is almost identical to the `Aircraft_Base_file.csv` file, but instead of an `AC_GROUP` column it has an `AC_GROUPNAME` column. This column contains a concatenated string with the engine type and number of engines.

Once you are done reviewing these source files, let's look at the steps involved in building the aircraft dimension script.

Loading the aircraft information

Load the Aircraft information into QlikView by following these steps:

1. Open the Airline Operations.qvw document we saved in the previous chapter and press Ctrl + E to open the script editor.

2. On the **Data** tab of the tool pane, make sure the **Relative Paths** checkbox is enabled.

3. Go the **Aircrafts** tab and delete all script from the tab.

4. Click the **Table Files** button in the tool pane and navigate to the `Data Files\CSVs` folder.

5. Select the file `Aircraft_Base_File.csv`.

6. Rename the fields by clicking on the column headers and replacing the text as follows:

Original name	New name
AC_TYPEID	%Aircraft Type ID
AC_GROUP	%Aircraft Group Type
SSD_NAME	Aircraft Name
MANUFACTURER	Aircraft Manufacturer
LONG_NAME	Aircraft Name Full
SHORT_NAME	Aircraft Name Abbreviated
BEGIN_DATE	Aircraft Begin Date
END_DATE	Aircraft End Date

7. Complete the **Table File Wizard** window by clicking on **Finish**.

8. Replace the **Directory;** text with [Aircraft Types]:, this will assign that name to the table.

The resulting code should look as follows:

```
[Aircraft Types]:
LOAD AC_TYPEID as [%Aircraft Type ID],
     AC_GROUP as [%Aircraft Group Type],
     SSD_NAME as [Aircraft Name],
     MANUFACTURER as [Aircraft Manufacturer],
     LONG_NAME as [Aircraft Name Full],
     SHORT_NAME as [Aircraft Name Abbreviated],
     BEGIN_DATE as [Aircraft Begin Date],
     END_DATE as [Aircraft End Date]
FROM
[..\Data Files\CSVs\Aircraft_Base_File.csv]
(txt, codepage is 1252, embedded labels, delimiter is ';', msq);
```

Note how the source filename and path are specified in a relative manner, that is, the location of the source file relative to the QlikView document. This happens because we enabled the **Relative Paths** checkbox. Had we disabled the checkbox, the full path and file name would have been used. For example, using relative paths is convenient when your document will be moved around from a development to a production environment.

Take a minute to review the rest of the script and see if your script matches.

Adding the aircraft groups

The next step is to enrich the Aircraft type data by adding the data from the
`Aircraft_Group.csv` file to it. To do this, follow these steps:

1. Place the cursor below the last line of the **Aircraft Types** load statement.

2. Click on the **Table Files** button in the tool pane and navigate to the `Data Files\CSVs` folder.

3. Select the file `Aircraft_Group.csv`.

4. Notice that the headers in this file are not automatically detected by QlikView.

5. Change the value of the **Labels** dropdown box to **Embedded Labels**.

6. Notice that the key column **Aircraft Group ID** does not match the name we've given to the corresponding column in the `Aircraft Types` table. Correct this by changing the name of the column to `%Aircraft Group Type`.

7. Complete the **Table File Wizard** window by clicking on **Finish**.

8. Replace the **Directory;** text with `[Aircraft Groups]:` to assign that name to the table.

9. Save the document by pressing the **Save** icon on the toolbar, *Ctrl + S*, or by selecting **File | Save Entire Document**.

   The resulting code should look like this:

   ```
   [Aircraft Groups]:
   LOAD [Aircraft Group ID] as [%Aircraft Group Type],
        [Aircraft Engine Type],
        [Aircraft Number Of Engines]
   FROM
   [..\Data Files\CSVs\Aircraft_Group.csv]
   (txt, codepage is 1252, embedded labels, delimiter is ';', msq);
   ```

Better "Save" than sorry

By default, when QlikView encounters errors during the reload of a document, it automatically closes the document and reloads the last saved version of the file. It can be a frustrating experience when you have just written a lot of script, only to see all of it lost because you forgot a semicolon somewhere.

One way to avoid this problem is by always first saving your script before reloading. This can be done by going to **File | Save Entire Document** from the menu, by pressing *Ctrl + S*, or by clicking on the **Save** icon in the toolbar.

Another more fail-safe way is to set QlikView to automatically save the file before each reload. To do this, close the script editor and open the **User Preferences** menu by selecting **Settings | User Preferences** from the menu, or by pressing *Ctrl + Alt + U*. In the menu, select the **Save** tab and tick the checkbox labeled **Save Before Reload**. It is also advisable to tick the checkbox **Use Backup** and set the field **Keep Last Instances** to **5**. This last option ensures that the last 5 versions of the QlikView file are kept.

To run the script and see what the result is, follow these steps:

1. Select **File | Reload**, press *Ctrl + R*, or click the **Reload** button on the toolbar to reload the script.

2. When the script has finished loading you will see the **Sheet Properties** dialog, click on **OK** to close it.

You will notice that two of our list boxes have gone missing, **Aircraft Group** and **Aircraft Type**. This has happened because the fields that were used for these list boxes were removed from the data model.

Let's remove the two list boxes and replace them with a single Aircraft multibox, by following these steps:

1. Right-click on the list box labeled **(unavailable)[Aircraft Group]** and select **Remove**. As this is a linked object, select **Delete All** to remove the object from all sheets.

2. Repeat the previous step for the list box labeled **(unavailable)[Aircraft Type]**.

3. Create a new multibox and add the **Aircraft Name**, **Aircraft Engine Type**, and **Aircraft Number of Engines** fields.

4. Style the multibox to look like the following image and position it below the **Carrier Name** list box.

5. Add the multibox to the **Analysis** and **Reports** sheets as a linked object by holding *Ctrl + Shift* while dragging the multibox onto the respective tabs.

6. Verify that the data is associated by selecting the **Name** field from the **Aircraft** multibox and checking if the **Engine Type** and **Number of Engines** drop-down lists are being updated.

Loading the second aircraft table

Now that we have loaded these two tables, let's load the final file, Aircraft_2010_Update.csv, into QlikView. Remember that this file is very similar to the Aircraft_Base_File.csv file. The only difference is that there is no ID for an Aircraft Group, just the actual Aircraft Group Name. We will load the file by following these steps:

1. Place the cursor below the last line of the current script.

2. Click on the **Table Files** button in the tool pane and navigate to the Data Files\CSVs folder.

3. Select the file Aircraft_2010_Update.csv.

4. With the exception of AC_GROUPNAME, rename the fields in the following manner.

Original name	New name
AC_TYPEID	%Aircraft Type ID
SSD_NAME	Aircraft Name
MANUFACTURER	Aircraft Manufacturer
LONG_NAME	Aircraft Name Full
SHORT_NAME	Aircraft Name Abbreviated
BEGIN_DATE	Aircraft Begin Date
END_DATE	Aircraft End Date

5. Complete the **Table File Wizard** window by clicking on **Finish**.

6. Replace the **Directory;** text with `[Aircraft Types 2010]:` to assign that name to the table.

7. If you did not turn on automatic saving, save the document by selecting **File | Save Entire Document** from the menu or by pressing *Ctrl + S*.

   The resulting script should look like this:

```
[Aircraft Types 2010]:
LOAD AC_TYPEID as [%Aircraft Type ID],
     AC_GROUPNAME,
     SSD_NAME as [Aircraft Name],
     MANUFACTURER as [Aircraft Manufacturer],
     LONG_NAME as [Aircraft Name Full],
     SHORT_NAME as [Aircraft Name Abbreviated],
     BEGIN_DATE as [Aircraft Begin Date],
     END_DATE as [Aircraft End Date]
FROM
[..\Data Files\CSVs\Aircraft_2010_Update.csv]
(txt, codepage is 1252, embedded labels, delimiter is ';', msq);
```

8. Reload the document by selecting **File | Reload** from the menu, or by pressing *Ctrl + R*.

9. Once the script is finished, click on **OK** to close the **Sheet Properties [Dashboard]** dialog.

10. Add the fields `AC_GROUPNAME` and `Aircraft Begin Date` to the **Aircraft** multibox.

When we interact with the **Aircraft** multibox, we notice that something strange is going on. There are three fields with overlapping information. `AC_GROUPNAME` contains information that is also shown in the **Engine Type** and **Number of Engines** drop-down lists. When we interact with the data, we will notice that any aircraft that has an **Aircraft Begin Date** field before 2010 is associated with the **Engine Type** and **Number of Engines** fields, while later models are associated with the `AC_GROUPNAME` field.

When we open the table viewer we notice that the data model contains a synthetic key table named **$Syn1**. We were introduced to synthetic keys in *Chapter 5, Data Modeling*. In the next section we will see a practical example of how to resolve this issue.

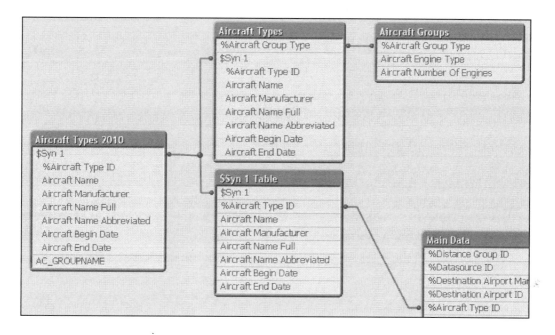

Making it all right

Remember how QlikView's associative logic works? It automatically associates fields that have the same name. And those associations between tables can only be based on a single field. Well, the **Aircraft Types** and **Aircraft Types 2010** tables that we loaded contain seven fields that match between these tables. To resolve this issue QlikView created a synthetic key by creating a key for each unique combination of the seven fields.

We will solve the problem by merging all these tables into a single **Aircraft Types** dimension table. The following schematic shows the general approach we will be taking.

We will begin by joining the **Aircraft Groups** table to the **Aircraft Types** table. We will then concatenate (or union, for SQL connoisseurs) the **Aircraft Types 2010** table to the result we got by joining the **Aircraft Groups** table to the **Aircraft Types** table. To achieve this, we follow these steps:

1. Go back to the script editor by pressing *Ctrl + E* or by selecting **File | Edit Script** from the menu.

2. Go to the LOAD statement for the file `Aircraft_Group.csv` and replace the text `[Aircraft Groups]:` with the text `LEFT JOIN ([Aircraft Types])`.

3. Next, go to the LOAD statement for the file `Aircraft_2010_Update.csv` and replace the text `[Aircraft Types 2010]:` with the text `CONCATENATE([Aircraft Types])`.

4. Replace the line reading `AC_GROUPNAME,` with `SubField(AC_GROUPNAME, ', ', 1) as [Aircraft Engine Type],` and press *Return* to create a new line.

5. On this new line enter `SubField(AC_GROUPNAME, ', ', 2) as [Aircraft Number Of Engines],`.

6. Beneath the LOAD statement for the file `Aircraft_Group.csv` add the following code: `DROP FIELD [%Aircraft Group Type] FROM [Aircraft Types];`.

The finished code should look like this:

```
[Aircraft Types]:
LOAD AC_TYPEID as [%Aircraft Type ID],
     AC_GROUP as [%Aircraft Group Type],
     SSD_NAME as [Aircraft Name],
     MANUFACTURER as [Aircraft Manufacturer],
     LONG_NAME as [Aircraft Name Full],
     SHORT_NAME as [Aircraft Name Abbreviated],
     BEGIN_DATE as [Aircraft Begin Date],
     END_DATE as [Aircraft End Date]
FROM
[..\Data Files\CSVs\Aircraft_Base_File.csv]
(txt, codepage is 1252, embedded labels, delimiter is ';', msq);


LEFT JOIN ([Aircraft Types])
LOAD [Aircraft Group ID] as [%Aircraft Group Type],
     [Aircraft Engine Type],
     [Aircraft Number Of Engines]
FROM
[..\Data Files\CSVs\Aircraft_Group.csv]
(txt, codepage is 1252, embedded labels, delimiter is ';', msq);



DROP FIELD [%Aircraft Group Type] FROM [Aircraft Types];

CONCATENATE([Aircraft Types])
LOAD AC_TYPEID as [%Aircraft Type ID],
     SubField(AC_GROUPNAME, ',', 1) as [Aircraft Engine Type],
     SubField(AC_GROUPNAME, ',', 2) as [Aircraft Number Of
     Engines],
     SSD_NAME as [Aircraft Name],
     MANUFACTURER as [Aircraft Manufacturer],
     LONG_NAME as [Aircraft Name Full],
     SHORT_NAME as [Aircraft Name Abbreviated],
     BEGIN_DATE as [Aircraft Begin Date],
     END_DATE as [Aircraft End Date]
FROM
[..\Data Files\CSVs\Aircraft_2010_Update.csv]
(txt, codepage is 1252, embedded labels, delimiter is ';', msq);
```

The following changes were made:

- By adding the LEFT JOIN ([Aircraft Types]) statement, we tell QlikView not to load the data from the Aircraft_Group.csv file to a separate table. Instead, it will be joined to the table specified between the parentheses. A join is made over the common fields between both tables, in this case [%Aircraft Group Type].

- By adding the CONCATENATE ([Aircraft Types]) statement, we tell Qlikview not to load the data from the Aircraft_2010_Update.csv file to a separate table. Instead, the rows are appended to the table specified between the parentheses. Fields that are not shared between tables, for example, the field [%Aircraft Group Type], get null values for the rows that are missing this field.

- The AC_GROUPNAME column contains both the **Engine Type** and **Number of Engines** fields, separated by a comma. The SubField(AC_GROUPNAME, ',', 1) as [Engine Type], expression uses the SubField function to split the AC_GROUPNAME string into subfields based on the ',' delimiter. The first subfield returns the **Aircraft Engine Type** table, the second subfield returns the **Aircraft Number of Engines** table.

- As we no longer require the [%Aircraft Group Type] key field, the DROP FIELD [%Aircraft Group Type] FROM [Aircraft Types]; statement is used to remove it from the **Aircraft Types** table.

To see the effect of our changes, let's reload the script by selecting **File | Reload** from the menu, or by pressing *Ctrl + R*.

After reloading has finished, open the **Table Viewer** window by selecting **File | Table Viewer** from the menu, or by pressing *Ctrl + T*.

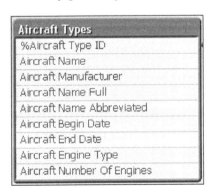

As we can see, all the source tables have been merged into a single **Aircraft Types** dimension table.

Manipulating tables

Now that we have seen an example of how QlikView script statements and functions can be used to load and combine data, let's look at some of the most common script statements for manipulating tables.

As we saw in earlier chapters, the LOAD statement is the main statement used to load data into QlikView.

The script we created in this chapter showed us two statements that can be used to combine data from different tables: JOIN and CONCATENATE. We will now look at these statements and others in some more detail.

The JOIN statement

The JOIN statement is a prefix to the LOAD statement. It is used to join the table that is being loaded to a previously loaded table. The two tables are joined using a **natural join**, this means that the columns in both tables are compared and the join is made over those columns that have the same column names. This means that if multiple columns are shared between tables, the match will be made over the distinct combinations of those columns.

By default, QlikView performs an **outer join**. This means that the rows for both tables are included in the resulting table. When rows do not have a corresponding row in the other table, the missing columns are assigned null values.

Let us consider the following two tables:

Table1				Table2		
A	B	C		B	C	D
1	1	1		2	2	2
2	2	2		3	3	3
3	3	3		5	5	5

These two tables share two columns, **B** and **C**. Then we use the following code to perform a regular join:

```
Table1:
LOAD * INLINE
[
A, B, C
1, 1, 1
2, 2, 2
3, 3, 3
```

```
];
JOIN

LOAD * INLINE
[
B, C, D
2, 2, 2
3, 3, 3
5, 5, 5
];
```

The result is the following table:

Table1 - JOIN			
A	B	C	D
1	1	1	
2	2	2	2
3	3	3	3
	5	5	5

As you can see, the overlapping columns, **B** and **C**, have been merged into single columns, and the fields **A** and **D** have been added from both tables. It is important to note that, as the second table is being joined to the first the name of the table stays **Table1**. It is also important to note that the rows that could not be joined, the first and the last, get null values for the missing values.

Make it explicit

When using just the bare `JOIN` statement, the join will be made to the table loaded directly before the `JOIN` statement. If the table to join to was loaded somewhere earlier in the script, that table can be joined to by supplying its name in parentheses. In our example this would be achieved by replacing `JOIN` with `JOIN (Table1)`. From the perspective of keeping our code easy to understand, it is preferable to always supply the name of the table to join to. While the load statement for the table to join to may be directly above now, this may change in the future. When that happens, the join is suddenly targeting another table.

The JOIN statement can be prefixed with the statements INNER, OUTER, LEFT, and RIGHT, which performs an inner, outer, left, or right join respectively. This has the following results:

- INNER JOIN: Only rows that can be matched between both tables will be kept in the result.

- OUTER JOIN: All rows will be kept in the result, rows that do not have a corresponding value in the other table will get null values for the fields that are unique to that table. When no prefix is specified, this is the default join type that will be used.

- LEFT JOIN: All rows from the first table and those rows from the second table that have a corresponding key in the first table, will be included in the result. When no match is found, null values will be shown for the columns that are unique to the second table.

- RIGHT JOIN: All rows from the second table and those rows from the first table which have a corresponding key in the second table, will be included in the result. When no match is found, null values will be shown for the columns that are unique to the first table.

Applied to our example tables, the results would be:

Table1 - INNER JOIN

A	B	C	D
2	2	2	2
3	3	3	3

Table1 - OUTER JOIN

A	B	C	D
1	1	1	
2	2	2	2
3	3	3	3
	5	5	5

Table1 - LEFT JOIN

A	B	C	D
1	1	1	
2	2	2	2
3	3	3	3

Table1 - RIGHT JOIN

A	B	C	D
2	2	2	2
3	3	3	3
	5	5	5

The KEEP statement

The KEEP statement works in the same way that the JOIN statement does, with a small difference. Instead of joining the result in a single table, the KEEP statement keeps both original tables and filters (keeps) rows in one table based on matching rows in another table. The same logic for INNER, OUTER, LEFT, and RIGHT KEEP applies here as did with the JOIN statement.

Let us consider the same two tables from the JOIN example:

Table1				Table2		
A	B	C		B	C	D
1	1	1		2	2	2
2	2	2		3	3	3
3	3	3		5	5	5

If we apply a LEFT KEEP statement to these two tables, like shown in the following code:

```
Table1:
LOAD * INLINE
[
A, B, C
1, 1, 1
2, 2, 2
3, 3, 3
];

Table2:
LEFT KEEP (Table1)
LOAD * INLINE
[
B, C, D
2, 2, 2
3, 3, 3
5, 5, 5
];
```

The result we get is the following two tables. As you can see, the last row from the original Table2 has been filtered out as it does not correspond to any of the rows in Table1:

Table1				Table2		
A	B	C		B	C	D
1	1	1		2	2	2
2	2	2		3	3	3
3	3	3				

The CONCATENATE statement

The CONCATENATE statement is also a prefix to the LOAD statement, but instead of matching and merging rows between tables, this statement appends the rows of one table to another table.

Let us again consider the same two tables from the previous example:

Table1				Table2		
A	B	C		B	C	D
1	1	1		2	2	2
2	2	2		3	3	3
3	3	3		5	5	5

We use the following code to concatenate the two tables:

```
Table1:
LOAD * INLINE
[
A, B, C
1, 1, 1
2, 2, 2
3, 3, 3
];

CONCATENATE (Table1)

LOAD * INLINE
[
B, C, D
2, 2, 2
3, 3, 3
5, 5, 5
];
```

The result is the following table:

Table1			
A	B	C	D
1	1	1	
2	2	2	
3	3	3	
	2	2	2
	3	3	3
	5	5	5

Notice how the rows from the second table were appended to the first table, and that non-matching fields have all been given null values.

Make it explicit too

As you can see in the example code, the CONCATENATE statement also supports explicitly specifying which table to concatenate to. For the same reasons named with the JOIN statement, it is a good idea to always do this.

The NOCONCATENATE statement

When two tables share the exact same columns, QlikView will automatically concatenate them. For example, when looking at the following code we could assume that the result would be two tables, Table1 and Table2.

```
Table1:
LOAD * INLINE
[
A, B, C
1, 1, 1
2, 2, 2
3, 3, 3
];

Table2:
LOAD * INLINE
[
A, B, C
4, 4, 4
5, 5, 5
6, 6, 6
];
```

However, in reality, as both tables share the exact same columns, QlikView will implicitly concatenate Table2 onto Table1. The result of this script is a single table.

We can prevent this from happening by prefixing the LOAD statement for Table2 with the NOCONCATENATE statement. This statement instructs QlikView to create a new table, even if a table with the same columns already exists.

Using MAPPING tables

The MAPPING statement provides an alternative to the JOIN statement in a very specific scenario: when you want to replace a single key value with a value from a lookup (mapping) table. To see how this works, let's enrich our **Aircraft Types** dimension table by adding the manufacturer's country. To do this, we open up the script editor and follow these steps:

1. Place the cursor directly above the LOAD statement for [Aircraft Types].

2. Click the **Table Files** button in the tool pane and navigate to the Data Files\CSVs folder.

3. Select the file Aircraft_Manufacturers.csv.

4. Set the **Labels** drop-down list to **Embedded Labels**.

5. Complete the **Table File Wizard** by clicking on **Finish**.

6. Replace the **Directory;** text with Map_Manufacturer_Country: to assign that name to the table.

7. On the next line, prefix MAPPING to the LOAD statement.

8. Now add a line below the line MANUFACTURER as [Aircraft Manufacturer], in the [Aircraft Types] LOAD statement.

9. On this line add the following script: ApplyMap('Map_Manufacturer_Country', MANUFACTURER, 'Unknown') as [Aircraft Manufacturer Country],.

10. Add a line below the line MANUFACTURER as [Aircraft Manufacturer], in the CONCATENATE([Aircraft Types]) LOAD statement.

11. On this line add the following script: ApplyMap('Map_Manufacturer_Country', MANUFACTURER, 'Unknown') as [Aircraft Manufacturer Country],.

The modified script for the mapping table should look as follows:

```
Map_Manufacturer_Country:
MAPPING LOAD Company,
     Country
FROM
[..\Data Files\CSVs\Aircraft_Manufacturers.csv]
(txt, codepage is 1252, embedded labels, delimiter is ';', msq);
```

By prefixing the LOAD statement with the MAPPING statement, we tell QlikView that we want to create a mapping table. This is a specific type of table that has the following properties:

- It can only have two columns, the first being the lookup value and the second being the mapping value to return.

- It is a temporary table. At the end of the script, QlikView automatically removes the table from the data model.

We then used the ApplyMap() function to look up the aircraft manufacturer's country while loading the Aircraft_Base_File.csv and Aircraft_2010_Update.csv files. The ApplyMap() function uses three parameters:

- The name of the mapping table to use, in our case this is the Map_Manufacturer_Country table

- The search value, a field value or expression from the source table, that is looked up in the mapping table. We used the MANUFACTURER field

- An optional value that specifies what value to use when no match is found in the mapping table; here we used the value Unknown. When no value is specified, the search value is returned.

> You may wonder why we are using the name MANUFACTURER in the ApplyMap() function, and not the name [Aircraft Manufacturer] that we renamed it to. This is because renamed fields only become known by the name after the entire LOAD statement has been executed.

Let's look at how this affects the data model:

1. **Save** and **reload** the document.
2. After reload is finished, remove the fields AC_GROUPNAME and Aircraft Begin Date from the Aircraft multibox.
3. Add the Aircraft Manufacturer and Aircraft Manufacturer Country fields to the **Aircraft** multibox.
4. Select the value **Unknown** from the Aircraft Manufacturer Country list-box.

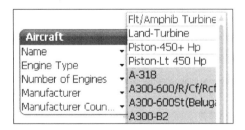

We will notice that there are four aircraft that have an unknown **Aircraft Manufacturer Country** field. When we look at the **Aircraft Name** drop-down list we can see that this is because there are generic aircraft classes for which there are no manufacturers listed.

Adding comments

The COMMENT statement can be used to add comments to tables and fields. These comments will be shown when hovering the mouse cursor over table and field names in various dialogs and the **Table Viewer** window, and are a very useful aid for understanding the data.

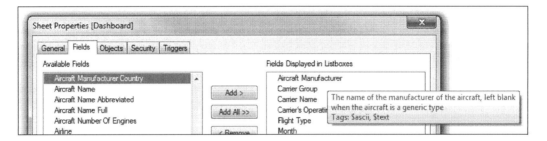

Comments can be added to a table by using the following code:

```
COMMENT TABLE [Aircraft Types] WITH 'Dimension containing information
on aircrafts, including engine types and configuration and
manufacturer';
```

Fields can be commented in the same manner:

```
COMMENT FIELD [%Aircraft Type ID] WITH 'Primary key of the Aircraft
Type dimension';
```

Of course, commenting each table and field individually in the script is quite a lot of work. Besides that, we often already have our table and field definitions stored outside of QlikView, why would we want to duplicate work? Fortunately, we do not have to. QlikView has the option to use mapping tables for the table and field comments.

Let's open the script editor and apply comments to our **Aircraft Types** dimension by following these steps:

1. Place the cursor beneath the last line of the `Map_Manufacturer_Country` mapping table.

2. Click on the **Table Files** button in the tool pane and navigate to the `Data Files\Excel` folder.

3. Select the file `Comments.xls`.

4. Check that the **Tables** drop-down box is set to `Tables$`.

5. Complete the **Table File Wizard** dialog by clicking on **Finish**.

6. Replace the `Directory;` text with `Map_Table_Comments:` to assign that name to the table.

7. On the next line, prefix `MAPPING` to the `LOAD` statement.

8. Place the cursor beneath the last line of the `Map_Table_Comments` mapping table.

9. Click on the **Table Files** button in the tool pane and navigate to the `Data Files` folder.

10. Select the file `Comments.xls`.

11. Check that the **Tables** drop-down box is set to `Fields$`.

12. Complete the **Table File Wizard** dialog by clicking on **Finish**.

13. Replace the `Directory;` text with `Map_Field_Comments:` to assign that name to the table.

14. On the next line, prefix `MAPPING` to the `LOAD` statement.

15. Place the cursor beneath the last line of the `Map_Field_Comments` mapping table.

16. Add the following two lines:

    ```
    COMMENT TABLES USING Map_Table_Comments;
    COMMENT FIELDS USING Map_Field_Comments;
    ```

Our resulting script should look like this:

```
Map_Table_Comments:
MAPPING LOAD TableName,
     Comment
FROM
[..\Data Files\Excel\Comments.xls]
(biff, embedded labels, table is Tables$);

Map_Field_Comments:
MAPPING LOAD FieldName,
```

```
      Comment
FROM
[..\Data Files\Excel\Comments.xls]
(biff, embedded labels, table is Fields$);

COMMENT TABLES USING Map_Table_Comments;
COMMENT FIELDS USING Map_Field_Comments;
```

We have now created two mapping tables and have instructed QlikView to use these tables to assign comments to the tables and fields, using the COMMENT TABLES and COMMENT FIELDS statements.

When we save and reload our document and open **Table Viewer** by pressing *Ctrl + T*, we should see the comments that we loaded when hovering over the fields of the **Aircraft Types** table.

Storing tables

Now that we have built our Aircraft Type dimension table, we can use it in our QlikView document. In an environment with multiple documents, it is very likely that we will want to re-use the same table in different apps. Fortunately, there is an easy way to export a QlikView table to an external QVD file; the STORE statement.

We can store the **Aircraft Types** table to a QVD file by adding the following piece of code at the end of our script:

```
STORE [Aircraft Types] INTO '..\Data Files\QVDs\
AircraftTypesTransformed.qvd' (qvd);
```

This tells QlikView to store the table [Aircraft Types] into the sub-folder DataFiles\QVDs with the filename AircraftTypesTransformed.qvd The .qvd suffix at the end of the statement tells QlikView to use the QVD format. The other option is (txt) to store the table in text format.

Renaming tables and fields

Renaming tables or fields in QlikView is done using the RENAME statement. The following code shows some examples of this statement:

```
RENAME TABLE [Aircraft Types] TO [Aircraft];
RENAME FIELD [%Aircraft Type ID]  TO [Aircraft ID];
RENAME FIELD [Aircraft Begin Date] to [Begin], [Aircraft End Date] to
[End];
```

As we can see in the third statement, we can also rename multiple fields within the same statement. We can also rename objects by using a mapping table, just like the one we used for the comments. The following code shows an example:

```
RENAME TABLES USING Map_Table_Names;
RENAME FIELDS USING Map_Field_Names;
```

Of course, we must not forget to load a mapping table before using this approach.

Deleting tables and fields

Deleting tables or fields is done using the DROP statement. The following code shows some examples of dropping table and fields:

```
DROP TABLE [Aircraft Types];
DROP FIELD [%Aircraft Group Type];
DROP FIELD [%Aircraft Group Type] FROM [Aircraft Types];
```

The first line deletes the table [Aircraft Types]. The second line deletes the field [%Aircraft Group Type]. The third line also deletes the field [%Aircraft Group Type], but only from the [Aircraft Types] table. If any other tables contain the same field, those are left unaffected.

Setting variables

As we saw in the previous chapter, a variable is a symbolic name that can be used to store a value or expression. Besides the frontend, variables can also be used within QlikView scripts. For example, we may want to use a variable called vDateToday, which we will set to the present day's date in our script:

```
LET vDateToday = Today();
```

The Today function is a built-in function that returns the present day's date. Once the variable has been set, we can use its value everywhere in our statements.

QlikView has two statements that can be used to assign a value to a variable, SET and LET. The difference between these two is that the SET statement assigns the literal string to the variable, while the LET statement first evaluates the string before assigning it. This is best illustrated with an example:

Statement	Value of vVariable
SET vVariable = 1 + 2;	1 + 2
LET vVariable = 1 + 2;	3

Controlling script flow

As we have seen before, QlikView script is executed from left to right and from top to bottom. Sometimes, however, we may want to skip certain parts of the script or execute a piece of script a few times in succession. This is where control statements prove useful.

A control statement is a conditional statement whose results determines which path will be followed. Let's open the script editor and follow these steps to conditionally load Main Data based on a variable:

1. Select the **Main** tab.

2. At the bottom of the script, add the following expression:

   ```
   SET vLoadMainData= 'N';
   ```

3. Select the **Main Data** tab.

4. Before the Main Data LOAD statement, create a new line that contains the following statement:

   ```
   IF '$(vLoadMainData)' = 'Y' THEN
   ```

5. At the bottom of the script, add the following statement:

   ```
   END IF
   ```

Now when we reload the script, we will notice that the Main Data table will not be loaded. Only when we change the value of the variable vLoadMainData to Y and reload the script will the Main Data table be included. Also notice that we are using Dollar Sign Expansion in the same way we've used it in the frontend earlier.

>
> Before continuing make sure that the value of vLoadMainData is set to Y in the script.

The control statement that we used in our example is IF .. THEN .. END IF. This checks If a certain condition is met; if it is, a piece of script is executed. As QlikView needs to know how much of the script should be executed, the statement is ended with END IF.

Other control statements of interest are:

Control statement	Explanation	Example
DO LOOP	Execute statements WHILE or UNTIL a condition is met.	DO WHILE i< 10 [executed while i is less than 10] LOOP
FOR NEXT	Use a counter to loop over statements.	FOR i = 1 TO 10 [executed for values 1 to 10] NEXT
FOR EACH NEXT	Loop over statements for each value in a comma separated list.	FOR EACH i IN A, B, C [executed for A, B and C] NEXT

IF
 	
THEN
 	
ELSEIF
 	
ELSE
 	
END IF
	Follow a different path based on which condition is met, this is the control statement we used in our example. The ELSEIF and ELSE conditions are optional.	IF i = 1 THEN
		
		[executed when i = 1]
		
		ELSEIF i = 2 THEN
		
		[executed when i = 2]
		
		ELSE
		
		[executed when i not 1 or 2]
		
		END IF

SWITCH CASE DEFAULT END SWITCH	Execute a different group of statements (CASE) based on the value of an expression. If no match is found for the value, the DEFAULT statements are executed.	SWITCH i CASE 1 [executed when i is 1] CASE 2 [executed when i is 2] DEFAULT [executed when i not 1 or 2] END SWITCH

A special type of control statement is the SUB .. END SUB statement. This defines a subroutine, a piece of script that can be called from other parts of the script. We will look into this in more detail later in the *Re-using scripts* section of this chapter.

Conditional functions

Often in QlikView, you want to modify the data based on a condition. For example, we may want to classify any aircraft that was present in the database before 1990 as "Classic", and classify everything from 1990 onward as "Current". Let's open the script editor and see how this is done:

1. Locate the `[Aircraft Types] LOAD` statement.

2. Add a comma behind the line `END_DATE as [Aircraft End Date]` and press *Return* to create a new line.

3. On the new line, put the following expression: `If(Year(BEGIN_DATE) < 1990, 'Classic', 'Current') as [Aircraft Age Classification]`

4. As the 2010 update only contains aircraft that are newer than 2010, we do not need to use the conditional expression, instead we can use a fixed value.

5. Add a comma behind the line `END_DATE as [Aircraft End Date]` and press *Return* to create a new line.

6. Put the following expression on this line: `'Current' as [Aircraft Age Classification]`

7. **Save** and reload the document.

8. Add **Aircraft Age Classification** field to the **Aircraft** multibox.

When we select the value **Classic** from the **Aircraft Age Classification** drop-down list, we see that only dates before the year 1990 are being selected.

The expression uses the `If` function as follows:

```
If(Year(BEGIN_DATE) < 1990, 'Classic', 'Current') as [Aircraft Age
Classification]
```

The `If` function takes three parameters:

- A condition, in our case `Year(BEGIN_DATE) < 1990`, which returns `true` if the year of the date is before 1990. Otherwise false is returned

- The expression to use if the condition is `true`: `'Classic'`

- The expression to use if the condition is `false`: `'Current'`

As we will see later, QlikView has many other conditional functions. However, the `If` function is the most common. For those who want to check the available conditional functions, select **Help | Help** from the menu, choose the **Index** tab, and search for **Conditional functions**.

Dealing with different data types

As we've seen in the previous section, QlikView offers a complete toolbox for dealing with data. In this section we will be looking at some of the most important operators and functions for dealing with strings, numbers, dates, and times.

Strings

Strings are pieces of text; in QlikView these are often used to provide context to the numbers. You may have noticed that in the script, strings are always enclosed between single quotes (').

String operators

The most common operation performed on strings is concatenating two or more strings together into a single string. This is achieved by using the & operator, for example:

```
[First Name] &' '& [Last Name]
```

This concatenates the values of First Name and Last Name, with a space between them, into a single string containing the full name.

String functions

The following table shows the most important string functions.

Function	Explanation	Example	Result
len(string)	Returns the length of a string.	len('QlikView')	8
left(string, number of characters)	Starting from the left of the string, returns the specified amount of characters.	left('QlikView', 4)	Qlik
right(string, number of characters)	Starting from the right of the string, returns the specified amount of characters.	right('QlikView', 4)	View

Function	Explanation	Example	Result

`mid(string, starting character, number of characters (optional))`	Returns a substring from the string, starting at the specified character. Optionally, the length of the substring can be specified. If no length is specified, the right-most part of the string (starting at the specified position) is returned.	`mid('QlikView', 5, 2)`
		
		`mid('QlikView', 5)`
			Vi
			
			View

`index(string, substring, occurrence (optional))`	Returns the position at which the substring is found in the string. If an occurrence is specified, QlikView will look for that specific occurrence, otherwise the first occurrence is assumed. If a negative number is supplied for occurrence, QlikView starts searching from the end of the string. If no match is found, the function returns 0.	`index('QlikView', 'i')`
		
		`index('QlikView', 'i', 2)`
		
		`index('QlikView', 'i', -1)`
			3
			
			6
			
			6

`upper(string)`	Converts the string to upper case.	`upper('QlikView')`	QLIKVIEW
`lower(string)`	Converts the string to lower case.	`lower('QlikView')`	qlikview
`capitalize (string)`	Capitalizes each word in the string.	`capitalize ('QlikView document')`	Qlikview Document
`replace(string, search string, replace string)`	Replaces the search string in the string with the replace string.	`replace('QlikView', 'Qlik', 'Click')`	ClickView

Function	Explanation	Example	Result
keepchar(string, characters to keep)	Returns the string without the characters that are not specified in the keep list.	keepchar('QlikView', 'ike')	ikie
purgechar (string, characters to purge)	Returns the string minus the characters specified in the purge list.	purgechar ('QlikView', 'ie')	QlkVw
textbetween (string, start text, end text, occurrence (optional))	Returns the substring found between the start and end text. If an occurrence is specified QlikView will look for that specific occurrence, otherwise the first occurrence will be assumed.	textbetween ('<Qlik><View>', '<', '>') textbetween ('<Qlik><View>', '<', '>', 2)	Qlik View
trim(string)	Returns the string without any leading and trailing spaces.	trim(' QlikView ')	QlikView
ltrim(string)	Same as the trim function, but only removes leading spaces.	ltrim(' QlikView ')	QlikView
rtrim(string)	Same as the trim function, but only removes trailing spaces.	rtrim(' QlikView ')	QlikView

Information on other string functions can be found by selecting **Help | Help** from the menu, choosing the **Index** tab, and searching for **String functions**.

Of course, all of these functions can be nested. For example, in our Airline Operations document, origin and destination airports follow the following naming convention:

```
[Name of town], [State or Country]: [Name of Airport]
```

For example:

```
New York, NY: John F. Kennedy International
```

or

```
Amsterdam, Netherlands: Schiphol
```

If we are only interested in extracting the actual name of the airport, the part behind the colon, we could use the following expression:

```
mid([Destination Airport], index([Destination Airport], ':') + 2)
```

In this example, we first use the `index` function to retrieve the position of the colon. We then tell the `mid` function to retrieve the string that starts two positions to the right of the colon (we don't want the colon or the trailing space).

Similarly, we can use nested functions to retrieve the name of the town:

```
left([Destination Airport], index([Destination Airport], ',') - 1)
```

This tells the `left` function to retrieve all characters up to the first occurrence of a comma.

Numbers and numeric functions

QlikView supports the basic arithmetic operators.

Operator	Explanation	Example	Result
+	Add	2 + 2	4
-	Subtract	10 - 5	5
*	Multiply	5 * 5	25
/	Divide	25 / 5	5

The following table shows some of the most important numeric functions:

Function	Explanation	Example	Result
Ceil()	Round up. Optionally, a parameter can be specified to indicate which multiple to round up to.	Ceil(2.5) Ceil(2.6, 0.25)	3 2.75
Floor()	Round down. Optionally, a parameter can be specified to indicate which multiple to round up to.	Floor(2.5) Floor(2.6, 0.25)	2 2.5
Round()	Round the number. Optionally, a parameter can be specified to indicate which multiple to round to.	Round(3.14) Round(3.16, 0.1) Round(3.14, 0.1)	3 3.20 3.10

Besides basic numeric functions, QlikView has an entire range of statistical, financial, and mathematical functions. An overview can be found by opening the **Help** file by selecting **Help | Help** from the menu, switching to the **Index** tab, and searching for **Script functions**.

Additionally, the **Functions** tab on the tool pane in the script editor also gives you access to the entire library of functions.

DUAL data type

Besides the usual data types, QlikView has a data type that can be interpreted as both a number and a string—the DUAL data type. This data type is often used for months, where a month field may return both an abbreviation (Jun) and a number (6). Dual values are created using the `Dual()` function. For example:

```
Dual('June', 6)
```

Date and time functions

Date and time are important attributes in a QlikView document. Being able to see how things have evolved over time is practically a mandatory requirement in any BI project.

It is important to understand that, underneath, the `DateTime` data type is represented by a floating point number.

For example, 12 noon on May 22nd 2012 is stored as 41,051.5. The whole number 41,051 represents the date; it is the number of days that have passed since December 31st, 1899. The fractional part 0.5 represents the time. As a day (24 hours) is 1, an hour is 1/24 and 12 hours is 12/24, which is equal to 1/2 or 0.5.

Knowing this, we can use many of the numeric functions that we saw earlier to perform date and time calculations. For example, we can use the `Floor()` function to remove the time information from a date.

Besides the numerical functions, QlikView has a broad range of functions that specifically deal with date and time. The following list shows the most common ones. For example, assume that Date equals 10.15 AM on May 22nd, 2012 , which is a Tuesday.

Function	Explanation	Example	Result
Year()	Returns the year part of the date.	Year(Date)	2012
Month()	Returns the month part of the date.	Month(Date)	5
Week()	Returns the ISO week number of the date.	Week(Date)	21
Day()	Returns the day of the month.	Day(Date)	22
Weekday()	Returns a number between 0 (Monday) and 6 (Sunday), representing the day of the week.	Weekday(Date)	1
Hour()	Returns the hour part of the time.	Hour(Date)	10
Minute()	Returns the minute part of the time.	Minute(Date)	15
Today()	Returns today's date, without a timestamp.	Today()	2012-05-22
MakeDate()	Creates a date from the supplied year, month, and day. If no day is specified, the first day of the month is assumed. If no month is specified, the first month of the year is assumed.	MakeDate(2012, 5, 22) MakeDate(2012, 5) MakeDate(2012)	2012-05-22 2012-05-01 2012-01-01

An overview of all date and time functions can be found by opening the **Help** file by selecting **Help | Help** from the menu, switching to the **Index** tab, and searching for **Date and time functions**.

Now that we have seen how we can use different statements, functions, and expressions to create QlikView scripts, it is time to see what options we have for debugging our script.

Debugging script

As with every form of scripting, writing QlikView scripts carries with it the risk of introducing bugs and errors. In this section, we will look at some of the available options to find and solve bugs in your script.

Syntax check

Improper use of syntax is a common cause of errors. Fortunately, QlikView has a feature that will catch these errors as they happen: **Syntax Check**.

As we saw earlier, QlikView script has syntax highlighting. Whenever incorrect syntax is detected, the statement is underlined in a red squiggly from that point onward. In practice, this means that often the error was made in the line that appears before the red underlined text. The following screenshot shows a piece of script with a syntax error, see if you can see what the error is.

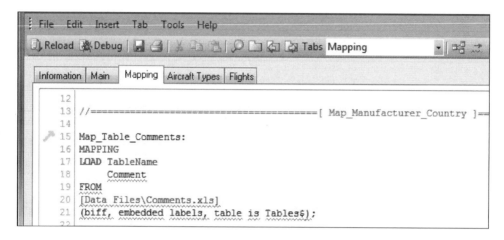

If you looked closely at the script in the previous picture, you will have noticed that there was a comma missing after the `TableName` column. This causes the statement to be underlined in red from that point onward.

Besides catching errors on-the-fly, we can also run a syntax check over the entire document by selecting **Tools | Syntax Check** from the menu, or by clicking the icon showing an arrow underlined in red, the right-most icon on the toolbar.

Saving logs to disk

When a reload is performed in QlikView, a log of all activity is shown in the **Script Execution Progress** window. A copy of this log can also be saved to disk so you can review it at a later time. If you haven't already set this up for the current example document, please follow these steps to generate log files:

1. Go to **Settings | Document Properties** to open the **Document Properties**.
2. On the **General** tab, check the **Generate Logfile** checkbox.

3. To create individual log files for each time the script is executed, check the **Timestamp in Logfile Name** checkbox.

4. Click on **OK** to close the **Document Properties** dialog.

Now, each time the script is run, an additional log file is created in the same folder as your QlikView document. The log file has the name of your document, with the date, time, and `.log` extension post fixed to it. For example `Airline Operations.qvw.2012_07_07_10_24_43.log`.

The script debugger

The **Debugger** offers some handy features to troubleshoot issues in your QlikView script. We can open the **Debugger** window, shown in the following screenshot, by clicking on the icon labeled **debug** on the toolbar, or by selecting **File | Debug** from the menu.

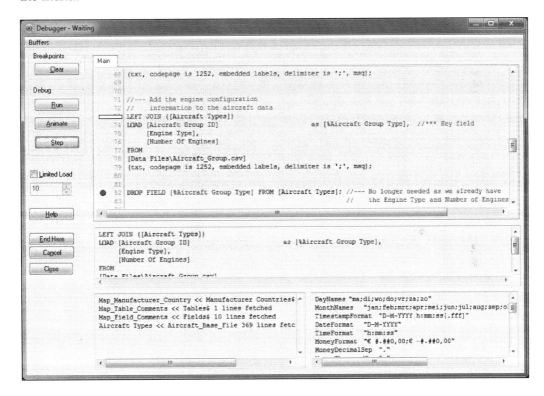

Besides buttons that trigger the various actions, the debugger dialog contains, from top to bottom, the following areas:

- The script from all tabs concatenated into a single script.
- The statement that is currently being executed.
- On the left, the script execution log file. This shows the same information as the **Script Execution Progress** dialog window during normal reload.
- On the right, the current values of the document's variables.

We can run the script in the following different ways:

- Using the **Run** button, which will run the script in the regular manner to the end, or until a breakpoint is reached.
- When clicking on the **Animate** button, the script is run in the regular manner, but a small pause is added after each step. This way the script execution can be monitored more easily.
- When the **Step** button is clicked, the script executes a single statement.

The statement that is currently being executed is marked with a yellow bar, in the preceding screenshot this can be seen on line **73**.

The following functions within the debugger are noteworthy.

Using breakpoints

Breakpoints are used to pause execution of the script at a particular point so that the intermediate state of the environment can be inspected without having to **Step** through the entire script.

A breakpoint is represented by a red dot, which is added by clicking on the row number. The preceding screenshot shows a breakpoint on line **82**. A single breakpoint is removed by clicking on it. We can remove all breakpoints by clicking on the **Clear** button.

Limited load

With their long load times, debugging scripts that load a lot of data can be rather cumbersome. This is where the **Limited Load** option proves useful. When this option is checked, QlikView will, for each statement, only load the number of rows that are specified in the input box.

 As a limited load does not load all data, it is important to note that lookups, mappings, and joins may not function correctly.

Tracing script

Another option that can be used to debug your scripts is the **Trace** statement. This statement is called from the script and can be used to write all sorts of (debug) information to the **Script Execution Progress** window.

For example, we can check if the amount of rows in the Aircraft Types changes after we add the left join command to the data from the Aircraft_Group.csv file to it. This is done by putting the following code before and after the statement.

```
LET vNoOfRows = NoOfRows('Aircraft Types');
TRACE >>> Number of rows in Aircraft Types: $(vNoOfRows);
```

The first line of this script uses the No Of Rows() function to assign the value of the number of rows in the Aircraft Types table to the vNoOfRows variable. The second line uses the TRACE statement to write this value to the **Script Execution Progress** window.

The result is shown in the following screenshot; we can see that there are **369** rows before and after the left join statement, in the table.

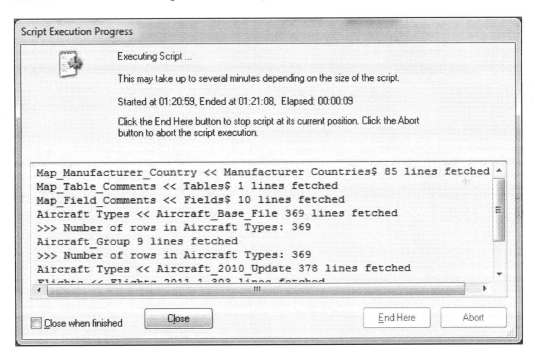

Now that we have seen the various options for debugging our QlikView scripts, it is time to think about how to keep things tidy and understandable.

Standardizing and organizing script

Have you ever experienced the following situation? A challenging problem presents itself. After many hours of thinking, developing, thinking some more, and developing some more, you have crafted a solution. "This is brilliant work!" you say to yourself, "It completely solves the problem, and in a very elegant way too."

Fast-forward a few months. A new business question presents itself and a small change to your original solution is required. You look at your original work, and after some poking around decide that you can make neither head nor tail of it."This is horrible work!" you say to yourself, "What was I thinking at the time?".

Did your script really go from brilliant to rubbish over the course of 6 months? Most likely not. You have just lost familiarity with the script. Fortunately, there are ways to ensure that you (and others) are able to quickly get up to speed when modifying existing QlikView script. The secrets are organizing your scripts and using naming conventions.

Using tabs

As we saw when we first looked at the script editor, the script can be split up into different tabs. It is advisable to divide your script into different tabs, each one focusing on a different functional area or table.

To add a tab, select **Tab | Add Tab** from the menu or click the **Add new tab button** on the toolbar. Tabs can be moved left and right by selecting **Tab | Promote** and **Tab | Demote** respectively, or by clicking the corresponding buttons on the toolbar.

Let's organize our script by opening the script editor and following these steps:

1. Select **Tab | Add Tab** from the menu.
2. Name the tab `Mapping` and click on **OK** to close the **Tab Rename** window.
3. Promote the **Mapping** tab so that it is in front of the **Main Data** tab.
4. Move all `MAPPING LOAD` statements (`Map_Manufacturer_Country`, `Map_Table_Comments`, and `Map_Field_Comments`) from the **Aircrafts** tab to the **Mapping** tab.
5. Create a new tab by clicking on the **Add new tab** button on the toolbar.
6. Name the tab `Comments` and click on **OK** to close the **Tab Rename** window.
7. Promote the **Comments** tab so that it is in front of the **Main Data** tab.
8. Move all `COMMENT` statements from the **Aircrafts** tab to the **Comments** tab.
9. **Save** the document.

Now the script is starting to look organized.

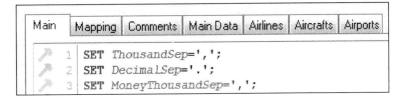

Comments

Comments can be added in the script in two ways. A single line can be assigned as a comment by prefixing it with //. For example:

```
// This is a single line comment
```

Additionally, multiple lines can be converted to comments by enclosing them between /* and */. Like this:

```
/* This is the first line of the comment
This is the second line of the comment*/
```

It is advisable to comment the following things:

- Table names: They makes it easy to understand which script belongs to which table

- General information: For example, who made this change, when, and also which field is being used as a key field in a JOIN statement

- Business logic: It describes what the business logic is and why you are taking a certain approach

An example of comments added to the **Aircraft Types** tab of our document is shown in the following image.

```
Information   Main   Mapping   Comments   Main Data   Airlines   Aircrafts   Airports

  1  //===================================[ Aircraft Types ]===================================
  2
  3  [Aircraft Types]:
  4  LOAD AC_TYPEID as [%Aircraft Type ID],
  5       AC_GROUP as [%Aircraft Group Type],
  6       SSD_NAME as [Aircraft Name],
  7       MANUFACTURER as [Aircraft Manufacturer],
  8       ApplyMap('Map_Manufacturer_Country', MANUFACTURER, 'Unknown') as [Aircraft Manufacturer Country],
  9       LONG_NAME as [Aircraft Name Full],
 10       SHORT_NAME as [Aircraft Name Abbreviated],
 11       BEGIN_DATE as [Aircraft Begin Date],
 12       END_DATE as [Aircraft End Date],
 13       If(Year(BEGIN_DATE) < 1990, 'Classic', 'Current') as [Aircraft Age Classification]
 14  FROM
 15  [..\Data Files\CSVs\Aircraft_Base_File.csv]
 16  (txt, codepage is 1252, embedded labels, delimiter is ';', msq);
 17
 18  //--- Add the engine configuration information to the aircraft data
 19  LEFT JOIN ([Aircraft Types])
 20  LOAD [Aircraft Group ID] as [%Aircraft Group Type], //*** Key field
 21       [Aircraft Engine Type],
 22       [Aircraft Number Of Engines]
 23  FROM
 24  [..\Data Files\CSVs\Aircraft_Group.csv]
 25  (txt, codepage is 1252, embedded labels, delimiter is ';', msq);
 26
 27  //--- No longer this key as we just joined the Engine Type and Number of Engines
 28  //     to the Aircraft Types table.
 29  DROP FIELD [%Aircraft Group Type] FROM [Aircraft Types];
 30
```

Adding an information tab

It is good practice to add an **Information** tab to your script. On this tab you document, amongst other things, information about who developed the document, what the goal of the document is, and when it was last modified. Additionally, a change log can be included to track which changes were made over time.

Take a moment to add an information tab to your document. An example template is shown in the following screenshot:

```
┌───────────┬──────┬─────────┬──────────┬───────────┬─────────┬───────────┬─────────┐
│Information │ Main │ Mapping │ Comments │ Main Data │ Airlines│ Aircrafts │ Airports│
├───────────┴──────┴─────────┴──────────┴───────────┴─────────┴───────────┴─────────┤
 1  /*****************************[ Information ]*****************************
 2
 3      Application:                 Airline Operations.qvw
 4
 5      Version:                     1.0
 6
 7      Author:                      Barry Harmsen      /   Mike Garcia
 8                                   barry@qlikfix.com  /   mike.garciam@gmail.com
 9
10      Date created:                May 1st 2012
11
12      Date last modified:          June 25th 2012
13
14      Goal of application:         HighCloud Airlines has the intention to enter the
15                                   US market. This application is intended to help
16                                   determine if this is a sensible business case at this
17                                   moment, by analyzing historical air travel data.
18
19
20      ---------------------------------[ Change log ]---------------------------------
21
22
23      Version:                     1.0
24
25      Date modified:               June 25th 2012
26
27      Modified by:                 Barry Harmsen
28
29      Changes:                     - Created new Aircrafts dimension table
30                                   - Cleaned up script by adding tabs and adding comments
31                                   - Added information tab
32
33
34      ---------------------------------------------------------------------------------
35
36      Version:                     0.1
37
38      Date modified:               May 1st 2012
39
40      Modified by:                 Mike Garcia
41
42      Changes:                     - Initial version, no changes
43
44
45  *********************************************************************************/
46
```

Script layout

Besides tabs, comments, and an information sheet, using a proper layout for your script greatly increases readability. It is recommended to use indentation to visualize the different levels in your script. It is also recommended to align all of your aliases (the field name after the `as` part in LOAD statements). Compare the following script to the commented script shown earlier and you will notice that it is much easier to read.

```
Information | Main | Mapping | Comments | Main Data | Airlines | Aircrafts | Airports

 1  //=========================== [ Aircraft Types ]===============================
 2
 3  [Aircraft Types]:
 4  LOAD
 5      AC_TYPEID                                   as [%Aircraft Type ID],
 6      AC_GROUP                                    as [%Aircraft Group Type],
 7      SSD_NAME                                    as [Aircraft Name],
 8      MANUFACTURER                                as [Aircraft Manufacturer],
 9      ApplyMap('Map_Manufacturer_Country', |
10              MANUFACTURER, 'Unknown')            as [Aircraft Manufacturer Country],
11      LONG_NAME                                   as [Aircraft Name Full],
12      SHORT_NAME                                  as [Aircraft Name Abbreviated],
13      BEGIN_DATE                                  as [Aircraft Begin Date],
14      END_DATE                                    as [Aircraft End Date],
15      If(Year(BEGIN_DATE) < 1990,
16         'Classic', 'Current')                    as [Aircraft Age Classification]
17  FROM
18  [..\Data Files\CSVs\Aircraft_Base_File.csv]
19  (txt, codepage is 1252, embedded labels, delimiter is ';', msq);
20
21  //--- Add the engine configuration information to the aircraft data
22  LEFT JOIN ([Aircraft Types])
23  LOAD
24      [Aircraft Group ID]                         as [%Aircraft Group Type], //*** Key field
25      [Aircraft Engine Type],
26      [Aircraft Number Of Engines]
27  FROM
28  [..\Data Files\CSVs\Aircraft_Group.csv]
29  (txt, codepage is 1252, embedded labels, delimiter is ';', msq);
30
31  //--- No longer this key as we just joined the Engine Type and Number of Engines
32  //    to the Aircraft Types table.
33  DROP FIELD [%Aircraft Group Type] FROM [Aircraft Types];
```

Naming conventions

Lastly, it is recommended to use naming conventions and to use these consistently throughout your script. We will now have a look at the naming convention that is being used for the documents in this book.

Table naming conventions

Tables that will be used in the final data model have a "business" name that is in plural. That means, a business user understands what is stored in the table. So instead of naming our table CST_DATA, we name it Customers. This also means that it is permissible to have spaces in our table names.

Mapping tables are prefixed with the word `Map` so that they are immediately recognizable as mapping tables. These tables can use technical names, for example, `Map_Manufacturer_Country`.

Temporary tables are tables that are not used in the final data model, they hold a temporary or intermediate result. We did not yet use any temporary tables in our examples, but when we use them they are prefixed with `TEMP`. For example, `Temp_Flights`.

Field naming conventions

Like tables that are used in the final data model, field names also have a business-friendly name. For example, `Aircraft Name` instead of `SSD_NAME`. As many of these names contain spaces, field names are enclosed in square brackets by default, even if they do not contain any spaces.

Key fields, fields that are used to link tables together, are prefixed with a % (percentage) sign. For example, `[%Aircraft Type ID]`.

Hiding fields

Key fields can cause confusion in the QlikView frontend. As these fields are used in multiple tables, they can return unexpected results when used in an aggregation function. It is therefore advisable to hide these fields from the frontend view.

There are two variables that can be used to hide fields: `HidePrefix` and `HideSuffix`. The first variable hides all field names that start with a specific text string and the second one hides all field names that end with a specific text string.

To hide our key fields, we can add the following statement at the start of our script: `SET HidePrefix='%';`

Measures, fields that contain amounts, are prefixed with a # (pound or hash) sign. For example, `[# Total Passengers]`.

Flags, fields that contain a Yes/No or 1/0 indicator, are prefixed with a _ (underscore) sign. For example, `[_Flight arrived on time]`.

Re-using scripts

When developing QlikView documents, we often have to apply the same set of logic or transformations to different data. I have often observed QlikView developers taking a copy-paste approach for re-using a script. While this approach may initially work, it does make the script a lot harder to maintain. When something needs to be changed, you need to change it in each instance of the script, running the risk of different versions of the same transformation process.

In this section, we will look at two better approaches for re-using data. The first is the use of **subroutines**, which can be used to re-use script within an document. The second is the use of **include files**, which enables re-use of script between different documents.

Subroutines

A subroutine is a reusable block of script that can be called from other places in the QlikView script by using the CALL statement. This block is formed using the SUB and END SUB control statements. Subroutines can contain parameters so that processing can be done in a flexible manner.

> As the QlikView script is processed in sequential order, the subroutine has to be defined before it can be called. Therefore, it is advisable to create subroutines as early as possible in the script.
>
> When executing the script, everything between the SUB and END SUB control statements is ignored by QlikView. The subroutine is only run when it is called via the CALL statement.

A good example of a candidate for a subroutine is the trace statement that we used earlier to write the number of rows in a table to the **Script Execution Progress** window. Let's see how we can package this into a subroutine. As we want our subroutine to be flexible, we will add a parameter to specify the table that we want to show a row count for.

We will create this subroutine by following these steps:

1. Open the script editor by pressing *Ctrl + E*.

2. Create a new tab called **Subroutines** and place it immediately after the **Main** tab.

3. Enter the following script.

```
SUB TraceRowCount (SourceTable)
// Writes the number of rows in SourceTable
// to the Script Execution Progress window.

  IF '$(SourceTable)' <> '' THEN
    LET vNoOfRows = NoOfRows('$(SourceTable)');
    TRACE >>> Number of rows in $(SourceTable): $(vNoOfRows);
    LET vNoOfRows = Null();
  ELSE
    TRACE >>> No table name specified;
  END IF

END SUB
```

4. Go to the **Aircrafts** tab.

5. Immediately after the first **Aircraft Types** load statement, enter the following statement: `CALL TraceRowCount('Aircraft Types');`

6. Add the same statement after the `LEFT JOIN ([Aircraft Types])` statement, just above the `DROP FIELD` statement.

Let's have a closer look at what this script does.

The subroutine is declared using the `SUB` control statement:

```
SUB TraceRowCount (SourceTable)
```

This tells QlikView that we want to declare a subroutine called `TraceRowCount`, which takes a single parameter: `SourceTable`. This parameter is passed into the subroutine as a variable, which only exists within the context of that subroutine.

The script checks if a value was given for the `SourceTable` parameter, if it has a value the number of rows is written to the **Script Execution Progress** window in the same way we saw earlier. If there is no value, an error message is returned.

The subroutine is ended using the `End Sub` statement.

 You may wonder why we used the `LET vNoOfRows = Null();` statement. By default, variables that are created in script are also available on the frontend. To prevent this, we delete the variable by assigning it the value `Null()`. This approach does not work for variables that already exist, in that case you will first have to delete them manually from the **Variable Overview** (opened by pressing *Ctrl + Alt + V* in the frontend).

On the **Aircrafts** tab, we used the `CALL TraceRowCount('Aircraft Types');` statement to show the number of records in the `Aircraft Types` table before and after joining the engine configuration information to it.

Including script files

As we have seen in the previous section, we can use subroutines to re-use pieces of script within a QlikView document. It is also possible to re-use script between documents by including external script files. Re-using script between documents is a worthwhile goal as it eases development and simplifies maintenance.

We will see how we can take the row count subroutine that we created in the previous section and turn it into an included script file that we can use in all of our documents. Let's follow these steps:

1. Open the **Script Editor** and navigate to the **Subroutines** tab.
2. Select and copy the entire `TraceRowCount` subroutine to the clipboard by pressing *Ctrl + C*.
3. Open Notepad (by pressing *Windows Key + R*, typing in `notepad` and pressing *Return*) or any other text editor.
4. Paste the `TraceRowCount` subroutine to Notepad.
5. Save the file to the same folder you used for the QlikView document and call it `TraceRowCount.qvs`.
6. Close **Notepad** and return to QlikView's **script editor** window.
7. Go to the **Subroutines** tab and remove the script for the `TraceRowCount` subroutine.
8. Select **Tab | Rename** from the menu and rename the tab to `Includes`.
9. Select **Insert | Include Statement** and select the `TraceRowCount.qvs` file.

The resulting code should look like this:

```
$(Include=tracerowcount.qvs);
```

This statement tells QlikView to include the contents of the script file in the current script.

> In this example, we put the script file in the same folder as the QlikView document. In a real environment, we would set up a folder structure with an `include` or `library` folder that contains all reusable scripts.

We've looked at how we can use `include` files to re-use script logic. As we will see in the next section, the same principle can also be applied to configuration settings such as file locations and database connection strings.

QlikView Components

Instead of creating your own library of scripts, you may also want to consider **QlikView Components (Qvc)**. Qvc is a free, open source script library. Its mission is to implement scripting best practices, improve the speed and quality of script development, and create a common ground between script developers.

Qvc contains subroutines and functions to automate tasks of intermediate complexity, such as creating calendars, incremental loads, and the creation of link tables to support multiple fact tables.

Qvc can be downloaded from `http://code.google.com/p/qlikview-components/`

Managing file locations and connection strings

In our current example documents, we have always referred to the `Data Files` folder for our source data. If, for any reason, this folder has to be moved somewhere else, we will have to manually change the source data path in many locations in many files.

Let's follow these steps to create an included script file to set the source data folder in a single location:

1. Open Notepad (by pressing *Windows Key + R*, typing in `notepad`, and pressing *Return*) or any other text editor.

2. Enter the following script:

   ```
   SET vFolderSourceData = '..\Data Files\';
   ```

3. Save the file to the same folder as your QlikView document and call it `Config.qvs`.

4. Close **Notepad** and return to QlikView's **script editor** window.

5. Go to the **Include** tab and place the cursor on the first line.

6. Go to **Insert | Include Statement** and select the `Config.qvs` file.

We have now created an include file that sets the `vFolderSourceData` variable to the path of the source data folder.

 In a real QlikView environment, it is advisable to specify paths in UNC format, for example: `\\myserver\source_data`.

Now all we have to do is replace every instance of the hardcoded file path with the new variable file path. To do this, follow these steps:

1. In the **Edit Script** window, select **Edit | Find/Replace** from the menu.
2. In the **Find What** input box enter `..\Data Files\`.
3. In the **Replace With** input box enter `$(vFolderSourceData)`.
4. Check the **Search all tabs** checkbox.
5. Click on the **Replace All** button.
6. Click on the **Close** button to close the dialog window.

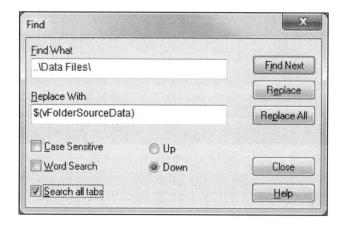

Every hardcoded instance of the source data folder is now changed to the `vFolderSourceData` variable. Now, if we need to change the folder location we only need to change it in a single place. Of course, the same logic can be applied for database connection strings.

Summary

We have come to the end of this chapter on scripting. We have learned how to navigate the script editor. We have seen the most important script statements, and have applied them to our Airline Operations project. We also picked up a few tips and pointers for working with different data types in QlikView, and for debugging, standardizing, and organizing our scripts. We ended this chapter by looking at script re-using, which makes our scripts easier to maintain.

In short, we learned about the Script Editor window, what the most important script statements are and how to use them, operators and functions for dealing with various data types, and what options exist to debug a script.

We also learned how to organize and standardize our script and how to re-use your script within and between QlikView documents.

Now that we have learned the basics of QlikView scripting, in the next chapter we will apply this new knowledge while learning about data modeling best practices.

9
Data Modeling Best Practices

In *Chapter 5*, *Data Modeling*, we started working with data modeling in QlikView and reviewed some guidelines to follow when designing a data model. Now that we have also reviewed how data manipulation via a script can be performed in QlikView, we are ready to expand on both topics and review some best practices to accomplish better and cleaner data model designs. We'll talk about how to overcome common modeling challenges, such as multiple fact tables, and look at various techniques for assuring that our data models are consistent and do not contain unnecessary data. Additionally, we will look at some best practices for dealing with date and time information.

We will learn how to:

- Make sure data models are consistent
- Work with complex data models and multiple fact tables
- Reduce storage requirements for a dataset
- Deal with date and time information

Let's get started!

Data consistency

The first set of best practices that we present on data modeling are those related to data consistency. This is one of the most important things we need to take care of when building QlikView documents. Let's look at some best practices that we can use to assure our data is concise and consistent.

Dealing with dimensions without facts

Sometimes, a dimension table can contain values that do not have any associated facts. To demonstrate this, let's take a second look at the data model we built in *Chapter 4, Data Sources,* and have been using ever since:

1. Open the `Airline Operations.qvw` file.

2. Launch the Table Viewer by selecting **File | Table Viewer** or by pressing *Ctrl + T*.

3. Hover the mouse over the `%Aircraft Type ID` field in the **Aircraft Types** table, pay special attention to the **Subset ratio** value.

4. Next, hover the mouse over the `%Aircraft Type ID` field in the **Main Data** table, again paying special attention to the **Subset ratio**. What you will notice is that the **Aircraft Types** dimension table has a subset ratio of **100%** for the field `%Aircraft Type ID`, while the **Main Data** table only has a **48%** subset ratio, seen here:

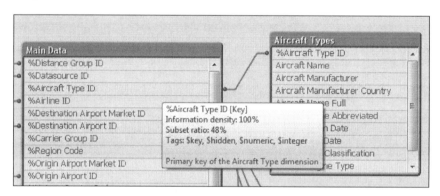

We learned earlier what this means: of all the distinct possible values for `%Aircraft Type ID`, **100%** of those values appear in the **Aircraft Types** dimension table, while only **48%** of the values appear in the **Main Data** table. In other words, only **48%** of aircrafts have actually made any flights.

Before we look at how to remove these aircraft types from the model, let's first quickly investigate which aircraft types have not logged any flights:

1. Close the **Table Viewer** window by clicking on **OK**.

2. Add a new sheet to the document by clicking on the **Add Sheet** button from the **Design** toolbar.

3. Once the new sheet is created, right-click on the workspace area and select **Properties....** Then, from the **Sheet Properties** window, activate the **General** tab and change the **Title** field to **Data Consistency**.

4. Now, navigate to the **Fields** tab and, from the **Available Fields** list on the left, highlight the **Year** field as well as the **Aircraft Type** field, and click on the **Add >** button. Then, click on **OK** and two new listboxes will be created.

5. We will now create a **Table Box**, so right-click on the workspace area again, but this time select **New Sheet Object | Table Box...**, as seen here:

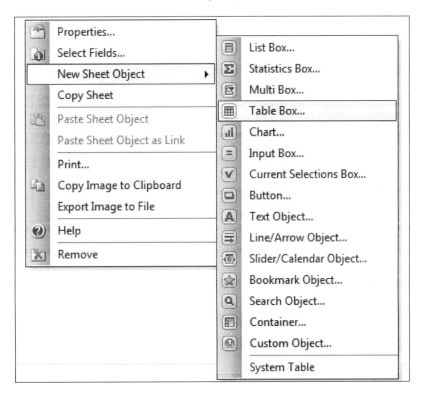

6. From the **New Table Box** window, enter **Flights** in the **Title** box.

7. Then highlight the following fields from the **Available Fields** list and click on the **Add >** button: %**Aircraft Type ID, # Air Time, # Available Seats, # Departures Performed**, and **# Departures Scheduled**.

   Remember to press the *Ctrl* key to highlight multiple fields at once.

8. Click on **OK**.

9. Right-click on the **Year** listbox and click on **Select All**. Notice that, by association, this reduces the aircraft types list and keeps only those that have logged flights in **2009, 2010**, and **2011** (the selected years).

10. Now, right-click on the **Aircraft Type** listbox and click on **Select Excluded** from the pop-up menu. This will switch our selection to those aircrafts that have not logged flights.

By looking at the **Flights** table box, shown in the following screenshot, we can see that the selected aircrafts indeed have no flight data associated with them:

Flights				
%Aircraft Type ID	# Air Time	# Available Seats	# Departures Perfo...	# Departures Sche...
007	-	-	-	-
008	-	-	-	-
009	-	-	-	-
020	-	-	-	-
024	-	-	-	-
029	-	-	-	-
031	-	-	-	-
032	-	-	-	-

Of course, it can be very useful for a business analyst to see which dimensions do not have any fact data associated with them. For that reason, it may be worthwhile to keep this information in the model. Whenever these types of issues present themselves, it is important to check with the business users what their wishes are.

For our example, we will remove the aircraft types that do not have any associated flight data. To do that, follow these steps:

1. Open the **Script Editor** window by selecting **File | Edit Script** in the menu bar, or by pressing *Ctrl + E*.

2. Go to the **Aircrafts** tab.

3. Locate the following Load statement:

```
[Aircraft Types]:
LOAD
    AC_TYPEID              as [%Aircraft Type ID],
    AC_GROUP              as [%Aircraft Group Type],
    SSD_NAME              as [Aircraft Name],
    MANUFACTURER          as [Aircraft Manufacturer],
    ApplyMap('Map_Manufacturer_Country',
                MANUFACTURER,
                'Unknown')    as [Aircraft Manufacturer
Country],
    LONG_NAME              as [Aircraft Name Full],
    SHORT_NAME            as [Aircraft Name Abbreviated],
    BEGIN_DATE            as [Aircraft Begin Date],
    END_DATE              as [Aircraft End Date],
    If(Year(BEGIN_DATE) < 1990,
        'Classic', 'Current')       as [Aircraft Age Classification]
FROM
[$(vFolderSourceData)CSVs\Aircraft_Base_File.csv]
(txt, codepage is 1252, embedded labels, delimiter is ';', msq);
```

4. From the preceding script, remove the semicolon (;) at the end and press *Return* to create a new line.

5. On the new line, type the following code:

```
Where Exists([%Aircraft Type ID], AC_TYPEID);
```

6. Now, locate the LOAD statement in which the `Aircraft_2010_Update.csv` table file is being loaded, and add the following Where clause at the end in a similar manner (the final semicolon gets replaced):

```
Where Exists([%Aircraft Type ID], AC_TYPEID);
```

7. **Save** and **Reload** the script.

The non-matching aircrafts are no longer in the data model after the reload. The code that we added to the script uses a WHERE clause combined with the Exists() function. We are essentially filtering out any records in which the AC_TYPEID field from the dimension table does not have a corresponding value in the %Aircraft Type ID field already loaded in the **Main Data** table.

The Exists() function takes two parameters:

```
WHERE Exists([%Aircraft Type ID], AC_TYPEID);
```

The first parameter specifies the field on which we need to check to see if there are any occurrences of the values contained in the second field, the one specified in the second parameter.

In some cases, the two fields being compared have the same name in both the input dimension table and the fact table already loaded. If that's the case, we could use a simplified, one-parameter, syntax as follows:

```
Where Exists([%Aircraft Type ID]);
```

Depending on how the field names from the input table are defined, we should use the appropriate syntax from the two presented above. The main advantage of the second scenario (one-parameter syntax) is that, when loading from a QVD, it will still perform as an optimized load, while the first scenario will not.

An alternative to using the Exists() function is the use of the KEEP prefix, which will be added before the LOAD keyword. As shown in the previous chapter, by using LEFT KEEP or RIGHT KEEP, we can limit the records being loaded to those that have a matching key in the already loaded fact table. A benefit of using this prefix is that the result set can be limited on multiple fields, while the Exists() function can only use a single field. However, script processing of the KEEP prefix can be a lot slower on larger data sets, so the Exists() function is the preferred method whenever possible.

Let's take another approach to dealing with this problem this time using the KEEP prefix.

An alternative approach

The previous example depends on the fact table being loaded before the dimension tables. It often makes more sense to load dimension tables first and fact tables later. In that scenario, the solution shown before will not work because the actual fact table has not yet been loaded at the time we load the dimension table. There is no way for us to "load only dimension values for which facts have been loaded." Therefore, the `Exists()` function cannot be used.

The alternative approach consists of first loading the entire dimension table and then reducing the record set based on the corresponding values in the fact table after the facts have been loaded. Let's see how this works by following these steps:

1. Open the **Script Editor** window again and go to the **Aircraft** tab.

2. Comment out the lines we added previously by selecting the code `WHERE Exists([%Aircraft Type ID], AC_TYPEID);` right-clicking on it, and selecting **Comment**.

3. Then, add a semicolon on the next line to ensure that the LOAD statement is properly ended.

4. Next, we need to make sure that the **Aircrafts** tab is run *before* the **Main Data** tab. With the **Aircrafts** tab still active, press *Ctrl + Q,T,P* simultaneously twice to promote it, or select **Tab | Promote** from the menu bar until the **Aircrafts** tab is placed to the left of the **Main Data** tab.

5. Next, activate the **Main Data** tab and, after the end of the corresponding LOAD statement, enter the following code:

```
Temp_Aircraft_Type_Dim:
RIGHT KEEP ([Aircraft Types])
LOAD DISTINCT
[%Aircraft Type ID]
RESIDENT [Main Data];

DROP TABLE Temp_Aircraft_Type_Dim;
```

6. **Save** and **reload** the script, and use the **Table Viewer** window to check the result.

The code we inserted creates a temporary table, `Temp_Aircraft_Type_Dim`, which contains all of the distinct `%Aircraft Type ID` values from the `Main Data` fact table. By using a `RIGHT KEEP` statement, the data in the original `Aircraft Types` table is reduced to only those rows that are associated with the `Main Data` table. After the `Aircraft Types` table has been truncated, we remove the temporary table.

> The `Left Keep` prefix can also be used, accompanying the `Load` statement corresponding to the `Aircraft Types` dimension table, if the `Main Data` table had been loaded first.

We will now be able to see that when all values from the **Year** listbox are selected, no aircrafts are being excluded in the **Aircraft Type** listbox.

A solo exercise

Most of the dimensions we loaded to the `Airline Operations` app in *Chapter 3, Seeing is Believing* and *Chapter 4, Data Sources* present the scenario described previously. That is, the subset ratio for most key fields in the `Main Data` table is lower than 100%.

The end users of our QlikView document, HighCloud Airlines, have decided that they don't need unused values in the dimension tables as it corresponds to either airlines that are no longer in operation or aircrafts that are no longer in use.

Take what you've learned in this section and reduce all of the dimension tables to contain only those values that appear in the fact table and save the updated document.

> The `Origin and Destination Airports` dimension tables perform a direct query to the source database. Therefore, the `Exists()` function cannot be used as described here. A QlikView function might not be interpreted as expected in a direct database query. Therefore, we need to use the `Left Keep` prefix approach in those two cases to achieve the expected result.

Once you've reduced the dimension tables and saved the document, take a look at the size of the QVW file and you'll see the impact of removing unnecessary data. In this case, the document size on disk will be reduced from around 55 MB to approximately 33 MB. This will also have a positive impact on RAM usage.

In the next section, we'll work with a side example, so you may now close the `Airline Operations.qvw` document.

Dealing with facts without dimensions

Of course, when dimensions can exist without related facts, the inverse can also be true. Let's look at how we can deal with facts that do not have any associated dimension values.

As you may have noticed in the **Table Viewer** window, our current example data model is a bit too tidy. There aren't any dimensionless facts. However, to illustrate the new scenario, we've prepared a side example for which you will find the corresponding datafiles in the `Airline Operations\Side examples\Chapter 9` folder. Make sure you have the `Flights.csv` and `Aircrafts.csv` files in the specified folder. Then, follow these steps:

1. Launch the QlikView program and create a new document. Save the document into the `Airline Operations\Side examples\Chapter 9` folder as `Dimensionless Facts.qvw`.

2. Next, go to the **Edit Script** window by pressing *Ctrl + E*, and load both the `Flights.csv` and the `Aircrafts.csv` files with the methods you've learned until now.

3. Explicitly assign a name to each table in the `Load` statement, using the corresponding filename.

4. When creating the `Load` statement for each table, you'll notice that there are no shared fields between them, at least not explicitly. Therefore, we'll need to rename the `AC_TYPEID` field in the `Aircrafts` table to `%Aircraft Type ID` so that an association is created between both tables through this field. To do this, use the `as` keyword as follows:

   ```
   AC_TYPEID as [%Aircraft Type ID],
   ```

5. You should now have the following code:

   ```
   Aircrafts:
   LOAD AC_TYPEID as [%Aircraft Type ID],
        [Aircraft Group],
        Manufacturer,
        [Aircraft Name],
        [Aircraft Short Name]
   FROM
   Aircrafts.csv
   (txt, codepage is 1252, embedded labels, delimiter is ',', msq);

   Flights:
   LOAD Year,
        [Month (#)],
   ```

```
            [%Aircraft Type ID],
            [# Departures Scheduled],
            [# Departures Performed],
            [# Available Seats],
            [# Transported Passengers],
            [# Transported Freight]
    FROM
    Flights.csv
    (txt, utf8, embedded labels, delimiter is ',', msq);
```

6. Save the entire document and then execute the script by clicking on the **Reload** button from the toolbar.

After finishing the script execution, if we open the **Table Viewer** window (*Ctrl + T*), we can analyze the subset ratio for the `%Aircraft Type ID` field, seen here:

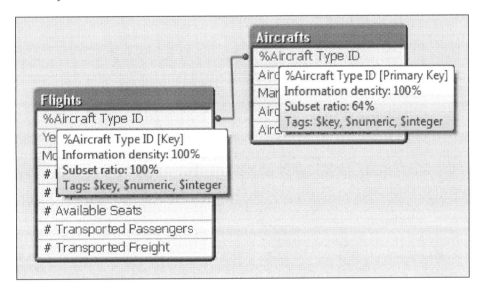

Notice that the subset ratio is **100%** in the `Flights` table, but below 100 percent in the `Aircrafts` table. In other words, there are now flights with no corresponding dimension data.

Having facts without an associated dimension is undesirable. When we use the dimension in a dashboard, facts that are not associated all get grouped under a hyphen symbol. Since this is basically a null value, this group of facts can not be easily selected by the user.

To illustrate this, let's create a new bar chart with the `Aircraft Group` field as dimension, which is an aircraft attribute, and `Sum ([# Departures Performed])/1000` as the expression. We will end up having something like the following:

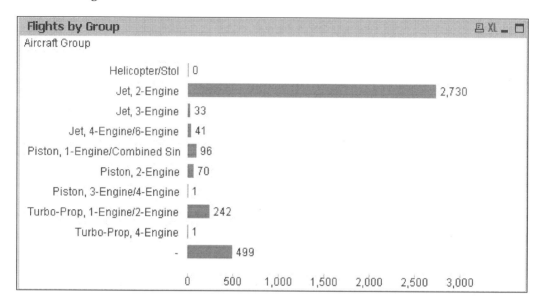

On the other hand, we cannot just remove these dimensionless records from the fact table as it will skew the total amounts.

While the appropriate response is always discussed with and decided by the business users, a very common approach is to add dummy dimension values to the dimension table. To do this in our current example, let's follow these steps:

1. Open the **Script Editor** window.

2. At the end of the script, add the following code:

```
Temp_Aircraft_Type_ID:
LOAD DISTINCT
    [%Aircraft Type ID] as Temp_Aircraft_Type_ID
RESIDENT [Aircrafts];
```

```
CONCATENATE ([Aircrafts])
LOAD DISTINCT
    [%Aircraft Type ID],
    'Unknown: ' & [%Aircraft Type ID]  as [Aircraft Name],
    'Unknown'                                      as [Aircraft
Group],
    'UNKNOWN'                                      as
[Manufacturer],
    '???'                                          as
[Aircraft Short Name]
RESIDENT Flights
WHERE NOT Exists(Temp_Aircraft_Type_ID, [%Aircraft Type ID]);

DROP TABLE Temp_Aircraft_Type_ID; // Clean up temporary table
```

3. **Save** and reload the document.

Here's what the added script does:

1. It copies all of the %Aircraft Type ID values from the Aircrafts
    dimension table into a separate, temporary field called Temp_Aircraft_
    Type_ID.

    ○   This separate field is necessary as we want to compare the Aircraft
        Type ID values from the Flights table against only the Aircraft
        Type ID values that exist in the Aircrafts table.

2. We append a dummy table segment to the Aircrafts table by using the
    WHERE NOT Exists(Temp_Aircraft_Type_ID, [%Aircraft Type ID])
    clause. This helps us load the missing aircrafts from the Flights table while
    also ruling out all aircrafts that are already stored in the original Aircrafts
    table, thus avoiding duplicates.

3. At the same time, for each of the missing ID's, a dummy record is created
    with (a variant of) the **Unknown** value for each corresponding attribute.

When checking the **Table Viewer** we'll see that the **Subset Ratio** value for %Aircraft Type ID is now **100%** on both tables. This can be verified by looking at the previously created chart, which now groups all of the **Unknown** values, as seen here:

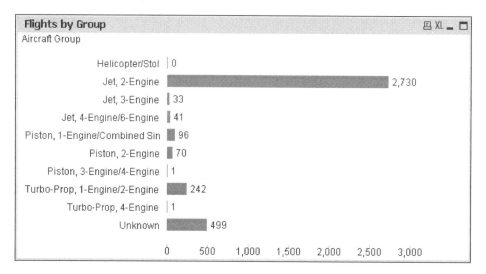

Additionally, when adding a new listbox with one of the various aircraft attributes, we can see that the **Unknown** values are being listed as well, as shown in the following screenshot:

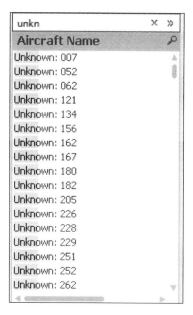

Save and close the Dimensionless facts.qvw file to continue.

Reducing storage requirements

While it is often tempting to include as much data as possible, this can also make your data model more complex than it needs to be. Additionally, as QlikView uses an in-memory database, it is also a good idea to not waste resources. RAM is still a much scarcer resource than disk-based storage.

Using number-based key fields

When linking between tables using key fields, it is advisable to use numbers as key values instead of text. The `AutoNumber()` script function can be used to generate a unique integer value for an expression or compound key, thus compacting the occupied RAM space.

Consider, for example, the following list of colors and their corresponding value assigned by the `AutoNumber()` function. As each new value appears in the list, a consecutive number is assigned. All subsequent appearances of the same value will take the value assigned to the first instance. For example, all appearances of the `Blue` color have been assigned the number 2, as it is the second value we encounter on the list:

Color	AutoNumber(Color)
Red	1
Blue	2
Green	3
Blue	2
Green	3
Yellow	4

A second parameter can be specified to handle more than one counter in the same script and indicate which one should be used to assign the values. For example, `AutoNumber(Color, 'Color')` would use a counter called `Color`. As QlikView is very efficient at compressing sequential numbers, it is advisable to use a different counter for each separate key.

It is important to note that the `AutoNumber()` function returns a number solely based on the load order. Encoding the same value in different QVW files might return different numbers. Therefore, it is not possible to use results of the `AutoNumber()` function sourced from multiple QlikView documents.

Removing unused fields

Removing unused fields from the data model is a quick win in most QlikView applications. It can save anywhere between a few to hundreds of MB on bigger documents. Text fields, in particular, can take up a lot of space.

As the developer, you will probably have an idea of fields that are definitely not being used. You can either remove those from the script, or comment them out if you want to play it safe.

An automated tool that can help you spot unused files is Rob Wunderlich's Document Analyzer. This QlikView document is used to process another QlikView document and indicate which fields are not being used anywhere in the layout or expressions. Since this tool does not always correctly identify unused fields, it is advisable to always perform a sanity check before deleting fields. However, as a starting point, this is an excellent tool. The QVW file can be downloaded from `http://robwunderlich.com/downloads/`.

Splitting high-cardinality fields

QlikView utilizes various algorithms to compress the data to a fraction of its original size. One way it does this is by storing only the unique values of a field. For example, a table containing a list of colors, in which some of the values appear more than once, would be compacted in the following manner:

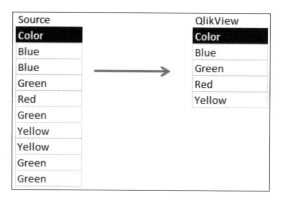

You can imagine that columns containing few distinct values (or, **low cardinality**) will be compressed much better than those with many distinct values (**high cardinality**).

If possible, it is worth considering if a high cardinality field can be split into multiple low cardinality fields.

Consider the example of a timestamp field, which contains a date and a time. If we were to load data corresponding to a single year, it could potentially lead to 31,536,000 unique timestamp values: 365 days x 24 hours x 60 minutes x 60 seconds.

However, we could also decide to split the timestamp into two fields: a date field and a time field. In this scenario the maximum number of unique values would be reduced to 86,765, that is, 365 days for the date field and 86,400 for the time field (24 hours x 60 minutes x 60 seconds). This is only 0.28 percent of the original volume, and can therefore have a tremendous impact on the document size, especially on larger data volumes.

> In some cases, the time component is not needed at all, so it's a good practice to simply truncate the timestamp value and keep only the date component. The Floor() function can be used to accomplish this, which removes the decimal part of a given numeric value.

Two more cases where this technique is applicable are phone numbers and big numbers. For example, if we have a measure that contains integer numbers ranging from 0 to 100,000,000, we can potentially end up with 100 million unique values. As an alternative, we could split the number into two 10,000 (the square root of 100 million) number ranges using the Div() and Mod() functions, shown here:

```
LOAD
    Div(BigNumber, 10000) as BigNumber1,
    Mod(BigNumber, 10000) as BigNumber2
FROM BigNumber;
```

The first expression in the preceding code performs an integer division of the value of BigNumber by 10,000. This means that only the resulting whole number is stored. The second expression performs a modulo operation, storing only the remainder of BigNumber divided by 10,000. Both of these fields have a potential of 10,000 unique values. That's 20,000 possible unique values when combined, or only 0.2 percent of the original list.

In the final application, we can then restore the original number by multiplying BigNumber1 with 10,000 and adding the remainder from BigNumber2:

```
(BigNumber1 * 10000) + BigNumber2
```

Of course, this calculation will be more processor-intense than a straightforward calculation on a single value. What works best "depends," so it is best to always perform a thorough test before implementing a solution like this.

Design challenges of data modeling

We will now provide some useful tips for dealing with more complex data models, specifically those used for dealing with multiple fact tables in a single QlikView document.

We will take a hands-on approach and we will continue using the `Airline Operations` document that we have previously used. The design challenge we will describe in this section will be aimed at integrating a new fact table into our data model, one that contains **Airline Employment Statistics**.

The Airline Employment statistics table

The table we will be adding to the data model contains monthly information about the number of employees per airline, separated by full time and part time, and also showing the equivalent total of full time employees.

The table contains the following fields:

- `Year`
- `Month`
- `%Airline ID`
- `%Unique Carrier Code`
- `Unique Carrier`
- `Carrier Code`
- `Carrier Name`
- `%Carrier Group ID`
- `# FullTime Employees`
- `# PartTime Employees`
- `# Equivalent FTEs`
- `# Total Employees`
- `Period`
- `Month (#)`

As you can see, all of the dimension fields are already part of the Airline Operations data model and the only new fields are those related to the actual measurements of employment.

Integrating multiple fact tables into one data model is one of the main challenges we can come across when designing a data model. This is, in fact, a very common scenario and we will present two ways of solving the task at hand:

1. By concatenating the two fact tables into one.
2. By creating a link table.

Let's see how each of these methods work and how the integration of this table will take place.

Concatenating fact tables

The first approach suggests that we should combine the two fact tables into one. This is a valid approach as all of the dimension fields of the new table are also present in the initial table.

We have already used the `concatenate` function in the previous example, and we will use it again to combine both fact tables.

This method will keep our data model simplified because there will be virtually no additional tables in it. However, we should keep in mind one important consideration: **structural asymmetry**.

Structural asymmetry

Although it is true that all of the dimension fields contained in the `Employment` table are present in the `Main Data` table, the opposite is not true: not all of the dimension fields in the `Main Data` table are present in the `Employment` table. There is an asymmetric structure between them.

This structural asymmetry needs to be kept in mind when creating the frontend of the document, simply because there will be analyses across certain dimensions that will be impossible to make. For example, we will not be able to create a chart that shows the number of employees by airport, as that dimension (airport) is not present on the `Employment` table, and there is no way to get that data into our document. However, we will be able to create, for instance, a chart that shows the number of employees by airline or by month or by year.

In hand with this difference in table structure, there is another point we should address: the `Main Data` table already contains `Year`, `Month`, and `Quarter` dimensions, and those dimensions are included as listboxes in the user interface to allow the user to filter through the data. However, the `Employment` data only contains the `Year` and `Month` fields, but *not* the `Quarter` field.

There is something we can do about this: simply add a calculated field to the Employment table before concatenating it to the Main Data table. In the end, both table segments contain the Quarter field. If we do not add the Quarter field to the Employment table, any user selection on this field will automatically exclude all of the employment data.

Natural and forced concatenation

Moving on to concatenating tables, as we saw in the previous chapter, there are two ways in which this operation can take place in QlikView:

- Natural concatenation
- Forced concatenation

Let's take a moment to revisit this subject and see how we can apply it to our fact tables.

Natural concatenation

Natural concatenation happens when two tables are loaded with exactly the same structure, that is, they contain the exact same fields (in both the number of fields and field names).

When this condition is met, QlikView automatically combines all tables that are similar and treats them as one logical table.

An example of this is shown in the next script:

```
Sales:
Load
 Region,
 Month,
 Year,
 [Total Amount]
From Sales2011.qvd (qvd);

Load
 Region,
 [Total Amount],
 Month,
 Year
From Sales2010.qvd (qvd);
```

As you can see, with the preceding script we are loading two tables into the data model and both tables are loaded from a different QVD file. The first table contains data for the year 2011, while the second table contains data for 2010. As they both have the same structure (field names), they will automatically be merged into one logical table in the QlikView data model. Also note that the order in which the fields are defined in the load script is not relevant for natural concatenation.

NoConcatenate

In case we want to avoid the default behavior whenever this circumstance is present in the script, we can add the `NoConcatenate` keyword as a prefix to the `Load` statement of the second table so that QlikView continues treating them as separate tables in the data model.

Forced concatenation

Forced concatenation happens when we explicitly define that two tables should be combined into one logical table in the data model, even if they don't have the same structure or field names.

This is the method we have used earlier in this chapter, where we used the Concatenate prefix to add the 'unknown' Aircrafts to the Aircrafts dimension table. It will be useful in this case as well as there are only a few shared fields between both tables.

As we also saw earlier, with the `Concatenate` prefix we can specify to which of the previously loaded tables the new table should be appended. This is done by adding the name assigned to the target table, enclosed by parentheses.

The following script shows how to explicitly concatenate two tables that do not have the same structure:

```
Sales:
Load
 Region,
 Month,
 Year,
 [Total Amount]
From Sales2011.qvd (qvd);

Concatenate (Sales)
Load
 Region,
```

```
    [Total Budget Amount],
    Month,
    Year
From Budget2011.qvd (qvd);
```

If we don't add the name of the original table (`Sales`, in the preceding example) to the `Concatenate` prefix, the new table will be concatenated to the table loaded immediately before it, no matter what that table is.

We recommend, as a best practice, to always explicitly define concatenation by adding the name of the target table to the `Concatenate` prefix, even if both tables have the same structure and would naturally be combined. This is mainly to avoid confusion and makes it easier for other developers, and yourself, to understand the script.

Concatenating the Employment Statistics table

Now that we've revisited the subject of table concatenation and described the considerations that we must keep in mind, let's put it into practice. We will be integrating the `Employment` table into the already designed data model for the Airline Operations document.

Follow these steps:

1. Make sure the `T_F41SCHEDULE_P1A_EMP.qvd` file is placed into the `Airline Operations\Data Files\QVDs` folder.

2. Open the `Airline Operations.qvw` document we've been working with.

3. Save the file with another name. Let's call it `Chapter 8_Concatenated tables.qvw`.

4. Go to the **Edit Script** window, activate the **Main Data** tab, and click on the **Add new tab** button from the toolbar.

5. The **Tab Rename** dialog window will appear, in which we will enter `Employment Data` and click on **OK**.

6. The new tab will be added to the right of the **Main Data** tab, which is particularly important for our example.

7. Using the **File Wizard** dialog (click on the **Table Files...** button), create the `Load` statement for the `T_F41SCHEDULE_P1A_EMP.qvd` file. Make sure the `Load` statement is added on the **Employment Data** tab created previously.

8. Add the new `Quarter` field as a calculated field to address part of what we discussed about structural asymmetry. The expression we will use for this is:

```
'Q' & Ceil([Month (#)]/3, 1) as Quarter
```

9. Add the `Concatenate` prefix to the load statement, specifying that the `Main Data` table is the one to which this will be appended. The added script should look as follows:

```
Concatenate ([Main Data])
LOAD Year,
     Period,
     [Month (#)],
     Month,
     'Q' & Ceil(Month/3, 1) as Quarter,
     [%Airline ID],
     [%Unique Carrier Code],
     [%Carrier Group ID],
     [Unique Carrier],
     [Carrier Code],
     [Carrier Name],
     [# Full Time Employees],
     [# Part Time Employees],
     [# Total Employees],
     [# Equivalent FTEs]
FROM
[..\Data Files\QVDs\T_F41SCHEDULE_P1A_EMP.qvd]
(qvd);
```

It is of fundamental importance that this script be added in a tab that is to the right of the **Main Data** tab, as we are referencing the `Main Data` table and. For that to work, the table must have been loaded previously, during the script execution. Remember that script executes sequentially from left to right.

10. Save the changes and reload the script.

As no actual tables have been added to the data model, the resulting model will look identical to the one we had before adding the script. The only difference will be the new fields that are included at the end of the `Main Data` table that correspond to the employment measures. Use the **Table Viewer** dialog to verify that the new fields have been added.

We have described the first approach for dealing with multiple fact tables in a data model. In the next section, we will present yet another option along with its pros and cons, so that you, as a Developer, can better decide which one will suit your needs best.

To continue, save and close the `Chapter 8_Concatenated tables.qvw` document.

Working with link tables

When we include two or more fact tables in a single QlikView document, it's very likely they all are somehow related and will, therefore, have some common dimension fields among them. However, as we've outlined before, in a QlikView data model, two tables should not be associated through two or more fields because it would generate a synthetic key.

So how do we incorporate two or more fact tables into one data model and treat them as two separate logical tables while, at the same time, avoiding the synthetic-key issue? At first sight, it can seem like both options are mutually exclusive, but there is a workaround which is to create a **Link Table**.

As its name implies, a link table essentially "links" two or more fact tables by taking all common fields out of the original tables and placing them into a new one (the link table).The new link table contains all possible combination of values for that set of fields and, through a unique key, is associated to the original tables.

A link table example

Take, for example, the following scenario:

- We are required to design a data model for analyzing Call Center Performance data, and have two fact tables: Operations and Payroll. Based on these tables, we need to be able to present cross-functional information in a QlikView dashboard.

- The Operations table has the following fields: Call ID, Timestamp, Employee ID, Supervisor ID, Department ID, Call Type ID, Customer ID, Call Duration, and Total Hold Time.

- The Payroll table has the following fields: Payroll ID, Employee ID, Department ID, Position ID, Amount.

- We also have the corresponding dimension tables to provide a description to the fields Call Type ID, Employee ID, Department ID, and Position ID.

If we let QlikView make the default associations, we would get the following data model:

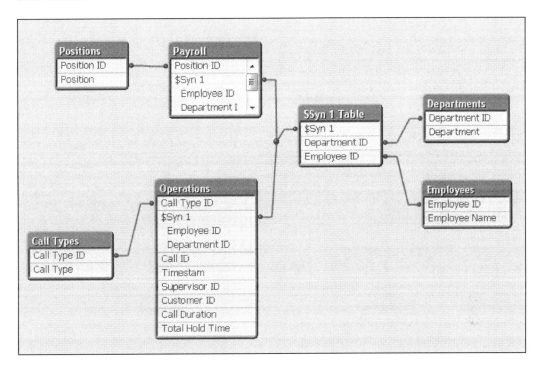

From the preceding image, we can observe that a synthetic key has been created because two fields (`Employee ID` and `Department ID`) are shared between the `Operations` table and the `Payroll` table.

To solve this challenge, we will remove the synthetic key by using a link table. As was mentioned earlier, the new link table will hold all combinations of the key fields that are common for both tables. We should also create a new compound key to connect the three tables.

Essentially, the link table replaces the synthetic key table, and in some cases, the result in both performance and design is exactly the same. However, it's a good practice to always "clean" the data model and remove all synthetic keys.

Our re-designed data model will look as follows, after applying the appropriate changes:

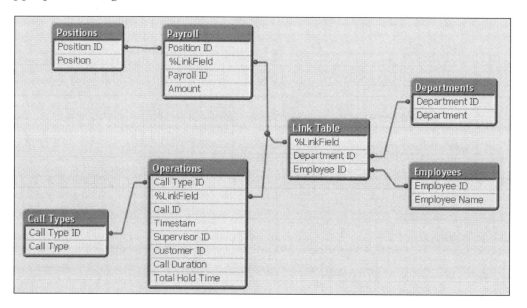

As you can see, the synthetic key has been removed and the `Payroll` and `Operations` tables are now connected to the `Department` and `Employees` dimension tables indirectly and through the link table.

When designing a data model using this method, we should always consider the following:

- The link table can become very large depending on the number of possible combinations that exist between or among the fields it's composed of.

- We must make sure that all of thecombinations that exist in both fact tables are also in the created link table. If they are not, the association between the fact tables and the link tables might be "broken" or missing for some records.

- For performance optimization, the link table should not have repeated records. Only one record per possible combination of values is needed.

- If the link table becomes immense, remember that QlikView needs to "walk" through the defined path between tables each time it needs to look for associations. An additional "hop" on this path, especially if it is through a large table, might slow calculation times for the end user.

Creating a link table in the Airline Operations document

Now that we've described the creation of link tables and its uses, let's put it into practice in our Airline Operations data model.

Remember that, in the previous section, we already added the `Employment Statistics` table to the Airline Operations data model by using the `Concatenation` method. We'll now do the same, but this time using the link table method. You can compare each of them and see for yourself their pros and cons.

Follow these steps:

1. Make sure the `T_F41SCHEDULE_P1A_EMP.qvd` file we used previously is already in the `Airline Operations\Data Files\QVDs` folder.

2. Open the `Airline Operations.qvw` document.

3. Save the file with another name. Let's call it `Chapter 8_Link tables.qvw`.

4. Head on to the script editor and add a new tab to the right-side of the **Main Data** tab. Name the new tab as `Employment Data`.

5. Using the **File Wizard** (click on the **Table Files...** button), create the `Load` statement for the `T_F41SCHEDULE_P1A_EMP.qvd` file. Name the table as `Employment Statistics`.

6. Identify the common fields between the `Employment Statistics` table and the already loaded `Main Data` table. The shared fields are:

    ○ `Year, Period, Month, Month (#), %Airline ID, %Unique Carrier Code, Unique Carrier, Carrier Code, Carrier Name,` and `%Carrier Group ID`.

7. For all of the shared fields listed above, identify those that will form a unique key. In this case, the fields that must be included in the unique key are:

    ○ `Period, %Airline ID, %Unique Carrier Code,` and `%Carrier Group ID`.

8. The fields we will leave out of the key will be:

    ○ `Year, Month, Month (#), Unique Carrier, Carrier Code,` and `Carrier Name`.

9. Create a new compound key on both of the tables by using the following script expression:

```
Period
& ' | ' & [%Airline ID]
& ' | ' & [%Unique Carrier Code]
& ' | ' & [%Carrier Group ID] as [%Key Field],
```

10. Add a new tab from the **Tab** menu and name it **Link Table**. Make sure this new tab is located to the right-side of both the **Employment Data** and **Main Data** tabs.

11. In the **Link Table** tab, add the following script:

```
[Link Table]:
Load Distinct
     [%Key Field],
     [%Key Field] as [%TEMP Key Field],
     Year,
     Period,
     [Month (#)],
     Month,
     Quarter,
     [%Airline ID],
     [%Unique Carrier Code],
     [%Carrier Group ID],
     [Unique Carrier],
     [Carrier Code],
     [Carrier Name]
   Resident [Main Data];

Concatenate ([Link Table])
Load Distinct
     [%Key Field],
     Year,
     Period,
     [Month (#)],
     Month,
     'Q' & Ceil([Month (#)]/3, 1) as Quarter,
     [%Airline ID],
     [%Unique Carrier Code],
     [%Carrier Group ID],
     [Unique Carrier],
     [Carrier Code],
     [Carrier Name]
   Resident [Employment Statistics]
   Where Not Exists([%TEMP Key Field], [%Key Field]);
```

```
Drop Field [%TEMP Key Field];
Drop Fields  Year,
    Period,
    [Month (#)],
    Month,
    [%Airline ID],
    [%Unique Carrier Code],
    [%Carrier Group ID],
    [Unique Carrier],
    [Carrier Code],
    [Carrier Name] From [Employment Statistics];

Drop Fields Year,
    Period,
    [Month (#)],
    Month,
    Quarter,
    [%Airline ID],
    [%Unique Carrier Code],
    [%Carrier Group ID],
    [Unique Carrier],
    [Carrier Code],
    [Carrier Name] From [Main Data];
```

With the preceding script we are doing the following:

a. Assign a name to the table: `Link Table`.

b. Create a list of distinct combinations of all shared fields from the previously loaded `Main Data` table, including the new `%Key Field`, by performing a **Resident Load** (more on Resident Loads in *Chapter 13, Advanced Data Transformation*).

c. Create a duplicate of the `%Key Field` attribute and name it `%TEMP Key Field`.

d. Concatenate a new list of distinct combinations of all shared fields from the previously created `Employment Statistics` table, including the new `%Key Field` attribute and adding a calculated field `Quarter`. From this new list we exclude all combinations that already exist on the first list earlier, using a `Where` clause.

e. Remove the `%TEMP Key Field` field from the data model, as it was only to be used in the `Where` clause.

f. Remove the shared fields from each fact table, except the `%Key Field` attribute, as they will now be stored in the link table.

12. Save the changes we made and reload the script. The new data model will be created and look as follows:

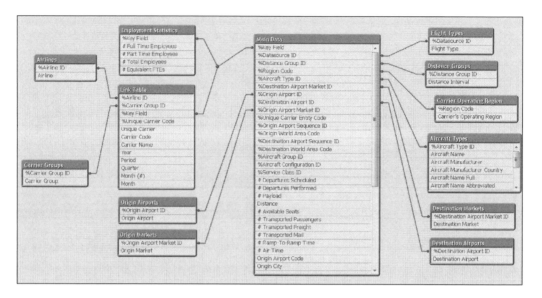

Two fundamental recommendations can be made regarding the creation of link tables:

- Always use the `Distinct` keyword when creating the link table. This is done so we are only loading dimension fields into this table and we should not have duplicate records.

- If the `Key` field is composed of several individual fields, it can be resource intensive for the application. In these cases, we could use the `Autonumber()` function described previously.

Proceed to save and close the document.

Finding a balance

We have outlined two ways for dealing with multiple fact tables in a data model. If we were to ask which of these methods is better, we would need to say, again, "it depends." There is no definite best, and the decision about which to use will depend entirely on the specific scenario where it has to be implemented.

When deciding on data model design, you should always ask yourself if the "structural asymmetry" we talked about before is something you could accept in your data model, or if the asymmetry is highly significant and therefore you would prefer to live with the "additional hop" in the data model.

Choosing between approaches can also impact the application's size. Take a look at both of the files created using each of the preceding methods and see which one is smaller in disk size .Can you guess why the link table approach produces a smaller file? It's because we've taken out some fields from the relatively large fact tables and placed them into a smaller link table.

For QlikView, both of these approaches are OK. They work as they should and there should not be calculation differences resulting from using them one over the other.

For the purpose of continuity throughout the rest of the book, we will be working with the new data model created using the first method: Concatenation. Therefore, make sure to integrate the `Employment Statistics` table to the original `Airline Operations` document by concatenating both fact tables as previously shown.

The master calendar

Finally, our last set of best practices on data modeling involves dealing with dates and times. When analyzing data, time often plays an important role. Initially, it's not much of the individual transactions and events that users are interested in, but rather the rolled up totals per period, or trends over multiple periods.

Source systems usually record the date at which a particular transaction or event took place, but do not contain any further information for time grouping. This makes sense, as transactional systems strive not to include redundant data. In our QlikView documents, however, we strive to make the selections and aggregations as easy as possible for our users. That is why, in addition to the original date, we include attributes such as the month, quarter, and year components in our data model.

Rather than placing these attributes directly in our fact table, as we've done until now, the best practice is to create a separate master calendar dimension table. The main advantage is that it lets us use the same master calendar for multiple fact tables. Another important benefit is that if the fact table is missing any intermediary periods, we can still create these in our master calendar. This way, when data is missing for a certain period, we would still be able to see that period in our document.

Follow these steps to add a master calendar table to our Airline Operations data model:

1. Open the `Airline Operations` document and go to the script editor.

2. Activate the **Main Data** tab. Then, locate the lines corresponding to the fields `Year`, `Quarter`, `Month (#)`, and `Month`.

3. Remove those lines so that these fields are not loaded. You can also comment out the lines instead of completely removing them.

   This way, we will only have the `Period` field in the fact table, which encodes both the `Year` and `Month` fields. We will then use the `Period` field to link the fact table to the calendar table.

4. Let's do the same with the `Employment Statistics` table. Activate the **Employment Data** tab and remove the `Year`, `Quarter`, `Month (#)`, and `Month` fields from the corresponding `Load` statement. Make sure the `Period` field is still loaded.

5. Insert a new tab directly after the **Employment Data** tab by simultaneously pressing *Ctrl + Q, T, A* or by selecting **Tab | Add Tab** from the menu. Name the new tab as **Calendar**.

6. On this tab, insert the following code:

```
//--- Select the lowest and highest periods
//from the Flights fact table.

Temp_Calendar_Range:
LOAD
     Num(Date#(Min(Period), 'YYYYMM'))as MinDate,
     Num(Date#(Max(Period), 'YYYYMM')) as MaxDate
RESIDENT [Main Data];
```

This code creates a temporary table that contains the lowest and highest periods from the `Main Data` table. As these values are originally in YYYYMM format, we need to convert them to a date value by using the `Date#()` function.

 The `Date#()` function essentially takes a string value representing a date and converts it to an actual date value based on the specified source format.

By using the `Min` and `Max` aggregations functions, the resulting fields will have the very first and very last date, respectively, appearing in the source table.

Once the corresponding date value has been obtained, it is then converted to its numerical representation (which is the number of days that have passed since December 31, 1899) using the `Num()` function. For instance, December 28, 2011, would be converted to 40905. This ensures that all of the dates can be treated as consecutive numbers.

Using these two dates contained in the temporary table, we will generate a master calendar that includes each month in them:

1. Add the following code at the end of the previous `Load` statement:

   ```
   //--- Assign the start and end dates to variables
   LET vMinDate = Peek('MinDate', 0, 'Temp_Calendar_Range');
   LET vMaxDate = Peek('MaxDate', 0, 'Temp_Calendar_Range');

   DROP TABLE Temp_Calendar_Range; // Cleanup
   ```

   Using the `LET` statement, we assign the lowest and highest dates to temporary variables. The `Peek()` function is, which we will learn more about in a later chapter, used to retrieve the values of these dates from the `Temp_Calendar_Range` table. After creating the variable, we will no longer need the `Temp_Calendar_Range` table, so it is deleted using the `DROP TABLE` statement.

2. The next step is adding the code that will create the actual master calendar table. Enter the following below the `Drop Table` statement:

```
[Master Calendar]:
LOAD DISTINCT
    Year(Temp_Date) * 100 + Month(Temp_Date) as [Period],
    Year(Temp_Date) as [Year],
    Month(Temp_Date) as [Month],
    Date(Temp_Date, 'YYYY-MM') as [Year - Month],
    'Q' & Ceil(Month(Temp_Date) / 3) as [Quarter]
;
LOAD DISTINCT
    MonthStart($(vMinDate) + IterNo() - 1) as Temp_Date
AUTOGENERATE (1)
WHILE $(vMinDate) + IterNo() - 1 <= $(vMaxDate);

//--- Remove the temporary variables
LET vMinDate = Null();
LET vMaxDate = Null();
```

You may notice that the first LOAD statement in the preceding script is missing a source. When no source is specified, QlikView uses the result of the next LOAD statement as the source. This is called a **Preceding Load**.

The script first creates a table with a single column called `Temp_Date`. By using the `AUTOGENERATE (1) WHILE $(vMinDate) + IterNo() - 1 <= $(vMaxDate)` statement, QlikView iterates over each day between the lowest (`vMinDate`) and highest (`vMaxDate`) period and creates one record per day.

By applying the `MonthStart()` function, a table containing every first day of the month for the intermediate period is created. The preceding load statement then loads the `Temp_Date` table and applies various date functions to it to create the final `Master Calendar` table. At this point, we also use an expression to create the dimension key `Period` by concatenating the year and month into a single number. For example, October 2011 will be stored as 201110. The `Period` field will then be used to associate the `Master Calendar` table and the fact table.

After the master calendar is created, the temporary variables are deleted by setting their value to `Null()`.

3. **Save** and **reload** the application and the final data model will be created, shown here:

As our data model only contains data on a monthly level, our master calendar contains relatively little data. Other applications are often built with data at a daily level. An example script for generating a day-based master calendar is included in the solution files for this chapter. An example script for generating a day-based master calendar is included in the solution files for this chapter. You can find this script inside the `Airline Operations\Side Examples\Chapter 9` folder, in the file `CreateCalendarFromField.qvs`.

A final note on data modeling

To close this chapter, we should insist on something that, if followed, will save you tons of hours spent guessing where a possible mistake might be. That is, always confirm, test, and validate that the changes you make to the data model result in what you expect.

It happens many times that we add a little table here and there, modify a field name, join two tables, or something similar and that "small" change modifies our data model a little, but the final calculations are affected greatly without us even noticing.

Always make sure the modification moves you forward instead of backward.

Summary

This brings us to the end of this chapter on data modeling best practices. If you haven't finished all of the exercises, don't worry, all of the solutions are included in the solution files.

To recap, in this chapter we learned how to deal with common consistency issues, such as facts without associated dimensions, and vice versa, how we can reduce storage requirements by using numeric keys, removing unused fields from our model, and by splitting high-cardinality fields.

We also learned how to approach two of the most common design challenges, concatenating two fact tables and creating link tables, and what the advantages of the different methods are.

Finally, we learned how to create a master calendar.

In the next chapter, we will learn some basic data transformation techniques that will help us cleanse source data and load data that isn't in a straightforward, tabular format.

10
Basic Data Transformation

At this point in the book, we've already covered topics related to data sources such as extraction, data visualization, scripting, and data modeling. These topics are all interconnected in the development process. We will now complement these four topics with a fifth subject that is of fundamental importance, and one that plays an essential role when developing QlikView apps, taking to an advanced level the lessons learned from all of the previous chapters: **Data Transformation**.

The topics we'll cover here will help us:

- Make the data sources adequate to meet our data model design requirements
- Deal with unstructured tables (such as Crosstables) and incorporate them into our data model

On we go.

Changing the source table structure

We've seen how the QlikView engine works and the importance of having a data model design that fully takes advantage of QlikView's associative algorithms. So, the first section of this chapter deals with **transforming** source tables to make them adequate for our data model. The different structure transformations we'll make are:

- "Cleansing" a dirty table
- Converting a Crosstable to a standard table
- Using hierarchy tables
- Loading generic tables

"Cleansing" a dirty table

As we've said before, it's not that uncommon for business users to require consolidated information from all sorts of different sources: the CRM, the company's Data Warehouse, Excel tables, Legacy systems, and so on. In these scenarios, the developer commonly faces the challenge of adapting a user file (Excel, CSV, TXT) that has either a non-standard structure or contains "dirty" data which needs to be removed, such as report headers or subtotal lines, and sometimes both.

Fortunately for us, QlikView's data extraction engine is powerful enough to be able to interpret these tables, cleanse them before loading and convert them into a standard table. However, for that to happen, we must specify the set of rules to follow when loading a certain file. These rules and conditions can be set via the **Transformation Wizard**, available when loading local table files and HTML web files.

To demonstrate how the Transformation Wizard works, we will be using a text file that has been provided along with this book, named `Production Planning - Legacy. txt`. Look for it inside the `Airline Operations\Side Examples\Chapter 10` folder.

> The exercises we will be doing in this chapter are just for demonstration purposes and will not affect our `Airline Operations.qvw` document.

File contents

The contents of the `Production Planning - Legacy.txt` file, as seen from a text editor, are shown in the following screenshot:

```
Report Date: May 27, 2012
Report Name: Production Planning
Generated by: System User

Date      Plant # Product Line ID Estimated Production   Date      Plant # Product Line ID Estimated Production
--------  ------- ------- ------- -------- ---------- -------   --------  -------
20120528         1        03      99      20120702         1        03       199
           1     04       85               1        04      185
20120529         2        04      112     20120703         2        04       82
20120530         2        03      103     20120704         2        03       93
20120601         1        05      108     20120705         1        05       68
Week 1 Total                      507     Week 6 Total                       627
20120604         1        03      173     20120709         1        03       73
           1     04       234     20120710         1        04      134
20120605         2        04      291     20120711         2        04       191
20120606         2        03      124     20120712         2        03       224
20120607         1        05      102              1        05      202
Week 2 Total                      924     Week 7 Total                       824
20120611         1        03      97      20120716         1        03       197
           1     04       193              1        04       93
20120612         2        04      102     20120717         2        04       202
20120613         2        03      82      20120718         2        03       182
20120614         1        05      96      20120719         1        05       196
Week 3 Total                      570     Week 8 Total                       870
20120618         1        03      199     20120723         1        03       190
20120619         1        04      142     20120724         1        04       132
           2     04       124              2        04      224
20120620         2        03      108     20120725         2        03       208
20120621         1        05      168     20120726         1        05       208
Week 4 Total                      741     Week 9 Total                       962
20120625         1        03      142     20120730         1        03       192
20120626         1        04      162     20120731         1        04       112
20120627         2        04      120              2        04      220
           2     03       134     20120801         2        03      234
20120628         1        05      78      20120802         1        05       178
Week 5 Total                      636     Week 10 Total                      936
```

The structure and contents of the file are described as follows:

- It has a 4-line header, with information about the report above the actual field names.

- Columns in the data area are delimited with tabs.

- Column labels are placed in the fifth line.

- After the column heading there is a "garbage" line intended to be a visual separator.

- The report shows daily data with a weekly subtotal.

- The report shows ten weeks of data, with five of them on the left and the other five placed on the right.

- Records with no specified date correspond to the same date as the previous record.

We have taken the preceding file as an example since it represents a very common way of pulling data out of certain particular systems. Even in popular ERP systems, such as SAP, reports can be generated in this manner. Of course, there may be ways to circumvent the unstructured report and go right to the source table, but in some cases access is a bit restricted.

So, let's start cleaning up this mess.

Working with the Transformation Step wizard

We will load this file into a new QVW file, so let's begin by creating a new QlikView document and saving it as `Production Planning.qvw`. This new file will be saved inside the `Airline Operations\Side Examples\Chapter 10` folder. After saving the file, make sure the `Production Planning - Legacy.txt` file is also at the same location.

Next, open the Script Editor (*Ctrl+E*) and bring up the **File Wizard** by clicking on the **Table Files...** button.

Then, browse to the folder in which the text file is stored, select it and click on **Open**. Right after that, the **File Wizard** will show the following window:

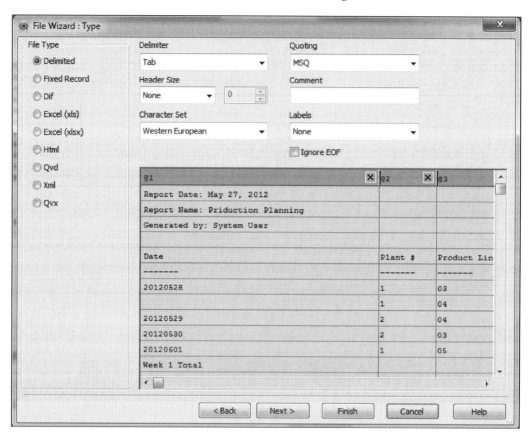

Make sure the parameters are set as shown in the preceding screenshot so that QlikView interprets the file correctly.

After clicking **Next >**, the **File Wizard: Transform** window will appear, showing a brief description about it and a warning:

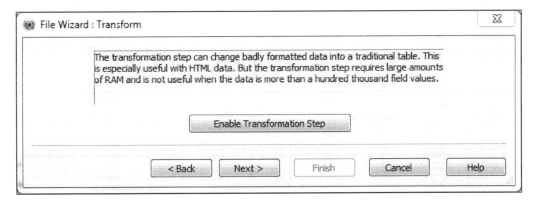

Essentially, the warning text indicates that the Transformation Step Wizard should not be used for large tables. In our case, the example file contains no more than 50 lines of data, so it won't be a problem for us this time and will rarely be when working with actual "dirty" reports.

Click on the **Enable Transformation Step** button to access the corresponding features. We will be presented with the following wizard:

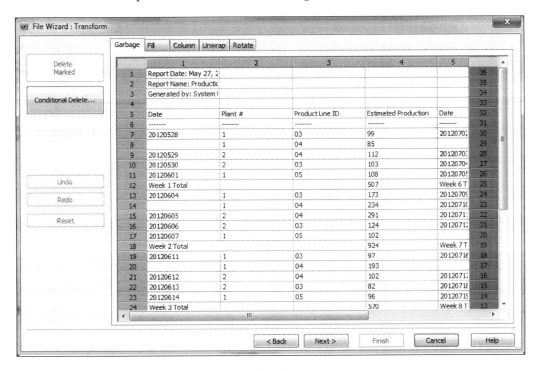

As you can see, the Transformation Step Wizard is split into several tabs, and each one is used to handle different scenarios. We will be using three of the five tabs, but will describe what all of them do and the types they could be used.

Throwing out the garbage

Our example file certainly has some garbage that needs to be thrown out. We will use the first tab of the Transformation step wizard to:

- Remove the heading rows (first 4 lines)
- Remove the visual separator between the column headings and the actual data
- Remove the weekly totals

Follow these steps to accomplish the above:

1. Click on each of the row numbers in the first four lines, as well as in the sixth line, one at a time. The entire row should be highlighted and the **Delete Marked** button should be enabled, as shown in the following screenshot:

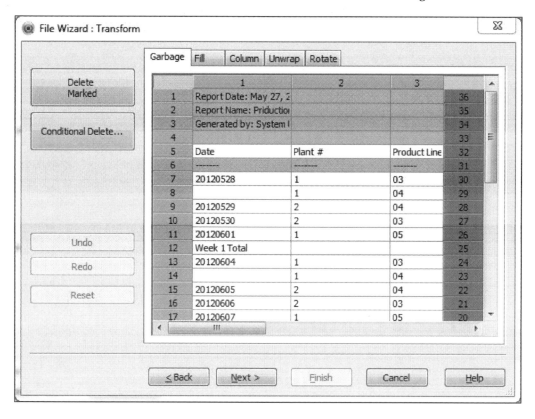

2. Click on the **Delete Marked** button to remove these rows. They should instantly disappear.

3. Now, click on the **Conditional Delete...** button to continue removing the weekly totals. A new window will appear, shown below, in which we will specify the condition on which the remaining rows should be removed.

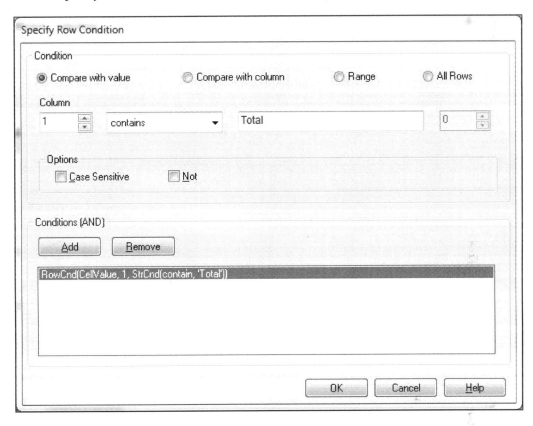

4. Make sure, as in the preceding screenshot, to set the following parameters:
   ○ The **Compare with value** radio button should be selected
   ○ The comparison operator will be set to **contains**
   ○ The comparison value will be the word **Total**
   ○ The **Case Sensitive** and **Not** options should be disabled

5. Click on the **Add** button to finish setting the condition and then click on **OK** to return to the previous window.

The preceding procedure will remove the garbage from our file, but that is not all we need to do.

Unwrapping table contents

There is another "formatting challenge" we will tackle with this file, which is, that data is split into two parts: the first five weeks are on the left side of the file and weeks 6 - 10 are on the right, occupying the same rows. So, we need to unwrap them.

Essentially, we want to move the data located on the right part of the table and place it below the data located on the left. To do that, we will activate the **Unwrap** tab from the Transformation Step wizard and follow these steps:

1. Use the bar-shaped cursor to mark the beginning of the "right" part of the table by clicking on the column border between columns 4 and 5. This will specify the separation, as seen in the following screenshot. If you don't see where the second part of the table begins, use the scrollbar to move to the right.

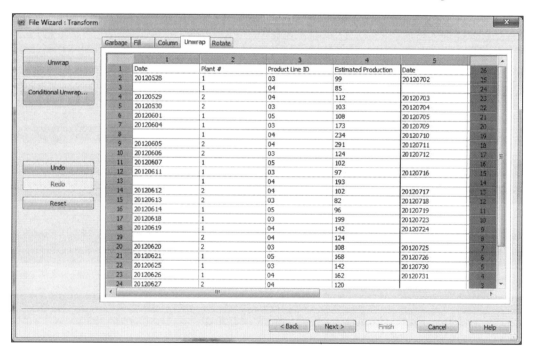

2. Click **Unwrap** to move the table content to the appropriate place. We should now see the following result:

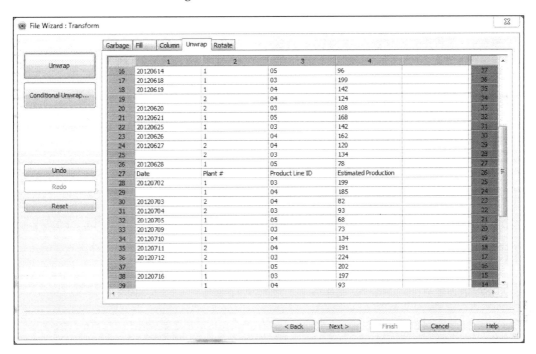

The preceding procedure leaves us with a new garbage line: the column headings corresponding to the unwrapped content (shown at line 27 in the preceding screenshot). To remove it, we need to go back to the **Garbage** tab and follow these steps:

3. Click on the **Conditional Delete…** button to specify the condition on which the rows should be removed.

4. From the **Specify Row Condition** dialog window, we will specify two conditions, joined with an **AND** operator. For the first condition, mark the following parameters:

   ° The **Compare with value** radio button should be selected

   ° The comparison operator will be set to **contains**

   ° The comparison value will be the word **Date**

   ° The **Case Sensitive** and **Not** options should be disabled

5. Click on the **Add** button to include the first condition and then continue setting the second condition with the following parameters:

   ° Select the **Range** radio button

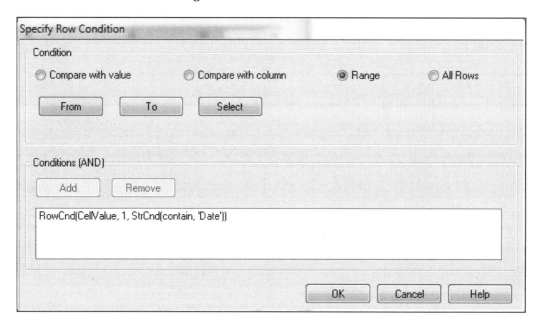

   ° Click on the **From** button and set the **Cell Index Position** to **2 From Top**. Then, click on **OK**.

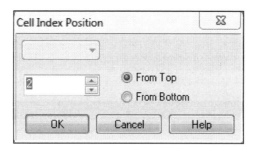

○ Now, click on the **To** button and set the **Cell Index Position** to **1 From Bottom**. Click on **OK**.

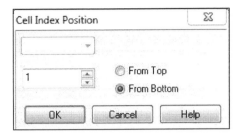

○ Click on the **Select** button and set the **Select** value to **1** and the **Skip value** to **0**. Click on OK:

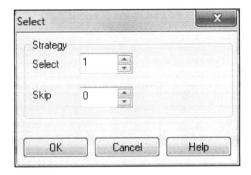

6. Click on the **Add** button to include this second condition and then click on **OK**.

Now, the two conditions will be evaluated and those rows that match both conditions will be removed.

We had to apply both conditions because if we had only specified the "contains Date" condition the first row would have been removed as well.

Furthermore, if we had deleted line 27 directly by marking it with the mouse and by clicking on the **Delete Marked** button, even though the effect would have been what we expected, the final code instruction would always look for line 27 and remove it, without first evaluating if that's actually a garbage line. What would happen when the report is updated? Who knows if the garbage line will still be line 27. You can't be sure. It's better to apply a certain logic so that even when you update the report, the code can automatically identify the garbage line.

Filling missing cells

As we previously said, there are records with no specified date. We will use the **Transformation Step Wizard** dialog to fill those values. Follow these steps:

1. Activate the **Fill** tab from the **Transformation Step Wizard** dialog.

2. Click on the **Fill...** button. The following wizard should appear:

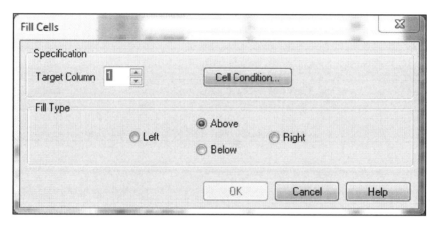

3. The **Target Column** field should be **1**, as that is where the date values are stored.

4. The **Fill type** will be **Above**, to take the value that is in the immediate previous record.

5. Click on the **Cell Condition...** button to specify which rows should be filled.

6. In the **Cell Condition** window, make sure the **Cell Value** field is set to **is empty** and the **Not** and **Case Sensitive** options are disabled. Click on **OK** twice to return to the **Transformation Step** window and see the result so far:

	1	2	3	
1	Date	Plant #	Product Line	26
2	20120528	1	03	25
3	20120528	1	04	24
4	20120529	2	04	23
5	20120530	2	03	22
6	20120601	1	05	21
7	20120604	1	03	20
8	20120604	1	04	19
9	20120605	2	04	18
10	20120606	2	03	17
11	20120607	1	05	16
12	20120611	1	03	15
13	20120611	1	04	14
14	20120612	2	04	13
15	20120613	2	03	12
16	20120614	1	05	11
17	20120618	1	03	10

Tabs: Garbage | Fill | Column | Unwrap | Rotate

As you can see, the missing cells now have the correct date value. Click on the **Next >** button to exit the **Transformation Wizard**.

From the **File Wizard: Option** dialog window, set the **Label** parameter to **Embedded Labels**, and then click on **Finish** to generate the final Load statement.

The final result

After specifying the transformation criteria, the corresponding Load statement is automatically generated and, as you will see, all of the settings are specified in the script itself.

The generated script looks as follows:

```
LOAD Date,
     [Plant #],
     [Product Line ID],
     [Estimated Production]
FROM
[Production Planning - Legacy.txt]
(txt, codepage is 1252, embedded labels, delimiter is '\t', msq,
filters(
Remove(Row, Pos(Top, 6)),
Remove(Row, Pos(Top, 4)),
Remove(Row, Pos(Top, 3)),
Remove(Row, Pos(Top, 2)),
Remove(Row, Pos(Top, 1)),
Remove(Row, RowCnd(CellValue, 1, StrCnd(contain, 'Total'))),
Unwrap(Col, Pos(Top, 5)),
Remove(Row, RowCnd(Compound,
RowCnd(CellValue, 1, StrCnd(contain, 'Date')),
RowCnd(Interval, Pos(Top, 2), Pos(Bottom, 1), Select(1, 0))
)),
Replace(1, top, StrCnd(null))
));
```

After reloading the script, we can open the Table Viewer window and see that we have a nicely formatted table with the Production Planning data:

Dialog			
Date	**Plant #**	**Product Line ID**	**Estimated Prod...**
20120528	1	03	99
20120528	1	04	85
20120529	2	04	112
20120530	2	03	103
20120601	1	05	108
20120604	1	03	173
20120604	1	04	234
20120605	2	04	291
20120606	2	03	124
20120607	1	05	102
20120611	1	03	97
20120611	1	04	193

As the code was generated and pasted into the script editor, every time the TXT report is updated we just need to re-run the script to update the data in the QlikView document, without having to go through of all the steps over again.

We've successfully loaded a "dirty" file into QlikView by taking advantage of one of its extraction capabilities. This capability broadens QlikView's ability to consolidate data from disparate sources and empowers the QlikView developer in the data model design process.

Other transformation tricks

Let's look at some other options the Transformation Step Wizard provides:

- **Column**: This tab allows us to copy data from one column, either in its entirety or based on conditions, and place it into other columns. We can also create new columns based on this copy.
- **Rotate**: This tab can be used to rotate an entire table to either side or by transposing it.
- **Context**: This tab is only available when loading HTML files and can be used to extract additional information about the cells, other than what is actually visible (for example, URL links, tags, and so on).

We've uncovered one of the Transformation tools available in QlikView, and now it's time to learn about other functions we can use when extracting data.

Loading a Crosstable

To be fair, the example we saw in the preceding section is possible but is actually rare. A more common example of a source table that is unfit for QlikView is the Crosstable.

In this section, we will describe what a Crosstable is for QlikView, why it's not suitable for a data model, and how can we transform it into a traditional table using QlikView's extraction engine.

A Crosstable example

Let's look at the following input table:

Department	Jan	Feb	Mar	Apr	May	Jun
A	160	336	545	152	437	1
B	476	276	560	57	343	476
C	251	591	555	195	341	399
D	96	423	277	564	590	130

As you can see, we have one field (column) for each month. We also have a `Department` field, with its corresponding field values in one single column. The values in the data area of the table are amounts. Let's assume they are `Sales` amounts.

The problem with this matrix-like structure is that if, for example, we want to obtain the total sales for each department, we would need to create an expression like the following:

```
Sum (Jan) + Sum(Feb) + Sum(Mar) + Sum(Apr) + Sum(May) + Sum(Jun)
```

At the same time, we wouldn't be able to create a trend chart, because all months are stored as different dimensions. So, we need to make it fit our purposes.

For us to use this table better in a QlikView data model, we need to convert it to a traditional table with the following structure:

Department	Month	Sales
A	Jan	160
A	Feb	336
A	Mar	545
A	Apr	152
A	May	437
A	Jun	1

This way, in our charts, we will be able to create expressions such as:

```
Sum(Sales)
```

Working with the Crosstable Wizard

Just as we did with our preceding example, we will load this file into a new QVW, so let's begin by creating a new QlikView document and saving it as `Crosstable example.qvw`. The new file should be saved in the `Airline Operations\Side Examples\Chapter 10` folder.

After saving the file, make sure the `Crosstable example.xls` file is also at the same location.

Next, open the **Script Editor** window and bring up the **File Wizard** by clicking on the **Table Files...** button.

Browse to the folder in which the example file is stored, select it, and click on **Open**.
Right after that, the file wizard will show the following window:

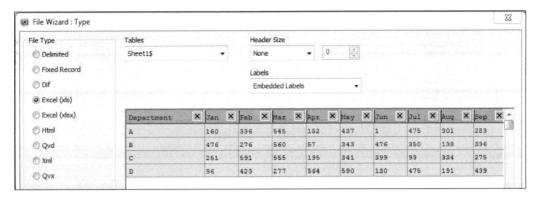

Make sure the appropriate parameters are set, as shown in the preceding screenshot,
so that QlikView interprets the file correctly.

Click on **Next >** twice and the already familiar **File Wizard: Options** dialog window
opens. Locate the **Crosstable...** button at the upper-right corner of the window, shown
in the following screenshot, and click on it.

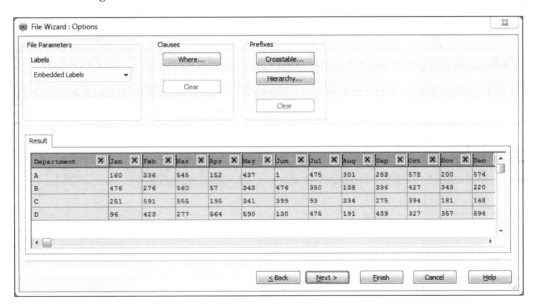

The Crosstable wizard only requires us to set three parameters, as shown below:

- Number of **Qualifier Fields**: Here, we specify the number of columns which precede the table Data Area (where the amounts are). In our case, there is only one Qualifier field: Department.

- **Attribute field**: This parameter is used to assign a name to the field that will hold the new dimension values resulting from the transformation. For this example, we will , set it to Month.

- **Data Field**: This indicates the name of the field that will hold the data values resulting from the transformation. We will name it Sales.

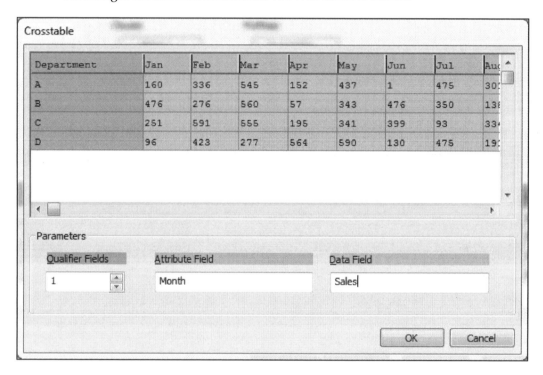

After clicking on **OK**, the **Result** tab, at the lower pane of the **File Wizard** window, will show a preview of the transformed table:

Department	Month	Sales
A	Jan	160
A	Feb	336
A	Mar	545
A	Apr	152
A	May	437
A	Jun	1
A	Jul	475
A	Aug	301
A	Sep	283
A	Oct	578
A	Nov	200
A	Dec	574
B	Jan	476

We can now click on **Finish** and the corresponding Load statement will be generated. The code looks like this:

```
CrossTable(Month, Sales)
LOAD Department,
     Jan,
     Feb,
     Mar,
     Apr,
     May,
     Jun,
     Jul,
     Aug,
     Sep,
     Oct,
     Nov,
     Dec
FROM
[Crosstable example.xls]
(biff, embedded labels, table is Sheet1$);
```

Notice there is a prefix to the `Load` keyword with the names of the new fields. After reloading the script, we will have a table with three fields (`Department`, `Month`, and `Sales`) ready to be used in a QlikView data model.

A solo exercise

We've covered the process of loading a Crosstable into QlikView, and now it's your time to put it into practice. We've prepared a table file for you to load into QlikView.

The filename is `Employment Statistics - CrossTable.qvd` and it is located inside the same `Airline Operations\Side Examples\Chapter 10` folder. It contains Airline Employment Data (number of total employees), which the same we used in the previous chapter, but with a Crosstable format.

The challenge for you consists of:

- Identifying the Qualifier fields
- Identifying the name of the Attribute field
- Generating the corresponding Load statement
- Determining how the transformed table can be loaded into the Airline Operations data model

Good luck!

Expanding a hierarchy

A hierarchy table is a common format to store information in a parent-child structure. The hierarchical nature of the table allows one value to be related to one or more values across the table, as a parent or as a child. In fact, one value can be related to one or more other values as a child and to one or more other different values as a parent.

The advantage of these tables is that they keep the information in a compact format, and QlikView is able to handle them, and expand its relations with a special function: **Hierarchy**.

In technical terms, the original table format is called an `Adjacent Nodes` table, while the resulting table is called an `Expanded Nodes` table.

A hierarchy example

Consider the following table which contains hierarchical information about regions of the world:

Parent	Child
World	Europe
World	North America
Europe	England
England	London
Europe	Italy
Italy	Rome
North America	United States
United States	Washington
United States	New York

The preceding data is the actual format in which the information is stored, but it can also be read as follows, for easier interpretation:

We can see that the shown hierarchy has 4 levels (World – Continent – Country – City). Each of these levels should be stored in a different field in the QlikView data model after expanding the hierarchy.

Working with the Hierarchy Wizard

Again, to demonstrate the concept, we will:

1. Create a new QlikView document and name it Hierarchy example.qvw.

2. Store the QVW file into the Airline Operations\Side Examples\ Chapter 10 folder.

3. Make sure the Hierarchy example.xls file is also at the same location.

4. Open the script editor window and bring up the **File Wizard** dialog with the associated example file.

5. In the first window of the **File Wizard**, make sure the following parameters are set before continuing:

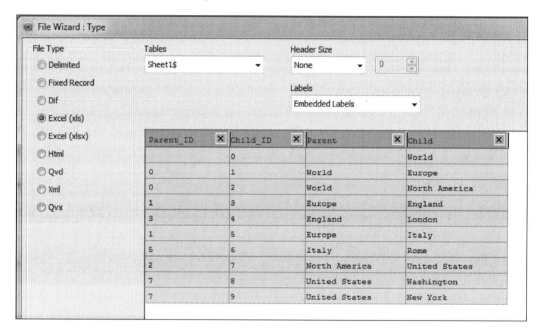

6. Then, click on **Next >** twice to get to the **File Wizard: Options** dialog window. Locate the **Hierarchy...** button at the upper-right corner of the window and click on it.

We will then set the parameters in the next window as follows:

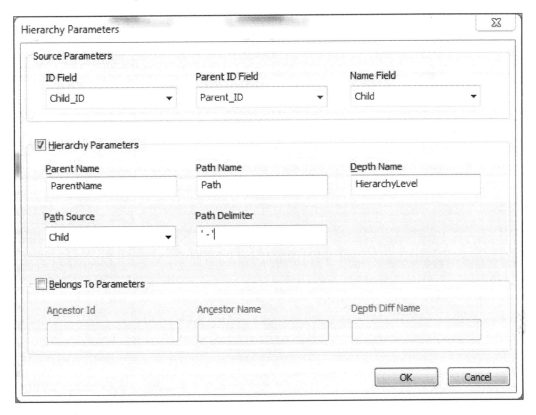

The three parameters at the top are mandatory, while the rest are optional.

 If the source fields have special characters in their field name, such as spaces, the Hierarchy Wizard will not enclose them between brackets in the resulting script, so you might need to add them after the script is generated.

From the preceding screenshot, we can observe the following fields:

- **ID Field**: This is the field that stores the IDs corresponding to the child nodes
- **Parent ID Field**: This is the field that stores the ID of the parent node
- **Name field**: This is the field that stores the name of the child node
- **Parent Name**: This is a string used to name a new field that will be created containing the names of the parent nodes

- **Path Name**: This is a string used to name a new field that will be created containing the list of nodes from the top level to the corresponding node

- **Depth Name**: This is the name to be assigned to a new field that will hold the number of levels for each expanded node

- **Path Source**: This is the field from the source table that contains the value that should be used to populate the hierarchy path

- **Path Delimiter**: This defines the string that should be used to separate the hierarchy values in the path

> If any of the optional parameters are left blank, the new field that uses the missing parameter will not be created when expanding the hierarchy.

Even if none of the optional parameters are going to be used, the **Hierarchy Parameters** checkbox should be marked for the script to be created, otherwise it will not be generated.

> We've also noted that, at the time of writing of this book, a bug in QlikView prevents the Depth field (`HierarchyLevel` in the preceding example) from being populated when using the wizard. Therefore, you may need to manually modify the resulting script in order to create the corresponding field, simply by adding the `Depth` parameter to the `Hierarchy` statement, as shown below.

After finishing setting the hierarchy parameters, click on **OK** to return to the **File Wizard** window, and then click on **Finish** to generate the resulting `Load` statement.

The resulting script for our example will look like this:

```
HIERARCHY(Child_ID, Parent_ID, Child, ParentName, Child, Path, ' - ',
HierarchyLevel)
LOAD Parent_ID,
     Child_ID,
     Parent,
     Child
FROM
[Hierarchy example.xls]
(biff, embedded labels, table is Sheet1$);
```

After reloading the script, we should have a new table in our data model with the following structure:

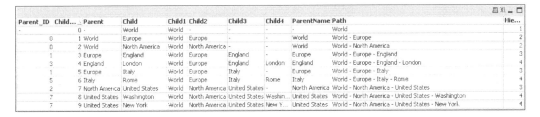

As you can see, the resulting expanded nodes table has one field for each hierarchy level, and one record for each node. Additionally, new fields have been created to show Path and Depth information.

In cases where one node has multiple parents, the expanded nodes table will have several records for these nodes.

Also, it's important to note that the expanded nodes table will exclude any orphan nodes, that is, nodes that have no connection to a top-level node. Only nodes connected to the highest hierarchy level will be kept in the final table.

Once we have a table with this structure, it is easy to use it on the frontend of the QlikView document, for example, within a pivot table or in a hierarchy dimension group.

The created fields can also be used in listboxes to make selections. In fact, let's quickly explore a feature in which we can add a tree-like view to a simple list box.

The tree-view list-box

With the resulting data from the above example, we will create a new list-box object by following these steps:

1. Select **Layout | New Sheet Object | List Box...** from the menu bar.

2. From the **New List Box** window, enter **Tree View** into the **Title** field.

3. Then, using the **Field** dropdown, select the `Path` field.

4. Still from the **General** tab, mark the **Show as TreeView** checkbox and enter a minus sign (-), with a leading and a trailing space, into the **With Separator** field.

5. Click on **OK** to create the new list box.

The new list box will be created. Here we are taking advantage of the hierarchical path created in one of the fields from the previous exercise. The tree-view list box only requires a field with the hierarchical definition for a set of values, and with each hierarchical level separated by a specific character. The separation symbol can be any character. In the preceding example, we used a minus sign along with a leading and a trailing space since that's how each value is separated in the actual data.

The following screenshot shows a side-by-side comparison of a "normal" list box and the tree-view list box. Both use the same field:

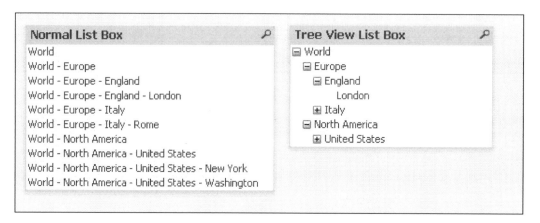

As you can see from the preceding screenshot, a tree-view list box is good at representing hierarchical levels, and provides an easy way to collapse/expand the hierarchy with the plus and minus icons to the left of each parent value.

When clicking a collapsed parent value, all of its children are selected as well.

Generic load

Another table structure we can come across when loading data into QlikView is what we call a generic table.

A generic table is commonly used to store attribute values for different objects. These attributes are not necessarily shared across all objects contained in the table, and that's one of the reasons why a traditional columnar structure is not used for these tables.

The following is an example of a generic table:

Object	Attribute	Value
Ball	Color	Yellow
Ball	Weight	120 g
Ball	Diameter	8 cm
Coin	Color	Gold
Coin	Value	$100
Coin	Diameter	2.5 cm
Hockey Puck	Color	Black
Hockey Puck	Diameter	7.62 cm
Hockey Puck	Thickness	2.5 cm
Hockey Puck	Weight	165 g

As you can see, there are several different attributes (color, diameter, weight, and so on) and only a few of them are shared among all objects. Some attributes, such as thickness, are only used for a single object.

Using the preceding structure, the table is kept from growing too large in terms of columns, regardless of new objects or attributes being added.

Using a traditional structure, the preceding table would have several columns (one for each attribute), and each time a new attribute is added, a new column should be added as well. Additionally, attributes (columns) that are not applicable for certain objects (rows), would have a corresponding null or blank value.

Loading a generic table into QlikView

When loading a generic table, we can use the GENERIC keyword so QlikView treats the table as such and converts its structure in a way that is more appropriate for the associative data model and is easier for user interaction.

Let's load this table into a new QlikView document using the GENERIC keyword:

1. Start by creating a new QlikView document and name it Generic Load.qvw.

2. Store the QVW file into the Airline Operations\Side Examples\ Chapter 10 folder.

3. Make sure the Generic DB.xls file is also at the same location.

4. Open the script editor and bring up the **File Wizard** dialog with the associated example file.

5. In the first window of the **File Wizard**, make sure the following parameters are set before continuing:

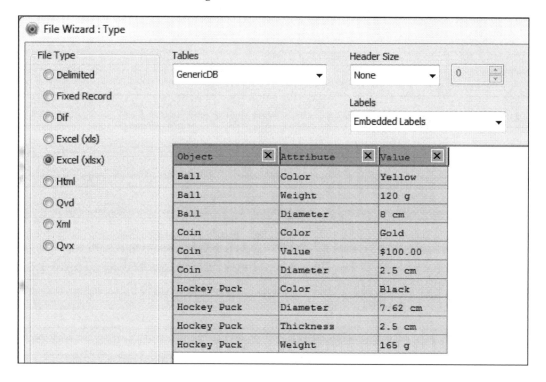

6. Then, click on **Finish** to close the **File Wizard** dialog window and generate the corresponding Load script.

7. Now, right before the LOAD keyword, enter the GENERIC keyword so that the final script looks as follows:

```
GENERIC
LOAD
    Object,
    Attribute,
    Value
FROM
[Generic DB.xlsx]
(ooxml, embedded labels, table is GenericDB);
```

8. Save the document and click on the **Reload** button from the toolbar.

By using the GENERIC keyword, QlikView will transform and process the contents of the generic table so that, in the end, we have all attributes stored in a separate field and associated to the corresponding object. The resulting data model for the preceding example is shown in the following screenshot:

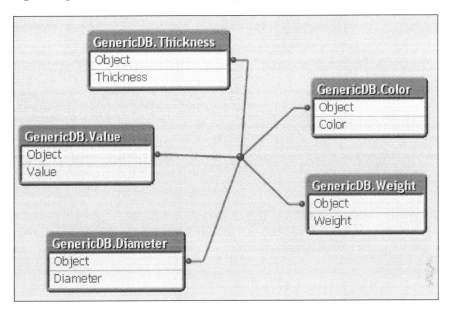

Each of the tables shown in the preceding screenshot will have only the necessary rows, depending on how many objects share the corresponding attribute.

With the new associated tables, we can add different list boxes to our QlikView document to allow the user to select different attributes and objects.

Summary

We have seen four different scenarios in which the source table is not suitable for a QlikView data model, and we have shown the tools QlikView provides to deal with those formats. We have learned how to use the Transformation Wizard to remove garbage from input tables, fill missing cells, and unwrap table files.

We also learned what a Crosstable is, why it's not fit for the QlikView data model, and how to transform it into a traditional table. We saw how to deal with hierarchical tables and identify parent and child nodes.

Finally, we learned what a generic table is and how to take advantage of QlikView's ability to transform its structure.

In *Chapter 13, Advanced Data Transformation*, we will look at more advanced techniques for transforming source data for use in different data model designs.

11
Advanced Expressions

The current frontend of our `Airline Operations` document is made up of charts that use straightforward aggregations, such as a `Sum` of values in a field. Dashboarding, however, often requires more complex calculations, depending on the nature of the data we are working with and the way some metrics should be calculated. Also, we often need to add certain context to the numbers; for instance, we might need to present the data in terms of relative growth (comparing current year versus last year), or create visualizations in a way that is not exactly "natural", in which case we could use calculated or synthetic dimensions.

In this chapter, we will dive into some of the complexities you can come across when developing a QlikView application. In summary, we will learn:

- To expand the use of variables
- To use conditional functions and `If` expressions
- To handle advanced aggregations

So let's get to it.

Using variables

Simply put, variables in QlikView are used to store data, either static or dynamic, and they can contain text, numbers, or any other data type. They are stored as a separate entity and are given a name to be able to reference them from any object in the whole document.

Even when one variable can store a single data value, their use can be extended to a much broader scope once we understand its inner workings.

At a general level, we can say that variables in QlikView are used in two different ways:

- To store a value or string either static or based on a formula. This type of variable can also be used to receive and interpret input from the user.

- To store an expression definition that can be used in charts. This is an approach we explored in *Chapter 7, Building Dashboards*.

The main difference between the previously mentioned options is that one calculates the output before sending it to the sheet object that makes use of the variable, whereas the other stores only the definition of the expression and the object using it is in charge of evaluating it and getting a result.

In this section, we will cover the use of variables up to an advanced level, but let's first get the basics in order and move on from there.

Creating a variable

We've already worked through the process of creating a variable in a previous chapter, and you've seen that it is fairly simple. However, let's make a quick review of the steps involved in using our `Airline Operations` document. Open the corresponding QVW file and create a new sheet so that we don't mess up the objects already created. Name this new sheet `Variables`.

After practicing with some examples in a separate sheet, we will apply the learned concepts by extending our **Dashboard** and **Analysis** sheets.

Now, go to the **Variable Overview** window by using the keyboard shortcut *Ctrl + Alt + V* or by clicking on the **Settings** menu and selecting the **Variable Overview...** option, as shown in the following screenshot:

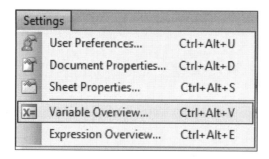

From this window, we are able to see the variables that have been previously defined. Click on the **Add** button and the **New Variable** dialog will appear, where we will type the name we want to assign to our new variable.

The default name is `Variable1`. Change it to `vTop` and click on **OK**. The variable will be created and we will now be able to assign a value to it. To do that, highlight the new variable by clicking on its name and, in the **Definition** pane on the lower part of the window, type the number `5`. Then, in the **Comment** field, add the following comment to describe what the variable is for:

```
Variable used to dynamically change the number of displayed values in
a Top N Chart.
```

It's important to first highlight the variable by clicking on its name before entering the variable's definition, otherwise the definition we enter will not be correctly applied.

Using variables in charts

Our new variable will, for now, contain a simple and static value. We will use that value to manipulate a chart. Specifically, this value will represent the number of carriers that should be shown in a bar chart, based on their number of flights. Only the top five carriers shall be shown.

Create a new bar chart with **Carrier Name** as dimension and `Sum([# Departures Performed])` as the expression. From the **Sort** dialog window, make sure the **Carrier Name** values are sorted by **Y-Value** in descending order.

Our new chart should so far look like the following screenshot:

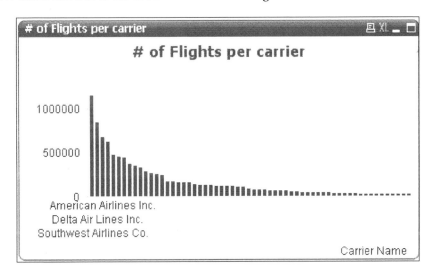

As you can see, the chart is a little clogged with bars in the limited space we have available. We need to limit the number of bars shown so that only the first *N* Carriers are visible. *N* is the number that our **vTop** variable holds.

Go to the **Chart Properties** window and activate the **Dimension Limits** tab. Enable the **Restrict which values are displayed using the first expression** checkbox. The configuration for the limit we will set is:

- The **Show only** radio button must be selected
- From the drop-down list, the **Largest** value will be selected
- On the **Values** field, we will enter our variable using the following syntax:
  $(vTop)
- The **Show Others** checkbox should be disabled

The previous configuration is shown in the following screenshot:

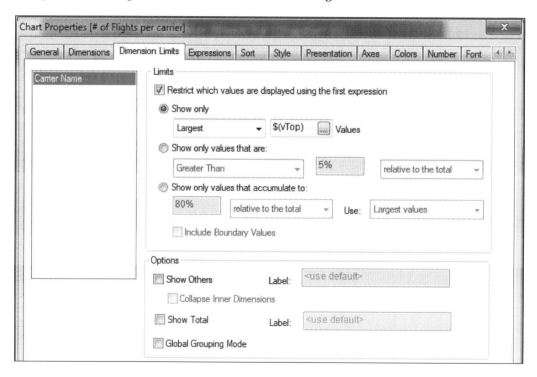

The syntax we used to enter the variable is called **Dollar Sign Expansion**. In this particular case, the variable could have been entered without the dollar sign, but there are some circumstances in which it is a must, so it's a good practice to always include it. We will talk about this syntax later in the chapter.

After finishing setting the previous configuration, click on **OK** and the chart will be more readable and will look like the following screenshot:

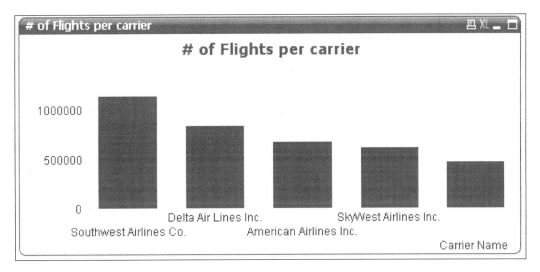

Change the chart's **Orientation** to **Horizontal** from the **Style** tab of the properties window so that it's even more readable.

Interactively changing a variable's value

The reason for using a variable to limit the number of dimension values shown in the chart is to enable the user to dynamically change it as pleased. There are two main layout objects through which a variable's value can be changed:

- The Input Box object
- The Slider object

We will describe the two of them and their uses.

Using the Input Box object

The Input Box is basically an Excel-like cell on which the user enters values. An Input Box can hold any number of variables, each one with its own associated cell.

To describe how it is used, click on an empty space of the sheet workspace and, from the **New Sheet Object** section, select **Input Box...**.

The **New Input Box** dialog window will appear and the **General** tab will initially be active. From the **Title** field, we can assign a display text to be placed on the object's caption bar. Type `Enter number of top values` into this field.

In the **Available Variables** list to the left, we will see all created variables. There is also a button to create a **New Variable**, which is very convenient if we previously forgot to add the variable we want to use.

We are going to add the **vTop** variable to the **Displayed Variables** list on the right. Do this by highlighting the variable's name and clicking on the **Add >** button. Once the variable is in the **Displayed Variables** list, highlight it and the **Label** field, located below, will be enabled. On this field, replace the name of the variable with `Top Values`.

There are other options that can be set in the rest of the tabs, but we can click on **OK** at this point and the object will be created with just what we need.

> Most of the other tabs hold settings that are similar to those used in other sheet objects, such as charts. For instance, we also have the **Presentation** tab or the **Layout** tab. We invite you to explore those tabs and change their settings based on what you've learned from previous chapters.

When the object is created, the input cell will have the number 5, which is the value we previously defined for our variable. If we click on the value cell, we will enter into edit mode and be able to change the variable's value; upon doing so, the chart will be instantly updated to reflect the change.

Change the variable's value to `10` using the **Input Box** object and see the effect on the chart.

> Resizing the **Input Box** object is achieved using the method previously described for resizing a multi box, which consists of simply resizing the label cell and the value cell individually.

Using the Slider object

Similar to the Input Box object, the Slider object is used to interactively change a variable's value from the frontend. The main difference is the way in which the user interacts with the object. The Slider object is a little more visual.

To create a **Slider** object, right-click on an empty space of the sheet workspace and, from the **New Sheet Object** section, select **Slider/Calendar Object....**

The **New Slider/Calendar Object** dialog window will appear and the **General** tab will be active. For a **Slider/Calendar** object, the **Input Style** option can be set to either **Slider** or **Calendar**. The **Slider** object is the one we will be using in this example, since the **Calendar** object is used to work with date values.

 It's important to note that this object can be used not only to interact with variables, but also to make field selections.

From the **Data** section, make sure to activate the **Variable(s)** radio button and select the **vTop** variable from the drop-down list. The **Mode** and **Value Mode** settings will be left with the default options.

We must set min and max values to delimit the slider's range of possible values. Set the **Min Value** option to 5 and the **Max Value** option to 30.

To specify that only integers should be used in the slider, enable the **Static Step** checkbox and set its value to 1.

Click on **OK** and the slider will be created in horizontal form. It can be changed to vertical, if desired, from the **Presentation** tab of the slider's properties.

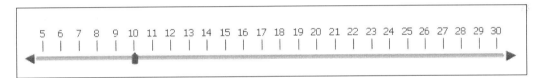

The initial value the slider will hold is the one we previously set the vTop variable to. To modify the value, click on the thumb tack and drag it to its desired value. The chart will automatically reflect any change made to the variable and, at the same time, the value stored in the **Input Box** object we previously created will be kept in sync with the **Slider** object, since both objects are using the same variable.

Using variables based on expressions

In the previous section, we used a variable to store a static value. That is to say, the value was not based on a calculation and therefore didn't respond to user field selections.

We will now create a variable with a dynamic value, one that responds to the document state and calculates an output value based on user selections. To keep this example as simple as possible, we will create a value that will hold and return the total number of FTEs based, on current selections, and use that value in a chart expression.

Go to the **Variable Overview...** window (*Ctrl + Alt + V*) and click on the **Add** button. From the **New Variable** window, type `vTotalFTEs` to name the new variable and click on **OK**.

Next, highlight the variable and type the following expression from the **Definition** pane:

```
=Sum([# Equivalent FTEs])
```

 Don't forget the equal to sign. This tells QlikView to calculate the variable across all dimensions regardless of the context in which the variable is used.

Click on **OK** to close the **Variable Overview...** window.

We will now proceed to create a new chart in the form of a straight table with **Carrier Name** as the only dimension and having the following expression:

```
Sum([# Equivalent FTEs]) / $(vTotalFTEs)
```

From the **Number** tab of the **Chart Properties** window, assign a two-decimal format and specify it to be shown as percentage.

These settings will result in a table with a list of carriers and the percentage of FTEs each of them contributes to the total. Notice we have included our `vTotalFTEs` variable as the divisor with the Dollar Sign Expansion syntax.

Since the variable holds a single value, all rows in the straight table will be divided by the same number, which represents the total number of FTEs employed by all reporting airlines; the numerator value, which is the number of corresponding FTEs, will be different for each carrier.

FTE % to Total	
Carrier Name	**FTE % to Total**
	100.00%
Federal Express Corporation	22.82%
American Airlines Inc.	12.81%
Delta Air Lines Inc.	12.75%
United Air Lines Inc.	8.45%
Southwest Airlines Co.	6.79%
Continental Air Lines Inc.	6.52%
US Airways Inc.	5.78%
JetBlue Airways	2.16%

Since the variable's value is an active calculation, the output value will respond to all user selections, and the chart will be updated to reflect the changes as well.

> There are other ways for achieving the above calculation, one of which is by using the TOTAL qualifier. We will describe how to use it in a later section.
>
> Another way is enabling the **Relative** checkbox in the **Expressions** tab.

Using variables to store expressions

So far, we've discussed variables that store a single static value and variables whose output value is based on a calculation. Now, it's time to take variables to a new level and expand their usability.

You may remember from *Chapter 7, Building Dashboards*, how we used variables to store expression definitions and then used them in charts. To expand on the topic, we will quickly review the theory and proceed to discuss the advantages of these types of variables and additional use cases.

Go to the **Variable Overview...** window and add a new variable, with the name of eFTEs. The contents of this variable will be:

```
Sum([# Equivalent FTEs])
```

Add the following comment to the variable:

```
Total Equivalent FTEs.
```

Notice the variable definition is almost the same as that of the vTotalFTEs variable we previously created. The difference, the equals sign at the beginning, though small, is in fact huge in terms of impact.

> When creating variables intended to store expression definitions, the equals sign must be omitted so that the calculation is performed on the chart side and not as the variable output.

After creating the variable, head on to create a new chart in the form of a straight table with **Carrier Name** as dimension and having the following expression:

```
$(eFTEs)
```

The new straight table will be created with the total number of FTEs for each carrier, just as if we had used a direct expression instead of a variable.

As discussed previously, the main advantage of using variables for handling chart expressions is that, when using the same expression across several sheet objects, it's easier to administer when a new change needs to be made to the expression. For instance, suppose the number of FTEs should now be shown in thousands; in this case, you just add the divisor to the variable definition and all charts are automatically updated to reflect the change.

Sometimes, one single chart requires the use of the same expression to define different properties; for example, to add a text in the chart with the expression result, or to define thresholds with different colors for each. The use of a variable to store the expression will ensure consistency across all these configuration settings.

Variable naming convention

We have now seen the different ways in which a variable can be used to interact with a QlikView document and to handle different chart's calculations. Before continuing let's review a quick guideline on variable naming convention.

It's important, when working with variables, to assign names based on certain "rules" to help better understand what each variable's purpose is, how it should be used, and to better administer them when the list of variables in a QlikView document grows.

The one basic rule in naming consistency is the use of predefined prefixes. For instance, you previously saw how we named the first two variables (vTop and vTotalFTEs) with the v prefix. A v prefix was used in naming those variables because the output is a single value, as opposed to the third variable we created (eFTEs) where we use the prefix e as the variable value is an expression.

Being consistent to this convention will ensure that even when the list of variables is long, any particular variable can be found on the list whether you are looking for an expression or a value-based variable.

The Dollar Sign Expansion syntax

We have been using a particular syntax to reference variables; it's called **Dollar Sign Expansion (DSE)**. Let's quickly describe how and why we should use this syntax.

You can see the role of the Dollar Sign Expansion syntax as that of simply evaluating a variable's contents, that is, calculate (expand) the result of the variable and then return the output value.

We said earlier that, when the variable's output value is simply a plain number (such as the **vTop** or **vTotalFlights** variables) the Dollar Sign Expansion is not actually required since there is actually nothing to "expand". However, it's good practice to always use DSE even when the variable to be expanded does not require it, because of the following two reasons:

- At any moment you might decide to change the variable's definition and modify it to one that does actually require DSE syntax

- So that your objects maintain consistency with respect to the use of variables

There are, however, cases in which the DSE is ineffective on its own. When the variable's output value is a text string, the result of the Dollar Sign Expansion will be a null or missing value because a text value cannot be interpreted numerically, so we need to either enclose the Dollar Sign Expansion into straight single quotes or simply not use DSE. An example would be:

- Variable name:

  ```
  vUsername
  ```

- Variable definition:

  ```
  =OSUser()
  ```

- Variable output (as literal value):

  ```
  Domain\Username
  ```

- When called from a sheet object (a text object, for instance) we should use any one of the following two expressions:

  ```
  ='User Name: $(vUsername)'
  ='User Name: '& vUsername
  ```

As mentioned before, using the DSE syntax and enclosing it in single quotes is the recommended approach in the previous example.

Dollar Sign Expansion with parameters

It is also possible to create variables with parameters and then call them via a DSE specifying the parameter's value, thus allowing extended flexibility and reusability of variables.

The way we create a variable with parameters is as follows:

1. Open the **Variable Overview...** window (*Ctrl + Alt + V*) and create a new variable. Name it `eDeparturesPerformed_VarUnit`.

2. The variable definition will be:

   ```
   Sum([# Departures Performed]) / $1
   ```

3. In the **Comment** field, enter `Variable to calculate the number of departures performed with variable divisor.`

4. Close the **Variable Overview...** window by clicking on **OK**.

We already have a similar variable, called `eDeparturesPerformed`, which is used to store an expression that calculates the number of flights performed in thousands. The difference this time is that we are inserting a parameter as the divisor. This parameter is represented by `$1`, and will allow us to use the same variable to obtain the corresponding expression and calculate the number of flights performed in millions (by defining the parameter as `1000000`), thousands (when the parameter is `1000`), units, and so on.

To use the above variable in an expression, start by creating a new chart in the form of a straight table with **Carrier Group** as the dimension and the following three expressions:

1. The first expression, labeled `# of Flights`, will be:

    `$(eDeparturesPerformed_VarUnit(1))`

2. The second expression, labeled `# of Flights (thousands)`, will be:

    `$(eDeparturesPerformed_VarUnit(1000))`

3. The third expression, labeled `# of Flights (millions)`, will be:

    `$(eDeparturesPerformed_VarUnit(1000000))`

The only difference in the previously mentioned expressions, apart from the label, are the parameter values inserted into the variable.

After properly formatting the expression values and the chart's presentation, we will have the following chart:

# of Flights			
Carrier Group	△ # of Flights	# of Flights (thousands)	# of Flights (millions)
	10,750,155	10,750.2	10.75
Commuter Carriers (air t...	733,959	734.0	0.73
Foreign Carriers	595,573	595.6	0.60
Large Regional Carriers...	41,014	41.0	0.04
Major Carriers (carriers...	6,129,188	6,129.2	6.13
Medium Regional Carrier...	25,154	25.2	0.03
National Carriers (carrier...	2,663,803	2,663.8	2.66
Small Certificated Carrie...	561,464	561.5	0.56

A variable can have any number of parameters defined, all specified with a dollar sign and a number that indicates the parameter's number: $1, $2, $3, and so on.

When expanding the variable, the parameters are specified by enclosing them in parentheses as a comma-separated list. For example, a variable with three parameters would be expanded as follows:

```
$(VariableName(30, 20, 50))
```

Where the values 30, 20, and 50 are inserted into the corresponding parameter's position in the variable definition.

Parameters in a variable can either be numbers or text; we can also arrange a parameter to receive a field name to be used in the calculation, or even receive values read from fields.

Double Dollar Sign Expansion

We've already discussed how storing expressions in variables can be a good idea for re-using expressions, easily manage changes in them, as well as for data consistency across sheet objects. We will push this idea a bit further by using those expression variables to allow the user to switch among different metrics at his/her convenience.

1. First, make sure the following expression variables are already in the `Airline Operations` document. If the variables are not yet defined, refer to *Chapter 7, Building Dashboards*, to find their definitions and apply them:

    ◦ eDeparturesPerformed

    ◦ eEnplanedPassengers

    ◦ eAirTime

2. Now, we will add a new island table to the data model via a `Load Inline` statement. Open the **Edit Script** window and add a new tab at the end of the script; name it `Metrics`. In this new tab, we will add the new table using the **Inline Data Wizard** dialog (**Insert | Load Statement | Load Inline**):

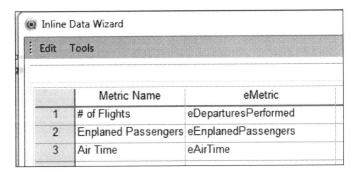

The corresponding script that will be generated will be:

```
LOAD * INLINE [
    Metric Name, eMetric
    # of Flights, eDeparturesPerformed
    Enplaned Passengers, eEnplanedPassengers
    Air Time, eAirTime
];
```

The first column of the previous table holds the metric names, which the user will be able to select from a listbox. The second column holds the corresponding expression variable names, used to calculate any of the selected metric.

1. Reload the script to add the new table to our data model.

2. Then, we will create a new listbox based on the **Metric Name** field and place it in the **Variables** sheet.

3. Once the listbox is created, select one of its values and enter the listbox properties window to enable the **Always One Selected Value** setting from the **General** tab. This way, we ensure that we will have something to calculate at all times.

> The **Always One Selected Value** setting can only be applied when there is one selected value in the listbox at the time the properties window is opened. Otherwise, it will be grayed out.
>
> Sometimes, this setting can be removed and might need to be reapplied if the document is reloaded with no data in the corresponding field (for example, in the case of a script error).

4. We are now going to create a new chart, whose expression will be dynamically changing based on the **Metric Name** selection. The settings of the new chart are as follows:

   ○ Select the **Pie Chart** option in the **Chart Type** section

   ○ Enter the following expression into the **Window Title** field:

   ```
   =[Metric Name] &' by Carrier Group'
   ```

   ○ Disable the **Show Title in Chart** checkbox

   ○ Set the dimension as **Carrier Group**

   ○ Set the following as the expression:

   ```
   $($(=eMetric))
   ```

   ○ From the **Presentation** window, enable the **Limit Legend** checkmark and set it to 15

Once the chart is created, we will be able to switch its active expression by selecting the desired metric from the **Metric Name** listbox.

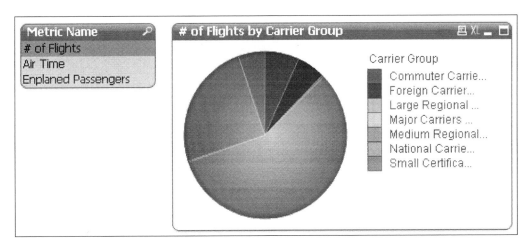

The metric selection based on a listbox works the same as having grouped expressions in the chart to be able to switch them with a cycle button (as described in *Chapter 3, Seeing is Believing*). However, the listbox selection makes it possible to change the metric on several charts at the same time, something that is not possible with the cyclic expression method.

Notice how we have also set a dynamic chart title that changes according to the metric selection.

We are performing two expansions before actually arriving at the calculation we need. The first, inner-most, Dollar Sign Expansion pulls the value from the island table corresponding to the user selection and indicates which variable the second, outer, Dollar Sign Expansion is going to evaluate.

Now that we have reviewed the different ways in which we can use variables in QlikView objects, let's complement the acquired knowledge by exploring other uses of advanced expressions.

Be sure to save the changes we've made to the
Airline Operations document before continuing.

Using the TOTAL qualifier

The TOTAL qualifier is added to aggregation functions to disregard chart dimensions and make the calculation over the entire record set as defined by the current selection state.

In a previous section, we calculated the percentage of FTEs each carrier performs relative to the total number of FTEs and we used a variable (**vTotalFTEs**) to store the divisor value. Instead of using a variable, the same calculation can be made using the following expression:

```
Sum([# Equivalent FTEs]) / Sum(TOTAL [# Equivalent FTEs])
```

When the preceding expression is used in a straight table with **Carrier Name** as the dimension, the numerator will calculate the value corresponding to each carrier, which will be different on each row of the table. The divisor will calculate the total number of flights made by all carriers, which will be the same for all rows of the table, therefore disregarding the dimension value.

Additional modifiers can be used along with the TOTAL qualifier to disregard only some of the dimensions in a chart, instead of all of them; that is, in cases where there is more than one dimension in a chart.

For instance, if the straight table described earlier, besides the **Carrier Name** dimension, also has the **Year** and **Month** dimensions, we can add any of those dimensions to a list of fields enclosed in angular brackets, and separated by a comma, to specify which of them should the TOTAL qualifier disregard.

Let's take the already created pivot table in the **Reports** tab of our Airline Operations document and add three new expressions to it to better illustrate how the TOTAL qualifier works. The three expressions we'll add, along with their labels, are:

- Participation to the whole:

  ```
  Sum([# Departures Performed]) / Sum(TOTAL [# Departures
  Performed])
  ```

  This expression will return the percentage of flights for a particular carrier, month, and year relative to the total flights of all carriers, and for all years and months available in the current selection state.

- Percentage versus the carrier's whole:

```
Sum([# Departures Performed]) / Sum(TOTAL <[Carrier Group],
Airline> [# Departures Performed])
```

This one will return the percentage of flights for a particular carrier, month, and year relative to the total flights performed by that carrier in all years and months available in the current selection state.

- Percentage versus the carrier's whole per year:

```
Sum([# Departures Performed]) / Sum(TOTAL <[Carrier Group],
Airline, Year> [# Departures Performed])
```

This will return the percentage of flights for a particular carrier, month, and year relative to the total flights performed by that carrier in that year, but for all months available in the current selection state that correspond to that same year.

The result is shown in the following screenshot:

Carrier Group	Airline	Enplaned passengers (millions)	Departures Performed (thousands)	Participation to the whole	% vs the Carrier's whole	% vs the Carrier's whole per year	Enplaned passengers (millions)	Departures Performed (thousands)
						Jan		Feb
Commuter Carriers (air...		0.911	59.89	0.2%	2.7%	8.0%	0.916	57.0
Foreign Carriers		5.413	47.61	0.1%	2.7%	8.5%	4.503	42.6
	Aerodynamics Inc.: AJQ	0.001	0.03	0.0%	2.5%	5.3%	0.001	0.0
	Aloha Air Cargo: KH	0.000	0.67	0.0%	2.8%	8.2%	0.000	0.6
	Asia Pacific: PFQ	-	-	-	-	-	-	-
	Avjet Corporation: 0WQ	-	-	-	-	-	-	-
	Capital Cargo International: ...	0.000	0.66	0.0%	2.2%	6.4%	0.000	0.6
	Casino Express: XP	0.014	0.14	0.0%	1.7%	8.1%	0.014	0.1
	Colgan Air: 9L	0.180	9.06	0.0%	8.3%	8.3%	0.172	8.3
	Compass Airlines: CP	0.252	4.91	0.0%	8.9%	8.9%	0.233	4.3
Large Regional Carriers (carriers with annual revenue of $20 million to $100 million)	Florida West Airlines Inc.: P...	-	-	-	-	-	-	-
	Gulf And Caribbean Cargo: ...	0.000	0.21	0.0%	5.3%	5.3%	0.000	0.2
	Lynden Air Cargo Airlines: L2	0.000	0.10	0.0%	2.0%	6.3%	0.000	0.1
	Lynx Aviation d/b/a Frontie...	0.064	2.01	0.0%	5.1%	7.9%	0.068	1.9
	National Air Cargo Group, 1...	-	-	-	-	-	-	-
	Northern Air Cargo Inc.: NC	0.000	0.45	0.0%	2.9%	9.1%	0.000	0.3
	Pace Airlines: PCQ	0.012	0.25	0.0%	15.4%	15.4%	0.010	0.2
	Ryan International Airlines:...	0.015	0.17	0.0%	16.1%	16.1%	0.012	0.1
	Tatonduk Outfitters Limited.	0.000	0.49	0.0%	2.3%	7.2%	0.000	0.4
	Tradewinds Airlines: WI	0.000	0.14	0.0%	8.2%	16.1%	0.000	0.1
	USA Jet Airlines Inc.: U7	-	-	-	-	-	-	-
	Vision Airlines: 0JQ	-	-	-	-	-	-	-
	Total	**0.538**	**19.29**	**0.1%**	**5.6%**	**8.2%**	**0.511**	**17.7**

The Aggr function

The output of the Aggr function can be likened to the list of values a straight table would display when evaluating an expression over a certain dimension. For instance, the following straight table has the **Flight Type** field as the dimension and Sum([# Departures Performed]) as the expression.

# of Flights	# of Flights
Flight Type	
	32,296,313
Domestic, US Carriers Only	27,889,508
International, US Carriers Only	2,663,621
International, Foreign Carriers	1,662,792
Domestic, Foreign Carriers	80,392

Essentially, the Aggr function creates a virtual straight table, similar to the earlier one, so that we can further process the list of values that would appear in the expression column, without even creating the actual object. The result of the Aggr function can be used to:

- Create a calculated dimension and perform a nested aggregation
- Perform additional aggregations based on the resulting set of values

Let's see examples for both of these.

Using Aggr for nested aggregation

Since HighCloud Airlines' users are interested in discovering key players in the industry from different perspectives, they now require a visualization object that clearly identifies carrier coverage of interstate routes.

To know how many interstate routes each carrier covers, we would simply create a chart similar to the following screenshot:

Interstate Routes by Carrier	Interstate Routes
Carrier Name	
	2,655
Delta Air Lines Inc.	1,145
Miami Air International	864
Southwest Airlines Co.	821
Federal Express Corporation	708
ExpressJet Airlines Inc.	707
USA Jet Airlines Inc.	688
American Airlines Inc.	637
SkyWest Airlines Inc.	609
Atlantic Southeast Airlines	591

Taking this a step further, we can ask a different, but in a way similar, question: If we were to classify carriers by the number of interstate routes they serve, how many carriers would fall under each category?

We could display a straight table with the number of **Interstate Routes** as the dimension and the number of carriers that fall under each "category" as the expression. The problem is that we don't have a "number of interstate routes" field in our data model, nor can we add it as a calculated field in the script because the calculation varies with each user selection; having a pre-aggregated field is simply not the answer.

What we can do is perform a nested aggregation that dynamically constructs the chart's dimension. To do that, follow these steps:

1. Create a new sheet to allocate the examples in this section; name it `Advanced Expressions`.

2. Then, click on the **New Chart** button from the design toolbar.

3. From the initial dialog window, select **Straight Table** in the **Chart Type** section and set the **Title** field to `Carrier Classification by # of Interstate Routes`.

4. Click on **Next** and, from the **Dimensions** dialog window, click on the **Add Calculated Dimension...**button.

5. The **Edit Expression** window will pop up and there we will enter the dimension's definition, based on the `Aggr` function. Type the following expression and click OK:

    `Aggr(Count(DISTINCT [From - To State Code]), [Carrier Name])`

    This expression will result in a list of values corresponding to the different number of interstate routes each carrier serves, which is basically the expression column in the straight table shown in the previous screenshot. That list will now be our chart's dimension.

6. From the **Dimensions** window, highlight the calculated dimension we just created from the **Used Dimensions** list and, in the **Label** field below, type `Interstate Routes`.

7. Then, click on **Next** to move on to the **Expressions** dialog window. On the **Edit Expression** window, enter the following and click on **OK**:

    `Count(DISTINCT [Carrier Name])`

    This expression will count all different carriers so that the final chart shows the number of carriers each interstate-routes classification has.

8. From the **Expressions** dialog window, assign the `# of Carriers` label to our expression.

9. Click on **Finish** and we will be left with the following chart:

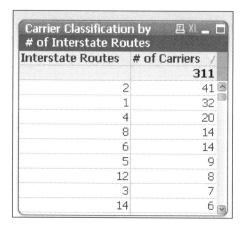

Interstate Routes	# of Carriers
	311
2	41
1	32
4	20
8	14
6	14
5	9
12	8
3	7
14	6

According to the table we see in the earlier screenshot, there are **41** carriers that fall into the two-route category. **32** more serve a single interstate route, **20** other serve **4** interstate routes, and so on.

To design such a table, as you just saw, it's not necessary to create any pre-aggregations in the source tables, nor is it required to have an "**Interstate Routes**" field per se. The chart, along with its calculated dimension, is completely self-contained and does not require other objects to function.

 In an upcoming section, we'll extend on the nested aggregation topic to group dimension values with the use of ranges.

A word on calculated dimensions

As useful as they are, calculated dimensions (such as the one we created earlier) are not performance-friendly. Besides delaying calculation time, they can sometimes prevent a chart's state from being cached to RAM, hence stopping QlikView's caching algorithm from coming into play.

As calculated dimensions are sometimes necessary for advanced aggregations, it is advisable to use this feature only when there is no other way of accomplishing certain visualizations. Whenever a calculated dimension can be created as a new field from the script, it is advisable to do so in order to use it in a more natural way in chart objects.

Aggregations over the Aggr output

It's also possible to perform additional aggregations over the result set that the Aggr function outputs. Let's look at the following example:

To build upon the insight gained from the previous example, suppose we want to use a text object to present the maximum, minimum, and average number of interstate routes served by all carriers; our starting point would, again, be the following chart:

Interstate Routes by Carrier	
Carrier Name	Interstate Routes
	2,655
Delta Air Lines Inc.	1,145
Miami Air International	864
Southwest Airlines Co.	821
Federal Express Corporation	708
ExpressJet Airlines Inc.	707
USA Jet Airlines Inc.	688
American Airlines Inc.	637
SkyWest Airlines Inc.	609
Atlantic Southeast Airlines	591

Since the chart is sorted by number of interstate routes in descending order, we can easily see that the maximum value, regarding number of interstate routes per carrier, belongs to **Delta Air Lines Inc.** and is **1,145**. To get the minimum value, we would sort the table in ascending order. To get the average value, however, it gets kind of tricky. Let's use the Aggr function to display all three values at once. Follow this procedure:

1. Click on the **Create Text Object** button in the design toolbar.

2. The **New Text Object** window will appear, with the **General** tab initially active. The text we want displayed by the object is entered into the **Text** field.

 If we want to define the display text based on an expression, the **Text** definition must begin with an equal to sign.

On the **Text** field, type the following expression:

```
=Max(Aggr(Count(DISTINCT [From - To State Code]), [Carrier Name]))
```

Notice that the Aggr function part in the earlier expression is the same as that which we used in the previous example to create the chart's dimension. We are now adding the Max aggregation function to obtain the largest number from the resulting list of values.

3. Click on **OK** to close the **New Text Object** dialog window. The text
   object should display **1145**.

We now have one of the three values we are interested in. To get the other two
values we will use essentially the same expression, only changing the Max function
with the Min and Avg functions to get the minimum and average values, respectively.

1. Right-click on the text object we just created and select **Properties**....

2. We will modify the **Text** definition to add the rest of the values. Replace the
   previous expression with the one that follows:

```
='Max Value: ' & Max(Aggr(Count(DISTINCT [From - To State Code]),
[Carrier Name])) & Chr(10) &
'Min Value: ' & Min(Aggr(Count(DISTINCT [From - To State Code]),
[Carrier Name])) & Chr(10) &
'Avg Value: ' & Avg(Aggr(Count(DISTINCT [From -
To State Code]), [Carrier Name]))
```

As you can see from this expression, it gets quite lengthy and the Count
function is used three times with the same parameters. In this case, it would
be a good idea to apply the expression-in-variable concept described earlier
in this chapter. Once a new eRoutes variable is created, the preceding
expression could be changed to the following:

```
='Max Value: ' & Max(Aggr($(eRoutes), [Carrier Name])) & Chr(10) &
  'Min Value: ' & Min(Aggr($(eRoutes), [Carrier Name])) & Chr(10)
  &
  'Avg Value: ' & Avg(Aggr($(eRoutes), [Carrier Name]))
```

3. Click on **OK** to apply the changes and the text object should display
   the following:

Max Value: 1145
Min Value: 0
Avg Value: 77.813505

A word on using the Distinct qualifier

In some of our previous expressions, we have used the Distinct qualifier in our Count aggregation function. The Distinct qualifier is used in this case to avoid duplicate counts. However, the use of this qualifier can make the calculation perform poorly as it causes the operation to be single-threaded.

In some cases, it is advisable to avoid using the Count function and the Distinct qualifier by creating a counter field in the script (a field with the value of 1) and then using a more direct aggregation such as Sum(RouteCounter) in the final chart's expression.

Getting the Average Load Factor per Route per Airline

HighCloud Airlines have a new requirement in which the Aggr function will prove useful. They want to know the average load factor percentage per airline, but over each route. In this case, a direct aggregation function like the Avg function will not give the result we need because of the additional "dimension" required in the calculation. To illustrate, take the following chart:

Average Load Factor per Route per Airline		
Carrier Name	From - To Airport ID	Load Factor %
		78.6%
40-Mile Air	11245 - 15236	10.3%
40-Mile Air	15236 - 11630	22.7%
40-Mile Air	11036 - 15236	0.8%
40-Mile Air	11630 - 12141	28.6%
40-Mile Air	12141 - 15236	25.1%
40-Mile Air	15236 - 11036	1.4%
40-Mile Air	15236 - 11245	11.7%
40-Mile Air	11630 - 15236	30.0%
Abaco Air, Ltd.	13289 - 13303	41.7%
Abaco Air, Ltd.	15147 - 13303	66.7%

In this chart, we can see the different routes each carrier serves along with the corresponding load factor. We should now take the individual load factor per route and perform an average operation over the list of values for each airline to obtain the value we are looking for.

We can't simply remove the **Route** dimension because even though we will get a grouped **Load Factor** % value for each airline, it will not be what we are looking for as the **Average Load Factor per Route per Airline** value is not the same as the **Load Factor per Airline** value. Instead, we will use the Aggr function to solve the requirement by entering the chart expression as follows:

```
Avg(Aggr($(eLoadFactor), Airline, [From - To Airport ID]))
```

Notice how we've included both dimensions in the Aggr function. Additionally, this function will also account for routes with zero or missing load factors, which are by default not shown in the straight table.

We will keep a second expression with the **Load Factor per Airline** value to show the difference in both calculations. The second expression column will have the following definition:

```
$(eLoadFactor)
```

Now, we can remove the **Route** dimension from our chart and we will get the following:

Average Load Factor per Route per Airline		
Carrier Name	Average Load Factor per Route	Airline's Global Load Factor
	59.9%	78.6%
40-Mile Air	14.5%	15.2%
Abaco Air, Ltd.	57.4%	50.2%
ABC Aerolineas SA de CV dba...	89.0%	91.5%
ACM AIR CHARTER GmbH	15.9%	16.0%
Acropolis Aviation Ltd.	27.2%	28.1%
Aer Lingus Plc	76.0%	77.0%
Aeroenlaces Nacionales, S.A....	60.9%	64.6%
Aeroflot Russian Airlines	79.1%	80.1%
Aerolineas Argentinas	80.9%	80.9%
Aerolineas Galapagos S A Aer...	68.3%	73.2%

With the use of the Aggr function, a QlikView document can be empowered enormously and we are able to accomplish things that are almost impossible with other tools, especially because all calculations are being performed on the fly.

 Be sure to save the changes we've made to the Airline Operations document before continuing.

Conditional functions

There are several conditional functions in QlikView that can be used in the frontend to give our charts a higher level of flexibility in terms of handling and presenting the data, both in expressions and dimensions. Let's go through some examples of these functions to enhance the analysis in our QlikView app.

The If function

Though sometimes neglected because of its high resource usage when compared to other methods (such as Set Analysis, which is covered in the next chapter), the If function has important uses when creating QlikView documents. Essentially, it is used when two or more different outputs should result from a single expression, depending on a condition that is evaluated to either be true or false.

In this section, we'll explain how it works and discuss a use case.

The syntax

As the first step, we should describe the syntax used by this function and the parameters it needs to work. If you've worked with Microsoft Excel previously, then it's very likely you well have come across the If function in a spreadsheet. The syntax of the If function in QlikView is almost the same as that in Excel. The function takes the following three parameters:

- Condition: An expression that, when evaluated, results in either true or false. Relational and logical operators are used to create the expression.

- Then: The expression or value set as the then parameter will be the output of the If function whenever the condition results in true.

- Else: The expression or value set as the else parameter will be the output of the If function whenever the condition results in false.

The pseudocode is:

```
if(condition , then , else)
```

The If function can also be used as a script function for creating calculated fields. The syntax would be the same.

Additionally, a nested If expression can be constructed in the following manner:

```
If(condition1, expr1,
  If(condition2, expr2,
  expr3))
```

A use case

You should be advised upfront that the If function is, in fact, resource heavy. It's often a good alternative to move all calculations based on the If function from the frontend to the script whenever possible and handle the results through calculated fields or flags in the data model. However, there are cases in which the calculation cannot be handled anywhere but in the frontend. Here, we describe one scenario in which you can take advantage of the If function's capabilities.

Heat charts

A heat chart is a cell matrix in which each individual value is color-coded based on a threshold. We will create one of those charts using the Airline Operations document to demonstrate the concept.

1. From the Airline Operations.qvw document, activate the **Analysis** tab. Then, click on the **Create Chart** button from the design toolbar.

2. From the **New Chart** dialog window, select the **Pivot Table** option in the **Chart Type** section and enter Load Factor % Heat Map in the **Title** field.

3. Click on **Next** and the **Dimensions** dialog will appear, from which we will add the Carrier Name, Year, and Month dimensions to our new chart. Click on **Next** to continue to the **Expressions** dialog window.

4. From the **Edit Expression** window, type the following expression:

    $(eLoadFactor)

5. Click on **OK** to close the **Edit Expression** window and, from the **Expression** dialog, type Load Factor % as the expression **Label**.

6. Next, we will define a background color from the expression's attributes. To do that, click on the small plus sign located next to the expression name in the **Expressions** dialog window. Highlight the **Background Color** attribute.

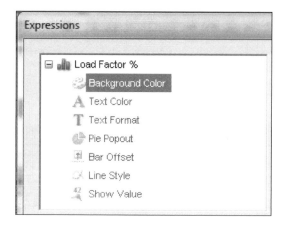

7. Once the attribute is highlighted, go to the **Definition** pane to the right and click on the ellipsis button to bring up the corresponding **Edit Expression** window.

   The expression we will define for this attribute is as follows:

   ```
   If([Load Factor %] >= 0.85, Green(),
     If([Load Factor %] >= 0.70, LightBlue(),
     LightRed()))
   ```

8. Click on **OK** to close the **Edit Expression** dialog.

    Notice how we are not recalculating the **Load Factor** % value but instead referencing the actual expression we created in the previous step, using the label we set. This will help us save some valuable CPU resources.

9. Next, highlight the **Text Color** attribute for the **Load Factor** % expression and, in the **Definition** pane, type `White()`. This will ensure that the cell text uses a white color to make it more readable within the three different background colors we previously defined.

    The "conditional formatting" functionality presented here can also be accomplished using the **Visual Cues** tab of the **Chart Properties** window. However, the **Visual Cues** option only supports up to three levels. Using the expression's attributes, we can define a more complex formatting condition, with four or more levels.

10. Click on **Next** six times until you get to the **Number** dialog window; set the following format to our expression:

    ○ **Fixed to 2 decimals**

    ○ **Show in percent (%)**

11. Click on **Next** three times to get to the **Caption** dialog window and enable the **Auto Minimize** option.

12. Click on **Finish**.

Initially, only the first dimension (**Carrier Name**) will be visible. Expand the other two dimensions and drag them to the top to create the matrix. The heat map should look like the following screenshot:

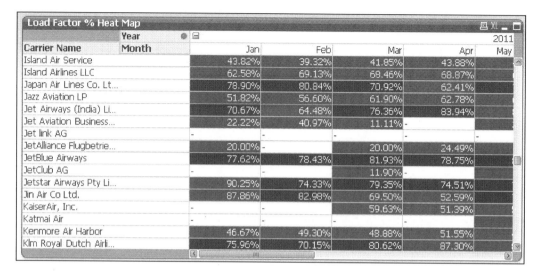

To accommodate the new chart into the **Analysis** sheet, enable the **Auto minimize** option in the **Passengers vs Mail** scatter chart. Then, resize and position the new heat chart to occupy the same space as the scatter chart.

Resize and position their corresponding minimized icons as well, just as we did with the **Reports** tab previously.

A solo exercise

It's time for a little challenge. We've defined the threshold with static limits (0.85 and 0.7). How can we make them variable, and how can we let the users define their own limits?

[The key is in the first section of this chapter.]

Building a heat chart with the Colormix wizard

In our previous example, we used the `Green()`, `LightBlue()`, and `LightRed()` color functions in conjunction with the `If` function to define the **Background color** attribute. Now, we will edit the attribute's expression to make use of the **Colormix Wizard** option and see if we can come up with a better looking heat chart.

1. Right-click on the pivot table we created above and select **Properties...**.

2. Then, navigate to the **Expressions** tab and click on the expand icon to reveal the attributes list. Double-click on the **Background Color** attribute to open the **Edit Expression** window, in which we will replace the current attribute's definition.

3. Clear the expression's current content and, from the **File** menu, select **Colormix Wizard...**.

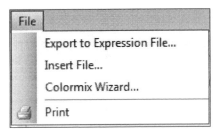

4. The **Colormix Wizard** window will pop up. Click on **Next** in the first dialog, which is just informative, and we'll enter **Step 1**, which is about defining the **Value Expression**.

5. Enter the name of the main expression, in our case `Load Factor %`, enclosed in square brackets. This expression will be used to determine the color and intensity that should be set on each cell.

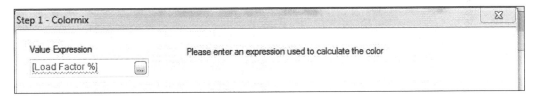

6. Click on **Next** to move on to **Step 2**, in which we will define the upper and lower limit specifications. The settings will be defined as follows:

   ° The **Auto Normalize** option will be disabled for us to explicitly define upper and lower limits, instead of using the chart's max and min values

   ° The **Upper Limit** value will be set to 1, which represents a 100 percent load factor level

   ° The **Upper Limit** color will be left as the default green

   ° The **Intermediate** color checkbox will be enabled, with a value of 0.75 and a blue color

   ° The **Lower Limit** value will be set to 0.5, which represents a 50 percent load factor level

   ° The **Lower limit** color will be left as default red

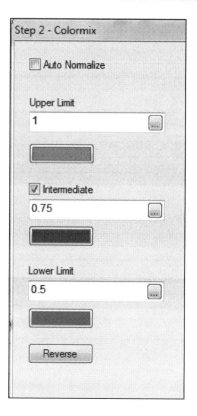

7. Click on **Next** to navigate to the third step in the wizard.

8. We will use the default values in the **Step 3** window (**Enhanced Colors** enabled and **Value Saturation** set to **Use Upper (Lower) Color**), so just click on **Finish** for the new color expression to be generated. The new expression, which will be automatically inserted into the **Edit Expression** window, should look like the following expression:

```
ColorMix2 (if(rangemin(1,rangemax([Load Factor
%],0.5))<0.75,-Sqrt(-(rangemin(1,rangemax([Load Factor %],0.5))-
0.75)/(0.75-0.5)),Sqrt((rangemin(1,rangemax([Load Factor %],0.5))-
0.75)/(1-0.75))), ARGB(255, 255, 0, 0), ARGB(255, 0, 255, 0),
ARGB(255, 0, 0, 160))
```

This expression uses a combination of different color functions, as well as nested If statements. Even though the expression looks complex, it shouldn't be a problem for us since it is auto generated by the **Colormix wizard**.

9. Click on **OK** in the **Edit Expression** window to apply the changes and then **OK** again from the **Chart Properties** window.

The modified heat map should now adopt the following look:

Load Factor % Heat Map						2011
Carrier Name	**Year** Month	Jan	Feb	Mar	Apr	May
JetAlliance Flugbetrie...		20.00%	-	20.00%	24.49%	
JetBlue Airways		77.62%	78.43%	81.93%	78.75%	
JetClub AG		-	-	11.90%	-	
Jetstar Airways Pty Li...		90.25%	74.33%	79.35%	74.51%	
Jin Air Co Ltd.		87.86%	82.98%	69.50%	52.59%	
KaiserAir, Inc.		-	-	59.63%	51.39%	
Katmai Air		-	-	-	-	
Kenmore Air Harbor		46.67%	49.30%	48.88%	51.55%	
Klm Royal Dutch Airli...		75.96%	70.15%	80.62%	87.30%	
Korean Air Lines Co....		81.34%	73.95%	74.55%	75.59%	
Kuwait Airways Corp.		69.12%	67.11%	67.53%	76.28%	
Lacsa		83.37%	77.89%	87.14%	82.32%	
Lan-Chile Airlines		81.80%	80.78%	78.76%	77.97%	
LAN Argentina		79.32%	76.37%	77.38%	78.51%	
Lan Ecuador		74.03%	74.88%	79.28%	73.48%	
Lan Peru Airlines		85.54%	85.90%	82.89%	82.01%	

If we compare the new chart to what we had previously, it's evident that the new look is more dynamic and has additional levels of intensity, thus providing a more detailed insight.

Numeric versus text comparisons

An important consideration when inserting comparisons into conditional functions is that text-based comparisons will be slower than numeric comparisons.

Take the following two expressions, for example:

1. `If(Month = 'January', expr1, expr2)`
2. `If(MonthNum = 1, expr1, expr2)`

The only difference is that the first expression is comparing the `Month` value as a literal value, that is, a text, while the second expression is performing the comparison based on a numeric value. The latter will be faster.

Similarly, it's also important to consider that, when defining a numeric comparison value, it shouldn't be enclosed in single quotes (`MonthNum = '1'`) as it will cause QlikView to treat it as a text-based comparison.

The Class function

Conditional functions are widely used in conjunction with numeric intervals either to find where a specific value falls in a set of ranges, or to group results into predefined bins. The `Class` function is particularly helpful in these cases.

Take, for example, the analysis we made in a previous section about the number of interstate routes per carrier. The initial chart is:

Interstate Routes by Carrier	Interstate Routes /
Carrier Name	**2,655**
Delta Air Lines Inc.	1,145
Miami Air International	864
Southwest Airlines Co.	821
Federal Express Corporation	708
ExpressJet Airlines Inc.	707
USA Jet Airlines Inc.	688
American Airlines Inc.	637
SkyWest Airlines Inc.	609
Atlantic Southeast Airlines	591

We can group the carriers based on the number of interstate routes they serve, only instead of using the individual number of routes, we can use intervals. Add the following expression to our chart:

```
Class(Count(Distinct [From - To State Code]), 100)
```

The result will be the following screenshot:

Interstate Routes by Carrier		
Carrier Name	Interstate Routes	Interstate Routes Interval
	2,655	**2600 <= x < 2700**
Delta Air Lines Inc.	1,145	1100 <= x < 1200
Miami Air International	864	800 <= x < 900
Southwest Airlines Co.	821	800 <= x < 900
Federal Express Corporation	708	700 <= x < 800
ExpressJet Airlines Inc.	707	700 <= x < 800
USA Jet Airlines Inc.	688	600 <= x < 700
American Airlines Inc.	637	600 <= x < 700
SkyWest Airlines Inc.	609	600 <= x < 700
Atlantic Southeast Airlines	591	500 <= x < 600

Essentially, the Class function takes the individual result of an expression, in this case the count of routes, and automatically creates the corresponding bin based on the bin width specified.

 The Class function only supports fixed bin widths.

We can take this further to use the Class function into a nested aggregation, by having a new straight table chart with the following calculated dimension:

```
Aggr(Class(Count(DISTINCT [From - To State Code]), 100), [Carrier
Name])
```

Add the following expression:

```
Count(DISTINCT [Carrier Name])
```

The result will be as seen in the following screenshot:

# of Carriers by Inter	
Routes Interval	# of Carriers
	311
0 <= x < 100	256
100 <= x < 200	14
200 <= x < 300	13
300 <= x < 400	9
400 <= x < 500	4
500 <= x < 600	7
600 <= x < 700	3
700 <= x < 800	2
800 <= x < 900	2
1100 <= x < 1200	1

As you can see, this one is easier to read than having all individual values listed in the dimension column.

The dimension values presented just now show the default format for the bin names. This is fixed within QlikView, but we can create our own custom format with the Replace function, as follows:

```
Replace(Aggr(Class(Count(DISTINCT [From - To State Code]), 100),
[Carrier Name]), '<= x <', ' - ')
```

This expression will result in the following dimension values:

Routes Interval	# of Carriers
	311
0 - 100	256
200 - 300	13
800 - 900	2
100 - 200	14
700 - 800	2
500 - 600	7
400 - 500	4
600 - 700	3
300 - 400	9
1100 - 1200	1

A solo exercise using the Class function

Now that you've seen how to create nested aggregations with the use of intervals, take a moment to create a chart to visualize the number of airlines falling into different load factor ranges with a bin width of 10 percent. Place it into the **Dashboard** tab.

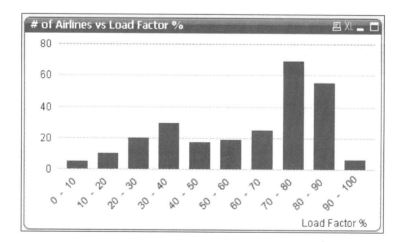

The fascinating thing about this chart is that when the user clicks one of the bars corresponding to a specific interval, all carriers that fall into that interval will be automatically selected. This selection would be made on the **Carrier Name** field, as the **Load Factor** % bins do not exist as a field in the data model. This combination of interactivity, associations, and complex calculations on the fly allows for further navigation and extends the discovery experience.

The Pick function

Another interesting and powerful conditional function available in QlikView is the `Pick` function. In a way, it can be said to act as a simplified nested `If`. The parameters this function takes are:

```
Pick(n, expr1, expr2)
```

Where `n` is an integer number that determines which of the subsequent expressions should be evaluated. `expr1` is an expression to be evaluated when n= 1 and `expr2` is an expression to be evaluated when n= 2

The same result of the `Pick` function can be accomplished using a nested `If`; for example:

```
If (n = 1, expr1, If(n = 2, expr2))
```

However, we can easily see that the `Pick` function is much simpler to use in this case and can even be lighter in terms of resource usage.

 The `Pick` function has no hard limit as to how many expressions it can hold.

Let's look at a practical example.

Using Pick with Dimensionality

One of the examples we described using the `Aggr` function required us to make a sub aggregation in the chart's expression to obtain the average load factor per airline per route. In the example, we used only one chart dimension, **Airline**, and the corresponding `Aggr` function only had two fields in the dimensions parameter: **Route** and **Airline**. However, the defined expression will not work as expected when a new dimension is added to the chart.

For instance, if we were to use a pivot table with several different dimensions, and in which the active dimensions are dynamically being expanded or collapsed, the sub-aggregation used to calculate the average load factor should be adapted with each new dimension arrangement; the correct aggregation expression will depend on which dimensions are visible in the pivot table.

To account for the different possible arrangements in the chart's dimensions, we will make use of the `Pick` function in conjunction with the `Dimensionality` function and the `Aggr` expression we previously used.

The `Dimensionality` function is used in pivot tables to indicate which level of aggregation is active in the pivot table for each of its segments or rows. For instance, if all dimensions are collapsed and only the first dimension is visible, then the `Dimensionality` function would return 1; if the first dimension is expanded, the `Dimensionality` function would return 2, and so forth.

The result of the `Dimensionality` function is row-specific, so we could have one row with one level of aggregation (depending on which of its dimensions are expanded) and another row with a different level. The `Dimensionality` function will account for each rows' aggregation level to provide the correct result. The following screenshot illustrates this concept, with the result of the `Dimensionality` function presented as the second expression column and color-coded for easier understanding:

Carrier Group	Airline	Aircraft Name	Departures Performed (thousands)	Dimensionality
Commuter Carriers (air taxi...			733.96	1
Foreign Carriers			595.57	1
Large Regional Carriers (carriers with annual revenue of $20 million to $100 million)	Aloha Air Cargo: KH	Boeing 737-10...	0.00	3
		Boeing 737-20...	7.75	3
		Saab-Fairchd 3...	0.24	3
		Total	8.00	2
	Asia Pacific: PFQ		0.71	2
	Avjet Corporation: OWQ		1.97	2
	Capital Cargo Internat...		8.59	2
	Total		19.26	1
Major Carriers (carriers with...			6,129.19	1
Medium Regional Carriers (...			8.91	1
National Carriers (carriers w...			2,644.94	1
Small Certificated Carriers (...			561.46	1
Total			10,693.30	0

The title of the screenshot is "The Dimensionality function".

So, to approach the presented scenario (of course, this will only keep working when users do not modify the pivot table by dragging dimensions), start by activating the **Aggr** sheet in the workspace and creating a pivot table with the following dimensions: **Flight Type**, **Carrier Group**, and **Carrier Name**, in that order. Then, enter the following expression:

```
Pick(Dimensionality() + 1,
        Avg(Aggr($(eLoadFactor), [From - To Airport ID])),
        Avg(Aggr($(eLoadFactor), [From - To Airport ID], [Flight
Type])),
        Avg(Aggr($(eLoadFactor), [From - To Airport ID],
                                                [Flight Type],
[Carrier Group])),
        Avg(Aggr($(eLoadFactor), [From - To Airport ID], [Carrier
Group],
                                                [Flight Type],
[Carrier Name]))
)
```

Label the created expression as `Avg Load Factor per Route`. Then, create another expression and enter the following:

```
$(eLoadFactor)
```

Label the new expression as `Direct Load Factor`. Then, navigate to the **Presentation** dialog window and enable the **Show Partial Sums** option for all three dimensions.

The resulting chart will be:

Avg Load Factor per Route				
Flight Type	Carrier Group	Carrier Name	Avg Load Factor per Route	Direct Load Factor
Domestic, Foreign Car... ⊞			55.4%	75.3%
	⊟ Commuter Carriers (... ⊞		55.2%	63.9%
	Large Regional Carriers (carriers with annual revenue of $20 million to $100 million)	⊟ Avjet Corporation	34.5%	31.3%
Domestic, US Carriers Only		Casino Express	63.0%	64.5%
		Lynx Aviation d/b/a Fro...	72.1%	64.2%
		National Air Cargo Grou...	23.8%	32.3%
		Tatonduk Outfitters Limi...	27.9%	27.9%
		Total	**40.3%**	**62.5%**
	Major Carriers (carrie... ⊞		72.6%	80.1%
	Medium Regional Car... ⊞		41.4%	48.7%
	National Carriers (car... ⊞		58.9%	76.0%
	Small Certificated Ca... ⊞		36.0%	55.0%
	Total		**55.7%**	**78.7%**
International, Foreign... ⊞			61.6%	78.8%
International, US Carri... ⊞			66.9%	77.9%
Total			**57.4%**	**78.6%**

We can compare the result from both expressions in this screenshot. A higher result in the **Direct Load Factor** % column means the low-occupancy routes have just a few flights that don't affect the overall result. However, the impact of those routes can still be seen in the **Avg Load Factor per Route** column since that's where all routes are equally accounted for, no matter the amount of flights performed.

For each Dimensionality level, the chart depicted earlier is using a different sub-aggregation to calculate the average load factor per route. Additionally, when Dimensionality is zero (the total row at the bottom), the chart is calculating the average for all routes, all carriers, and all flight types. We used Dimensionality() + 1 as the n parameter of the Pick function because otherwise there would be no way of adding an expression for when Dimensionality() equals zero.

Since the expression's definition is based on a certain, predefined, arrangement of the dimensions in our pivot table, we must be cautious when using an expression like this because it will yield unexpected results when the dimensions are re-ordered by the user (for by dragging the corresponding columns).

A tip on copying expressions

We will close this chapter on advanced expressions by sharing a tip that can save you quite some time when developing QlikView documents. You have noticed that, when defining a chart's expressions, we not only define the formula, but also expression attributes, number format, presentation, labels, alignment, and so on. It is very common that, when using more than one expression in a chart (a straight table, for instance), two or more of these expressions are very similar in terms of formatting and sometimes also in the formula itself.

In those cases, we can simply copy and paste an expression within the **Expressions** tab of the **Chart Properties** window to replicate the entire expression definition and then adjust whichever parameters or definitions we need to, thus saving a great deal of time and work.

To do this, simply right-click on the name of the expression you want to replicate and right-click again on the blank space below the expressions list to paste it.

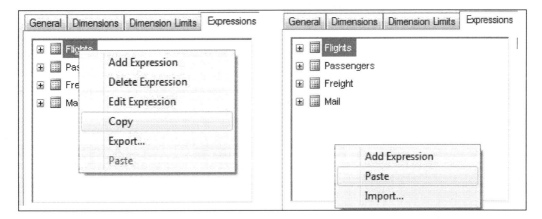

Summary

We've come to the end of this chapter where we've been able to use some advanced techniques for data aggregation and advanced expressions. We have learned how to use variables in QlikView and embed them into expressions.

We also learned the use of conditional expressions, with the If function, to output results based on logical comparisons.

Finally, we learned how to use advanced and nested aggregations in charts.

In the next chapter, we will be learning about Set Analysis, one of QlikView's most powerful functionalities, and how it can be used for Point In Time reporting.

12
Set Analysis and Point In Time Reporting

Comparing performance metrics over a period of time is one of the most fundamental tasks expected from any BI solution. There are a few ways to deliver these sort of comparisons in QlikView, but the most flexible and dynamic ones involve the use of Set Analysis. Set Analysis, by itself, is a powerful tool that can be used for not only for Point In Time Reporting, but for many other complex calculations.

In this chapter, we will expand on what we've learned from all of the previous chapters, and introduce the following new concepts:

- Set Analysis and modified record sets
- Point In Time Reporting
- Comparative analysis with alternate states

We will approach these topics with the use of some practical examples. Given the harshness of the syntax we are going to use, and the complexity of the expressions that can be built with Set Analysis, we recommend you to have a lot of patience and dedication to the subject at hand. Even with the best reference material, Set Analysis can take a while to master—so don't lose heart!

The magic of Set Analysis

We will now introduce one of the most powerful tools you, as a developer, have at your disposal when creating QlikView documents. We must say upfront that, as with anything, the excessive use of Set Analysis in chart expressions can yield poor performance or low response times. However, we should also know that, when used effectively, it can have a positive impact in both performance and user experience.

In this section, we will cover topics such as when to use Set Analysis, why you should use it, what the correct syntax is, and we will provide common examples and several tips and tricks for maximizing performance as well.

What is it for?

Set Analysis is a great feature in QlikView that lets you, as a developer, take control over what your charts display and allows calculations that wouldn't be possible otherwise, at least not as dynamically. To understand its inner workings, we can compare it to how selections that are made using listboxes work.

With UI selections, we can say that whatever is selected affects the entire document, and all of the charts only display information associated with the set of data corresponding to those selections; plain and simple. In a way, that is basically what Set Analysis does. It restricts, predefines, or extends the set of data that charts base their calculations on. Using a set expression, we can, for instance, specify that a certain chart should perform an aggregation only based on records that meet a set of criteria in certain fields (for example, `Region A` and `Region B` from the `Region` field), even if the non-matching values are part of the user's selected record set. We can also use Set Analysis to expand the selections made by the user to show, for example, results of the previous year even when it has not been actually selected. For example, when the user selects the year 2012 and a table displays data for 2012 in one column and 2011 in the other.

 The modified record set specified in a set expression affects only the expression in which it is being used, not the entire document.

That is the whole concept. However, it is sometimes not as simple to tell our chart to "show the numbers of the previous year/month/period" as it would be using selections. In Set Analysis, we need to specify the modified record set using an expression with the correct syntax.

These are some situations in which the use of Set Analysis is practical:

- To compare results for two different time periods in one single view based on the same selection state

- To restrict or exclude certain value(s) in a field from the calculation

- To create a cumulative sum or YTD (Year-To-Date) result, even if the user selects only one month

- To disregard selections in a certain field that may not be applicable to calculate a particular metric

- To essentially ignore all selections

- To use the set of data returned by a Bookmark, even when the Bookmark is not activated

- To replace `If` expressions that make use of lots of hardware resources

- A mix and match of all of the above

We will first work our way through the Set Analysis syntax, after that we will apply the concepts to achieve something that is a must in almost every QlikView document: Point In Time Reporting.

Syntax and examples

The details for creating a `set` expression are outlined in the following step-by-step procedure:

1. We start off by defining the base expression. Say we want to sum the total number of flights performed. So, we will begin with the following:

   ```
   Sum([# Departures Performed])
   ```

2. Then, we need to construct the `set` part of the expression. It is the set expression in which we specify the record set we want to use in our calculation. The set definition is placed just after the first parenthesis in the base expression, before the field name, and will be enclosed in curly brackets:

   ```
   Sum({set expression} [# Departures Performed])
   ```

3. After the first curly bracket, we define a set identifier by adding either a dollar sign (which means the alternative record set will be initially based on the current selections), the number 1 (meaning we will use the full record set of all the data contained in the document, ignoring all user selections) or the ID of a bookmark (which uses the selection stored in the bookmark). To illustrate our example, we will use the dollar sign identifier, since it is the most common. We will now have:

   ```
   Sum({$} [# Departures Performed])
   ```

 Note that the dollar sign can be omitted, since it is the default identifier, and the set expression will not be affected. However, it is good practice to use it to maintain consistency.

4. Right after the dollar sign, we define the fields that will play the role of **set modifiers**. This is the part in which we specify what to add or exclude from the initial record set. The entire set of field-value definitions will be enclosed in angle brackets (< >) and the syntax is `FieldName = {NewValue}`. Different variations to this syntax are described as follows:

   ○ `FieldName = {value}`: when the `NewValue` parameter is a numeric value, it is specified as such with no additional modifications

   ○ `FieldName = {'TextValue'}`: when the `NewValue` parameter is text, we should enclose it in straight single quotes

   ○ `FieldName = {"SearchString"}`: if we want to use a search string as the value definition, we should enclose it in straight double quotes

The value definition can also be a set of different values, in which case each element is separated by a comma.

 We can also refer to the `NewValue` parameter as the `Element List` parameter.

Once we add the set modifiers, our set expression will be complete and have the following structure (shown as pseudocode for illustration purposes):

```
Sum({$<Field1 = {NewValue1}, Field2 = {NewValue2}>} [# Departures
Performed])
```

Taking our base expression as a starting point, here are some examples:

- `Sum({$<[Carrier Group] = {'Foreign Carriers'}>} [# Departures Performed])`

  This will result in the total number of flights performed, but only taking into account the record set defined by the current selections ($), and where the `Carrier Group` field has a value of `Foreign Carriers`. All other Carrier Groups are excluded.

  In this example, if the user has specifically selected a different value in the `Carrier Group` field, that selection will be overridden and the calculation will be made based on the modified record set. It's important to convey this fact to the end users of the QlikView document and add pointers in the user interface as to what each calculation is being based on so that the use of Set Analysis doesn't negatively affect the user experience.

- `Sum({$<Year = {2010}>} [# Departures Performed])`

  This will use a record set based on current selections ($) where the `Year` is `2010` even if the user selects something else in the `Year` field.

- `Sum({$<Year = {"20*"}>} [# Departures Performed])`

  This will use a record set based on current selections (`$`) where the `Year` matches the search string `"20*"`, meaning all years that begin with `20` will be taken into account.

- `Sum({$<Year = {">=2010"}>} [# Departures Performed])`

  This will use a record set where the `Year` is greater than or equal to `2010` to calculate the number of flights. A search string is used in the field value definition.

- `Sum({$<[Carrier's Operating Region] = {'Domestic', 'Latin America'}, Year = {2010}>} [# Departures Performed])`

  This will use a record set based on the current selections where the `Carrier's Operating Region` field is either `Domestic` or `Latin America`, and only those records corresponding to the year `2010`.

  Notice how two elements in the field value definition have been separated by a comma.

- `Sum({1<[Carrier's Operating Region] = {'Domestic', 'Latin America'}, Year = {2011}>} [# Departures Performed])`

  In this expression, the only difference from the preceding example is the use of the number `1` as the set identifier. The calculation will use the entire document record set as a starting point, disregarding all user selections, but take into account only those records where the `Carrier's Operating Region` is either `Domestic` or `Latin America`, and will only look at those records corresponding to the year `2011`.

- `Sum({$<[Carrier's Operating Region] = {'Domestic', 'Latin America'}, Year = >} [# Departures Performed])`

  In this expression, there is no modifier value assigned to the field `Year`. The calculation will use a record set initially based on the current selections, but disregard the selections made in the `Year` field, and where the `Carrier's Operating Region` is either `Domestic` or `Latin America`.

Internally, QlikView evaluates the field value definitions in Set Analysis in the same manner as conditional expressions are evaluated (but usually faster), to determine if a specific record should be part of the calculation or not. Therefore, the same rule discussed previously about numeric versus text-based comparisons applies for Set Analysis. That rule: using a set modifier based on a text-based field (`Month = {'Jan'}`, for instance) is slower than using its numeric equivalent (`MonthNum= {1}`).

Similarly, it's also important to consider that, when defining a numeric comparison value, it shouldn't be enclosed in single-quotes (`MonthNum = {'1'}`) as it will cause QlikView to treat it as a text-based comparison.

Using variables in set expressions

It's sometimes convenient to make use of variables in set expressions to make them even more dynamic. We've previously discussed how variables alone are used. We will now go through some examples of Set Analysis expressions that make use of variables instead of hard-coded field values.

As before, we use the Dollar Sign Expansion syntax inside the field value definition or element list. If, for instance, our variable contains a number, we would type the set analysis expression as follows:

```
Sum({$<Year = {$(vLastYear)}>} [# Departures Performed])
```

On the other hand, if our variable contains text, our expression would be:

```
Sum({$<[Carrier Group] = {'$(vInterestGroup)'}>} [# Departures
Performed])
```

If we want to use a variable's value as a search string, the expression would be:

```
Sum({$<[Aircraft Group] = {"$(vSearchAircraftGroups)"}>} [# Departures
Performed])
```

We have just gone through a basic introduction on the topic, but there is a lot more to know about Set Analysis. Let's move to the next part and discover some more of it.

Dynamic record sets

In the previous section, we reviewed some basic examples using set modifiers with explicit (hardcoded) field value definitions. Our next step will be about making our modified record set dynamic and based on the user's current selections, that is, using a calculated field value definition. By doing so, the alternative record set will dynamically change depending on what the user selects.

To embed actual calculations into the field value definition in a set expression, we use the Dollar Sign Expansion (DSE) syntax. The final expression would be as follows:

```
Sum({$<Year = {$(=Max(Year))}>} [# Departures Performed])
```

As you can see, it is just as if we were using a variable, just with an additional equal sign and the expression itself. Here, the DSE function is to evaluate the enclosed calculation and the set expression will only use the output value in the set modifier.

 We should never forget the equal sign when embedding calculations in set expressions. Otherwise, the embedded calculation will not be evaluated.

If we want to get the record set corresponding to the previous year to whatever year the user selects, we would use:

```
Sum({$<Year = {$(=Max(Year)-1)}>} [# Departures Performed])
```

In this case, the DSE is first calculating the last possible year from the current selections record set. It goes back one year and the output is then passed to the set modifier as the field value definition. Anytime the user changes his selections, the set modifier is changed as well.

> At this point, we must reinforce our recommendation that it is very important to let the user know exactly what records the calculation is taking into account. By doing so, we will avoid confusion as it might result counter-intuitive for the user to see values being calculated that are not associated to his selections.

The same concept also works with Quarters, Months, Days, and so on. However, additional considerations need to be made for some fields. For example, if we were to use the previous calculation for the Month field, Max(Month) - 1 would not work if the user selects January. The expression would return zero, which is not a valid month. Although we can easily build an expression that returns the number 12 instead of zero (with the use of the If function, for instance), we will provide an even simpler and straightforward solution for this scenario in an upcoming section of this chapter (Point In Time Reporting).

More assignment operators

All of the preceding examples use set expressions which have predefined field values in the element list definitions, overriding the user selections on the specified fields. However, in some cases, we will need to first take the actual record set that the user has selected and, from there, modify it by adding or removing certain values. To do that, we need to use a different assignment operator in the field-value definition, instead of the equal sign. The available assignment operators are:

- =: This is what we have been using, and it simply redefines the selection for a certain field.

- +=: This operator implicitly defines a union between the selected field values and the ones we specify in the element list.

- -=: This operator implicitly defines an exclusion of the values we specify from the values the user has selected.

- `*=`: This operator is used to define the corresponding field values based on the intersection between what the user has selected and the values we specify. That is, the resulting record set will be the values that "intersect" or are present in both the user's selection and the values we explicitly define in our element list.

- `/=`: This one is used to define a symmetric difference (XOR), and the resulting record set will contain the values that are present in either one set (the user's selections or the explicitly defined values), but not in both.

Let's walk through some examples to better understand the assignment operators:

- `Sum({$<Year += {2007, 2008}>} Sales)`

   This expression will return the sales for the years the user has selected and also for the years 2007 and 2008 whether they are selected or not.

- `Sum({$<Product -= {'Product X'}>} Sales)`

   This expression will return the sales for the products the user has selected, but exclude records corresponding to `Product X`.

- `Sum({$<Product *= {'Product X', 'Product Y'}>} Sales)`

   This expression returns the sales for the current selection, but only for the intersection of currently selected products, and products `X` and `Y`.

- `Sum({$<ProductNumber *= {"48*"}>} Sales)`

   This expression returns the sales corresponding to the current selections, but only for the intersection of the currently selected products and all of the products whose number begins with `48`.

Set operators

Set modifiers, the part of the set expression that is enclosed in angle brackets, can also be constructed by combining several different element lists in the field value definition. Furthermore, the entire set expression can be composed using several different set modifiers. This is accomplished using set operators.

The different set operators that can be used are:

- `+`: Union
- `-`: Exclusion
- `*`: Intersection
- `/`: Symmetric difference

The exclusion operator (-) can also be used as a unary operator to retrieve the complement set.

The set operators work in a manner similar to the assignment operators described in the previous section. Let's review some basic examples:

- `Sum({$<Year = {2007, 2008} + {"<=2000"}>} [# Departures Performed])`

  This expression will return the total flights performed in the years 2007, 2008, plus all of the years that are less than or equal to 2000.

- `Sum({$<[Carrier's Operating Region] = {'Latin America'},Year = {2011}> + <[Carrier's Operating Region] = {'Domestic'},Year = {2010}> - <[Carrier Group] = {'Foreign Carrier'}>} [# Departures Performed])`

  This expression will result with the total number of flights performed during 2011 by carriers operating in Latin America plus flights performed during 2010 by carriers operating as Domestic, but exclude Foreign Carriers from both sets.

  This is one of those calculations that wouldn't be possible with simple selections.

Just as in arithmetic operations, parentheses can be used to enclose different set operations and ensure they are evaluated in the correct order.

Using element functions

There are two special functions that can be used in set expressions to implicitly specify an element list. The functions are:

- `P()`: To use all possible values in a field as the element list
- `E()`: To use all excluded values in a field as the element list

A quick example:

- `Sum({1<Year = p(Year)>} [# Departures Performed])`

  This expression will use the full set of data disregarding all user selections (because the specified set identifier is the number 1), but take into account those records corresponding to the years that the user has selected. In other words, only selections made on the Year field are considered.

For more examples, head to the **Help** menu in QlikView, select **Contents**, and activate the **Index** tab from the left pane to search for **Set Analysis**. There is also a document on QlikCommunity that explores additional examples: http://community.qlikview.com/docs/DOC-1867

The possibilities are endless. Take a moment to try it out in the Airline Operations document and see for yourself what you can do with Set Analysis. In the solution file corresponding to this chapter, we've included an additional sheet, named Set Analysis, with different examples of Set Analysis uses.

Point In Time Reporting

One of the most common use cases of Set Analysis is **Point In Time Reporting**. Having the ability to perform period-over-period analysis is a basic requirement in any BI tool and is easily performed in QlikView with the aid of set expressions. However, needless to say, Set Analysis is also amazingly useful for the fulfillment of other special requirements.

Let's combine the acquired knowledge and apply it to add Point In Time Reporting to our Airline Operations document.

The challenge

HighCloud Airlines' executives require a dashboard to easily compare different performance indicators in a period-over-period basis. The different period comparisons they need are:

- Current Year-To-Date indicators versus the same period last year
- Current month versus same month last year
- Current month versus previous month

The comparisons should be dynamic and based on the user's selections. So, if the user selects October 2010, the corresponding comparisons should be:

- From January through October 2010 versus January through October 2009
- October 2010 versus October 2009
- October 2010 versus September 2010

At the same time, all user selections across the different Airline, Aircraft, or Airport attributes must be taken into consideration in all point-in-time analyses.

Let's work some Set Analysis magic.

Defining the set modifiers

We'll start tackling each requirement by first defining the set modifiers each period comparison would need. For that, we must remember that the current time-related fields in which the user is able to make a selection are Year, Quarter, Month, and Period.

However, not always will the user have explicitly selected values in all fields. There can be selections in Year only, for instance, or Year and Month, or only Month, or even no selection whatsoever.

The set modifiers we define when building our expressions need to account for all of the possible scenarios and always show a clear result. This will ensure the user is not confused as to what filters are being applied when navigating the document.

Even if the user has not made specific selections on all time-based fields, we can easily infer a period in which to base our comparisons by taking the most-recent period from the list of associated values. Let's suppose the user has the following selection state:

- Year = 2010
- Quarter = Q2

From the previous example, we can infer that the "current month" (our base period) is June 2010, as it is the most recent period in the list of possible values.

If, on the other hand, the user has nothing selected at all, we will take December 2011 as our base period, as it is the latest month available in the dataset.

Obtaining the base period record set

A simple Max(Period) expression will help us get the base period in all scenarios, as the Period field contains both the Month and Year components. Therefore, the set modifiers that we would use to get the record set corresponding to the base period in each of the required comparisons are:

- Current Year-To-Date indicators:

  ```
  <Period = {"<=$(=Max(Period))"}, Year = {"$(=Max(Year))"}, Quarter
  = , Month = >
  ```

  This set modifier will result in a record set containing all of the periods that are less than or equal to the current period, and belong to the current year, which would be all Year-To-Date records.

- Current month:

```
<Period = {$(=Max(Period))}, Year = , Quarter = , Month = >
```

This set modifier will result in a record set corresponding to only the current period.

We have defined some "disregard" fields in our set modifiers because, depending on user's selections, the base period we are trying to retrieve might already be excluded from the active record set. Therefore, we need to override the restricting selections to be able to access the periods we need.

Now that we have the base period, we are halfway through. We just need to construct the set modifier for the compare-to period, which is a little trickier to obtain and will naturally be different for each different period comparison.

Obtaining the compare-to period record set

The easiest of the compare-to periods to obtain is the "previous month." We would use something such as `Max(Period) - 1` to obtain its value. However, this expression doesn't always work for our purposes. As pointed out previously, when our base period is January, the previous month obtained using the above expression would be an nonexistent one. For example, if the current period value is 201101 (remember the field is in YYYYMM format), the expression would return 201100.

One way we could solve it is adding an `If` function to the expression to account for those particular scenarios:

```
If(Right(Max(Period) - 1, 2) = '00', (Max(Year) - 1) & '12',
Max(Period - 1))
```

However, this is very impractical, so here is another approach: instead of using the actual period numeric representation in the YYYYMM format, we can assign each of the period a new numeric ID using the `Autonumber()` function in the script. That way, all periods in the calendar table will have a consecutive number assigned with which we can easily use in our frontend calculations. Follow these steps:

1. Open the `Airline Operations.qvw` document and launch the **Edit Script** window.

2. Activate the **Calendar** tab and modify the `Master Calendar Load` script by adding the following code between the table name and the first `LOAD DISTINCT` statement:

```
Load
   *,
   AutoNumber(Period, 'PeriodID') as [PeriodID]
   ;
```

3. **Save** and **reload** the script to apply the changes.

   We simply added a new preceding Load statement to create a new `PeriodID` field by taking the result in the `Period` field, which is being created in another preceding Load, and applying the `Autonumber()` function to it using a `PeriodID` counter. As the calendar is being populated in ascending order, each new period will have a `PeriodID` value that is the consecutive to its previous period.

4. Create a temporary table box with all of the calendar-related fields to better visualize the contents of the `Master Calendar` table. It should look as follows:

PeriodID	Period	Year	Month	Year - Month	Quarter
1	200901	2009	Jan	2009-01	Q1
2	200902	2009	Feb	2009-02	Q1
3	200903	2009	Mar	2009-03	Q1
4	200904	2009	Apr	2009-04	Q2
5	200905	2009	May	2009-05	Q2
6	200906	2009	Jun	2009-06	Q2
7	200907	2009	Jul	2009-07	Q3
8	200908	2009	Aug	2009-08	Q3
9	200909	2009	Sep	2009-09	Q3
10	200910	2009	Oct	2009-10	Q4
11	200911	2009	Nov	2009-11	Q4
12	200912	2009	Dec	2009-12	Q4
13	201001	2010	Jan	2010-01	Q1
14	201002	2010	Feb	2010-02	Q1
15	201003	2010	Mar	2010-03	Q1

The `Autonumber()` function will only create the correct IDs in **chronological** order when the calendar table is being loaded or populated in **ascending** order. If that's not the case, an alternative formula to generate a consecutive `PeriodID` field in the script would be:

```
(Year(Temp_Date) - 1)  * 12 +
Num(Month(Temp_Date))
```

This formula will, for example, assign the value 24120 to December 2010, and 24121 to January 2011, and so on.

Now that we have the corresponding `PeriodID` field, we can use a simple expression to retrieve the value for the previous periods. This will account for every scenario:

```
Max(PeriodID) - 1
```

The corresponding set modifiers to obtain the compare-to periods are:

- Previous Year Year-To-Date

```
<PeriodID = {"<=$(=Max(PeriodID)-12)"}, Year = {"$(=Max(Year) -
1)"}, Quarter = , Month = , Period = >
```

This set modifier subtracts 12 from the current period's ID field to obtain the corresponding period from last year. It also subtracts 1 from the `Year` value to obtain the previous year. As we are now using the new `PeriodID` field, the old `Period` field is specified as an ignored-selections field.

- Same month last year

```
<PeriodID = {"$(=Max(PeriodID)-12)"}, Year = , Quarter = , Month =
, Period = >
```

By subtracting 12 from the current period's ID, we obtain the corresponding month from last year.

- Previous month

```
<PeriodID = {"$(=Max(PeriodID)-1)"}, Year = , Quarter = , Month =
, Period = >
```

By subtracting 1 from the current period's ID, we obtain the previous month's record set.

Now that we have defined our set modifiers, it's time to construct the expressions.

Constructing the expressions

Using the base and compare-to set modifiers that we just defined, our final expressions will be as described here.

 The following examples use the `# Departures Performed` field in the aggregation function, but it can be changed to obtain any other indicator.

The following expressions are constructed in the following form to obtain a variance percentage:

```
(BasePeriod / CompareToPeriod) - 1
```

- Current Year-To-Date versus the same period last year

```
(Sum({$<PeriodID = {"<=$(=Max(PeriodID))"}, Year =
{"$(=Max(Year))"}, Quarter = , Month = , Period = > } [#
Departures Performed])
    /
```

```
Sum({$<PeriodID = {"<=$(=Max(PeriodID) - 12)"}, Year =
{"$(=Max(Year) - 1)"}, Quarter = , Month = , Period = > } [#
Departures Performed]))
    - 1
```

- Current month versus same month last year

```
(Sum({$<PeriodID = {"$(=Max(PeriodID))"}, Year = , Quarter = ,
Month = , Period = > } [# Departures Performed])
    /
Sum({$<PeriodID = {"$(=Max(PeriodID) - 12)"}, Year = , Quarter = ,
Month = , Period = > } [# Departures Performed]))
    - 1
```

- Current month versus previous month

```
(Sum({$<PeriodID = {"$(=Max(PeriodID))"}, Year = , Quarter = ,
Month = , Period = > } [# Departures Performed])
    /
Sum({$<PeriodID = {"$(=Max(PeriodID) - 1)"}, Year = , Quarter = ,
Month = , Period = > } [# Departures Performed]))
    - 1
```

 The preceding expressions are used to obtain the variance percentage from one period to the other. To obtain the actual numbers corresponding to each period, or the net change, these expressions can be adjusted.

However, the expressions alone are nothing if we don't create some charts to make use of them. Take a moment to create some visualization objects, such as gauge charts, straight tables, and so on, that allow HighCloud Airlines' executives to get the performance overview they need in terms of period-over-period relative growth.

 We have included some chart examples in the solution file corresponding to this chapter.

Enabling additional period comparisons

The same concept used to build the `PeriodID` field can be used for the `QuarterID` field. We can easily and seamlessly create a lot of expressions for Point In Time Reporting after we've created the `Calendar` table with at least the following fields: `Year`, `Month`, `Quarter`, `PeriodID`, and `QuarterID`.

Take a moment to add the `QuarterID` field to the master calendar table by using the following script expression:

```
AutoNumber(Year & Quarter, 'QuarterID') as [QuarterID]
```

Therefore, the final `Master Calendar Load` script will be:

```
[Master Calendar]:
Load
   *,
   AutoNumber(Period, 'PeriodID') as [PeriodID],
   AutoNumber(Year & Quarter, 'QuarterID') as [QuarterID]
   ;
LOAD DISTINCT
   Year(Temp_Date) * 100 + Month(Temp_Date) as [Period],
   Year(Temp_Date) as [Year],
   Month(Temp_Date) as [Month],
   Date(Temp_Date, 'YYYY-MM') as [Year - Month],
   'Q' & Ceil(Month(Temp_Date) / 3) as [Quarter]
   ;
LOAD DISTINCT
   MonthStart($(vMinDate) + IterNo() - 1) as Temp_Date
AUTOGENERATE (1)
WHILE $(vMinDate) + IterNo() - 1 <= $(vMaxDate);
```

Save and **reload** the script to apply the changes.

More Point In Time Reporting examples

Let's quickly review some common Set Analysis expressions that we can use when required. The following expressions calculate the total number of flights for different specific periods of time:

- YTD (Year-To-Date) flights:

```
Sum({$<PeriodID = {"<=$(=Max(PeriodID))"},
         Year = {$(=Max(Year))},
         Quarter = ,
         Month = ,
         Period = >} [# Departures Performed])
```

- QTD (Quarter-To-Date) flights:

```
Sum({$<PeriodID = {"<=$(=Max(PeriodID))"},
         QuarterID = {$(=Max(QuarterID))},
         Year = ,
         Quarter = ,
         Month = ,
         Period = >} [# Departures Performed])
```

- MTD (Month-To-Date) flights:

```
Sum({$<PeriodID = {$(=Max(PeriodID))},
            Year = ,
            Quarter = ,
            Month = ,
            Period = >} [# Departures Performed])
```

> The preceding MTD expression is actually a current-month expression. To construct a MTD expression, we should also include a Date field, which we don't have in our example document.

- Previous Month flights:

```
Sum({$<PeriodID = {$(=Max(PeriodID) - 1)},
            Year = ,
            Quarter = ,
            Month = ,
            Period = >} [# Departures Performed])
```

> When the QlikView document contains data at a daily level, the previous month calculation can be defined to only account for the same number of days as the days so far in the current month. This would be done adding a new field value definition, based on a Date or Day field, to our set modifier.

- Previous Quarter flights:

```
Sum({$<QuarterID = {$(=Max(QuarterID) - 1)},
            Year = ,
            Quarter = ,
            Month = ,
            Period = >} [# Departures Performed])
```

- Flights for the same Month of the previous Year:

```
Sum({$<PeriodID = {$(=Max(PeriodID) - 12)},
            Year = ,
            Quarter = ,
            Month = ,
            Period = >} [# Departures Performed])
```

- Flights for same Quarter of the previous Year:

```
Sum({$<QuarterID = {$(=Max(QuarterID) - 4)},
            Year = ,
            Quarter = ,
            Month = ,
            Period = >} [# Departures Performed])
```

- YTD flights for the previous Year

```
Sum({$<PeriodID = {"<=$(=Max(PeriodID) - 12)"},
          Year = {$(=Max(Year) - 1)},
          Quarter = ,
          Month = ,
          Period = >} [# Departures Performed])
```

- Flights for rolling-12 months:

```
Sum({$<PeriodID = {">=$(=Max(PeriodID)-11)<=$(=Max(PeriodID))"},
          Year = ,
          Quarter = ,
          Month = ,
          Period = >} [# Departures Performed])
```

There you have it, a complete set of formulas to help you create Point In Time Analysis in your QlikView documents in a very simple fashion. We invite you to try them out with the Airline Operations document and build some context around the already created dashboard.

Storing set expressions into variables

Period-over-period comparisons are widely used in QlikView documents and, as you've seen, they can get somewhat messy. Instead of writing the set expression each time for every expression in which it is used, it's a good practice to store its definition in a variable, which can then be called from anywhere in the QlikView document where it's required.

Take, for example, the following expression. It calculates the number of flights Year-to-Date, based on user's selections:

```
Sum({$<PeriodID = {"<=$(=Max(PeriodID))"},
          Year = {$(=Max(Year))},
          Quarter = ,
          Month = ,
          Period = >} [# Departures Performed])
```

From the preceding calculation, we can take the set modifier part (the part which is enclosed in angle brackets) and define it as a new variable, called vSetYTD. Then, we would use this new variable into a modified version of the expression presented above as follows:

```
Sum({$<$(vSetYTD)>} [# Departures Performed])
```

Look closely. You'll see we are inserting the set modifier into our formula with the use of the Dollar Sign Expansion syntax, which results in the exact same expression as the original.

The reason for only storing the set modifier without the angle brackets in the variable definition is to allow for the flexibility to include additional modifiers in the end expression. For example, we can extend the set expression as follows:

```
Sum({$<$(vSetYTD), [Carrier's Operating Region] = {'Latin America'}>}
[# Departures Performed])
```

By adding expression-specific set modifiers, all of the other expressions using the base set variable remain unaffected.

Furthermore, we can define all of the set expressions used for period comparisons so that they are ready to be used when required from any given expression:

Variable name	Variable definition
vSetYTD	PeriodID = {"<=$(=Max(PeriodID))"}, Year = {$(=Max(Year))}, Quarter = , Month = , Period =
vSetQTD	PeriodID = {"<=$(=Max(PeriodID))"}, QuarterID = {$(=Max(QuarterID))}, Year = , Quarter = , Month = , Period =
vSetMTD	PeriodID = {$(=Max(PeriodID))}, Year = , Quarter = , Month = , Period =
vSetPreviousMonth	PeriodID = {$(=Max(PeriodID) - 1)}, Year = , Quarter = , Month = , Period =

Variable name	Variable definition
vSetPreviousQuarter	QuarterID = {$(=Max(QuarterID) - 1)}, Year = , Quarter = , Month = , Period =
vSetLYMTD	PeriodID = {$(=Max(PeriodID) - 12)}, Year = , Quarter = , Month = , Period =
vSetLYQTD	QuarterID = {$(=Max(QuarterID) - 4)}, Year = , Quarter = , Month = , Period =
vSetLYYTD	PeriodID = {"<=$(=Max(PeriodID) - 12)"}, Year = {$(=Max(Year) - 1)}, Quarter = , Month = , Period =
vSetRolling12	PeriodID = {">=$(=Max(PeriodID)- 11)<=$(=Max(PeriodID))"}, Year = , Quarter = , Month = , Period =

Once we have defined all of the preceding variables, the creation of new expressions for period comparisons will be a very straightforward process.

Set expressions with parameters

We will expand the concept a bit further by incorporating what we discussed in the previous chapter about variables with parameters and apply it to a set expression. Let's follow these steps:

1. Open the **Variable Overview...** window (*Ctrl + Alt + V*) and create a new variable. Name it vSetPreviousNMonth.

2. The variable definition will be:

```
PeriodID = {$(=Max(PeriodID) - $1)},
Year = ,
Quarter = ,
Month = ,
Period =
```

Look closely and you'll notice that the new variable is almost the same as the one defined previously, called vSetPreviousMonth. The difference between both variables is that we are now inserting a parameter into the PeriodID value definition. This parameter is represented by $1, and will allow us to use the same set variable to obtain the corresponding record set either for the previous month (when the parameter's value is 1), for two months ago (when the parameter's value is 2), and so forth, all using the same set variable.

To use the preceding variable in an expression, start by creating a new chart in the form of a straight table with **Carrier Group** as the dimension and the following three expressions:

1. The first expression, which we will label as Current Month Flights, will be:

   ```
   Sum({$<$(vSetPreviousNMonth(0))>} [# Departures Performed])
   ```

2. The second expression, which we will label as Flights Previous Month, will be:

   ```
   Sum({$<$(vSetPreviousNMonth(1))>} [# Departures Performed])
   ```

3. The third expression, which will be label as Flights Two Months Ago, will be:

   ```
   Sum({$<$(vSetPreviousNMonth(2))>} [# Departures Performed])
   ```

The only difference among the preceding expressions, apart from the label, is the parameter's value inserted into the variable.

After properly formatting the expressions' values and the chart's presentation, we will have the following chart:

Carrier Group	Current Month Flights	Flights Previous Month	Flights Two Months Ago
	879,559	846,485	893,962
Major Carriers...	510,026	486,557	508,956
National Carrie...	217,773	210,652	219,263
Commuter Car...	57,789	56,819	61,644
Foreign Carriers	50,738	47,806	50,641
Small Certificat...	38,171	39,898	48,506
Large Regional...	3,044	2,875	2,943
Medium Regio...	2,018	1,878	2,009

Awesome!

We can even take this one step further. We previously said that period comparisons are widely used in almost any QlikView document, but what we've done with the preceding procedure is define the variables in one document. What about all of the other documents? Do we need to create each of these variables over and over again for each of our QlikView documents? Well, let's discuss an alternative.

Portable set expressions

Now that set expressions are handled via variables, we can automate the process of creating these variables, instead of doing it all manually. We will use an `include` statement to create the variables during script execution and by using a text file shared across different QlikView documents.

To begin, we will create a text file, containing the code used to define each variable. The contents of our text file will be:

```
Let vSetYTD = 'PeriodID = {"<=' &Chr(36) & '(=Max(PeriodID))"},'
&Chr(10) &
'Year = {' &Chr(36) & '(=Max(Year))},' &Chr(10) &
'Quarter = ,' &Chr(10) &
'Period = ,' &Chr(10) &
'Month = ';

Let vSetQTD = 'PeriodID = {"<=' &Chr(36) & '(=Max(PeriodID))"},'
&Chr(10) &
'QuarterID = {' &Chr(36) & '(=Max(QuarterID))},' &Chr(10) &
'Year = ,' &Chr(10) &
'Quarter = ,' &Chr(10) &
'Period = ,' &Chr(10) &
```

```
'Month = ';

Let vSetMTD = 'PeriodID = {' &Chr(36) & '(=Max(PeriodID))},' &Chr(10)
&
'Year = ,' &Chr(10) &
'Quarter = ,' &Chr(10) &
'Period = ,' &Chr(10) &
'Month = ';

Let vSetPreviousMonth = 'PeriodID = {' &Chr(36) & '(=Max(PeriodID) -
1)},' &Chr(10) &
'Year = ,' &Chr(10) &
'Quarter = ,' &Chr(10) &
'Period = ,' &Chr(10) &
'Month = ';

Let vSetPreviousQuarter = 'QuarterID = {' &Chr(36) & '(=Max(QuarterID)
- 1)},' &Chr(10) &
'Year = ,' &Chr(10) &
'Quarter = ,' &Chr(10) &
'Period = ,' &Chr(10) &
'Month = ';

Let vSetLYMTD = 'PeriodID = {' &Chr(36) & '(=Max(PeriodID) - 12)},'
&Chr(10) &
'Year = {' &Chr(36) & '(=Max(Year)-1)},' &Chr(10) &
'Quarter = ,' &Chr(10) &
'Period = ,' &Chr(10) &
'Month = ';

Let vSetLYQTD = 'QuarterID = {' &Chr(36) & '(=Max(QuarterID) - 4)},'
&Chr(10) &
'Year = ,' &Chr(10) &
'Quarter = ,' &Chr(10) &
'Period = ,' &Chr(10) &
'Month = ';

Let vSetLYYTD = 'PeriodID = {"<=' &Chr(36) & '(=Max(PeriodID) -
12)"},' &Chr(10) &
'Year = {' &Chr(36) & '(=Max(Year)-1)},' &Chr(10) &
'Quarter = ,' &Chr(10) &
'Period = ,' &Chr(10) &
'Month = ';

Let vSetRolling12 = 'PeriodID = {">=' &Chr(36) & '(=Max(PeriodID) -
11)<=' &Chr(36) & '(=Max(PeriodID))"},' &Chr(10) &
'Year = ,' &Chr(10) &
'Quarter = ,' &Chr(10) &
'Period = ,' &Chr(10) &
'Month = ';
```

When defining our set variables in the script, we must be very cautious because of the presence of the dollar sign inside the variable's text. If we were to use the dollar sign directly inside the variable's definition, QlikView would interpret it as something to be expanded in the process, causing the load script to fail. Therefore, we have avoided the insertion of this symbol and used a string function instead. Chr(36) results in the dollar sign, as it is the ASCII character used to represent the symbol. The resulting string is concatenated to the rest when the variable is defined.

We have also inserted line breaks with the Chr(10) function.

We will name the text file as SetVariables.txt and store it in the same location as the Airline Operations document.

A copy of the finished SetVariables.txt has been included into the Airline Operations\Apps folder.

Now that we have the text file, we will include it into our script using the following statement:

```
$(Include=SetVariables.txt)
```

Relative or full paths can be used with the Include statement. Double-check the file path when using this statement, as there are no error messages when the specified file is not found.

When we run the script, the corresponding variables will be created and are ready to be used on the chart's expressions. The same statement could be used on any QlikView document to make them execute the same SetVariables.txt script and share the same set variables across them.

An alternative method for defining variables in an external file and loading them into QlikView is described in Barry's blog at http://www.qlikfix.com/2011/09/21/storing-variables-outside-of-qlikview/. Be sure to check that out too.

Set variables and the Master Calendar

As the set variables created with the preceding script are based on field names, all of those fields must exist (preferably in a Master Calendar table) in the document that uses the variables, otherwise they will not work as expected. Therefore, we advise you to integrate both the set variables and the Master Calendar scripts into a single, generic script stored in a text file to be called from any QlikView document, ensuring consistency and functionality.

Comparative analysis with alternate states

In addition to time-based comparisons, there are other scenarios in which the comparison of two different sets of data can help enhance the analytical capabilities of a QlikView document. In this section, we will present a feature available in QlikView since version 11 which makes it easy to create highly dynamic comparative scenarios that enables business discovery in an entirely new way.

A comparative analysis example

Let's discuss one of these scenarios by using our Airline Operations document. Suppose we want to compare how the number of international flights arriving at the city of Chicago, IL, and performed by US carriers, compares to the number of domestic flights departing from Chicago and bound to the State of California, performed by US Carriers as well. If we were to see this comparison in a bar chart and over time, we would have the following:

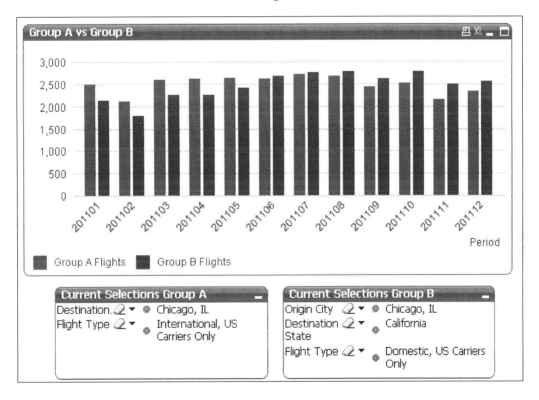

In the preceding example, the total flights in **Group A** (represented by the blue bars) correspond to those coming from outside the US, arriving at Chicago, and performed by US carriers, as depicted in the corresponding current selections box on the left. **Group B** (represented by the brown bars) covers flights departing from Chicago, bound to California, and performed by US carriers as well, as depicted in the current selections box on the right.

We can easily see how the amount of flights performed by **Group A** is greater to that of **Group B** during the first five months of 2011, it is almost equal during June and July, and it is lower during the rest of the year.

Alternate states step-by-step

We have been able to define two different record sets and compare the corresponding results side-by-side by enabling the **alternate states** functionality. To see how this works, let's build the preceding chart, step-by-step, by following this procedure:

1. Open the `Airline Operations.qvw` document we have been working with.
2. Click on the **Add Sheet** button from the **Design** toolbar to create a new sheet.
3. Right-click on an empty space of the worksheet area of the new sheet and select **Properties...**.
4. From the **Sheet Properties** window, activate the **General** tab and enter **Comparative Analysis** into the **Title** field.
5. Click on **OK** in the **Sheet Properties** window.
6. Now, navigate to **Settings | Document Properties...** and activate the **General** tab from the **Document Properties** window.
7. Then, click on the **Alternate States...** button and a new pop-up window will appear , as seen here:

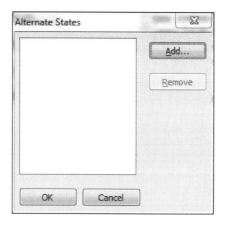

8. From the **Alternate States** window, click on the **Add...** button and enter **Group A** into the **New State Name** window. Then, click on **OK** to create the new alternate state and get back to the **Alternate States** window.

9. Click on the **Add...** button once more in the **Alternate States** window to create a new state, and name it **Group B**.

10. Click on **OK** to close the **Alternate States** window and on **OK** again to exit the **Document Properties** window.

    At this point, we have defined two different states: **Group A** and **Group B**. Each of these states will be used to save the two different record sets we want to analyze, which will be given by user selections in a set of listboxes we will now create.

11. Add the following listboxes by right-clicking on an empty space from the worksheet area and clicking on **Select Fields...** from the context menu:

    Origin Country, Origin State Code, Origin City, Origin Airport, Destination Country, Destination State Code, Destination City, Destination Airport, and **Flight Type**.

12. Now, create a container object with all of the above-listed listboxes in it.

13. From the **General** tab of the container object properties window, select **Group A** in the **Alternate State** drop-down list, as seen here:

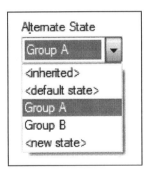

 This drop-down list is available in the sheet object once the **Alternate States** feature has been enabled by defining at least one alternate state from the **Document Properties** window. If no alternate state has been previously created, the drop-down list will not be visible.

14. Enter **Origin and Destination - Group A** as the container object's title and click on **OK** to close the **Container Properties** dialog window.

15. Now, clone the container object just created by copying it to the clipboard (right-click on **Copy to Clipboard** and go to **Object**) and then pasting it again (right-click on the sheet workspace area and select **Paste Sheet Object**).

16. Access the properties window corresponding to the new copy of the container object and change the alternate state from **Group A** to **Group B**. Change the title as well to **Origin and Destination - Group B**.

17. After arranging the presentation of the two container objects just created, we should have the following:

What we've done is define two sets of listboxes to control selections and indicate which data each alternate should state take into account. As the state of all new objects, by default, set to **inherited**, all of our listboxes are using the alternate state defined in the next higher-level object, which is the container into which they were placed.

> Any selection made on one state does not affect any other state.

By using container objects to accommodate the various listboxes related to origin and destination dimensions, we are able to save some valuable screen space and keep an ordered layout in our document.

We will now create a bar chart to visualize the comparison of the two record sets:

1. Before continuing, copy the listboxes corresponding to **Year**, **Quarter**, and **Month** from one of the other sheets and place them into the new **Comparative Analysis** sheet as linked objects.

2. Now, create a new chart by clicking on the **Create Chart** button from the **Design** toolbar and setting the following properties:

   ° **Chart Type**: **Bar Chart**
   ° **Window Title**: **Group A vs Group B**
   ° **Show Title in Chart**: Disabled
   ° **Dimension**: **Period**
   ° **Expression 1**:

   Label: **Group A**

   Definition: Sum({ [Group A] * $} [# Departures Performed])
   ° **Expression 2**:

   Label: **Group B**

   Definition: Sum({ [Group B] * $} [# Departures Performed])
   ° **Primary Dimension Labels**: With diagonal orientation
   ° **Number Format Settings**: **Integer** for both expressions

At this point, our chart will respond to user selections on either state and show the corresponding comparisons. Let's select the following values in each of the alternate states:

- Group A:

   ° **Flight Type**: **International, US Carriers Only**
   ° **Destination City**: **Chicago, IL**

- Group B:

   ° **Flight Type**: **Domestic, US Carriers Only**
   ° **Origin City**: **Chicago, IL**
   ° **Destination State Code**: **CA**

- **Year**: **2011**

   The selection in **Year** is made in the default document state, as the corresponding listbox has not been associated to either alternate state. This selection will apply to both chart calculations.

Our comparative analysis chart will now show the trend we discussed previously. Let's now look at how we constructed the preceding expressions.

State-based expressions

The syntax we used is very similar to the one we described when we introduced Set Analysis. In this case, the [Group A] and [Group B] parameters are the equivalent of a set identifier. To quickly recap, the two different set identifiers we described previously are:

- $ (Dollar symbol): This set identifier is used to base the calculation on the default current selections.

- 1 (number one): This set identifier is used when the calculation should be based on the entire document data, disregarding any selections made by the user.

Similar to these two, we can use any defined alternate state as set identifiers in our expressions so that the calculation is based only on selections made on listboxes (or objects) linked to that specific state.

The syntax, apart from the set identifier (or state identifier), is basically the same as with Set Analysis. This means we can integrate additional set modifiers into our state-based expressions. We can also use the same set operators described in the *Set operators* section in this chapter.

Combining alternate states and the default state

In the two expressions we just created, we are using the Intersection set operator to further restrict our calculation and use a modified record set. Take, for example, the expression corresponding to group A:

```
Sum({[Group A] * $} [# Departures Performed])
```

With this expression, the calculation will be based on both the selections made on the alternate state named Group A and the selections made on the default state. In other words, that is, only the data found in both record sets is considered in the calculation. This is especially useful when we only need a few fields to differentiate each alternate state (like the origin and destination dimensions), while selections in all other fields should be equally considered in all alternate states. In our case, we are using the intersection operation to be able to take into account selections made on the Year, Quarter, and Month fields.

We must be careful, though, when using set intersections in our state-based expressions. For this to work appropriately, no conflicting selections should be made in the default state over the fields we have also defined in our alternate states.

However, you want to play it safe, there is another way in which we could construct our expressions:

- Group A:

    ```
    Sum({[Group A]<Year = p(Year), Quarter = p(Quarter), Month =
    p(Month)>} [# Departures Performed])
    ```

- Group B:

    ```
    Sum({[Group B]<Year = p(Year), Quarter = p(Quarter), Month =
    p(Month)>} [# Departures Performed])
    ```

The preceding expressions will only consider the selections made in the Year, Quarter, and Month fields from the default document state and add them to all selections made on the corresponding alternate state. By doing so, we ensure that all of the selections made in any other field outside the alternate state are not taken into account.

 Element functions are described in the *Using element functions* section of this chapter.

Applying alternate states to layout objects

By default, all layout objects (that is, charts, listboxes, sheets, and so on) use an **Inherited** state unless specifically overridden via its properties window. Sheet objects can inherit states from a higher-level object, such as a sheet or a container object.

There is another state that can be specifically applied to any sheet or sheet object: the default state. The QlikView document is always in the default state.

Additionally, once the alternate states feature has been enabled, we can create new alternate states from any layout object by selecting the **<new state>** option from the **Alternate States** drop-down list.

Document navigation with alternate states

Just as with Set Analysis, the use of alternate states can become a bit confusing for the end users if we are not careful. It is very important to develop our QlikView documents in such a way that every state-based object is properly labeled. This will help the user to easily identify how each calculation is being performed and the record set it is based on.

One way we can do this is by adding current selections boxes to represent each alternate state at any given time. Look at the image with which we started this section and you'll see how important they are.

Clearing selections in an alternate state

By default, all of the buttons in the navigation toolbar affect all states. That is, when we click on the **Clear** button, all selections from all states are cleared. Similarly, the **Back** and **Forward** commands apply to all selections in all of the states.

However, it is possible to clear the selections in one specific state without affecting the others. This is accomplished via a menu item found under the **Clear** button drop-down menu, as shown below:

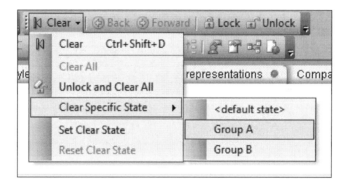

Always validate

Set expressions and alternate states can can get very complex, so it's a good practice to always validate the results thoroughly. Here are a few ways in which we can do that:

- When using calculations in the element list definition, take the individual calculation out of the set expression and enter it into a text object to visualize its result and ensure that it's what you expect.

- Once the set expression or state, has been constructed, play around and make a few selections to see how each affects the calculation and ensure it's what the user would expect.

- When you've arrived at a result using a set expression, replicate the base expression, without the set portion, and try to arrive at the same result using only selections. If everything is correct, the result should always be the same, unless of course the modified record set cannot be replicated using selections only.

Summary

We've come to the end of this chapter in which we've been able to use some advanced expression techniques and Set Analysis to build period-over-period comparisons. We have learned the syntax and variations of a set expression.

We also learned how to construct and use Set Analysis expressions to enable time period comparisons, and also how to use some time-saving techniques to re-use set expressions across different documents.

Finally, we learned how to use alternate states for comparative analysis.

Let's now move on to the next chapter, which expands on the concept of data transformation at an advanced level.

13
Advanced Data Transformation

In this chapter we will dive into advanced transformation functions and techniques available through QlikView's extraction engine. This will allow you, as a developer, to finely process the source data and turn it into a clean design, while at the same time keeping an efficient script.

The goals of this chapter are:

- To provide an overview of the most commonly used data architectures that can ease QlikView's development and administration
- To describe the available functions for data aggregation
- To learn how to take advantage of some of QlikView's most powerful data transformation functions.

Data architecture

Now that we have a decent amount of QlikView development experience under our belt, we will introduce the concept of data architecture. This refers to the process of structuring the different layers of data processing that exist between the source tables and the final document(s). Having a well-designed data architecture will greatly simplify the administration of the QlikView deployment. It also makes the QlikView solution scalable when new applications need to be developed and when the QlikView environment grows. There can be a lot of different data architectures, but in this section we will discuss two of the most commonly used in QlikView enterprise deployments.

Two-stage architecture

The following diagram depicts the two-stage architecture:

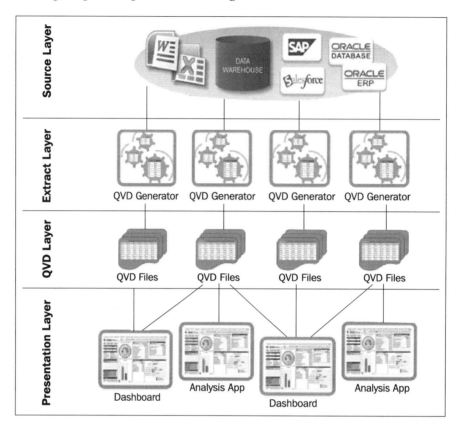

The two-stage architecture is composed of the following layers:

- **Source Layer**: composed of the source databases and original tables.
- **Extract Layer**: composed of QlikView documents, containing mainly script. These are used to pull the data from the source layer and store it into QVD files. The extraction scripts can either create a straight copy of the source tables to store them into the corresponding QVD files, or perform certain transformations before storing the result.

- **QVD Layer**: the set of QVDs resulting from the Extract Layer. These QVDs become the data sources used by the final QlikView document.

- **Presentation Layer**: the set of QlikView documents used to provide the data to the end user. These QlikView files will use the QVDs created in the previous layer as data sources, and sometimes perform additional transformations to create the final data model. No database calls are performed from the presentation layer.

The advantages of using this approach and having a QVD Layer are reuse and consistency. This approach promotes re-use because, in deployments where multiple documents make use of the same source data, the original database (Source Layer) is not overloaded with redundant requests. At the same time, the re-use process ensures consistency across all different QlikView documents that make use of the same data.

> If you look closely, you'll notice that this architecture is the one we've been using in the previous chapters, since we've mainly loaded data into our QlikView document from previously-created QVDs.

This approach is mainly used when the source data is good enough to be included into the QlikView data model with little or no modification. However, when major data transformation is needed, the administration gets a little messy with this architecture since it is not clearly defined at which stage these transformations take place.

Three-stage architecture

Now, let's take a look at the three-stage architecture:

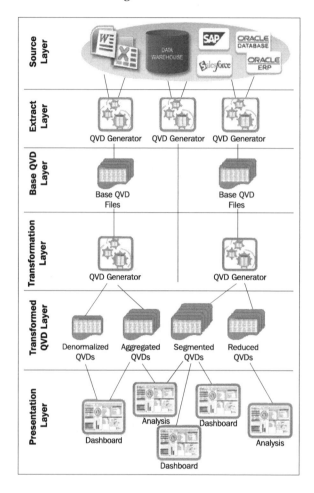

In this architecture, two additional layers are added: **Transformation Layer** and **Transformed QVD Layer**. The role of these two additional layers is to hold all transformations that need to be performed upon the source data before it can be integrated into the target data model.

This also suggests that all base QVDs will ideally keep a straight copy of the source table, which will optimize the extraction process. Then, the Transformation Layer, in which several base QVDs will be combined to create denormalized QVDs, performs any required aggregation or segmentation, and adds new calculated fields or composite keys to prepare the transformed QVDs for a clean and simple load into the final data model.

Since the documents in the Presentation Layer will use the transformed QVDs, and sometimes some base QVDs that required no modification, and will (ideally) read them "as-is", optimized loads will be ensured at this stage.

QVDs can also be reused with this architecture when the data model of two or more QlikView documents require the same source data.

 This approach is the one we will work from this point onwards since new transformations will be made to our base QVDs.

A well-designed data architecture, as those presented in this section, can also enable the possibility of having different QlikView teams working at different stages. For example, IT developers can prepare the base and transformed QVDs, while business teams can make use of those to build the end documents without requiring access to the source database.

Setting up our environment

Now that we've discussed the advantages of using the three-stage architecture, let's take a moment to set up our Windows folder structure following the described guidelines.

By copying the files corresponding to this chapter into your **QlikView Development** folder, you will have a structure like this:

The **0.Includes** folder is used to store re-usable code that is called from the end documents via an `Include` statement. The **1.Source Data** folder represents the Source Layer; this folder is used because our source database is composed of CSV files but wouldn't be required otherwise. The **2.Workbooks** folder holds all QVD Generators (QVW files) for both the Base Layer and the Transformation Layer. The **3.QVD** folder is used to store the resulting QVD files from both the Base Layer (using the **Source** subfolder) and the Transformation Layer (using the **Transformed** subfolder). The **4.Applications** folder represents the Presentation Layer.

Inside these folders, you will find all source tables in CSV format, as well as the extract QVWs and the base QVDs used in previous chapters. We will work directly with the Transformation Layer in the coming sections.

Loading data already stored in QlikView

The first lesson in advanced data transformation will be about optimizing loads when processing data. If you remember from *Chapter 4, Data Sources*, we discussed the various ways in which we can pull data from different sources into QlikView. We also described how we can take advantage of the QVD file format to store and read data in super-fast mode. Now, we will describe yet another way of reading source tables, but this time the "source" will be QlikView itself. There are different cases in which this approach will prove useful and we will describe two scenarios to perform it:

- Accessing data already stored in a QlikView data model (QVW file) from a separate QlikView document. We will call this approach *Cloning a QlikView data model*.

- Accessing data from the same QlikView document in which the data model resides. We will call this approach *Loading from RAM*.

Cloning a QlikView data model

This concept refers to the ability of replicating the data model of an already created QlikView document and placing it into another QlikView document without accessing the original data source. In technical terms, it's a **Binary load**. Once the data model is cloned by the second QlikView document, it can be manipulated further, integrated into a bigger data model (that is, adding more tables to it), or even reduced by removing some of its tables or data.

Suppose we have a QlikView file, with an already constructed data model and all of the composing tables properly associated. We now want to use this same model in another QlikView document, adding just a few more tables. The process for binary loading a QVW is as follows:

1. Create a brand new QlikView document and save it to the disk.

2. Open the **Edit Script** window (*Ctrl + E* or **File | Edit Script...**)

3. Click on **QlikView File...** button, located in the **Data** tab.

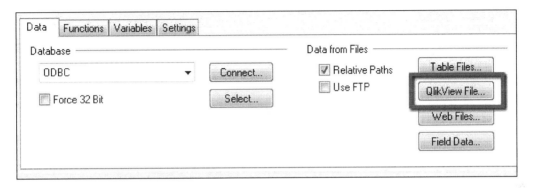

4. Browse to the QlikView file we want to read and click on **Open**.

5. A new script statement will be created at the top of the active script tab, which will be something like `Binary [file name.qvw];`

 The `Binary` statement must be the first statement to be executed in the script, so it has to be always at the top of the first (left-most) script tab. Also, only one binary load is allowed in a QlikView script.

6. At this point, we can add more tables to the already-loaded data model as we would normally do. After reloading the script, the data model will now be in the new QlikView document, along with any other added tables.

 A `Binary` load statement is the fastest way to load data into a QlikView document.

In the environment we've been working throughout the book, can you find a use case for a `Binary` load? Which would it be?

I can think of one. For example, we have an initial QlikView document with the `Airline Operations` data (the one we constructed in *Chapter 3, Seeing is Believing*). Based on this initial data model, we can create a new QlikView document, to which we will only add the `Employment` data (used in *Chapter 9, Data Modeling Best Practices*). As a result, we would have one `Airline Operations` document accessed by certain users, and another with the same data but with additional information about airline employment, which might be treated as confidential and accessed by another group of users.

As a side note, we must point out that binary loads are used in yet another approach to data architecture. We will not discuss it in-depth, but suffice to say that the new layer is composed of QlikView documents consisting of only a data model without any frontend objects, referred to as "QlikMarts". These QlikMarts then become the source for the QlikView documents in the Presentation Layer.

Loading from RAM

In some cases, we will need to read the same table more than once in a single script execution. This means, querying the database (or QVDs) and pulling data from it, and then reprocessing that same data after the first read in order to make it adequate for our data model. Since the data is being stored in RAM after each query during the script execution, we can use that RAM-stored data instead of going directly to the original data source. This is accomplished via a **Resident load**.

Resident load

The keyword `Resident` can be likened to the keyword `From` in a query. The difference is that the `Resident` keyword is used to reference the data in RAM model, that is, all the tables that have been previously read in the preceding queries of the same script. The process for achieving this is as follows:

1. First, we must load data from a data source (any database or table file described in the previous sections), so we create the corresponding query in the script. An example would be:

```
SalesData:
LOAD
    InvoiceNumber,
    Date,
    SalesPerson,
    Department,
    Amount as InvoiceAmount;
SQL SELECT * FROM DataBaseName.dbo.Sales;
```

Note that we have defined a table name, at the beginning of the query, so that we can use it to reference the table later on. We have also renamed the `Amount` field to `InvoiceAmount`.

2. Next, we add a subsequent query, in the same script, to access the table already in RAM using the `Resident` keyword. In this case, we will also aggregate the data using a `Group By` clause, which is a data transformation technique explained later in this chapter.

```
SalesTotals:
LOAD
   Department,
   Sum(InvoiceAmount) as TotalAmount
Resident SalesData
Group By Department;
```

Note that, when referencing a table that is now part of the QlikView data model, we must use the field names with which they have been defined, which might not necessarily be the same names as in the source table. In this case, we are using `InvoiceAmount`, a name that was defined in the previous query. The same applies for table names.

As a result, we will have two tables in our data model; one with all the data at an atomic level, the product of the first query, and the other as an aggregated version of the `SalesData` table with totals by `Department`, the product of the `Resident`load we constructed in conjunction with the `Group by` statement.

Aggregating data

While QlikView shines in dealing with massive data volumes, sometimes we just do not need to load everything at an atomic level. Data aggregation can, for example, be used in deployments where document segmentation by detail is needed, in which case two documents are created to serve different user groups and analysis needs: one document will have all data with the highest level of detail and another one will have a similar data model but with aggregated (reduced) tables. This way, users are better served by keeping a balance between performance and analysis needs.

In this section, we will implement a document segmentation scenario by aggregating the **Flight Data** table to create a second document intended for executive users, who only require summary data.

Aggregating the Flight Data table

When aggregating data, the first step is always to define which dimension fields will be left out and which ones will be kept in the summarized table. We should analyze this question by looking at the data from the ground up, that is, by reviewing each dimension from the most granular to the most general. The following list shows the most important dimension fields in the Flight Data table, sorted by granularity:

- **Airport (Origin** and **Destination)**
- **City**
- **State**
- **Country**
- **Aircraft Type**
- **Aircraft Group**
- **Airline / Carrier**
- **Carrier Group**
- **Region**
- **Month**
- **Quarter**
- **Year**

If we analyze how removing each dimension would individually affect the result of the summarization process, we can find that the most impact would come from removing the **Airport** dimensions, both Origin and Destination, since those are the ones with the greatest granularity. At the same time, we can say that the **Airport** dimension does not add much value to the analyses we are looking to deliver in our document, so it's a good choice to leave it out.

> Dropping dimensions from the data directly impacts the analyses that can be made in the resulting QlikView document. Therefore, the decision to leave out certain fields for the sake of summarization should always be discussed with the end user.

We could remove additional dimensions, for example, **Aircraft Type** or **Carrier**, but as we move up the detail ladder to the most general dimensions, those dimensions become more and more important to accomplish different analyses.

We must add that leaving dimensions out should be a thorough decision process, thinking both in terms of analytical requirements and the aggregation rate we can achieve. For example, removing the Country dimension would not result in any substantial aggregation if we keep the State field. Also, what happens if we remove the Airport dimensions but keep Origin City and Destination City? What happens is, not surprisingly, that the table will not be significantly reduced since both fields keep a close relation and their granularity is almost the same (there is only one airport in most cities). Therefore, and for the sake of simplicity, we will also leave out all city, state, and country fields.

Finally, before proceeding, we should keep in mind how many records the original table has, in order to be able to measure how much reduction we achieved in the summarization. In our case, the `Flight Data` table originally contains 1,256,075 rows.

Moving on to the aggregation process, follow these steps:

1. Create a new QlikView document and save it inside the `2.Workbooks` folder with the name `Transform - Flight Data.qvw`.

2. Go to the **Script Editor** window, click on the **Table Files...** button in the tool pane and navigate to the `3.QVD\Source` folder.

3. Select the `Flight Data.qvd` file and click **Finish** on the **File Wizard** window.

4. From the generated `Load` script, find the lines corresponding to those fields related to origin and destination airports and erase them. The fields we should remove are:

   ○ `%Origin Airport ID`
   ○ `%Origin Airport Sequence ID`
   ○ `%Origin Airport Market ID`
   ○ `%Origin World Area Code`
   ○ `%Destination Airport ID`
   ○ `%Destination Airport Sequence ID`
   ○ `%Destination Airport Market ID`
   ○ `%Destination World Area Code Distance`
   ○ `Origin Airport Code`
   ○ `Origin City`
   ○ `Origin State Code`
   ○ `Origin State FIPS`
   ○ `Origin State`
   ○ `Origin Country Code`
   ○ `Origin Country`

- ° Destination Airport Code, Destination City
- ° Destination State Code
- ° Destination State FIPS
- ° Destination State
- ° Destination Country Code Destination Country
- ° From - To Airport Code
- ° From - To Airport ID
- ° From - To City
- ° From - To State Code
- ° From - To State

5. Next, from the list of fields we have kept, we need to identify those that are dimensions and those that are measures. Our measure fields are:

   - ° # Departures Scheduled
   - ° # Departures Performed
   - ° # Payload
   - ° # Available Seats
   - ° # Transported Passengers
   - ° # Transported Freight
   - ° # Transported Mail
   - ° # Ramp-To-Ramp Time
   - ° # Air Time

6. The aggregation functions will be applied to these fields, that is, we will sum the # of Departures, or sum the # Transported Passengers. Identify where each of the listed fields are in the created load statement and replace the field name with the following expression:

   Sum (*Field Name*) as *Field Name*

   where Field Name represents each of the listed measures.

    Be careful not to remove the comma that separates each field definition and remove the comma from the last listed field, before the From keyword.

7. Finally, we will add a Group By clause to the end of the Load statement, and list *all dimension fields* that have been kept in the script, separated by a comma.

8. We will also add a table name preceding the Load keyword.

9. In the end, the `aggregation` script will look like this:

```
Flights:
LOAD
    [%Airline ID],
    [%Carrier Group ID],
    [%Unique Carrier Code],
    [%Unique Carrier Entity Code],
    [%Region Code],
    [%Aircraft Group ID],
    [%Aircraft Type ID],
    [%Aircraft Configuration ID],
    [%Distance Group ID],
    [%Service Class ID],
    [%Datasource ID],
    [Unique Carrier],
    [Carrier Code],
    [Carrier Name],
    Year,
    Period,
    Quarter,
    [Month (#)],
    Month,
    Sum([# Departures Scheduled]) as [# Departures Scheduled],
    Sum([# Departures Performed]) as [# Departures Performed],
    Sum([# Payload]) as [# Payload],
    Sum([# Available Seats]) as [# Available Seats],
    Sum([# Transported Passengers]) as [# Transported
Passengers],
    Sum([# Transported Freight]) as [# Transported Freight],
    Sum([# Transported Mail]) as [# Transported Mail],
    Sum([# Ramp-To-Ramp Time]) as [# Ramp-To-Ramp Time],
    Sum([# Air Time]) as [# Air Time]
FROM
[..\3.QVD\Source\Flight Data.qvd]
(qvd)
Group By
[%Airline ID], [%Carrier Group ID], [%Unique Carrier Code],
[%Unique Carrier Entity Code], [%Region Code], [%Aircraft Group
ID],
[%Aircraft Type ID], [%Aircraft Configuration ID], [%Distance
Group ID],
[%Service Class ID], [%Datasource ID], [Unique Carrier], [Carrier
Code],
[Carrier Name], Year, Period, Quarter, [Month (#)], Month;
```

10. Next, we will just save the changes and reload the script.

The resulting table will turn our 1,256,075 rows into only 100,091. A brief example of what just happened is shown in the following screenshot:

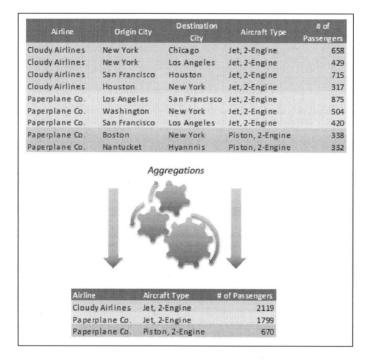

Notice how the totals remain the same for both tables.

A smaller table will occupy fewer resources (RAM and CPU) and, therefore, calculations will be faster. If the performance gain attained with data aggregation doesn't mean reducing business value and/or functionality for the end user, then it's a winning approach any day.

The Transformation output

We have loaded the base QVD containing flight data and transformed it by applying aggregations, now what? Well, the next steps would be to store the transformed table, using the store command, into a new QVD file that will reside in the 3.QVDs\ Transformed folder.

After that, a new data model could be created in the Presentation Layer based on the Airline Operations document, but using the newly aggregated QVD and without the Origin and Destination dimensions. This new QlikView document is intended to serve the users who only need summarized information about the Airline Operations document.

Aggregation functions

Of course, QlikView offers more aggregation options than summing. The most commonly used options are shown in the following table:

Function	Explanation	Example
Sum()	Sums numeric expressions. Optionally a DISTINCT qualifier can be added, this will cause the function to ignore duplicate values.	Sum(DISTANCE) Sum(DISTINCT AIR_TIME)
Min()	Returns the lowest value within a numeric range. Optionally a rank can be specified, this will return the nth lowest number. So 2 returns the second lowest number.	Min(DISTANCE) Min(DISTANCE, 2)
Max()	Returns the highest value within a numeric range. Optionally a rank can be specified, this will return the nth highest number. So 2 returns the second highest number.	Max(PASSENGERS) Max(PASSENGERS, 2)
Only()	If the aggregation of a value returns only a single value, that value is returned, otherwise the function returns null. For example, when an expression contains the values {1, 1, 1} then the Only() function will return 1. If an expression contains the values {1, 2, 3} then the Only() function returns null.	Only(SEATS)
MinString()	Similar to the Min() function, but applied to text strings. Also, it does not have the optional rank parameter.	MinString(MANUFACTURER)
MaxString()	Similar to the Max() function, but applied to text strings. Also, it does not have the optional rank parameter.	MaxString(MANUFACTURER)
Concat()	Concatenates all the values of an expression into a single string, which is separated by a delimiter given as a function's parameter. Has an optional DISTINCT qualifier which will set the function to ignore duplicate values.	Concat(AIRPORT_NAME, ';') Concat(DISTINCT MANUFACTURER, ',')
Count()	Counts the number of items in the input expression. Has an optional DISTINCT qualifier that sets the function to ignore duplicate values. Instead of an expression an * (asterisk) can also be used to count the number of rows.	Count(AIRCRAFT_NAME) Count(DISTINCT AIRCRAFT_NAME)

Sorting tables

We will now introduce the Order By statement, which is added to a Load statement and is used to sort an input table based on certain fields. There is one major condition for the Order By statement to work: it must be applied to a Load statement getting data from a Resident table, not from a table file or any other source.

Some databases can receive Order By instructions in the Select query, but in this section we will only deal with Order By statements on the QlikView side.

The Order By statement must receive at least one field name over which the ordering will be performed and, optionally, the sort order (either ascending or descending). If the sort order is not specified along with the field name, the default sort order will be applied, which is ascending.

An example script of an Order By statement at play is:

```
Load
 Region,
 Date,
 Amount
Resident SalesTable
Order By Date asc;
```

In this script, we are loading three fields (Region, Date, and Amount) from a previously loaded table, named SalesTable, and, as the table is being read, the data is being ordered by Date from older to newer records (ascending).

Ordering the Order-By fields

An important point to consider when using the Order By statement, is that not only can one field be specified as the sorting value, we can also, for instance, sort the table by Date from older to newer and by Amount from largest to smallest. The order in which we specify the sorting fields will determine the output of the operation. Take, for example the following two scripts:

```
A:
Load
 Region,
 Date,
 Amount
Resident SalesTable
Order By Date asc,
Amount desc;

B:
Load
```

```
    Region,
    Date,
    Amount
Resident SalesTable
Order By Amount desc,
Date asc;
```

The difference between both scripts is the Order by clause. Look closely and you will find that, in script A, the Date field takes precedence in the ordering of the data, while in script B, Amount is the first ordering field.

Take a moment to think what you would expect as the output of both scripts. You'll discover that the output of each script can be translated to plain English as:

- In script A, the table is first ordered by Date from oldest to newest and then, for each date, the corresponding records are sorted by Amount in the descending order

- In script B, the table is first ordered by Amount of the transaction, biggest amounts at the top, and, for records with the same amount, they get ordered by Date from oldest to newest

Normally we will want the table to be sorted by Date first and Amount as a second sorting value. It's important to take this into account when adding it in to our QlikView scripts.

 As a final remark, remember to drop the table on which the Resident load was based if it is no longer needed.

The Peek function

Another tool we'll add to our collection in this set of data transformation techniques is the Peek function. The Peek function is an inter-record function that allows us to literally peek into previously-read records of a table and use its values to evaluate a condition or to affect the active record (the one being read).

The function takes one mandatory parameter, the field name into which we will "peek", and two optional parameters, a row reference and the table in which the field is located.

For example, an expression like:

```
Peek('Date', -2)
```

This expression will go back two records in the currently-being-read table, take the value on the Date field and use it as a result of the expression.

Or take this other expression:

```
Peek('Date', 2)
```

In this expression instead of "going back" two records, we will take the value in the Date field from the third record from the beginning of the current table (counting starts at zero).

We can also add a table name as the third parameter, as in the following expression:

```
Peek('Date', 0, 'Budget')
```

This expression will return the value that the Date field stores on the first record in the Budget table.

Merging forces

On their own, the Order By statement and the Peek function are already powerful. Now, imagine what happens when we combine both of these tools to enhance our input data. In this section, we will use both of these functions to add a new calculated field to our Employment table (the one we integrated to our data model in *Chapter 9, Data Modeling Best Practices*).

A refresher

The Employment table provides information regarding the monthly number of employees per airline. The total number is split between part and full time employees, and it also shows the total **FTEs** (**Full Time Equivalent**).

The objective

The executives of HighCloud Airlines have asked the QlikView team to create a report that shows the monthly change in number of employees in a line chart to discover and analyze peaks in the employment behavior of each airline.

Getting it done

First, how do we find the total change in number of employees for this month compared to the last? Well, we take the number of employees in the current month and subtract the number of employees we had in the previous month. If the number is zero, it means there was no change (no one fired!), if the number is greater than zero, it means we have new hires in the house; last, and hopefully the least, if the number is less than zero, it means we will be missing some colleagues.

To add this field to our `Employment Statistics` table, and following the best practices we previously discussed, we will create a new QlikView document, used for transformations, and save it inside the `2.Workbooks` folder. Name this file as `Transform-Employment Data.qvw`. The resulting table will then be saved as QVD inside the `3.QVD\Transformed` folder.

Loading the table

Once you have the new QlikView document created, saved and still open, go to the **Edit Script** window (*Ctrl + E*) and perform the following steps:

1. Add a new tab to the script by clicking on the **Tab** menu and selecting **Add Tab...**.

2. From the **Tab Rename Dialog** window, type `Initial Load` as the name of the new tab and click on **OK**.

3. Use the **File Wizard** dialog to load the **Employment Statistics** table from the corresponding QVD file (`T_F41SCHEDULE_P1A_EMP.qvd`) stored in the `3.QVD\Source` folder.

4. Click on **Finish** on the first dialog window of the **File Wizard** dialog since no alterations will be made to the file on the initial load.

5. Assign the table a name by typing `Temp_Employment:` before the `Load` keyword of the generated script. Remove the `Directory;` statement if necessary.

6. Now, add a new tab to the right of the **Initial Load** tab, by clicking on **Add Tab...** from the **Tab** menu.

7. In the **Tab Rename Dialog** window, type `Transformation` as the name of the tab and click on **OK**.

8. Once in the **Transformation** tab, we will create the script to load the previously created `Temp_Employment` table via a `Resident` load. We will also name this new table as `Employment`. Write the following code:

```
Employment:
Load
        [%Airline ID],
         Year,
        [Month (#)],
        [# Total Employees],
        Period,
        Month,
        [%Unique Carrier Code],
        [Unique Carrier],
        [Carrier Code],
        [Carrier Name],
        [%Carrier Group ID],
        [# Full Time Employees],
        [# Part Time Employees],
        [# Equivalent FTEs]
    Resident Temp_Employment;
```

We are now ready to add the transformation functions to the table. It's important to note that, if we reload the script at this point, the new employment data will never be created because of the Natural Concatenation feature we talked about in *Chapter 9, Data Modeling Best Practices*, since both the `Temp_Employment` table and the `Employment` table will have exactly the same number of fields as well as the same field names. However, with the functions we will apply, and the new fields we will add, this structural similarity will be lost and we will not need to add the `NoConcatenate` keyword.

Sorting the table

Using the techniques learned in the *Sorting tables* section of this chapter, we will set the load order of the `Resident` table using the `%Airline ID`, `Year`, and `Month #` fields. The earlier script will be modified to:

```
Employment:
Load
        [%Airline ID],
        Year,
        [Month (#)],
        [# Total Employees],
        Period,
        Month,
```

```
        [%Unique Carrier Code],
        [Unique Carrier],
        [Carrier Code],
        [Carrier Name],
        [%Carrier Group ID],
        [# Full Time Employees],
        [# Part Time Employees],
        [# Equivalent FTEs]
    Resident Temp_Employment
    Order By [%Airline ID], Year, [Month (#)];
```

Take note of the order in which the sorting fields are defined. The ordering output is: all records will be first sorted by %Airline ID, for each airline, the records will then be sorted by Year in ascending order, and then, for each year, the records will be sorted by Month from first to last. In our case, the %Airline ID sorting can be either ascending or descending, it doesn't matter. However, Year and Month # must be sorted in ascending order, which is the default if no sort order is specified.

Peeking previous records

The final step will be to take the sorted table and start comparing adjacent months to find out the difference in number of employees between them. We've seen how the Peek function will bring a value from previous records, but in our case it gets a little trickier, since we need to be careful not to peek into and compare records corresponding to different airlines. An If expression should be used in conjunction with the Peek function. The adjustment we will make to the previous script will result in:

```
Employment:
Load
    If(
        [%Airline ID] = Peek('%Airline ID', -1),
        [# Total Employees] - Peek('# Total Employees', -1),
        0
        ) as [# Delta Total Employees],
        [%Airline ID],
        Year,
        [Month (#)],
        [# Total Employees],
        Period,
        Month,
        [%Unique Carrier Code],
        [Unique Carrier],
        [Carrier Code],
```

```
        [Carrier Name],
        [%Carrier Group ID],
        [# Full Time Employees],
        [# Part Time Employees],
        [# Equivalent FTEs]
    Resident Temp_Employment
    Order By [%Airline ID], Year, [Month (#)];
```

We are almost ready to reload our script and see the result. We just need to add a Drop statement to remove the Temp_Employment table from RAM after using it in the Resident load script. Add the following code at the end of the **Transformation** tab:

```
    Drop Table Temp_Employment;
```

After this, save the changes we've made to the QlikView document and hit **Reload** (or press *Ctrl+R*). The script will perform the transformation and, after it's finished, we can open the **Table Viewer** window and preview the resulting **Employment** table. Here is what we'll see:

%Airline ID	Year	Month (#)	# Total Employ...	# Delta Total E...	Period	Month
19386	2009	01	29084	0	200901	Jan
19386	2009	02	29138	54	200902	Feb
19386	2009	03	29084	-54	200903	Mar
19386	2009	04	29849	765	200904	Apr
19386	2009	05	26281	-3568	200905	May
19386	2009	06	27289	1008	200906	Jun
19386	2009	07	26710	-579	200907	Jul
19386	2009	08	26576	-134	200908	Aug

From the **Preview** dialog window, we can see how the very first airline (**19386**) has had an erratic behavior in their headcount. In February 2009, they had a bump of **54** employees, and in the following month their headcount dropped by the same amount. Then, a massive reduction of **3568** took place in May 2009.

Now that we've added the # Delta Total Employees field, let's add the corresponding delta fields for part-time and full-time employees, as well as FTEs. We will also add the store command to save the output table to a QVD file.

Our modified script will be:

```
Employment:
Load
    If(
        [%Airline ID] = Peek('%Airline ID', -1),
        [# Total Employees] - Peek('# Total Employees', -1),
        0
        ) as [# Delta Total Employees],
    If(
        [%Airline ID] = Peek('%Airline ID', -1),
        [# Full Time Employees] - Peek('# Full Time Employees', -1),
        0
        ) as [# Delta Full Time Employees],
    If(
        [%Airline ID] = Peek('%Airline ID', -1),
        [# Part Time Employees] - Peek('# Part Time Employees', -1),
        0
        ) as [# Delta Part Time Employees],
    If(
        [%Airline ID] = Peek('%Airline ID', -1),
        [# Equivalent FTEs] - Peek('# Equivalent FTEs', -1),
        0
        ) as [# Delta Equivalent FTEs],
    [%Airline ID],
    Year,
    [Month (#)],
    [# Total Employees],
    Period,
    Month,
    [%Unique Carrier Code],
    [Unique Carrier],
    [Carrier Code],
    [Carrier Name],
    [%Carrier Group ID],
    [# Full Time Employees],
    [# Part Time Employees],
    [# Equivalent FTEs]
 Resident Temp_Employment
Order By [%Airline ID], Year, [Month (#)];

Drop Table Temp_Employment;
Store Employment into [..\3.QVDs\Transformed\Employment Statistics.
QVD]
```

Adding these fields to our table makes it easier to perform more in-depth analyses, such as the ones shown in the following screenshot:

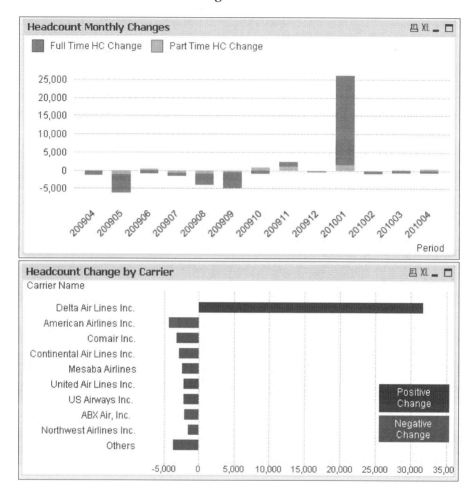

From the previous charts we can see that, while most carriers experienced a downsize in headcount from April 2009 to April 2010 (the selected dataset), **Delta Air Lines Inc.** grew its staff by about 32,000 employees in the same period.

By integrating this data into the final data model, may be able to find correlations between hires, downsizings, # of flights, enplaned passengers, flight occupancy, and so on. This enables the QlikView users at HighCloud Airlines to better make business decisions.

A solo exercise

By now, you are well armed, so what about a little challenge?

We've already added the fields for Monthly Headcount Change. How would we go about adding new fields for Quarterly Headcount Change and Annual Headcount Change? What information can you get from the resulting data?

Dealing with slowly changing dimensions

A slow changing dimension is one whose values vary across undefined time periods, that is, it can have different meanings depending on the time period context.

To illustrate the concept, consider the evolution of Joey, a support technician employee in a given company, over a certain period of time. When Joey joined the company, he had the Junior Support Technician position. Then, after one year, he gets promoted to Senior Technician. And now, one year later, has become the Support Manager.

Now, imagine you want to visualize the number of cases resolved by the entire support team over a three-year period and find out how many of those cases were resolved by junior technicians, how many were resolved by senior technicians, and how many were resolved by the support manager. If, for reporting purposes, we take Joey's current status in the company, all cases he has resolved in the last three years will be logged as if they were resolved by the Support Manager, which is not quite accurate. We should, instead, identify which positions Joey has had and the specific time frame for each of them. Then, count the corresponding number of cases he resolved on each support role and report it. Quite a task if we are dealing with tables of a respectable size.

To tackle challenges like these, we can make use of the `IntervalMatch` script function.

We will adapt our example to the `Airline Operations` data we've been working with, so make sure you have the `Carrier Decode.qvd` file in the `3.QVD\Source` folder.

The Carrier Decode table

Let's start by taking a closer look at the `Carrier Decode` table and its contents. If we were to open the table in Excel this is what we would see:

Airline ID	Carrier Code	Carrier Name	Unique Carrier Code	Unique Carrier Entity	Unique Carrier Name	Carrier World Area	Carrier Group ID	Region Code	Start Date	End Date
20195	WI	Tradewinds Airlines	WI	6884	Tradewinds Airlines	10	4	Domestic	01/02/98	31/12/99
20195	WI	Tradewinds Airlines	WI	16884	Tradewinds Airlines	10	4	International	01/02/98	31/12/99
20195	WI	Tradewinds Airlines	WI	6884	Tradewinds Airlines	10	1	Domestic	01/01/00	31/12/10
20195	WI	Tradewinds Airlines	WI	16884	Tradewinds Airlines	10	1	International	01/01/00	31/12/10
20195	WI	Tradewinds Airlines	WI	6884	Tradewinds Airlines	10	4	Domestic	01/01/11	31/12/11
20195	WI	Tradewinds Airlines	WI	16884	Tradewinds Airlines	10	4	International	01/01/11	31/12/11
20195	WI	Tradewinds Airlines	WI	6884	Tradewinds Airlines	10	1	Domestic	01/01/12	
20195	WI	Tradewinds Airlines	WI	16884	Tradewinds Airlines	10	1	International	01/01/12	

As you can see, the table extract shown in the screenshot contains the data corresponding to one particular carrier: **Tradewinds Airlines**. The first seven columns of the table are not relevant for us right now, so let's focus on the remaining four. We have a **Carrier Group ID** column which tells us if the carrier is catalogued as a Major, Large, Medium Carrier, and so on. We also have a **Region Code** column to indicate if the record corresponds to the domestic or international entity of the carrier (one carrier can perform both types of flights). And last but not least, we have a **Start Date** column and an **End Date** column, which will be the main fields we will use to deal with the slowly changing nature of this particular dimension. Those values indicate in which time frame the particular record is valid.

For example, the first two records shown earlier have a validity period from January 98 through December 99, in which Tradewinds Airlines was catalogued as a Medium Regional Carrier (**Group ID = 4**). Then, from January 2000 all the way through December 2010, the carrier was playing as a Large Regional Carrier (**Group ID = 1**). Afterwards, and until December 2011, it rolled back to the Medium Regional Carrier category but ascended back up as a Large Regional Carrier again for an undefined time.

When reporting Tradewinds Airlines' operations, we must take into account the carrier's classification in place (**Carrier Group ID** field) depending on the time period(s) being analyzed. Dealing with this is not trivial, so let's get going and create some **IntervalMatch** magic.

If we look at the original Flight Data table, we can see that we already have a `%Carrier Group ID` field in it, which is the same to that shown in the `Carrier Decode` table. However, to demonstrate how the `IntervalMatch` function can be useful, let's assume the field is not already in the fact table and that we must obtain it from the `Carrier Decode` table.

IntervalMatch magic

Because of the associative nature of the data model, and the dynamic nature of the queries a QlikView user performs, interval-based dimensions cannot be "queried" as one would with SQL-syntax queries. That's OK, since the associative engine can also handle such dimensions, just with a different, associative-based, approach. Let's see how.

Since the dimension value is dependent upon a time frame, the basic concept is that the key field, through which the dimension is associated with the rest of the data model, must be composed of both the dimension ID and a time element.

We refer to "time element" as the individual pieces into which an interval can be split.

The splitting of intervals means that one interval-based record in a table will be converted to several element-based records. If, for instance, an interval encompasses the equivalent of three time elements, the individual record will then be expanded into three different records, one for each of the corresponding time elements.

Expanding the intervals

The `IntervalMatch` function splits discrete, numeric-based, intervals based on two inputs:

- A table composed of two fields: one for the start of the interval and one for the end of the interval
- A list of values representing the individual data points into which the intervals will be split (the time element), according to their matching

All intervals must be closed, that is, they all must have an end value.

Let's look at a basic example to better illustrate the concept. Suppose we have the following intervals table:

ID	Start	End
A	6	8
B	2	15
C	9	20
D	1	8
E	8	15
F	10	15
G	6	9
H	8	9

We also have a list of the individual data points to associate the data with. The list of data points we will use has 20 values (from 1 to 20).

 Make sure a file called `Intervals.xlsx` is in the `1.Source Data\Examples` folder. It contains both tables described above and is the one we will be using.

To apply the `IntervalMatch` function, follow these steps:

1. Create a new QlikView document, name it `Intervals example.qvw`, and save it inside the `2.Workbooks\Examples` folder.

2. Go to the **Script Editor** window and click on the **Table files...** button to load the table called **Elements** from the `Intervals.xlsx` file.

3. Name the loaded table as `Elements`. The script so far should look as follows:

```
Elements:
LOAD
    Element
FROM
[..\..\1.Source Data\Examples\Intervals.xlsx] (ooxml, embedded
labels, table is Elements);
```

4. Next, create a new `Load` statement under the one we just created, this time loading the **Intervals** table from our Excel file.

5. Modify the `Load` statement by:

   ○ Removing the `ID` field.

   ○ Adding the `IntervalMatch` prefix as follows:

```
IntervalMatch(Element)
```

6. Create a `Drop` statement at the end of the script to remove the `Elements` table from the data model.

7. The final script should look like:

```
Elements:
LOAD
    Element
FROM
[..\..\1.Source Data\Examples\Intervals.xlsx]
(ooxml, embedded labels, table is Elements);

Intervals:
IntervalMatch (Element)
LOAD
    Start,
    End
```

```
FROM
[..\..\1.Source Data\Examples\Intervals.xlsx]
(ooxml, embedded labels, table is Intervals);

Drop Table Elements;
```

8. Now, save the changes and reload the script.

After the script execution, we will end up with one table containing all the expanded intervals and three fields: Element, Start, and End. If we add three listboxes to our workspace, one for each of the fields, and a table box to see the intervals, we will be able to appreciate the associations created by the IntervalMatch function. Some of these associations are depicted in the following screenshots.

When selecting the first interval (**1** through **8**), we see that the elements associated to that interval are all the numbers from **1** through **8**:

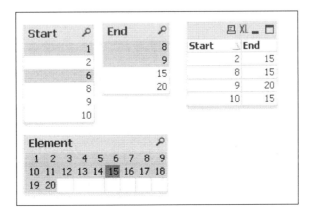

Then, if we select **15** in the **Element** listbox, we will see the four intervals containing that element within. All other intervals are now excluded:

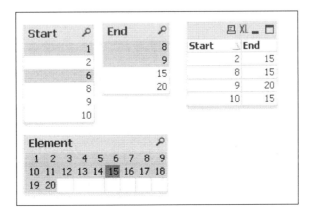

Finally, the actual output table, the one we now have in the data model, looks like this:

Start	End	Element
1	8	1
1	8	2
1	8	3
1	8	4
1	8	5
1	8	6
1	8	7
1	8	8
2	15	2

Some considerations

When working with the `IntervalMatch` function, it is important to keep the following in mind:

- This function is resource heavy, so, depending on the size of the input intervals table and the elements list, you should first consider if the machine you are working with will be able to handle the operation. Otherwise, you may need to break the work in parts.

- The intervals might enclose elements that are not actually needed in the data model, and we must ensure those elements are not considered when expanding the intervals, so that we save CPU and RAM resources. To do this, the elements list we input in the `IntervalMatch` function should only contain the required elements.

- Similarly, the intervals table should contain unique records, with no duplicates, to save resources. If one interval is present twice, then the `IntervalMatch` function will split it twice. Using the `Distinct` keyword will help us in this matter.

- When using the intervals table, the fields must be specified in the correct order: the start value before the end value.

Applying IntervalMatch to the Carrier Decode table

Now that we've seen an example of how the `IntervalMatch` function works, we are ready to apply the learned concepts to the `Carrier Decode` table we discussed earlier.

As a quick recap, our main objective will be to add the `Carrier Group ID` field from the `Carrier Decode` table to the `Flight Data` table. When retrieving the ID value for each of the records in the fact table, we must consider the date on which the corresponding fact took place so that the correct value is assigned. Therefore, the key between the fact table and the `Carrier Decode` table will be composed of a time element (a `Date` field) and the `%Unique Carrier Entity Code` field, which exists in both tables.

Let's follow these steps:

1. Create a new QlikView document; name it as `Transform - Carrier Decode.qvw` and save it inside the `2.Workbooks` folder.

2. Go to the **Edit Script** window and add a new tab. From the **Rename Tab** dialog, type `Facts data` as the tab's name.

3. Once in the new tab, click on the **Table File...** button and browse to the `Flight Data.qvd` file, located inside the `3.QVD\Source` folder.

4. After selecting the file and clicking on **Open**, click on **Finish** in the **File Wizard** window to create the corresponding `Load` statement.

5. Name the table to be loaded as `Flight Data` by typing it before the `Load` keyword and enclosing it within square brackets. Don't forget the colon at the end of the name.

6. Now we will create a new calculated field to build a date representation of the `Period` field. Use the following expression to create the new field:

   `Date#(Period, 'YYYYMM') as Date`

7. We will rename the original `%Carrier Group ID` field from the `Flight Data` table to `OLD_Carrier Group ID`, so that we can use the new field resulting from the transformation instead.

8. The rest of the script will not be modified, so our `Load` statement should be:

```
[Flight Data]:
LOAD
Date#(Period, 'YYYYMM') as Date ,
[%Carrier Group ID] as [OLD_Carrier Group ID],
[%Airline ID],
    [%Unique Carrier Code],
    [%Unique Carrier Entity Code],
    [%Region Code],
    [%Origin Airport ID],
    [%Origin Airport Sequence ID],
    [%Origin Airport Market ID],
    [%Origin World Area Code],
    [%Destination Airport ID],
    [%Destination Airport Sequence ID],
```

```
        [%Destination Airport Market ID],
        [%Destination World Area Code],
        [%Aircraft Group ID],
        [%Aircraft Type ID],
        [%Aircraft Configuration ID],
        [%Distance Group ID],
        [%Service Class ID],
        [%Datasource ID],
        [# Departures Scheduled],
        [# Departures Performed],
        [# Payload],
        Distance,
        [# Available Seats],
        [# Transported Passengers],
        [# Transported Freight],
        [# Transported Mail],
        [# Ramp-To-Ramp Time],
        [# Air Time],
        [Unique Carrier],
        [Carrier Code],
        [Carrier Name],
        [Origin Airport Code],
        [Origin City],
        [Origin State Code],
        [Origin State FIPS],
        [Origin State],
        [Origin Country Code],
        [Origin Country],
        [Destination Airport Code],
        [Destination City],
        [Destination State Code],
        [Destination State FIPS],
        [Destination State],
        [Destination Country Code],
        [Destination Country],
        Year,
        Period,
        Quarter,
        [Month (#)],
        Month,
        [From - To Airport Code],
        [From - To Airport ID],
        [From - To City],
        [From - To State Code],
        [From - To State]
FROM
[..\3.QVD\Source\Flight Data.qvd]
(qvd);
```

9. Now, let's create a new tab by clicking on the **Add new tab** button on the toolbar. The new tab will be named `Intervals`.

10. In this new tab, we will enter the following script:

```
[Carrier Decode]:
IntervalMatch (Date, [%Unique Carrier Entity Code])
LOAD
    [Start Date],
If(Len([End Date]) < 1, Today(1), [End Date]) as [End Date],
    [Unique Carrier Entity] as [%Unique Carrier Entity Code]
FROM
[..\3.QVD\Source\Carrier Decode.qvd]
(qvd);
```

With the preceding script, a new table is being created as the result of the `IntervalMatch` operation. In this case, we are using the extended syntax of the function so that the resulting table has one record for each combination of interval (`Start Date` and `End Date`), data point (`Date`), and dimension (`%Unique Carrier Entity Code`) value.

 When using the extended syntax, all fields specified as the function's parameter must exist in the previouslyloaded fact table, as well as listed in the `Load` statement to which it is being applied.

We are also ensuring that all intervals are closed, which is a requirement of the `IntervalMatch` function, by using a conditional expression. Whenever an open interval is encountered, the date of when the script is executed will be set as the `End Date`field for that interval.

11. Now that we have expanded the intervals, let's associate the dimension value we are interested in (`%Carrier Group ID`) so that we can incorporate it into the fact table. Do this by entering the following code below the previous one:

```
Inner Join ([Carrier Decode])
LOAD
[Start Date],
If(Len([End Date]) < 1, Today(1), [End Date]) as [End Date],
    [Unique Carrier Entity] as [%Unique Carrier Entity Code],
    [Carrier Group ID] as [%Carrier Group ID]
FROM
[..\3.QVD\Source\Carrier Decode.qvd]
(qvd);
```

With the preceding script, we are simply adding the new field (%Carrier Group ID) to the result of the IntervalMatch operation. This leaves us with a table containing all possible combinations of Interval, Date, Unique Carrier Entity ID, and the corresponding %Carrier Group ID value.

12. We will now end the transformation process by joining the expanded-intervals table to the fact table so that the %Carrier Group ID field is added to it. Enter the following script below the previous one:

```
Left Join ([Flight Data])
Load
 Date,
 [%Unique Carrier Entity Code],
 [%Carrier Group ID]
Resident [Carrier Decode];

Drop Table [Carrier Decode];
Drop Field Date;
```

The Join operation is performed by matching both the Date and %Unique Carrier Entity Code fields between the two tables. In the end, we issue a Drop statement to get rid of the Carrier Decode table since we don't need it anymore. We also drop the Date field from the Flight Data table since it was only needed during the IntervalMatch operation.

13. Now that the transformation has taken place and the new %Carrier Group ID field has been added to the fact table, we can store the result into a new QVD file and drop it from RAM with the following two statements:

```
Store [Flight Data] into [..\3.QVD\Transformed\Transformed -
Flight Data.qvd];
Drop Table [Flight Data];
```

Ordering, peeking, and matching all at once

In the earlier sections, we have discussed three different functions commonly used in data transformation. We will now present a use case in which all three functions will complement each other to achieve a specific task.

The use case

We know that the `IntervalMatch` function makes use of closed intervals already defined in a table. What happens if all we have is a start date? To illustrate this scenario, look at the following screenshot:

Airline ID	Carrier Code	Carrier Name	Unique Carrier Code	Unique Carrier Entity	Unique Carrier Name	Carrier World Area Code	Carrier Group ID	Region Code	Start Date
20195	WI	Tradewin(	WI	6884	Tradewinds Airlines	10	4	Domestic	1-Feb-1998
20195	WI	Tradewin(	WI	6884	Tradewinds Airlines	10	1	Domestic	1-Jan-2000
20195	WI	Tradewin(	WI	6884	Tradewinds Airlines	10	4	Domestic	1-Jan-2011
20195	WI	Tradewin(	WI	6884	Tradewinds Airlines	10	1	Domestic	1-Jan-2012
20195	WI	Tradewin(	WI	16884	Tradewinds Airlines	10	4	International	1-Feb-1998
20195	WI	Tradewin(	WI	16884	Tradewinds Airlines	10	1	International	1-Jan-2000
20195	WI	Tradewin(	WI	16884	Tradewinds Airlines	10	4	International	1-Jan-2011
20195	WI	Tradewin(	WI	16884	Tradewinds Airlines	10	1	International	1-Jan-2012

As you can see, the `End Date` field has disappeared. However, there is a way for us to guess it and assign the corresponding value, based on the start date of the immediate following record. That is, if one record starts on 1-Feb-1998 and the immediate following starts on 1-Jan-2000, it means that the first interval ended on 31-Dec-1999, right?

In order for us to calculate the end date, we need to first sort the table values so that all corresponding records are contiguous, then "peek" at the start value from the next (or previous, if ordered backwards) record, subtract one day and that will be our new end date. After that, we are now able to use the `IntervalMatch` function to expand those intervals.

To complete the challenge, make use of the same `Carrier Decode` table we have used previously, only ignore the `End Date` field as if it was not there. You will also be able to compare your results with those we came up with in the previous section.

Good Luck!

Incremental loads

Another important advantage of designing an appropriate data architecture, is the fact that it eases the construction and maintenance of incremental load scenarios, which are often required when dealing with large data volumes.

An incremental load is used to transfer data from one database to another efficiently and avoid the unnecessary use of resources. For instance, suppose we update our Base QVD Layer on a Monday morning, pulling all transactions from the source system and storing the table into a QVD file. The next morning, we need to update our Base QVD layer so that the final QlikView document contains the most recent data, including transactions generated in the source system during the previous day (after our last reload). In that case, we have two options:

1. Extract the source table in its entirety.
2. Extract only the new and/or modified transactions from the source table and append those records to the ones we previously saved in our Base QVDs.

The second option is what we call an **Incremental Load**.

The following diagram depicts the process of an incremental load at a general level, when a Base QVD Layer is used:

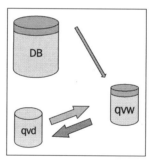

The process of performing an incremental load in QlikView varies in complexity depending on the nature of the source table. At a general-level, we would approach the task by following these steps:

1. We first query the source database using a Where clause with the appropriate logic so that only *new or updated records* are extracted.

2. Once the new records are read, we can *append the ones we previously saved* in QVDs by using the `Concatenate` function.

    ○   In this second load, a `Where` clause might be required with the appropriate logic so that previously-saved records that were updated in the source table, and therefore read in the first load (step 1), are not read again; by doing so, we will avoid inconsistencies with the data.

3. Finally, once the two tables are concatenated, we save it to the corresponding QVD file, thus replacing the old one.

The basic requirement for an incremental load to be possible is that the new or updated records in the source table can be identified. We can easily identify the target records if the source table has a `ModificationTime` or `Created on` field (or similar) and stores the corresponding timestamp or date for each record. This is often the case in production environments, but sometimes this field is not available.

An example pseudocode script that performs the aforementioned procedure is shown as follows:

```
Let vLoadTime = Num(Now( ));

QV_Table:
SQL SELECT
    PrimaryKey,
    Field_A,
    Field_B
FROM Source_Table
WHERE ModificationTime >= $(vLastLoadTime)
AND ModificationTime < $(vLoadTime);


Concatenate (QV_Table)
LOAD
    PrimaryKey,
    Field_A,
    Field_B
FROM OurFile.QVD
WHERE NOT EXISTS(PrimaryKey); /* This where clause is used to
ignore keys that already exist in QV_Table, which are new versions of
existing records. */

If ScriptErrorCount = 0 then

    STORE QV_Table INTO OurFile.QVD;
    Let vLastLoadTime = vLoadTime;

End If
```

In the script we just saw, we use two variables, vLoadTime and vLastLoadTime, to keep track of when the script was last executed and query the database accordingly. These variables are stored as numeric values, rather than using their timestamp representation, to avoid issues regarding date formats. We must ensure the database recognizes the ModificationTime comparison in numeric format, otherwise we should adapt it accordingly. We also use the system variable ScriptErrorCount to ensure that the QVD file and the variable vLastLoadTime are only updated when the previous script is executed without errors.

The process outlined earlier accounts for two scenarios:

- When the source table is only updated by inserting new records (*Insert-Only* scenario)
- When the source table is updated either by inserting new records or by updating existing ones (*Insert and Update* scenario)

There is, however, a third scenario: when the source table can be updated either by inserting new records, updating existing ones, or deleting existing records (*Insert, Update, and Delete* scenario).

When records can be deleted from the source table, the complexity of the incremental load increases and additional steps might be required in the process. One approach that can be implemented, is to perform a second load from the source database, this time pulling the entire list of record IDs (primary keys), without the rest of the fields, and then perform an Inner Join operation with the updated table (the one resulting from the second step in the earlier process) to discard deleted records before saving the new QVD file.

To account for this scenario, the following code should be inserted above the If ... Then ... Else statement in the example script presented previously.

```
Inner Join SQL SELECT PrimaryKey FROM Source_Table;
```

Having an incremental load logic in our *Extract Layer* can help reduce the amount of data being transferred over the network from server to server during the extraction process. It also helps to significantly reduce the time it takes for the extraction to be completed.

When implementing an incremental load, it's essential to monitor and validate the process to ensure that the logic employed in the extraction is appropriate and the data stored in the QlikView document is consistent with the data stored in the source table.

Summary

We've come to the end of an intense chapter. I hope you have followed the topics and, if not, I highly recommend to go back to read those sections which you found most difficult, so that you learn the concepts at full.

In this chapter, we have learned the importance of having a well-designed data architecture, how to load data from another QlikView document or previously loaded table in RAM, and also data aggregation functions and their uses.

We then learned how to order tables during load, how to calculate fields based on previously read records, how to deal with slowly changing dimensions to incorporate those tables into the associative data model, and finally the general process to perform an incremental load.

In the following chapter, we will continue exploring some front-end functionalities that can help us improve the user experience for our apps.

14

More on Visual Design and User Experience

In the chapter on building dashboards, we looked at the various QlikView objects and how we can create and configure these objects. This chapter will expand your knowledge further, not aiming for mere technical competency, but it will also giving you some solid rules of thumb that will help you create good QlikView documents.

This chapter consists of two sections. The first focuses on some best practices for creating a consistent user interface in QlikView.

The second section looks at how we can add additional interactivity to our documents.

Let's get started.

Creating a consistent QlikView UI

As mentioned earlier in the *Building Dashboards* chapter, we will want to make sure that the user interface, which includes language, layout, and design, is as consistent as possible. A consistent user interface makes it predictable for the user, they will have a better understanding of how things work, and will feel more in control.

Before you start, understand the users and their goals

Before you start designing your QlikView document and the UI, it is key that you first understand the users and their goals. Only when you are familiar with the goals of the document can you design an interface that will help the users achieve those goals.

One straightforward example, which we've seen while developing our document, is to place objects in the same location if they're being used on multiple sheets. If, for example, the current selections box is always in the same place, then the user will immediately know where to look for it. The linked object feature is the best way to enforce this.

Screen resolution

One of the big no-no's in dashboard design is to create a dashboard that occupies more space than the user's screen size. This will require the user to scroll around to see the information.

 If, for whatever reason, you need to create a dashboard that occupies more space than is available on screen, it is good to keep in mind that vertical scrolling is better than horizontal scrolling. Most users will be used to vertical scrolling from their web browser.

The easiest way to prevent this is to find out what default screen resolution is used by your users. Or, if there is more than one, what the lowest common denominator is. When this resolution is known, you can design all of your sheets and documents to fit within it.

 If your screen resolution does not match the target screen's resolution, you can use the **View | Resize Window** option from the menu to resize your QlikView document window to the most common screen resolutions.

Background image

One way to give your document a consistent look-and-feel on each sheet (and even between documents) is to use a background image. Usually, a background image has a few predefined panels where objects can be placed. The following image shows an example of a background image:

 The previous image does feature quite thick borders. In the
interest of reducing non-data pixels, you will probably want to
use a more minimalistic background in your own designs.

When setting up a background image, either at the **Document Properties** or **Sheet
Properties** level, it is important to configure the following settings:

- **Image Formatting** should be set to **No Stretch**
- **Horizontal** should be set to **Left**
- **Vertical** should be set to **Top**
- **Background Color** should be set to a color that matches the background
  color of the image so that the edges of the background image blend in with
  the rest of the background

 QlikView Developer Toolkit

Creating a background image can be done using an image
editor such as Photoshop. If you do not have access to an image
editor, or if you're not really artistically inclined, QlikView
installation has the Developer Toolkit included. This toolkit
can be found in the folder `C:\Program Files\QlikView\`
`Examples\Developer Toolkit` and includes around 100
predefined backgrounds to use in your QlikView documents.

Of course, you can use multiple background images to fit the different requirements of the sheets in your document. For example, you can use a background with two horizontal panels for your dashboard sheet, while using a background with three vertical panels for your analysis sheet.

Themes

While using background images can go a long way in standardizing the look and layout of your QlikView document, when you really want to standardize—for example, to enforce a corporate style—themes are what you need.

A theme is stored in an external XML file with a `.qvt` extension. It contains separate sections for each type of object, document, sheet, and the various sheet objects. For each of these objects, the object-specific properties are stored, as well as caption and border properties and print settings. You can even store only part of the settings, for example, adding the font type of a chart's axis to a theme while ignoring its font color.

The following diagram shows the Theme File structure. Notice that there is a separate section for each type of Sheet object:

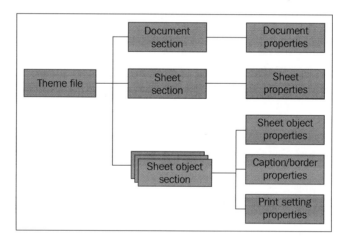

A theme is created using the **Theme Maker Wizard** and can contain settings for as many or few objects as you want, from a single setting for a single chart type to the entire look-and-feel of the document.

Applying themes

As theme files store properties at various levels (document, sheet, and object), we can apply them at various levels too. Let's start with a practical example that shows how to apply a theme to a complete document:

1. Open the `NoTheme.qvw` file that is located in the folder `4.Applications\Examples`.

2. Go to **Settings | Document Properties | Layout**.

3. Click on the **Apply Theme** button and select the `HighCloudCorporate_finished.qvt` file from the folder `0.Includes\Themes`.

The result now looks similar to the style we've been using in our own documents. Notice how, among other things, the background image, colors, and caption settings have changed once we applied the theme:

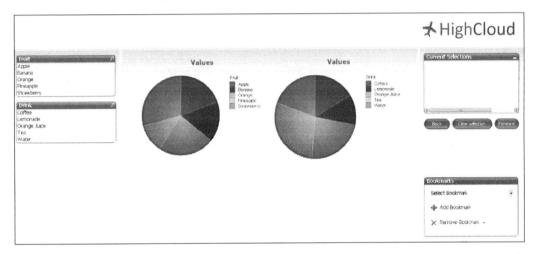

As was said before, themes do not always need to be applied to the entire document.

We can apply a theme to a single sheet, by selecting **Settings | Sheet Properties** and clicking on the **Apply Theme** button on the **General** tab.

We can also apply a theme to a single object (or a group of objects, if we first select them) by opening the **Object Properties** window (right-click on the object, or group of objects, and select **Properties...**) and clicking on the **Apply Theme** button on the **Layout** tab.

Now that we've seen how to apply themes, let's see how we can create them.

Creating themes

A theme is always created by copying the properties of documents, sheets and sheet objects which were already created. As we already spent quite some time styling our document, we can use it as a base for a HighCloud corporate theme.

 Creating a theme to style a complete document is no small task and involves a lot of repetitive steps. For the sake of brevity, we will only create the document and sheet sections of the theme, along with the theme for two sheet objects.

We will start by adding the document settings.

Adding document properties

Let's follow these steps to create the first iteration of our HighCloud corporate theme, based on the document properties:

1. Select **Tools | Theme Maker Wizard** from the menu.

2. Click on **Next** to go to the **Step 1 – Select theme file** dialog window.

3. Ensure that the radio button is set to **New Theme** and that **Template** is set to **<None>**.

4. Click on **Next**, this will open a dialog window to save our theme file.

5. Browse to the folder 0.Includes\Themes and name the theme file HighCloudCorporate.

6. In the **Step 2 – Source selection** dialog window, select **Document** from the **Source** drop-down list and click on **Next**.

   We have now reached the **Step 3a-Object type specific properties** dialog window, seen in the following screenshot. Depending on which type of object we've chosen, this dialog will show all properties that we can export to the theme file. Note there are some omissions to what can be exported to a theme, and some of the legends in the list are not entirely helpful with defining what it is you are theming.

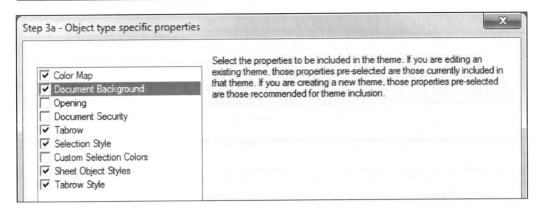

7. Enable the checkboxes so that they look like the preceding screenshot and click on **Next**.

8. Click on **Finish** to close the **Theme Maker Wizard** wizard and save the theme.

We have now reached the end of the **Theme Maker Wizard** dialog for the document properties. Before we start on the sheet properties theme, let's first look at the final dialog window of the wizard. In the **Step 5 - Save theme** dialog window, seen in the following screenshot we can decide if we want to set the created theme as a default for the current document, or set it as a default for all new documents. We've skipped this option for now, but when you have created your own corporate theme, it may be worthwhile to set it as a default theme for all new documents.

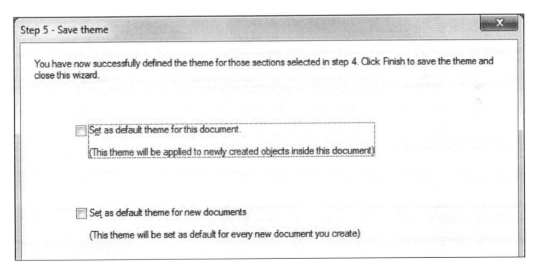

> **Out of style**
>
> You can always reset the default theme for the document by selecting the **Settings | Document properties** from the menu and changing the **Default Theme for New Objects** drop-down on the **Presentation** tab.
>
> To reset the default theme for all new documents, select **Settings | User Preferences** from the menu and change the **Default Theme** drop-down list on the **Design** tab.

Now that we've added the document properties, in the next section we will add the sheet properties.

Adding sheet properties

Let's follow these steps to add the sheet properties to our template:

1. Select **Tools | Theme Maker Wizard** from the menu and click on **Next** to open the **Step 1 – Select theme file** dialog.

2. Set the radio button to **Modify Existing Theme** and select **Browse** from the drop-down list.

3. Select the `HighCloudCorporate.qvt` file that we created earlier, and click on **Next** to open the **Step 2 – Source selection**.

4. From the **Source** drop-down menu, select the object **Sheet Document\ SH03 – Dashboard**. (The **SH03** part may be different in your document.)

5. Click on **Next** to go to **Step 3a – Object type specific properties**.

   As we can see in the following screenshot, the objects listed in this dialog window are different from those listed at the document level. Also note that, as we are modifying an existing theme, the options that are shown as selected are those that are currently already included in the theme. These were inherited from the document-level properties.

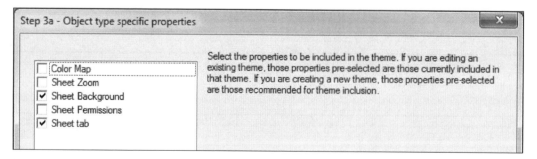

6. Enable the checkboxes for **Color Map** and **Sheet Zoom** and click on **Next**.

7. Click on **Finish** to close the wizard and add the sheet properties to the `HighCloudCorporate.qvt` theme file.

Adding sheet object properties

Now that we have added the sheet properties to our template, we will add the properties for two sheet objects: the list box and the pie chart. First, let's add the pie chart by following these steps:

1. Select **Tools | Theme Maker Wizard** from the menu and click on **Next** to open the **Step 1 – Select theme file** dialog.

2. Set the radio button to **Modify Existing Theme** and select **Browse** from the drop-down list.

3. Select the `HighCloudCorporate.qvt` file that we have been working on in the previous exercises, and click on the **Next** to **open Step 2 – Source** selection.

4. From the **Source** drop-down menu, select the object **Chart Document\ CH26 – Market Share**. (The **CH26** part may be different in your document.)

5. Enable all three checkboxes: **Object Type Specific**, **Caption Border**, and **Print Settings**.

6. Click on **Next** to go to **Step 3a – Object type specific properties**.

7. This dialog is the same as we saw when we were adding the document and sheet properties to the template. Leave all of the settings set to their default value and click on **Next** to go to **Step 3b – Caption and border settings**.

As the name implies, in the **Caption and border settings** dialog window, shown below, we can select which settings are related to borders and captions. As we will see later, we can apply these settings not only to the object we're adding to the template, but also for other objects. In practice, this means that when we create a complete document template we will only need to add these properties twice; once for objects with a caption, such as listboxes, and once for objects without a caption, such as charts.

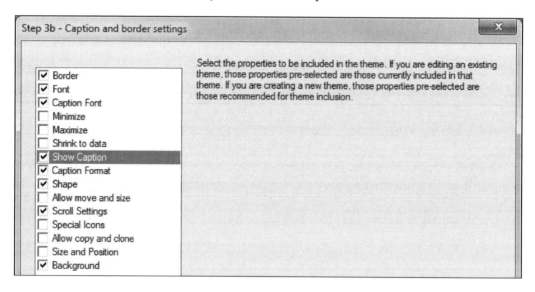

8. Enable the **Show Caption** checkbox, this will ensure that our caption settings (or more specifically, no caption settings) will be included in the template.

9. Click on **Next** to go to **Step 3c – Printer settings**.

10. Leave all of the settings to their default value and click on **Next** to go to **Step 4 – Insertion of properties in theme**.

In this dialog window, shown in the following screenshot, we can specify which objects we want to apply the **Caption & Border** and **Printing** settings to.

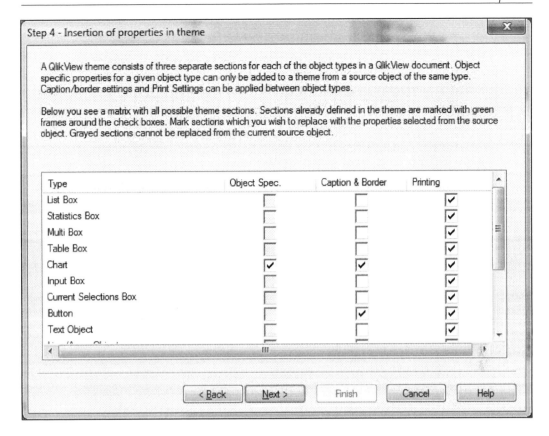

Let's follow these steps to add the **Caption & Border** and **Printing** settings to every object that needs similar styling:

1. In the **Caption & Border** settings column, select the **Button, Line/Arrow Object, Slider/Calendar Object, Container, Chart** and **Search Object** checkboxes. None of these objects by default need a caption.

2. In the **Printing** column, select every object to apply the same print settings to each object.

3. Click on **Next** and then on **Finish** to save the theme.

We have now added the properties for the pie chart to our template, which already contained the document and sheet properties.

Separate themes for separate objects

As you can see in the **Insertion of properties in theme** dialog window, the settings for all charts are stored in a single **Chart** type. This can create difficulties when you want to apply different settings to different charts. For example, showing a grid for line charts, but hiding it for bar charts. In that case, it is easier to create separate theme files for each of your chart objects.

A solo exercise

By now, you have probably spotted the pattern of creating and adding settings to a theme file, so it is time for a little solo exercise. We still need to add the list box properties based on the **Flight Type** list box to our theme. Make sure to pay special attention to the **Show Caption** setting as we want to ensure that a caption is displayed on our list boxes. Besides the list box, make sure to apply the **Caption & Border** settings to the following objects as well:

- Statistics Box
- Multi Box
- Table Box
- Input box
- Current Selections Box
- Bookmark Object

If you are able to successfully complete this exercise, then you have all of the skills necessary to create and modify your own themes.

You can test your new theme file by applying it to the `NoTheme.qvw` file that we used earlier in this chapter.

Additional interactivity

Besides properly styling your QlikView documents, how your document responds to user interaction is also critical to ensuring a pleasant user experience. Fortunately, most of the interaction is already built into the list boxes, charts, and so on, but there are a few options that can help you make your document even more polished.

We will first look how we can make QlikView respond to certain events by using triggers and actions. We'll then see how we can create an advanced search expression that lets us search for data in a flexible manner. We will see how we can use these advanced search expressions to send out alerts when predefined conditions are met. We will end this section by looking at how to conditionally calculate or show an object.

Triggers

By using **triggers**, QlikView lets us respond to certain **events** (for example, when a sheet is selected) with an **action**. Triggers can be defined at various levels.

Check before deploying to QlikView Server

Not all triggers and actions are supported when deploying your document to QlikView Server. When your goal is to deploy to QlikView Server, first check the QlikView Reference Guide (included with your QlikView installation) during development to see if the triggers and actions you are using are supported, or take the practical approach and test it with a test document.

Document triggers

At the document level (which can be opened by selecting **Settings | Document Properties | Triggers**), we can set **Document**, **Field** and **Variable Event Triggers**:

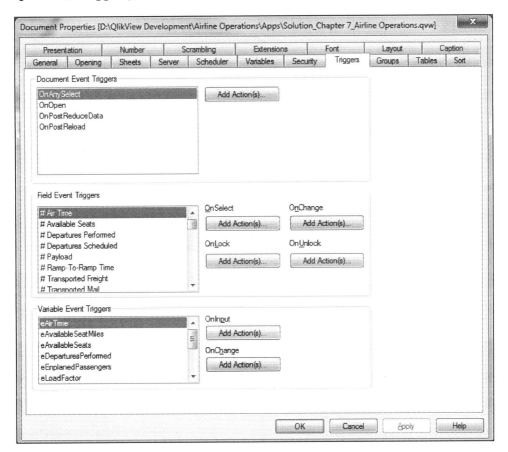

Before we look at the individual triggers, let's first look at a practical example. Follow these steps to always select the year 2011 when opening the document:

1. Select **Settings | Document Properties | Triggers** from the menu.

2. Select **On Open** from the list of **Document Event Triggers**.

3. Click on **Add Action(s)**.

4. In the **Actions** dialog, click on **Add**.

5. In the **Add Action** popup, select **Clear All** in the **Action** list box and click on **OK**.

6. In the **Actions** dialog, click on **Add** again.

7. In the **Add Action** popup, select **Select in Field** in the **Action** list box and click on **OK**.

8. In the **Field** input box type `Year`.

9. In the **Search String** input box type `2011`.

10. Click on **OK**.

    Notice how the **On Open Document Event Trigger** trigger has been postfixed with **<Has Action(s)>**. This indicates that an action is associated with the trigger.

11. Click on **OK** to close the **Document Properties** window.

12. In the **Year** list box, select **2009** and **2010**.

13. Select **File | Save** from the menu to save the document.

14. Select **File | Close** to close the document.

15. Reopen the document.

You will now notice that the document will open with the year 2011 selected, even though we saved it with 2009 and 2010 selected. This happens because, upon opening of the document, the **OnOpen** event is triggered. This event kicks off the two actions we defined, first clearing all selections and then selecting the year 2011.

Besides triggers on the document, we can also define triggers on fields and variables. All triggers which can be set in the **Document Properties** window are shown in the following table:

Trigger type	Trigger name	Description
Document event	OnAnySelect	This is triggered any time a selection is made in any field in the QlikView document.
	OnOpen	This is triggered when the QlikView document is opened. This will not work when opening the document in the AJAX client.
	OnPostReduceData	This is triggered when the Reduce Data command has been used.
	OnPostReload	This is triggered when the QlikView document has been reloaded.
Field event	OnSelect	This is triggered when a selection is made in the selected field.
	OnChange	This is triggered when the selection in the selected field is changed because of a selection made in another field.
	OnLock	This is triggered when the field is locked.
	OnUnlock	This is triggered when the field is unlocked.
Variable event	OnInput	This is triggered when a new value for the variable is directly entered (for example, in an input box).
	OnChange	This is triggered when the value of the variable is changed because of a change in other variables or the selection state.

Sheet triggers

Besides document triggers, we can also set triggers at the sheet level. To set these triggers, select **Settings | Sheet Properties | Triggers** from the menu, shown in the following screenshot. We can define two events:

- **OnActivateSheet** is triggered when the sheet is activated

- **OnLeaveSheet** is triggered when the sheet is deactivated (another sheet is selected)

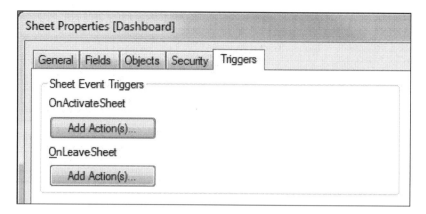

Now that we have seen how triggers work, let's see what actions we can attach to them.

Actions

Throughout this book, we have used actions in various places and objects, for example, while creating our **Back**, **Clear Selections**, and **Forward** buttons. Let's now take a closer look at actions and what their possibilities are.

Besides triggers, actions can be attached to the following objects:

- Buttons
- Text Objects
- Gauges
- Line/Arrow Objects

As we have seen, from the **Actions** dialog window we can add an action by clicking on the **Add** button, seen in the following screenshot. Deleting an action is done by clicking the **Delete** button. The **Promote** and **Demote** buttons are used to change the sequence in which the actions are executed.

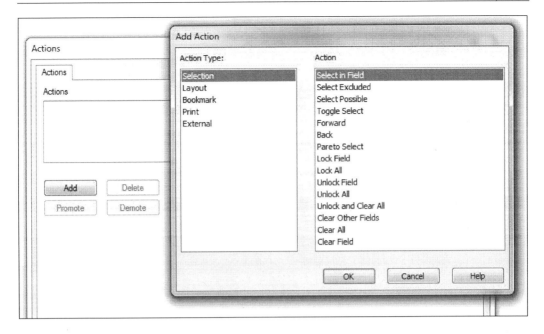

When we click on the **Add** button, we are taken to the **Add Action** dialog window. In this menu we can select an action from a few select **Action Types**.

Referring to sheets and other objects

Actions that need to perform a certain operation on a sheet or object, such as a sheet object, report or bookmark, will refer to it by an ID. This ID can often be found on the **General** tab of the object, shown in the following screenshot. It is good practice to give your objects recognizable (and predictable) names so that you do not need to switch back and forth when setting up actions.

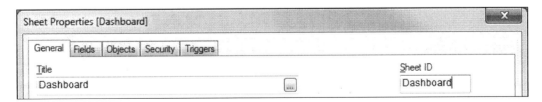

The following table lists all of the action types, associated actions, and their function:

Action type	Action	Description
Selection	Select in Field	Selects the value(s) in the specified field.
	Select Excluded	Selects the excluded (gray) value(s) in the specified field.
	Select Possible	Selects the possible (white) value(s) in the specified field.
	Toggle Select	Toggles between the current selection and the current selection with the addition of the selected value(s) in the specified field.
	Forward	Moves the selection one step forward. This is only possible if you went back one or more steps first.
	Back	Moves the selection one step back.
	Pareto Select	Based on an expression, selects the top X percent of values in the specified field.
	Lock Field	Locks the selection on the specified field.
	Lock All	Locks the selection on all fields.
	Unlock Field	Unlocks the selection on the specified field.
	Unlock All	Unlocks the selection on all fields.
	Unlock and Clear All	Unlocks the selection on all fields and clears all selections.
	Clear Other Fields	Clears the selections on all fields, except for the one specified.
	Clear All	Clears the selections on all fields.
	Clear Field	Clears the selections on the specified field.
	Copy State Contents	Copies the state from the source to the target state. This option is only visible when alternate states have been defined.
	Swap State Contents	Transfers the states between the two specified alternate states. This option is only visible when alternate states have been defined.
Layout	Activate Object	Activates the specified object.
	Activate Sheet	Activates the specified sheet.
	Activate Next Sheet	Activates the sheet to the right of the current sheet. It is recommended to use Activate Sheet instead since during development sheets might be positioned in between, leading to wrong results.
	Activate Previous Sheet	Activates the sheet to the left of the current sheet. It is recommended to use Activate Sheet instead.

Action type	Action	Description
	Minimize Object	Minimizes the specified object.
	Maximize Object	Maximizes the specified object.
	Restore Object	Restores the specified object.
	Set State Name	Assigns the specified state to the specified object. This option is only visible when alternate states have been defined.
Bookmark	Apply Bookmark	Applies the specified bookmark.
	Create Bookmark	Creates a bookmark from the current selection.
	Replace Bookmark	Replaces the specified bookmark with the current selection.
Print	Print Object	Prints the specified object to the specified printer (if not the default printer).
	Print Sheet	Prints the specified sheet.
	Print Report	Prints the specified report to the specified printer (if not the default printer).
External	Export	Based on the current selections, exports data from the specified fields to a file or the clipboard.
	Launch	Launches an external application.
	Open URL	Opens a URL in the default web browser.
	Open QlikView Document	Opens another QlikView document. We can transfer our selections to this second document, enabling **document chaining**.
	Run Macro	Runs a macro.
	Set Variable	Sets the value of the specified variable.
	Show Information	Shows the associated information (loaded via INFO or BUNDLE LOAD) for the specified field.
	Close This Document	Closes the current document.
	Reload	Reloads the current document.
	Dynamic Update	Executes a dynamic data update statement.

Now that we've seen how triggers and actions work, let's have a look at how we can use advanced search expressions to perform more detailed searches.

Advanced search expressions

Up until now, we have mostly used static text when performing searches in list boxes. While this type of search is usually good enough, sometimes we need our searches to be a little more fine-grained. This is where **advanced search expressions** are useful.

Let's start with a practical example. As HighCloud is still in the process of deciding which US cities to include in their network, analysts want to keep track of destination cities based on the following criteria:

- Cities that have been destination to flights originated outside the US
- Only cities within the US
- Their global load factor needs to be 80% or more

Follow these steps to create this search expression:

1. Locate the **Flight Information** multi box and click on the **Destination City** drop-down to open the list of values.

2. Right-click anywhere on the list and select **Advanced Search**.

3. In the **Search Expression** input box, enter the following expression:

```
=[Origin Country] <>'United States' and
[Destination Country] = 'United States' and
$(eLoadFactor) >= 0.8
```

4. Click on **Go** to apply the selection and then click on **Close** to close the **Advanced Search** dialog.

When we open the **Destination City** drop-down list, we can see that a selection has been made. These are the cities that have an occupancy of 80% or more for incoming international flights. We can also see that, instead of a list of fixed values, our advanced search expression is shown in the **Current Selections** box, seen here:

In our example, we used the **Advanced Search** dialog to enter the search expression. If you already know what expression you want to enter, it is also possible to just select the list box or drop-down, press the = key and enter the expression directly.

A solo exercise

Try to create an advanced search expression that selects all carriers that have between 70 and 80 percent occupancy, and have transported more than 10 million passengers.

 Note that advanced search expressions need to start with the equal (=) sign, otherwise the expression will be interpreted as regular text.

Dynamic bookmarks

Advanced search expressions are useful not only for ad hoc searches. When we create a bookmark based on an advanced search expression, the resulting bookmark will be dynamic. This means the advanced search expression is reinterpreted every time the bookmark is selected.

Let's see how this works by creating a bookmark which will always select the top ten carriers by number of enplaned passengers:

1. Clear all selections.
2. Right-click on the **Carrier Name** list box and select **Advanced Search**.
3. In the **Search Expression** input box enter the following code:

   ```
   =Rank($(eEnplanedPassengers)) <= 10.
   ```

4. Click on **Go** to perform the search, check that this changes the selection in **Carrier Name**.
5. Click on **Close** to close the **Advanced Search** dialog.
6. Select **Bookmarks | Add Bookmark** from the menu.
7. Enter **Top 10 carriers by transported passengers** as the **Bookmark Name**.
8. Check the **Make bookmark apply on top of current selection** checkbox.
9. Click on **OK** to save the bookmark.

We now have a bookmark that, based on the current selection, will always select the top ten carriers based on the number of transported passengers.

Alerts

QlikView can be used to slice and dice our data in any way we wish. However, there are times when we do not want to do all of the discovery ourselves, but instead want to be alerted when a certain threshold is exceeded. This is where **alerts** are useful.

An alert can be triggered by three events: after the document is opened, after it is reloaded, or after data reduction. The alert can show a pop-up message or send an e-mail to one or more recipients.

Before diving deeper into alerts, we will first look at a practical example. We will set up an alert that will notify us with a pop-up when the average occupancy for the top ten carriers, based on number of transported passengers, falls below 85%. Let's follow these steps:

1. Select **Tools | Alerts** from the menu.
2. Click on the **Add** button.
3. In the **Description** input box enter **Top 10 carriers load factor** %.
4. Select **Top 10 carriers by transported passengers** from the **Bookmark** drop-down list.
5. In the **Condition** input box, enter `$(eLoadFactor) < 0.85`.
6. In the **Message** input box, enter the following message: **The average load factor % has fallen below 85% for the top 10 carriers**.
7. Enable all events, **On Open**, **On Post Reload**, and **On Post Reduce**.
8. Click on **OK** to close the **Alerts** dialog.
9. Select **File | Save** to save the document.
10. Select **File | Close** to close the document.
11. Reopen the document.

As the condition we set is always true (occupancy for the top ten carriers is around 80 percent), when we reopen the document we will see the following alert pop up:

The average load factor % has fallen below 85% for the top 10 carriers.

Let's take another look at the **Alerts** dialog, shown below in the following screenshot, to see what other options are available:

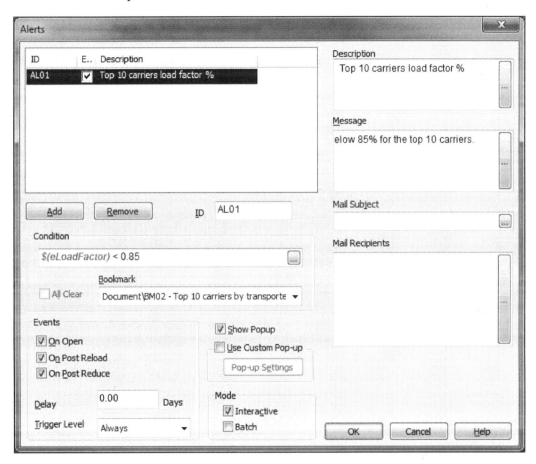

The top-left corner of the dialog displays all of the alerts that have been defined. For each alert, we see its unique **ID**, a checkbox to **Enable** or disable it, and the **Description** field for the alert. Alerts can be added or removed from the list by using the **Add** and **Remove** buttons. The **ID** input box can be used to assign an alternative ID to an alert.

As we saw when we defined our alert, the **Condition** input box is where we put the condition to test. By default, this condition is tested against the current selections. We can override this setting by either enabling the **All Clear** checkbox, which will test the condition against all data in the document, or by specifying a **Bookmark** against which to test the condition, as we did in our previous exercise.

In the **Events** group, we can define when the alert is checked: after opening the document (**On Open**), after reload (**On Post Reload**), or after data reduction (**On Post Reduce**).

In the **Delay** input box, we can specify how many days to wait after an alert is triggered before triggering the alert again. This is to avoid receiving the same alert over and over.

The **Trigger level** drop-down menu offers another option to suspend the triggering of alerts. **Always** is the default option and means that the alert will always be triggered when the condition is met. By selecting **Message Changes**, the alert will only be triggered when the value of the **Message** or **Mail Subject** changes. Of course, this only works when using a calculated expression for these fields. By selecting **State Changes**, the alert will be triggered only once and will be suspended until the alert condition is not met.

As we saw in our example, checking the **Show Popup** checkbox will show a popup when the alert is triggered. We can customize the popup by checking **Use Custom Pop-up** and clicking on **Pop-up Settings**.

In the **Mode** group, we can decide if an alert should be checked when a user uses the document (**Interactive**, that is, opened in QlikView Desktop by a user) or when an automated process, such as QlikView Publisher, uses the document (**Batch**).

In the **Description** input box, we can define a name or description for the alert. The **Message** input box contains the message that needs to be displayed when the alert is triggered. Note that both of these input boxes can also contain dynamic expressions.

Besides showing a popup, an alert can also be sent out via an e-mail. We can define the **Mail Subject** and the **Mail Recipients** fields.

> In order to send mail from QlikView Desktop, an e-mail account and server need to be defined under **Settings | User Preferences | Mail**. When deploying the application to QlikView Server, there are similar mail settings that need to be entered into the QlikView Management Console.

Now that we've seen how alerts work, let's look at the conditional display and calculation of objects.

Conditionally showing and calculating objects

While building our dashboard, we already saw how we can conditionally hide or show a text object. As you may have already discovered, this does not only work for text objects, but for any sheet and sheet object, and even for dimensions and expressions within charts.

For sheet objects, the conditional show input box is located on the **Layout** tab of the object properties. For sheets, it's located on the **General** tab of the **Sheet Properties** window.

For charts, within the **Chart Properties** window, conditional showing of dimensions can be set using the **Enable Conditional** checkbox located on the **Dimensions** tab. For chart expressions, conditional showing can be set using the **Conditional** checkbox on the **Expressions** tab.

Conditional showing of objects can make your document much more user-friendly. You can, for example:

- Show visual cues to make users aware of potential issues.
- Hide objects which, based on the current selection, would display incorrect information. For example, a sheet that displays information on an individual carrier that would not display correctly if more than one carrier is selected.
- Combined with buttons and variables, you can further refine the user interface. For example, showing and hiding groups of objects within the same sheet, or simulating pop-up windows.

Let's look at a small practical example in which we will add a sheet that will only be visible when a single carrier is selected:

1. Select **Layout | Add Sheet**.
2. Using **Layout | Promote** or the **Promote** button on the toolbar, move the sheet until it is next to the **Reports** sheet.
3. Press *Ctrl* + *Alt* + *S* to open the **Sheet Properties** dialog.
4. Use the following expression for the **Title** of the sheet =`'Details for '&` `[Carrier Name]`.
5. Click on **OK** to close the **Sheet Properties** dialog.

Notice how the sheet tab says **Details for**, without including a carrier name. This happens when there is more than one carrier selected. QlikView will only display the name when a single carrier is selected. Let's make this right:

1. Press *Ctrl + Alt + S* to open the **Sheet Properties** dialog.

2. In the **Show Sheet** group, select the **Conditional** radio button.

3. Enter the expression:
   ```
   count(distinct [Carrier Name]) = 1
   ```

4. Click on **OK** to close the **Sheet Properties** dialog.

If your selection contained more than one carrier, you will immediately notice that the sheet disappears, as the expression counts the number of unique carrier names that is selected. Only when you select a single carrier, or make a selection that is associated with a single carrier, will the sheet be shown.

Show all sheets and objects

Ctrl + Shift + S overrides all conditional show conditions, immediately making all hidden sheets and objects visible. This is a very useful key combination to remember during development. Be very careful to undo this change before moving your application into a production environment.

Besides conditionally showing objects and sheets, we can also add a **calculation condition** to our charts. When a calculation condition is added to a chart, it will only be calculated when the condition is met. Use cases for the calculation condition include:

- Preventing the calculation of charts which have specified requirements with regards to the current selection. For example, a chart that compares two carriers should only be calculated when two carriers are selected.

- Preventing the calculation of charts which would need a great amount of resources. For example, a straight table with hundreds of thousands of rows. No one is going to read them all and they require a lot of resources to be displayed.

Let's look at an example of the second use case. On the **Reports** tab, we created a pivot table that shows passengers and departures by airline and period. Let's see how we can use a calculation condition to only calculate the chart when less than 25 airlines are selected:

1. Right-click on the **Passengers/departures per Airline/Period** pivot table and select **Properties**.

2. Select the **General** tab.

3. In the **Calculation Condition** input box enter the following expression:

   ```
   Count(Distinct [Carrier Name]) <= 25
   ```

4. Click on the **Error Messages** button.

5. In the **Custom Error Messages** dialog, select **Calculation condition unfulfilled** from the list of **Standard Messages**.

6. In the **Custom Message** input box, enter `Please select fewer than 25 carriers for this pivot table to be calculated`.

7. Click on **OK** to close the **Customer Error Messages** dialog.

8. Click on **OK** to close the **Chart Properties** window.

If you have more than 25 carriers selected, instead of the pivot table, you will now see a blank square with the error message that we entered. Selecting 25 carriers or less automatically recalculates and displays the pivot table.

By now, you have seen much of what QlikView has to offer in additional interactivity.

Summary

This brings us to the end of this chapter.

In this chapter, we have learned how to create a consistent QlikView UI by using a fixed screen resolution, background image, and themes.

We also learned how to add additional interactivity to our documents by using triggers, actions, advanced search expressions, dynamic bookmarks, alerts, calculation, and show conditions.

In the next and final chapter, we will look at a very important aspect of developing QlikView documents, how to properly secure them, and prevent unwanted access.

15
Security

Until now, we have focused our efforts on getting data into QlikView and presenting it in dashboards, analyses, and reports. Our documents were open to anyone with access to QlikView. As QlikView documents can contain huge volumes of sensitive data, in a real world scenario, leaving your data unsecured might be a very risky proposition.

In this chapter, we will focus on how we can secure our QlikView documents. We will first look at how we can make parts of the script only accessible to a limited group of developers. Next, we will see how we can ensure that only authorized users have access to our document. We will finish this chapter by looking at how we can set different permissions for authorized users and can limit which data a user can interact with.

Specifically, in this chapter you will learn:

- How to create a hidden script that is only accessible to a select group of developers
- How to allow only authorized users to open your document
- How to limit what a user can do and see within your document

Time to start locking things down!

Hidden script

When QlikView script is being executed, the results of the actions are written to the **Script Execution Progress** window (and, if enabled, the log file). While this is a very useful feature to see what happened during reload, sometimes you do not want certain things (for example, login credentials) to be visible to everyone. In fact, sometimes you do not even want all developers to have access to the entire script. This is where the **hidden script** comes into play.

The hidden script is a password protected part of the script. It is always the left-most tab (and cannot be moved), so it is executed before the regular script is reloaded. Anything that is executed within the hidden script is not written to the log.

> Logging for the hidden script can be turned on by checking the **Show Progress for Hidden Script** checkbox on the **Security** tab of the **Document Properties**. Note that this will allow others to use the debugger to step through the hidden code. Since this defeats a main point for using hidden script, it is not advisable to use this option.

The following screenshot shows us the **Edit Script** window:

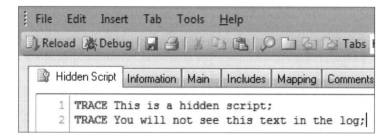

Let's add a hidden script to our document by following these steps:

1. Open our `Airline Operations.qvw` document.

2. Open the **Script Editor** window.

3. Go to **File | Create Hidden Script** in the menu.

4. Enter the password `hidden` twice and click on **OK** to create the hidden script.

5. On the **Hidden Script** tab, enter the following statements:

   ```
   TRACE This is a hidden script;
   ```

6. Save and reload the document.

Notice how the TRACE statement does not show up in the log file.

Reopening hidden script

When the password for the hidden script has been entered, the script remains visible in the **Edit Script** window. The script is hidden when the document is closed and other developers will not be able to see it without entering the password. To reopen a hidden script, select **File | Edit Hidden Script** from the menu and enter the password. Also, be aware that the password for hidden script cannot be recovered, so be sure to keep the password in a safe place.

In the next section, we will see how we can use a hidden script to securely set up user authorization.

Section access

Setting up user authorization under QlikView is generally referred to as **section access**, named after the statement that initiates the authorization section of the script. In section access, fields are loaded with details on which user is allowed which access rights. These fields are loaded in the same way as any other field in QlikView and can be sourced from an inline table, database, or external file.

Better Save than sorry (2)

It is strongly recommended to make a backup copy of your QlikView document before setting up section access. If anything goes wrong during the setup of section access, you will not be able to open your document anymore. Be very careful!

Besides using an inline table, database, or external file, there is also the option of storing and maintaining section access information under QlikView Publisher. Logically, this is no different than storing a table file with section access information in a (semi-)shared folder or, for example, on SharePoint. The data is loaded into the QlikView document as a web file.

As this book is focused on development within QlikView Desktop, storing section access information in QlikView Publisher is out of scope, but it is a good idea to take note of.

Let's start with a simple exercise that protects our QlikView document with a username and password:

1. Press *Ctrl + E* to open the **Edit Script** window.

2. Go to **File | Save Entire Document As** in the menu.

3. Save the file as `Airline Operations SA.qvw`.

4. Now that we've created a separate copy of the file, select the **Hidden Script** tab.

5. Go to **Insert | Section Access | Inline** from the menu.

6. In the **Access Restriction Table Wizard** dialog click on the **Basic User Access Table** button and click on **OK**.

7. In the **Inline Data Wizard** dialog, enter the data from the following table:

ACCESS	USERID	PASSWORD
ADMIN	ADMIN	ADMIN123
USER	USER	USER123

8. Click on **OK** to close the **Inline Data Wizard** dialog.

The following script should have now been generated:

```
Section Access;
LOAD * INLINE [
    ACCESS, USERID, PASSWORD
    ADMIN, ADMIN, ADMIN123
    USER, USER, USER123
];
Section Application;
```

As we can see, the script is started with the `Section Access` statement, which indicates to QlikView that we will be loading user authorization data. This data, `ACCESS`, `USERID`, and `PASSWORD`, is loaded in the next step using an inline table. The script is ended with the `Section Application` statement, indicating that QlikView should return to the regular application script.

We used a hidden script tab to create our section access. When using regular script, any user with privileges to view the script has full access to either the user credentials in plain text (when using an inline table), or to the location of the access files (when using an external table file). By using a hidden script, we can limit who will be able to see the section access script, adding an extra layer of security.

Another thing that you may have noticed is that all field names and field data are written in uppercase. While technically this is not necessary for data loaded from an inline table, any data loaded in section access from an external source must always be in uppercase. For the sake of consistency, it is a good idea to always load all data in uppercase in the section access area.

Now that we've seen how a basic section access example is set up, let's see if it works by following these steps:

1. Save the document by selecting **File | Save Entire Document** in the menu.
2. Click on **OK** to close the **Edit Script** dialog.
3. Close QlikView Desktop by selecting **File | Exit** in the menu.
4. Reopen QlikView and the `Airline Operations SA.qvw` file.
5. In the **User Identification** input box, enter `admin`.
6. In the **Password** input box, enter `admin123`.

If everything was set up ok, you should now be back in the document. Feel free to repeat these steps and enter wrong usernames and passwords to verify that QlikView will deny access to the document.

> QlikView will only verify your user credentials once during each session. You can verify this by closing the document and reopening it, without exiting QlikView Desktop. QlikView will not ask for your username and password the second time. Only when you completely close and reopen QlikView Desktop will you be asked for your credentials again. This is important to remember when changing and testing section access.

Section access fields

Access rights can be defined based on (a combination of) various criteria. In the previous example we used the ACCESS, USERID, and PASSWORD fields, but as we saw in the **Access Restriction Table Wizard** dialog, there are more options, as seen here:

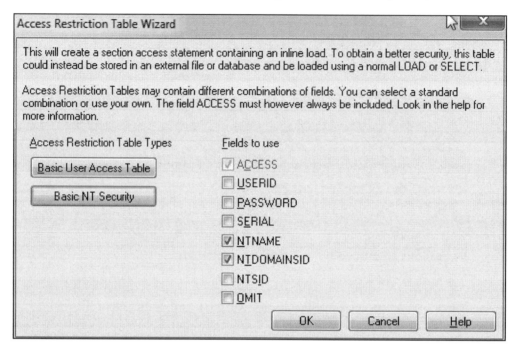

These options, and their description, are listed in the following table:

Field name	Description
ACCESS	A required field that defines the access level for the user. Access level can either be **ADMIN**, for administrator level access with privileges to change anything in the document, or **USER**, for (restricted) user level access.
	Opening the document via QlikView Server ignores the **ACCESS** setting, so every user is treated as having **USER** level access.
USERID	If set, QlikView will prompt for a user ID. This is not the same user ID as the Windows user ID.
PASSWORD	If set, QlikView will prompt for a password. This is not the same password as the Windows password.
SERIAL	A QlikView serial number, this can be used to tie a document to one or more QlikView license numbers.

Field name	Description
NTNAME	An NT Domain User Name or Group Name.
	Please note that the Domain Name needs to be prefixed, so, for example: `DOMAINNAME\NTNAME`
NTDOMAINSID	A Windows NT Domain SID, which is code that identifies the Windows Domain. It uses a value in the form of `S-1-5-21-479397367-1589784404-1244202989`.
	Only users that are logged on to the specified domain will be able to open the document. Be very careful when using this option. An upgrade to your network may mean that you get locked out of your document.
	The value for **NTDOMAINSID** can be entered in the script editor by going to **Insert | Domain SID**.
NTSID	A Windows NT SID, code which identifies a user using a value in the form of `S-1-5-21-479397367-1589784404-1244202989-1234`.
	As with the **NTDOMAINSID** field, be very careful when using this option since a change may lock you out of your document.
	This value can be found by opening command prompt (*Windows Key* + *R*, entering `CMD`) and typing `wmic useraccount get name,sid`.
OMIT	The name of a field that should be excluded for the user.

Note that just about any combination of fields is allowable. For instance, if just **NTNAME** and **PASSWORD** is defined, the domain user will need to be logged on correctly and provide the password associated with their domain account in section access. Also, it is valid to just have **USERID**, so only a name needs to be given to get access, regardless of domain user, and there will be no prompt for a password.

Order in which fields are checked

QlikView first checks if the fields `SERIAL`, `NTNAME`, `NTDOMAINSID`, or `NTSID` grant the user access to the document. Only if no match is found, or if these fields are not set, does QlikView prompt for a `USERID` and `PASSWORD` (if set).

In the next section, we'll look at how we can use section access to restrict the data that users can see.

Reduction fields

Besides the fields listed in the previous section, we can associate additional fields with the security fields to reduce the set of data that individual users have access to. Let's follow this example and see how we can limit the flight type (and associated flights) that are available to different users:

1. Open the **Edit Script** dialog and select the **Hidden Script** tab.

2. Update the inline `Section Access` table so it contains the following information:

ACCESS	USERID	PASSWORD	%FLIGHTTYPE
ADMIN	ADMIN	ADMIN123	*
USER	DF	DF123	DOMESTIC_FOREIGN
USER	DU	DU123	DOMESTIC_US
USER	IF	IF123	INTERNATIONAL_FOREIGN

3. Next, place the cursor after the `Section Application` statement.

4. Go to **Insert | Load Statement | Load Inline** in the menu.

5. In the **Inline Data Wizard**, select **Tools | Document** data.

6. In the **Import Document Data Wizard** window, select the field **Flight Type**.

7. Make sure that **Values to import** is set to **All Values** and click on **OK**.

8. Add **Flight Type** as a column header, and add a second column header for **%FLIGHTTYPE**.

9. Fill the table so it looks like the following table:

%FLIGHTTYPE	Flight Type
DOMESTIC_FOREIGN	Domestic, Foreign Carriers
DOMESTIC_US	Domestic, US Carriers Only
INTERNATIONAL_FOREIGN	International, Foreign Carriers
INTERNATIONAL_US	International, US Carriers Only

10. Click on **OK** to close the **Inline Data Wizard** dialog.

The resulting script should look like this:

```
Section Access;
LOAD * INLINE [
    ACCESS, USERID, PASSWORD, %FLIGHTTYPE
    ADMIN, ADMIN, ADMIN123, *
    USER, DF, DF123, DOMESTIC_FOREIGN
```

```
        USER, DU, DU123, DOMESTIC_US
        USER, IF, IF123, INTERNATIONAL_FOREIGN
];
Section Application;

LOAD * INLINE [
    Flight Type, %FLIGHTTYPE
    "Domestic, Foreign Carriers", DOMESTIC_FOREIGN
    "Domestic, US Carriers Only", DOMESTIC_US
    "International, Foreign Carriers", INTERNATIONAL_FOREIGN
    "International, US Carriers Only", INTERNATIONAL_US
];
```

In this script, we've created the `%FLIGHTTYPE` field. This field exists in both the section access part of the script as well as in the actual data model, thereby acting as a bridge field between these two sections. Through association, we can now limit what a particular user can access within the data model.

> **Basing an inline table on existing data**
> One nice feature in the **Inline Data Wizard** dialog is the ability to load the contents of an already loaded field by using **Tools | Document Data**. This can be very useful when we want to group the values of an existing field.

You may notice that for the `ADMIN` user, we used an asterisk (*) instead of a `%FLIGHTTYPE` value. When we use an asterisk, it means that the user gets access to all values listed in the reduction field. In this case, that means that `ADMIN` gets access to the `DOMESTIC_FOREIGN`, `DOMESTIC_US`, and `INTERNATIONAL_US` flight types, but not to the `INTERNATIONAL_FOREIGN` flight type, since that is not listed in the section access table.

If we want the `ADMIN` user to be able to access the `INTERNATIONAL_FOREIGN` flight type as well, we will need to add an additional line referencing the `INTERNATIONAL_FOREIGN` flight type to the section access inline table. Let's do that now:

1. Create a new line after the line `ADMIN, ADMIN, ADMIN123, *`.

2. On this new line, enter the following values: `ADMIN, ADMIN, ADMIN123, INTERNATIONAL_US`.

3. Go to **File | Save Entire Document** to save the document.

4. Click on the **Reload** button to reload the script.

In this exercise, we reduce the data model based on a single field. To reduce the data model on multiple fields, we can simply add another reduction column to the section access table and add a bridge field to the data model.

One important caveat to be aware of in this scenario is that the reduction will be performed over the intersection of all fields. If, for example, we give a user access to the `Domestic, US Carriers Only` flight type and to the `Jet` engine type, the user will only be able to see domestic flights carried out by US carriers using a jet-powered aircraft. Any flights that were made using another engine type will be excluded.

Although we have now finished the script part of setting up section access with reduction fields, we will need to make a few more changes before we can see the results. Let's head over to the frontend.

Initial data reduction

We will need to tell QlikView to perform an **Initial Data Reduction** when opening the document. When using initial data reduction, QlikView removes all of the data the user does not have access to, based on the authorizations in section access.

Using initial data reduction is very important. Not using it means that everyone with access to the document has access to all of the data. This means he entire point of using section access is all but lost.

Let's follow these steps to set up initial data reduction for our document:

1. Open the **Document Properties** window by pressing *Ctrl* + *Alt* + *D*.
2. Go to the **Opening** tab, and select the **Initial Data Reduction Based on Section Access** checkbox.
3. Make sure that the **Strict Exclusion** checkbox is checked.
4. Check the **Prohibit Binary Load** checkbox (seen in the following screenshot).
5. Click on **OK** to close the **Document Properties** dialog.
6. Go to **File | Save** in the menu to save the document.

☑ Initial Data Reduction Based on Section Access

　　☑ Strict Exclusion

　　☐ Initial Selection Based on Section Access

☑ Prohibit Binary Load

We have now set up the document to, upon opening, exclude all of the data that the user does not have access to. Let's have a closer look at the options that we set in the Document Properties:

- **Initial Data Reduction Based on Section Access**: This option enables initial data reduction for the document.

- **Strict Exclusion**: When set, QlikView denies access to users whose data reductions fields cannot be matched to values in the data model. This does not apply to ADMIN users, who will instead get access to the entire data model. It is recommended to always enable this option to prevent unwanted access to data within the document.

- **Prohibit Binary Load**: When set, it is not possible to load the document into another QlikView document using a binary load. It is recommended to always enable this setting unless you are using a multitiered data architecture that uses binary loads, for example, when using QlikMarts.

When a document containing section access is loaded into another document using binary load, the new document will inherit the section access of the original application. Take a minute to try logging in as the DUDF and IF users and see how the data is reduced to show only the authorized flight types. After that, reopen the document and log in as the ADMIN user, we'll need the privileges to make our next changes.

Omitting fields

While looking at the fields in the **Access Restriction Table Wizard**, you may have noticed that there is one field that is a little different from the others: the OMIT field. While all of the other fields are used to identify a user, the **OMIT** field is used to remove fields from the data model for the specified user.

In the next exercise, we will create a new user, NOCARRIER, and will remove the Carrier Name field for this user. Let's follow these steps:

1. Open the script editor by pressing *Ctrl + E* and select the **Hidden Script** tab.

2. Update the section access INLINE table by adding the OMIT field.

3. Set the value of the new OMIT field to null for all existing users, by adding a comma (,) at the end of each ADMIN and USER line.

4. Add a new user at the bottom of the list by entering the following script:

```
USER, NOCARRIER, NOCARRIER123, *, Carrier Name.
```

5. Go to **File | Save Entire Document** to save the document.

6. Click on the **Reload** button to reload the script.

The resulting script should look like this:

```
Section Access;
LOAD * INLINE [
    ACCESS, USERID, PASSWORD, %FLIGHTTYPE, OMIT
    ADMIN, ADMIN, ADMIN123, *,
    ADMIN, ADMIN, ADMIN123, INTERNATIONAL_US,
    USER, DF, DF123, DOMESTIC_FOREIGN,
    USER, DU, DU123, DOMESTIC_US,
    USER, IF, IF123, INTERNATIONAL_FOREIGN,
    USER, NOCARRIER, NOCARRIER123, *, Carrier Name
];
```

We've created a new user, NOCARRIER, whose password is NOCARRIER123. This user has access to all flight types, but cannot see the Carrier Name field.

 Notice that the values in the OMIT column do not need to be in upper case, instead they need to match the exact case of the field names that you want to omit.

We'll test if this works according to plan, but this time we will use another method. Let's follow these steps:

1. Keep your current QlikView application (the program) and document open.

2. Start a second copy of QlikView from the start menu or your quick launch shortcut.

3. If you get an **Auto Recover Files Found** warning, click on **Close** to close it.

4. Go to **File | Open** and select the Airline Operations SA.qvw file.

5. When prompted for a user id and password, enter NOCARRIER and NOCARRIER123 respectively.

If everything went well, we should see that the **Carrier Name** listbox is empty, and that the field is marked as **(unavailable)**.

By opening a second copy of the QlikView software and testing our file in that, we've significantly reduced the risk of getting locked out of our document. If anything is wrong, we can just revert back to the document that we did not close after saving and make the required changes to section access before repeating the process to try again. Using this approach is highly recommended.

Association works in section access too

So far we have been using a single table to store our section access data. However, we can use multiple, associated tables as well.

For example, when we want to OMIT multiple fields for a single user, we need to add each field on a separate line. We can do this within the single table that we've been using so far. However, a better alternative is to remove the OMIT field from the first table and create a second, associated table that contains the USERID and OMIT fields.

Now that we've seen how we can limit who has access to our document, and what they can see, we will now look at how we can restrict what users can do within the document in the next section.

Document-level security

User privileges can be set on two levels within QlikView, at the document level and at the level of individual sheets. We can open the document-level user privileges by pressing *Ctrl + Alt + D* to open the **Document Properties** dialog and selecting the **Security** tab. This tab is shown in the following screenshot:

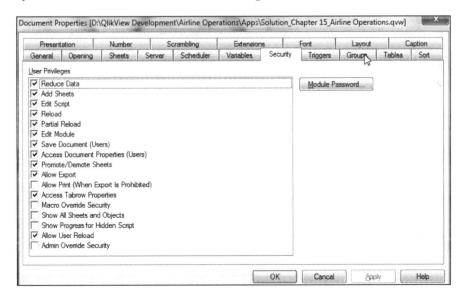

The following table lists and describes the document-level security settings:

User privilege	Description
Reduce Data	Allows users to reduce data using **File | Reduce Data**.
Add Sheets	Allows users to add new sheets by going to **Layout | Add Sheet**.
Edit Script	Allows users to edit the script by going to **File | Edit Script**. It is advisable to not enable this setting.
Reload	Allows a full reload of the document by going to **File | Reload**. As this will always return a full data set, ignoring any section access, it is not advisable to enable this setting.
Partial Reload	Allows users to perform a partial reload by going to **File | Partial Reload**. As this will always return a full data set, ignoring any section access, it is not advisable to enable this setting.
EditModule	Allows users to edit macros by going to **Tools | Edit Module**. It is not advisable to enable this setting.
Save Document (Users)	Allows users with USER privileges to save the document by going to **File | Save**. As this may risk a user overwriting the document with a document containing a reduced data set, it is not advisable to enable this option.
Access Document Properties (Users)	Allows users to open the document properties by going to **Settings | Document Properties**. While it is recommended to disable this setting, even when users have this privilege they will not be able to see the **Sheets**, **Server**, **Scheduler**, **Security** and **Scrambling** sheets.
Promote/Demote Sheets	Allows users to promote and demote sheets by going to **Layout | Promote Sheet** and/or **Layout | Demote Sheet**.
Allow Export	Allows users to export and print data, or to copy it to the clipboard.
Allow Print (When Export Is Prohibited)	If the **Allow Export** checkbox is disabled, setting this option will allow users to still print data.
Access Tab row Properties	Allows users to access the tab row properties.
Macro Override Security	Allows users to bypass all security settings when executing commands from a macro. It is recommended to disable this setting.
Show All Sheets and Objects	Allows users to override all conditional show expressions on sheets and objects by pressing *Ctrl + Shift + S*. It is recommended to disable this setting.
Show Progress for Hidden Script	Shows progress for the hidden script in the **Script Execution Progress** dialog. It is not advisable to enable this setting.

User privilege	Description
Allow User Reload	If the **Reload** checkbox is enabled, selecting this checkbox will prevent users with USER privileges from reloading the document. It is recommended to enable this setting.
Admin Override Security	When set, all security settings for the document and sheets are ignored when a user with ADMIN privileges opens the document, it is advisable to enable this setting.

Besides these settings, the **Module Password** button lets us password protect our macros with a password.

 It is important to note that these user privileges are applied to all users (excluding those with ADMIN privileges). Within QlikView Desktop, it is not possible, for example, to allow one user to export data while not allowing another user to do this.

Besides the document level, we can also set security privileges at the sheet level, as the next section will explain.

Sheet-level security

At the sheet level, we can also determine what actions our users are allowed to make. The sheet-level privileges can be opened by selecting **Settings | Sheet Properties** in the menu and selecting the **Security** tab. This tab is shown in the following screenshot:

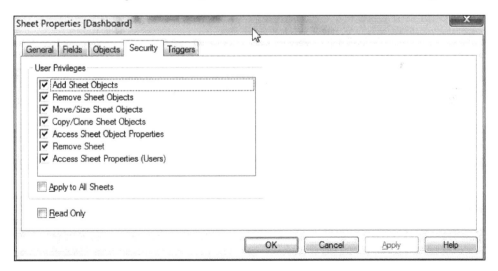

The following table lists and describes the various user privileges that can be set at the sheet level:

User privilege	Description
Add Sheet Objects	Allows users to add new sheet objects.
Remove Sheet Objects	Allows users to remove any of the sheet objects, not just the ones that they created.
Move/Size Sheet Objects	Allows users to move and size sheet objects. On sheets where we do not want the users to move or size any of the objects, this option is a lot more convenient than deselecting **Allow Move/Size** on each individual sheet object.
Copy/Clone Sheet Objects	Allows users to create a copy of existing sheet objects.
Access Sheet Object Properties	Allows users to access the Sheet Properties dialog.
Remove Sheet	Allows users to delete the sheet.
Access Sheet Properties (Users)	Allows users to access the **Properties** pages of objects on the sheet.

By selecting the **Apply to All Sheets** checkbox, we can apply the currently selected privileges to all sheets in the document.

Summary

We have come to the end of this chapter on security, in which we first saw how we can determine which users get access to our document. We then looked at how we can restrict the data that different users have access to. We ended this chapter by looking at how we can set user privileges at the document and sheet levels.

Specifically, in this chapter we learned how to create a hidden script and also that it is very important to create a backup before introducing Section Access.

We also learned how to add Section Access to your document and how to identify users on different criteria, such as **USERID**, **PASSWORD**, but also QlikView's **SERIAL** number or **NTNAME**.

Finally, we learned how we can use Section Access to dynamically reduce the data that is available to the user and how to set user privileges at the document and sheet levels.

With the end of this chapter, we have also reached the end of this book. Over the course of this book we've learned how to create scripts to extract data from various data sources, transform it, and load it into QlikView. We've also learned how to create and style frontend objects for use in dashboards, analyses, and reports, and how to perform complex calculations and Point In Time reporting. Finally, we've learned how to properly secure our data.

We hope that after reading this book and performing the various exercises you feel confident that you have acquired the skills that you need to start developing your own QlikView documents. We wish you good luck in your endeavors and welcome you to the community of QlikView developers!

Index

U

use borders checkbox 136
use case
about 362
heat charts 362-364
user controls
adding, in list boxes form 47, 48
USERID field 484

V

values
modifying, for variables 341
variable naming convention 346
variables
about 337
creating 195, 196, 338, 339
naming convention 346

set expressions, storing 394, 395
used, for storing expressions 345
using 338
using, based on expressions 343-345
using, in charts 339-341
using, in set expressions 382
values, modifying 341
Variables tab, Edit Expression window 160

W

web resources
accessing, via APIs 67
Qlik REST Connector 67
Qlik Web Connectors 67
What-If scenarios 149
where clause wizard 88, 89
workspace
preparing 34